HE INVENTED INDIAN

THE INVENTED INDIAN
Cultural Fictions and Government Policies

Edited by
James A. Clifton

Transaction Publishers
New Brunswick (U.S.A.) & London (U.K.)

First paperback edition 1994

Copyright © 1990 by Transaction Publishers,
New Brunswick, New Jersey 08903

Library of Congress Catalog Number: 89-20676
ISBN: 0-88738-341-6
Printed in the United States of America

Library of Congress Cataloging-in-Publication Data

The Invented Indian: Iconoclastic essays / James A. Clifton, editor.
   p. cm.
   ISBN: 0-88738-341-6 (cloth); 1-56000-745-1 (paper)
   1. Indians of North America—Public opinion.   2. Indians of North
America—Government relations.   3. Public opinion—United
States.   4. Stereotype (Psychology)—United States.
I. Clifton, James A.
E98.P99I58   1990
305.8'97—dc20   89-20676
                                                              CIP

IN MEMORY OF
Lynn Ceci (1930—1989)
John A. Price (1933—1988)
Absent Friends, Lost Colleagues,
Resolute Scholars

"Next, then," I said, "make an image of our nature in its education and want of education, likening it to a condition of the following kind. See human beings as though they were in an underground cave-like dwelling with its entrance, a long one, open to the light across the whole width of the cave. They are in it from childhood with their legs and necks in bonds so that they are fixed, seeing only in front of them, unable because of the bond to turn their heads all the way around. Their light is from a fire burning far above and behind them. Between the fire and the prisoners there is a road above, along which we see a wall, built like the partitions puppet-handlers set in front of the human beings and over which they show the puppets."

"I see," he said.

"Then also see along this wall human beings carrying all sorts of artifacts, which project above the wall, and statues of men and other animals wrought from stone, wood, and every kind of material; as is to be expected, some of the carriers utter sounds while others are silent."

"It's a strange image," he said, "and stranger prisoners you're telling of."

"They're like us," I said, "for in the first place, do you suppose such men would have seen anything of themselves and one another other than the shadows cast by the fire on the side of the cave facing them?"

—Plato's *Republic*,
Book VII,
Allan Bloom, trans.

Contents

List of Illustrations

Acknowledgments

My special, personal, and professional thanks go to Patricia Albers, Phillip Alexis, Benedict Anderson, Jo Allyn Archambault, James Axtell, John Baker, Donald Bahr, the late Robert and Mary Catherine Bell, Charles Bishop, John Boatman, Edward M. Bruner, James Canaan, Edison Chiloquin, Charles Cleland, the late Judge James Doyle, Jeanne Kay, Igor Kopytoff, Adam Kuper, James Janetta, Gail H. Landsman, Nancy O. Lurie, Buck Martin, James McClurken, J. Anthony Parades, Curtis Pequano, Paul Prucha, Tomatsu Shibutani, Bernard Sheehan, Donald Smith, William Sturtevant, Stanley J. Tambiah, Catherine Tierney, Flora Tobabadung, William Wabnosah, and Hiroto Zakoji. With a few exceptions, all of these have provided much positive grist for the mill of my thinking, directly and indirectly serving as sources of insight and enlightenment, as critics and intellectual buttresses, but they are in no manner responsible for the results. And I am also grateful to those few whose useful contributions to my practical education deserve anonymity for having acted—in the awful language of contemporary pop-sociology—as "negative role models"; but I have learned from them, too. A great many years ago, Lt. Col. Hideyose Gomi of Imperial Japan's *Kempei Tai*, gave me an unforgettable lesson in the fine distinction between education and propaganda, for which I will always remain appreciative.

To Theodore S. Stern I owe much too large a debt, for thirty-five years of higher education. For an advanced course in the intricacies of the Indian business, my thanks to the fourteen fine, independent minded, creative thinkers who contributed their essays to this book. However, on none of them should be loaded any culpability for the interpretations and conclusions I express in chapters One and Two.

To the Klamath, Southern Ute, Ute Mountain Ute, Potawatomi, Fox, Sauk, Menomini, Shawnee, Kickapoo, Chippewa, Ottawa, Brotherton, Wyandot, Huron, Miami, Oneida, Winnebago, Stockbridge-Munsee, and Delaware—of Oregon, Colorado, Kansas, Iowa, Wisconsin, Minnesota, Indiana, Ontario, and Quebec, individually and *en masse*, for the opportunities to learn about and from them since 1957, my lasting appreciation.

And to the Great Lakes Intertribal Council, the Federal District Court of Wisconsin and Michigan, and the now defunct Indian Claims Commission, my gratitude for providing me the opportunity to do what my friend and colleague John Messenger calls "observant participation" in their chambers.

Over the years my studies of North American Indians have been supported by the Social Science Research Council, the National Institute of Mental Health, the National Science Foundation, the Canadian Ethnology Service, the State of Michigan, the Cleveland Foundation, the Wenner-Gren Foundation, and, most recently, the National Endowment for the Humanities. I thank all of them.

And, above all others, to Faye, for wise counsel and everything else.

1

Introduction: Memoir, Exegesis

James A. Clifton

Though the biography of this book is still incomplete, a sketch of its genesis is proper, to help readers understand its lineage and anticipate the temperament of our offspring. This vita must remain unfinished for now, since only others can decide the later career of what the authors and editor have produced. While the contributors all write from the basis of their own experience and expectations, as editor, merely one of the parents, I can speak mainly of my own thoughts about the whole and the experiences which propelled them, from the first arousal of desire through conception up to the point of delivery.

Thirty-two years ago, as an apprentice anthropologist, I was invited to participate in an interdisciplinary team study of the effects of "termination" on the Klamath Indian tribe of Oregon. The termination policy (one of the American state's cyclical attempts to resolve its "Indian problem" by scrapping subvention and management of the affairs of these client communities) was then in flower; and the Klamath were one of the two largest such corporate groups where this plan was fully implemented. My host, exemplar, and mentor in this research was Professor Theodore S. Stern, who modeled for his students the highest standards of professional integrity, rigor in scholarship, disciplined truth-telling, humane concern for others, and personal generosity.

I then had no experience with Indians, personal or semi-professional, and was largely untutored in conventional anthropological knowledge about them. I was not driven toward identification with Indians by inner compulsion and harbored not the slightest conviction that I might or should act as their liberator. I had not set off to live with Indians in order to discover myself. I was not even interested in Indians per se. I

1

was, however, much committed to studying people, especially their so-
cial-cultural dynamics and resistance to change, hopefully among the
societies of the islands of Micronesia, not the ethnic insularities of North
America. However, because the Klamath were then facing major, externally imposed alterations in their status and situation, the invitation
to live and learn among them seemed to be a marvelous opportunity to
pursue knowledge and to master some of the rudiments of my craft (see
Stern 1966; Kamber 1989).

When a novice among the Klamath, with only scanty second-hand
knowledge about and few convictions concerning Indians, there came
the first glimmerings of intellectual passion—several puzzling, half-formed
questions—long before there were means or opportunity for consum-
mation. The causes for this were a few simple, on-the-spot observations.
Among the wealthiest of North American Indians, for instance, their
median family income much exceeded that of their neighbors and my
own (the young Klamath men and women I knew best sometimes kindly
expressed concern about *my* impoverishment). Yet a great many, about
40 percent, lived elsewhere, when there was no apparent, pressing economic need for them to do so. Within the reservation community, nonetheless, there were large differences in wealth and living standards,
though overall they were an enterprising, prosperous, self-reliant population.

Moreover, in the late 1950s they were not a culturally homogeneous
little community. Their indigenous ancestors did include mostly Klamath
proper, smaller numbers of closely related Modoc, and fewer Northern
Paiute; but their pedigrees also contained numerous forebears of diverse
European and other not-native ancestry. Much of their history of interactions with outsiders, as Felix Keesing had perceptively said of the
Menomini, was "written on their faces." In the still popular old American folk nomenclature, many were called "halfbreeds" or "mixed-bloods,"
labels of Euroamerican origin accepted and used regularly by the Klamath themselves. But in the anthropological thinking of the time the
pronounced intracommunity variations in values and behaviors were
said to represent differences in "level" or "degree" of acculturation.

The latter interpretation was based on the still commonly unrecognized assumption that these (and other) modern Indian groups are derived *exclusively* from culturally homogeneous ancestral, native North
American populations. As novice anthropologist, at the time I was bothered by the uncritical use of what I saw as American racial labeling and
ahistorical assumptions about collective ancestry and heritage that I
suspected might be faulty. But I could not then plainly specify the
underlying issues, much less think clearly about resolving them with

data and ideas. It was a long time before I understood that at the heart of this conceptual quandary lay the confusion of anthropology's favorite grand abstraction—Culture (in the partitive sense)—with the histories and heritages of a population. Thus, research observation and academic curiosity were accompanied by conceptual frustration, which bred a desire for intellectual resolution not easily or quickly sated.

Of more importance to my later thinking, in this period came a separate, provocative observation. As part of the legislative compromise laying out the details of the actual termination process, each adult Klamath had a choice, for self and for minor children. One option was to elect to "remain" as members of a reconstituted corporate (tribe-like) organization, with their per capita shares of collectively owned resources held in common in trust under state law. The second option allowed them to "withdraw," to go their individual (more accurately, family) ways, to voluntarily disaffiliate themselves from association with the new social entity, and to collect and personally control their per capita shares of the reservation community's joint assets, which were considerable.

The behavior of the Klamath at the time did not square with the political rhetoric of "tribalism," which holds that "the Indian" has some sort of inherited, mystic compulsion to belong to a "sovereign" corporate organization under outside government protection. For of the Klamath only 3.5 percent voted explicitly for the protected joint membership option, that is, for the perpetuation of "tribalism," a percentage swelled by the addition of the 19 percent who did not or could not vote (in addition to the many indifferent and fewer hard-case hold outs, mainly individuals deemed incapable of managing their own affairs—familyless elderly, orphaned children, the mentally disabled, etc.). The vast majority—77 percent—promptly withdrew and went their several ways, not without some anxiety about this major change in their status, which is not to say that the Klamath population, a Klamath identity, or their communities simply disappeared. Historically, I later learned, the Klamath were by no means either the first or the only Indian population to vote with their feet about remaining in "tribal" organizations, buffered from their larger social environment by a special, segregated status in the federal system. Indeed, in 1980 the "remaining" members of the Klamath tribe themselves cashed in their shares of joint assets for payments of $170,000 each.

After leaving Oregon, I spent two years living and researching among the Southern Ute of Colorado. I found these Ute a strikingly solidary group with a large, resource rich reservation, and an impressively efficient and successful system of government and economic management—with some inputs from federal authorities—about which there were then few strong, conspicuous complaints (Clifton 1965). The following year, in Kansas, I began a study of the Prairie Potawatomi, a small community transplanted over a century before from their old Great Lakes area estate, a group dramatically different from the Klamath and Ute. I was now well sensitized to some aspects of the plurality of differences between Indian communities.

These Potawatomi were dirt poor. For that matter they owned little enough of soil, and that consisted of some small scattered allotments on the remains of their old reservation. Unlike the Klamath and Ute, they exhibited almost no political-economic cohesion, except in violent opposition to any effort on the part of the federal government to deal with, even to deliver services to them. Internally, their affairs were disrupted by chronic, bitter, self-destructive infighting. They contrasted with the Klamath and Ute in other salient ways as well. They mostly still used their old language; in culture they were profoundly natavistic; and they deliberately shunned associations with the assimilated marginal people—the "mixed-bloods"—who lived elsewhere but stridently claimed rights as Prairie Potawatomi Indians (Clifton 1977).

First among the rights these outsiders claimed was access to per capita shares of the substantial Indian Claims Commission award the culturally conservative Potawatomi had for years been litigating. The latter when I met them were preoccupied with shaking the Great Treaty Tree to harvest a major windfall for themselves alone. Since these nativists were fewer than eight hundred, whereas the outside claimants numbered several thousands, they faced a considerable economic as well as a major political threat. Eventually, the insider-outsider conflict was resolved, externally, by fiat issuing from the Commissioner of Indian Affairs and his Assistant. These officials signaled the legitimacy of the outsiders as Potawatomi (by American racial definition), and approved the new Constitution they prepared. So far as I understood what was going on at the time (1964–1965), the culturally hard-shelled Potawatomi were having their political backs broken across the knees of others' visions for their future.

When I first knew them, the elder Kansas Potawatomi leaders were obsessed by a few shared fantasies. They were dreaming (literally so, night and day) that soon an Indian agent would arrive with a buckboard laden with strongboxes overflowing with silver and gold coins, which he would then hand over to them to do with as they wished. They thought they remembered this had been the custom a century earlier. They envisioned also that, if only they persisted in resolute opposition, the United States government would leave them strictly alone to manage their own internal political affairs, except periodically to deliver additional boxes of coins and other services they demanded and expected. Although I did not then entirely understand it, there in the thinking of these Potawatomi elders—in starkly explicit, paradigmatic form—lay the fundamental, conflicting elements of the goals of most modern Indian groups. Whether authentically native and officially recognized, or feigned Indians of invented identity aspiring to federal recognition, legal status, and a key to the treasury, these central aims are few. Simply put, they are: obtaining absolute political autarchy while perpetuating utter fiscal dependence.

About this time I began pondering whether *being* federally recognized Indian (as in the instance of both the Potawatomi-by-definition and the Potawatomi-by-culture) and *not being* government-defined Indian (as in the case of the withdrawing Klamath) both had as much or more to do with something as mundane as money (and other, symbolic incentives) than with an innate proclivity for protecting and perpetuating ethnic heritage. Being Indian, I reasoned, likely involved periodic access to substantial bonanzas of various kinds. And at the heart of being Indian in this legalistic sense, I suspected, lay a profoundly ambivalent psychosocial dependency relationship.

In any regard, like other anthropologists of my generation, I quickly discovered that short-term ethnographic field studies had serious limitations for anyone interested in long-term social and cultural processes. The cross-sectional analysis of facts drawn from contemporary communities such as the Potawatomi raised questions that could only be answered with comparative, longitudinal, proper historical research. Eventually settling in Wisconsin, close to the old heartland of the Potawatomi and their neighbors I embarked on field and archival studies of other Potawatomi and kindred groups, a style of enquiry by then dignified with the new title of "ethnohistory."

Following the historical tracks of the Kansas Potawatomi's ancestors led me onto the trail of those peoples who had influenced them. My additional comparative historical research included studies of the Ojibwa, Ottawa, Wyandot, Shawnee, Emigrant New York Indians in Wisconsin, and other peoples of indigenous or European origin (or some mixture of all of the above), with whom the Potawatomi had been endlessly entangled for over three centuries in the complex and changing cultural-geographic matrix encompassed by the Great Lakes-Ohio Valley region.

I write at a time when public confession of serious anthropological lapses has become chic. Though unlike some others involved with Indians I have never tried out the part of messiah or prophet of doom, I will admit that on several occasions I have acted in the capacity of advocate of Indian rights. Educated in the old tradition of Roger Bacon's aphorisms, I was convinced that if creating knowledge was worthwhile, finding some practical use for it was nearly as grand. At first I failed to recognize that what Bacon had in mind was improved navigation skills and increased crop production, not directly helping special-interest groups with social problems in competition with their adversaries.

By way of example, for the time they had given and the courtesy shown me, I felt an obligation to the culturally conservative Kansas Potawatomi, worse yet, a personal identification with their interests. Thus when called on for help in their efforts to fend off being overwhelmed by "newcomers," I tried to intervene on their behalf by persuading federal officials of the superior merits of their case. This modest effort did the old conservatives little good, and myself less, especially so since the outsiders quickly became dominant insiders. What I ran up against in Washington, I saw later, was the beginning of a policy that has since been institutionalized as an integral branch of the developing Indian rights industry. Now an important sideline for underemployed applied anthropologists, geographers, historians, and federal administrators, this involves the forging by legal reincarnation of the maximum feasible number of Indians, however obscure and questionable their ethnic antecedents. These include contingents of individuals being recruited and enrolled in existing, officially long-recognized tribes (as happened to the Kansas Potawatomi), and hundreds of recently resurrected "forgotten tribes" or "lost nations" seeking "status clarification," that is, the stamp of federal approval on and specially privileged political economic support of their resuscitated or contrived identities (Paredes 1974; Porter 1986).

Similarly, I was later called on to act as "expert" witness on behalf of the Michigan and Wisconsin Potawatomi in their appeal before the Indian Claims Commission. My inclination to be helpful, to put knowledge to practical use, again got me in some difficulty. At stake were millions of dollars: the attorneys for the Oklahoma and Kansas Potawatomi wanted all of it for their clients, leaving none for the smaller eastern communities. Convinced that the historical and anthropological facts led to a different conclusion, I soon discovered that being a witness under such circumstances was rather like the predicament of Christians in a Roman arena: pugnacious gladiators on the one side, ravenous lions the other. Striving to hold to academic standards of truth telling did my reputation no good among the Kansas Potawatomi, now suddenly quadrupled in population, since the commission's decision cost them part of the spoils. And my testimony greatly annoyed an Indian Claims tribunal commissioner. One of North Carolina's born again "Lumbee Indians," a man like his multitude of kin deeply committed to diluting and broadening the federal definition of Indianness, he had a particular stake in recognizing the rights of "Indians by blood" (see Henige 1984).

However, this and several later ordeals in federal courtrooms where Indian treaty rights cases were at issue provided me with an opportunity for "field" observations not ordinarily available to an academic. In these trials by history (i.e., law office history), watching the highly skilled, forceful attorneys serving the Indian cause at work was a thoroughly eye-opening experience. From them I learned much about the selective use and suppression of historical and anthropological evidence, systematic distortion of facts in support of a preconceived "theory of the case," the dexterous manipulation of judicial and public sentiments, perfectly astounding hyperbole, and the most outrageous fabrications. Watching some "experts" approach the witness stand with hats in hand, and others demur when caustically coached about how and what they should testify to, balking myself when pressed to distort or suppress interpretations and sources, I concluded that in Indian treaty rights cases the standards of evidence and logic are not what they are elsewhere, especially so in scholarly work.

The paramount aim, at last I had explained to me by an unusually impetuous counsel, was not veracity but to win at all costs. These particular attorneys were interested in neither truth nor social consequences, except those of obtaining for their clients the largest short-term benefits attainable—money and power. Rather than a quest relying on reasoned probity and a careful array of all relevant evidence in search of justice, these were purely political contests, I concluded (Clifton 1987). Over the past twenty-five years, the federal courtrooms have been arenas for many such exciting, generally unbalanced duels on behalf of Indian clients, mostly victorious. About the tactics used in similar struggles before state legislatures and in Congress I have only second-hand knowledge, never having served as anyone's lobbyist, but the legions of advocates for Indian prerogatives have been at least equally successful in these other political arenas.

Along the way, between 1971 and 1976, I had another, longer round of experience in a helping role, attempting to service the expressed needs of Indians. In this period I organized and administered a University Year for Action program throughout Wisconsin—mostly health, education, and economic development projects in nine of Wisconsin's ten Indian reservation communities. Managing this university-based VISTA/ Peace Corps-like program brought me into prolonged contact with the several parties then battling for control of the future of the eleventh Wisconsin Indian community, the Menomini, who like the Klamath had been the other major Indian group "terminated" several years earlier. When I first visited them, someone had erected a billboard alongside the major highway leading into the new Menomini County. It read, "We Will Make It!" Some years later, after the party lobbying for "restoration" had achieved victory in Congress, this sign was taken down, and a new one erected in its place to confront travelers through the newly reestablished Menomini Reservation. It read, "We Didn't Make It!" This suggests that Indians are not incapable of either large aspirations or self-irony.

Watching this process of Menomini retribalization, while trying to deliver some basic development and social services, was always instructive and often stormy. Having learned some lessons the hard way, with some special knowledge of the pitfalls laying in wait for strangers in situations of embittered factionalism, I tried to maintain a neutral, even-handed stance as regards the cabals and their corrosive, violent infighting. Avoiding earlier mistakes, I discovered that I had to find some intellectual profit when committing new ones. So with my anthropological eyes open I learned much more—of the political-economic relationships between Indian factions and outside interests, for example.

The leaders of the large "restorationist" camp (mainly educated, middle-class, off-reservation women), on one side, were the protégées of the liberal wing of Wisconsin's Democratic party, spurred on also by flotsam on the rising tide of militant paleface feminism. The leaders of the small "pro-termination" party (all elder, mainly male, upper middle-class managers and entrepreneurs), in their turn were aided and abetted by the conservative wing of Wisconsin's Republican party. And at the third point of this political triangle, the leadership of the late-coming, ferociously belligerent, recently improvised "Warriors Society" (mainly young, urban, lower-class males and the women who adored them) were covertly coached in their deftly played confrontational tactics by a political splinter-group—Wisconsin's tiny band of zealous Trotskyites. These hostiles were also helped quietly by various academic Marxists of the credit-card and other doctrinal varieties. And on the fringes, unsuccessfully seeking a lodgement for their own agenda, occasionally arrived representatives of AIM—the national American Indian Movement— talking about a replay of Wounded Knee II. They were joined by a perfectly weird medley of the other protest groupies who invariably show up when storms brew in Indian Country (see Schultz 1973; Smith 1973).

This phenomenon has a respectable scholarly name, "reciprocal exploitation." On the one hand, the three main Menomini factions were actively milking their external supporters of whatever they could get.

In turn, each collaborating with its chosen clique, the outside interest groups were playing out their own special agendas. Whatever the "Menomimi people" needed or wanted was nearly irrelevant; all the outsiders had lofty, alternative visions of their future, the internal leaderships dreams of power. The real folks—Menomini and everyone else watching the fireworks on the nightly news—were barely something more than an audience for political dramas. With no political agenda in mind, and, I recognized, little more than economic band-aids and aspirin in hand, my efforts at *nonpartisan* dealings for the Action project proved impossible. Any help delivered to a service program controlled or coveted by one party was defined as a mortal, dastardly boot to the innards of their opponents.

Trying to project an appropriately modest image of what the *Action* program could realistically deliver or accomplish, I was surprised to find it defined as a major natural resource. Along the way, I was assailed by a republican congressman/real estate developer for promoting the interests of "communist Indians," rejected by the liberal restorationists when I explained I could not deliver the entire budget of the Action program into their hands, and threatened with "fragging" by "warriors," one of whom—costumed in what seemed to me hand-me-down Apache garb from an old John Wayne movie—showed up at my campus door one afternoon flashing his little pistol at me.

Even in such circumstances it is possible to extract useful scholarly knowledge: maybe *only* under such conditions can some types of insights be acquired. Dealing with the Menomini and other Wisconsin Indian communities in these years provided numerous opportunities for validating earlier assessments, developing new questions, and disabusing myself of lingering misconceptions. An example of each, in order. Almost invariably, what the leaders of Wisconsin Indian communities wanted most of *Action* was aid in obtaining dollars, the more the better. Improved grantsmanship was at the top of the technical aid demanded, and I soon recognized that whatever goals granting agencies specified for their awards, the main incentive seen in them by Indian applicants was additional income. Like many academic institutions and the military-industrial complex, Indian organizations were adapted to increasing their standard of living by harvesting "soft money" (Clifton 1976).

So far as better appreciating Indians' own views about external social relationships, once the Action program ended and I no longer had resources to deliver, I received a message from a long-acquainted tribal booster. He was calling politely to explain the facts of anti-poverty program life to me. Always, previously, he had come personably to my office as he made his regular diplomatic rounds hustling resources for the programs he represented. He now phoned to say goodbye, he explained; adding, not quite apologetically, "Jim, remember, Indians don't have friends." I responded, "Yes, I understand perfectly. You have family, enemies, and allies." "You've got it," he answered, hanging up. What he did not say explicitly was that people formerly used as allies can quickly be redefined as enemies.

While engaged in this business, after listening several times to various Menominis make a peculiar public utterance, the same in substance if not exact phrasing, I started to ask stronger questions about the nature of Indian psychosocial identity and dependency. The setting was always a rally, during the course of which someone would rise and give a short speech. The words ran like this: "It's like yesterday I looked in the mirror and I was an Indian. Now I look in the mirror and I do not know what I am. That's what termination did to me." These were not simply the idiosyncratic sentiments of a few individuals: the audiences always seconded such declarations by acclamation. The facts of a powerful sense of identity dissolution were plain. To be really content with a legitimate sense of ethnic self, these individuals proclaimed, they had to have federal I.D. cards. I knew of no other ethnic group where social and personal identity was so hugely dependent on external, governmental certification.

In the same period a different transaction led to much better appreciation of what I as an anthropologist should properly be doing. A little group of Indians approached me for aid in writing a grant application, and for my support in getting it approved, inadvertently giving me a compelling lesson in professional ethics. The funds granted, they explained, would be spent to help them perpetuate the practice of their traditional religion. The application was rejected, on the grounds that, being a Christian foundation, the Board could not see fit to spend a donor's money in support of a "heathen religion." I will admit that this response temporarily sent me into a classic anthropological huff, which dissipated when I realized that the foundation's turndown was not the central issue. Why did these Indians need someone else's *money* to carry out their sacred rituals? Never in the history of this group had they ever needed a *grant* to pray, sacrifice, feast, and chant. Either I had unthinkingly allowed myself to get involved in perpetrating a hoax, or I was helping to perpetuate and increase dependency. The applicants were, unmistakably, loading their fund-raising hooks with mystical bait. This was a small moment-of-truth; the foundation's disapproval of this grant-dance, for me, spelled ethical relief.

For readers unfamiliar with the ins-and-outs of American Indian policy over the past two centuries, especially so the extraordinary reversals and transformations in dealings between Indians and other Americans in the past thirty years, let me underscore the sense of the few key points in the foregoing memoir. First, working as a field anthropologist, my experience with Indians began while the federal government was set on a policy, once and for all time, of ending its government-to-government relationship with Indian "tribes," and its stewardship over the daily welfare of Indian individuals, however piecemeal and abortive implementation of that policy may have been. In government circles called "termination," and popularly called "assimilation" (now a particularly nasty expletive in Indian and allied academic circles) or "cultural genocide," in my judgment this policy is better construed, in analytic ways, as one of political decolonization and social integration.

Then, starting in the late 1960s, and reaching its apogee in the later 1970s, that policy was quickly blown away and an entirely different one launched, a policy missile rather grandly but passionately called "sovereignty" and "self-determination" by both its Indian beneficiaries, if that is what they are, and their many allies. Again in analytic phrasings, this new policy might better be seen as political-social segregation and the perpetuation of economic-cultural dependency. Quite by accident, I happened to be on the ground observing the execution of both the former policy—the Klamath termination case, and the emergence and institutionalization of the latter one—the Menomini restoration example. These two are now generally considered landmarks in this momentous recent transmutation of the place of the Indian in American society and culture.

The preceding commentary *is not* intended as an authoritativeness bestowing "I was there, an eyewitness" story, the most common pose assumed by field anthropologists (and TV journalists) in their reporting mode. On the contrary, having sufficiently indicated theoretical doubts, conceptual frustration, and trial-and-error learning, it should be apparent that I was convinced—deeply immersed as I was in one or another case study—that my vision was much foreshortened. I could not see far enough with enough depth perception to get these small events into the focus of larger ones. The easiest chore for field anthropologists is to develop much understanding of "their people," and the most common snare they encounter is to become too closely identified with "their welfare." The really difficult tasks are: to develop historical, comparative, contextual, and processual comprehension; to maintain enough disciplined detachment to avoid getting trapped by the moral-intellectual quandaries of combining contradictory research and helping roles; to resist whatever personal temptations there are to play-act at being a

Lord Benevolent or Lady Beneficent; to eschew manipulating relationships with Indians so as to satisfy one's own political values.

The commentary *was* intended to suggest some of the stimulating
features of the course that led to this book. After some years of experience with the complexities of Indian affairs and the affairs of Indians
seen on the local, community level, it was glaringly apparent that my
understanding was missing in critical respects: about those larger, so-
cietal or national (and international) forces which acted on Indians (and
others) generally, and about the historical-developmental backdrop to
the contemporary scene.

Researching the historical experiences of the Kansas Potawatomi and
their neighbors helped, immeasurably. Of all the issues bearing on modern Indian affairs, for instance, few are more important than what are
called "Indian treaties" and "treaty rights." To my surprise, I discovered
that the Potawatomi had negotiated more than fifty such agreements,
with British imperial and American national authorities, far more than
any other indigenous North American society. This required close study
of the social-historical contexts of such negotiations, the substance of
their stipulations, and their consequences. And from 1634 onward the
Potawatomi and those peoples associated with them had met and somehow coped with nearly every known alien policy initiative bearing on
the situation and status of native North American peoples. From French
fur trade merchantilism and employment as mercenaries in colonial
wars, these adaptations ran on through two centuries of experience
countering efforts of marginal people such as missionaries, traders, Indian agents, the Métis, and "Potawatomi by blood" to intrude themselves and to dominate their institutions and economy. Their experiences
required their adapting to the American state's civilization, removal,
reservation, allotment, reorganization, claims payment, urban reloca-
tion, and termination initiatives—right down to the most recent separatist mini-state development and cultural-political resurrection policies
(Clifton 1984).

Such culture historical studies were greatly illuminating, since they
led to awareness of an important cyclical pattern in American Indian
policy, which has ebbed and flowed from separatist to integrationist
peaks and troughs regularly for two centuries. Thus in the 1970s, when
I listened to leaders of the Menomini restoration movement boast that
they were the first Indians ever to have been terminated, then to have
sought and achieved restoration of "tribal Indian status," I knew this
was not so, and was moved to remark to that effect. In the 1830s and
1850s American policy had also cycled from separatist to integrationist
and—for some—back again. Some Potawatomi, among others, had

been "terminated" one year, and "determined" several years later. A similar longer term integration phase began in the 1860s and ran through the early 1930s, only to be reversed with another step toward "Indian Reorganization" or segregation. This "Indian New Deal" effort to create culturally, economically, and politically viable new Indian corporate organizations, pushed by the utopian visionary, John Collier, was temporarily halted in the post–World War II years with the integrationist policy affecting the Klamath when I encountered them. But during the Vietnam War period came another, this time massive, reversal with a swing into another separatist phase, which propels us into the present.

Lest a useful point be missed, let me emphasize the implications of a matter that may have gone unnoticed in the preceding paragraph. By attempting to broaden the historical horizons of the Menomini leaders about precedents for their own not inconsiderable accomplishments in regaining their legal Indian status, I was violating one of the most stringently observed canons governing the behavior of those who work among Indians. Among aficionados who retain some sense of professional humility, this powerful proscription is sometimes called the Eleventh Commandment (though not in mixed-company). Every vocation has its Eleventh Commandment, to be sure, but in the Indian business it reads: "Thou Shall Not Say No to an Indian." In commenting on the Menomini leaders' strutting, I had in mind suggesting some sense of historical proportion, for they were expressing a strong conviction that their problems were over. The historical experiences of other communities that had experienced such a shift in federal fortunes was that all later experienced severe problems, as, indeed, have the Menomini themselves in the past dozen years.

Lest it be assumed that I was interfering in the supreme right of Noninterference of a group of innocent, hapless primitives bent on constructing some transcendental mythography, I will observe that none of the urbane Menomini who heard my remark had less than a high school diploma, and they included a B.S., an M.S.W., and an Ll.D. However, this does not make observance of this norm any more uncommon among or less obligatory upon those who deal with Indians, whatever the latters' ancestries or educational attainments. This Eleventh Commandment has many corollaries (for example, Indians Always Utter Ultimate Truths), and is accompanied by other norms and taboos of deferential conduct. These standards of etiquette are ordinarily voiced and enforced most strongly by not-Indians, especially those who vehemently project their personal support of the "Indian cause." And such canons are vigorously applied not only in face-to-face interactions with Indians but to what is said elsewhere or written about them. The taboo on scholars writing anything that is likely to annoy native peoples is one expression of this explicitly partisan, condescending ethos. A sample of the verbal sanctions addressed to or said about accused nonconformers who distress modern Indians or their allies is contained in the appendix.

The invention, growth, and establishment of this ethos, and of sanctions applied to produce conformity to it, over the past three decades formed the ideological components of a much changed new role for scholars. The expectations for this role are applied to those seeking knowledge about, to others hoping to service what they see as the true needs of Indians, and to those absorbed in a muddled, patronizing combination of both activities. This ethos, the associated sanctions, and the role expectations are now regnant in all institutions involved in the Indian business. These include scholarly organizations, commercial and academic presses, private and public foundations and universities, independent research institutes, the profession of Indian law, the mass media, state and federal governments, and the numerous special-interest advocacy organizations that promote the interests of the Indian, whether as narrow specialty or as sideline to their own central, separate concerns. In structure and operation, this system functions as an interlocking directorate, with Indians and their active supporters positioned in key places in all the seemingly separate circles of information and other resource production, management, and distribution.

This type of support network did not appear suddenly in the mid-1960s out of the historical blue, as some of its participants gripped by a high moral fervor claiming to be on the side of the angels want to believe (Washburn 1988:548–56, 570–72; Porter 1986). It has several prototypes and is characterized by much continuity with similar, older complexes. The "Indian Rights" organizations of the late nineteenth and early twentieth centuries, for example, is one of these (Prucha 1984 II:611–30, 940–68; Washburn 1988:430–58), as is the "Indian Ring" of the late nineteenth century (Prucha 1984 I:586–89). More than a century ago the "Indian Ring" badge was struck by Christian ideologues and pinned on a supposed junta made up of immoral, greedy traders, ranchers, state and federal legislators, and Indian leaders, all allegedly bent on economic exploitation of the helpless native, systematically manipulating the Bureau of Indian Affairs to this end.

Having invented the slur, the good Christian ladies and gentlemen of the past century—who construed their part as being dedicated to the salvation of their chosen underdogs in the struggle for survival, committing themselves morally to the political-economic liberation of the Indian—would have been mortally offended to have the tag pasted on themselves. But of course they had their own vested agenda, self-interested rewards, and alliances in their crusade. Even more so would today's heirs of such coalitions be disturbed if characterized as the "New Indian Ring."

Yet they are like their forerunners in several salient ways, structurally and ideologically. The powerfully idealized sense of mission is only one of these. The recognition that rewards of many different kinds await those who deal with Indians is another. A driving sense of opportunity for realization of the self is a third. The equating of Indian with victim, whether to be rescued or to be further manipulated, is yet one more. An emphasis on the most severe, accusatory, self-serving moral contrasts to set present reformers off against their predecessors and competitors is still another likeness drawing attention to the historical and cultural continuity between modern and earlier organizations committed to making something of or out of the Indian. One common point of widespread agreement between representatives of today's New Indian Ring seeking to establish a distinct ethical identity for themselves, for example, is the declaration that their forerunners were colonialist exploiters, whereas they are anti-colonialist benefactors. Down forced acculturation and assimilation! Up Indian sovereignty, self-determination, and nationalism!

And the old and the new Indian Rings—the networks of supporters, advocates, and exploiters—are alike, as well, in borrowing from a powerful model in the natural sciences to derive a key metaphor for use as a central rationalization in their political philosophies. For both older Christian reformers and those such "philanthropists" accused of being exploiters, the jointly shared trophe was, of course, Social Darwinism. For the contemporary Indian Ring the dominant metaphor has become (cultural) relativism, lifted from Albert Einstein's *General Theory* and uncritically applied to ethical issues and political affairs, as nearly seventy years ago the *London Times* and Walter Lippman forecast would happen (Lippman 1922:70).

However, to understand the genuine affinities of the new and the old "Indian Rings" we must look behind the rhetoric of such labeling to their continuities and discontinuities, expressed in prosaic, dispassionate social science terms. These consist of political, economic, organizational, and cultural features. One piece of the cultural dimension must come first. This consists of the construction and use of highly stereotyped images of "the Indian" as a foil, manipulated politically either to denigrate or to enhance European and American institutions and self-concepts. What has changed between the late nineteenth century (and, for that matter, the eighteenth) and this one is the nature of the institutions and values that are criticized. There are, however, some continuities in this respect. One constant theme has been disquiet about structures of subordination and inequality, with neatly fashioned, imaginative portraits of the Indian used as models for Paradise Lost or, in our time among the "counter-culture," as a fantasy of an Eden that might be regained (Washburn 1988:570–72).

The name of the game played by Indian Rings has been and is interest group politics, their aims the ordinary ones of manipulating power and controlling resources. Historically, this has regularly included some mix of geopolitical, governmental, bureaucratic, ecclesiastical, commercial, legal, suffragist (now feminist), recreational, environmentalist, diplomatic, international, state, economic, and intellectual/academic (with anthropology in recent years losing its older near monopoly), and other involvements (Washburn 1988:5–238). Although native societies have never lacked political acumen and at least some capacity for fending off or manipulating these parties to their own advantage (Viola 1981), over the past half-century the character of the play has greatly changed. This is so because of the recent "empowerment" of Indians in the United States and Canada, acquired in part with substantial aid and instruction from other interest groups. A century ago Indians were rarely seen attending conferences at Lake Mohonk, then a favorite watering hole of the charitably minded Christian elite promoting what they defined as Indian Rights (Washburn 1988:301–23). Today, a conference about Indians without Indians prominent on the agenda or, even better, acting as sponsor-hosts is nearly an impossibility. During the past half-century Indians have created countless local, regional, national, and international organizations from which bases they conduct their own lobbying (Joe 1986). To meetings of these now come churchmen, statesmen, feminists, environmental activists, and academics—as supplicants, soliciting coalitions, seeking favors, checking their approval ratings.

The economic dimension, broadly speaking, has always been and continues to be of special importance in the operations of Indian Rings, old and new. The five-century-old competition for acquisition of, access to, or protection of Indian owned *natural* resources continues today, if necessarily in attenuated form given the decline of the Indian land base. However, as the Indians' earthly assets have been depleted, their huge occult and cultural reserves have been vastly enhanced in value and marketability. The process of commodifying Indians and their heritages began on Columbus' return voyage, grew steadily through the nineteenth century, and accelerated greatly in our own time with the rise of mass communications, the vast expansion of public popular culture, and the increased appeal of things and ways supposedly ancient, exotic, indigenous, and "alternative" (see Kopytoff 1986). The production and exchange of many of the goods and services which form the content of what is called "pan-Indianism," perhaps better trademarked "Mac-Indianism," in large part represents one aspect of this "marketing of heritage" (Dominguez 1986).

However, in an era when job security, fringe benefits, and pensions are conspicuous in nearly everyone's thoughts, we must see Economic Man in the competition of Indians themselves for positions in governments and academic life. At least as much so, this is also true of the rivalry between Indians and everyone else for the manufacturing, advertising, and distribution of information about Indian culture and history, by whatever means it is disseminated—in newsprint, in theatricals, or across the podium. Embroiled in such contests are the numerous academic disciplines that have, over the past three decades, discovered opportunities in things Indian, and that are scrambling for a piece of the action in Native American Studies programs. The Indian's transcendental resources and heritage, many are discovering, possess a fabulous advantage over oil-bearing shales, timberlands, and condominium sites. Rather than being finite, they are infinitely replenishable—indeed, capable of perpetual expansion—limited in quantity, substance, and style only by the ingenuity of their inventors, delivered in annually exhibited new improved models as the consumer's wants dictate. Moreover, trafficking in such commodities during the Information Age is not yet quite so heavily weighted with the moral opprobrium retrospectively cast on milking profits from Indian real estate during the Industrial Age.

The organizational features of the Indian Rings, old and new, are implicit in the foregoing. Fundamentally, these are little more than those of a special interest lobby, one operating within the structure of state and regional politics of the United States (and Canada). In the past century Indian communities most often petitioned their grievances and sought advantage severally, separately, and directly. Written petitions, memorials, and appeals delivered to key decision-makers in the seats of power were then much favored. But preferred far more were visitations by Indian delegations representing distinct "tribal" constituencies seeking face-to-face conferences with top power-wielders in Washington and Ottawa (Viola 1981). The main arenas where advantage was sought were the ordinary quadripartite ones: the executive branch, the legislature, the courts—and public opinion. If Indians were not precisely the first to invent the role and to employ a paid press agent—as the Prairie Potawatomi did in 1845, when they set out for Washington to swing public opinion in their favor—they were among the early pioneers in the employment of such advocates (Clifton 1977:331–38). Attorneys, missionaries, congressmen, traders, interpreters, and an occasional founding anthropologist were also much favored as allies in such influence and political-edge seeking undertakings. Parallel to but very nearly independent of these numerous molecular Indian lobbies were the several prominent Indian Rings proper, the evangelicals and the entrepreneurs with their own agendas for Indians.

Early in our century, new Indian-bred organizations representing common interests began emerging, in some part bringing together formerly separate "tribal" level lobbying efforts. This trend accelerated rapidly in the post–World War II years, resulting in today's proliferation of local, regional, national and international native rights associations, which now perform on many political stages including the global. These still multiplying lobbying organizations have taken on many ideological hues, from the most conservative to extremist (or, at least, wildly bombastic). However, they are now founded, managed, and run almost exclusively by established Indian elites, or by upwardly mobile, ambitious parvenus. Notwithstanding rivalries and the differences between them in proclaimed goals, styles, and preferred tactics, when hard-pressed they will always stand at least temporarily united against their chief adversary, "the Whiteman." Their involvement with not-Indian groups has never ended; only its nature and extent has changed. Loyal not-Indian boosters have been relegated to stand-by, on-call technical or advocacy services—to a support role. These consist of many specialized professionals such as academics and attorneys, established institutions such as major foundations and church groups, various special function lobbying organizations such as environmentalists and New Age cultists, willing celebrities, and a mass of ordinary citizens. The services of some combination of these auxiliary forces can be mobilized rapidly and deployed in defense of whatever pressing issue is foremost at any one time. As in the nineteenth century so in ours: the Indian Rings are organized as political lobbies organized as networks and hierarchies of coalitions and alliances. What has changed is that elite Indians, now power-holders in their own right, dominate the writing and implementation of their agendas.

In our contemporary world no well organized, highly committed interest group with major political, economic, and other goals can survive, much less prosper, without a distinctive set of images of sufficient allure to sustain solidarity, invigorate potential supporters, beguile power-holders, captivate opinion makers, disarm adversaries, and mystify the masses (see Landsman 1987 and 1988). Over the past half century the New Indian Ring—in all its permutations, combinations, and subdivisions—has successfully accomplished the invention of just such a set of collective representations.

This is the second, major piece of the cultural dimension. It is the *product* of this influential network of information producers, image promoters, and opinion shakers. Edward M. Bruner characterizes this product as the recently developed "dominant narrative structure," a preferred story-line about the Indian, and above all else about the relationships between the Indian and the Whiteman, past and present (Bruner 1986: 19–20, 139–142). So often pressed on the unsuspecting public is this now overwhelmingly favored, pivotal, multivalent epic that it has become the substance and soul of a specialized part of North American mass culture: what Americans are convinced they "know" about the Indian. Professor Bruner emphasizes that this narrative structure is a "unit of power," since its creation, embellishment, and promulgation advances the interests of those who claim flesh-and-blood kinship with the narrative's protagonist, the Indian.

Bruner remarks that "Anthropologists and Indians are co-conspirators" in creating and performing this narrative. In line with my previous suggestions, I think he gives too much credit to anthropologists and not enough to Indians for the responsibility of fabricating the narrative. Accomplices, after all, are rarely of equal standing. Clearly, contemporary Indians are the primary political-economic royalty owners of this major work of cultural fiction. Besides, over the past several decades Indians have become central actors in editing and revising, in garnishing, enlarging, and serializing the narrative's substance, busily occupied with inventing their own preferred images. Without question, many anthropologists have had a significant part in ghostwriting and circulating large parts of the account; but since the 1950s they have had increasing help from other academics—mostly historians, joined by some sociologists, many literary specialists, and occasional political scientists and geographers. And the interests of anthropological and other lesser contributors are now largely derivative and secondary, that of increasingly subordinate loyalists, sometimes employees, taking second place to the Indians whose fortunes are more directly at stake.

Bruner provided us only a listing of the central themes and code words found in this dominant narrative structure. Not surprisingly, these are: exploitation, oppression, struggle, resistance movements, ethnic resurgence, liberation, victimization, colonialism (and neo- or internal colonialism), cultural persistence, cultural pluralism, nationhood, a New Golden Age, and the like. He does not provide a plot outline or a synopsis of the narrative. Because *The Invented Indian* critically addresses some of the most striking subplots and themes of this narrative structure, a synopsis of the whole story is important. In chapter 2 I will offer a compiled version of the story-line, together with a running critical, analytic commentary on a few of its principal elements. However, readers must appreciate that this is a living narrative, constantly being revised. As I write these paragraphs, for instance, I learn that the Native Alaskans, apparently increasingly dissatisfied with the long-term results for their special interests of the Alaska Native Claims Settlement Act (see Prucha 1984 II:1131–34), are now complaining that they have been made into "second-class Indians." They now seek sovereign or reservation status for their corporate estates, and a "citizen-plus" position in the state and federal system. Not to be outdone or ignored, in the fiftieth state of the union there is a movement underway to have the Native Hawaiians—now called the "Newest Lost Tribe"—reclassified as Indians, so that they, too, may hold and occupy reservations with federal subvention and protection (Houghton 1986). Obviously, for political fictions, as for purely literary ones, success spawns imitation.

These characterizations about the network of parties involved in the modern Indian business must be read as tentative and hypothetical. They emerged over the years as part of my persistent puzzlement— sometimes amazement—about Indians, their own activities, and what was said and done about them by others, whether historically or on the contemporary scene. Altogether, the experiences related in the memoir and the preliminary formulations amounted to increased motivation for a hopefully substantial creative act, one waiting an opportunity for realization. *The Invented Indian* has a slightly older sibling. Following up on an old interest in marginal individuals, cultural frontiers, and the use of biography as a research technique, and committed to interdisciplinary team efforts, I assembled a predecessor (Clifton 1989).

Two experiences in developing and arranging the publication of that book taught me considerably more about orthodoxy among those who truly believe in and support what Bruner calls the dominant narrative structure. First, in library research I discovered that in published biographies of Indians (a social category now defined generously), the spirit and style of Parson Mason Locke Weems was alive and flourishing (for example, Edmunds 1980; Liberty 1978; Lurie 1985). Published biographical studies of Indians, by and large, were mainly about notables and celebrities. Sterling contributions to the dominant narrative structure, these are thickly larded with the code words and themes listed above, featuring many virtues but displaying few warts. This inference concerned those who *prepare* new examples of the genre.

The second experience involved a small skirmish with one of those central figures who *control* the production and distribution of acceptable examples of the preferred narrative structure, an editor of an Indian series for a university press. After examining the manuscript for *Being and Becoming Indian*, this party complained that the questions raised therein were a "minefield" certain to antagonize many Indians, adding that the book was probably not suitable, implying too controversial for this publisher. Whether it was I never discovered conclusively, for after too many months of indecisive waiting, on enquiry I was informed the manuscript was lost or strayed after being put in the hands of a reviewer.

Having had some training in and practical experience with real minefields, I thought the series editor's analogy apt but misapplied. True minefields are entirely passive weapons, emplaced and employed to *defend* strategic positions and to impede an enemy's freedom of movement. They are, moreover, almost useless unless actively defended by fire. Otherwise, it is easy to dig or blow them up. My collaborators and I were not *laying* a minefield, we were charting a path through one created by others, identifying and marking some of the intellectual hazards we found along the way. That editor, also a tenured professor at a reputable university, did not take kindly to my further remarks about university press censorship.

Both experiences furnished further stimulation. Having confronted some of the defenses of an orthodox position added fuel to my hankering for taking another, stronger, analytic path through the shields fortifying the dominant narrative about Indians. The opportunity for developing this book came shortly thereafter, during an informal meeting of some anthropologists where the discussion focused, warmly so, on the current state of Native American studies and advocacy roles. Somewhere along the line I remarked to the effect that, if this was where we stood, if scholars have helped to invent a new, politically acceptable image of and for the Indian, then it would be an academically responsible thing to assemble some iconoclastic essays. The discussions became more heated. Soon thereafter the assembly divided, with departing loyalists issuing some comments about irreverence and heresy. A concept, title, and embryonic plan for *The Invented Indian* were conceived.

Thirty years' experience had convinced me that this could not be a singleton undertaking. The variety of questions and issues involved were entirely too complex, heavy, and specialized for that even to be considered. Following the meeting where the book's plan emerged, I had a few loyal companions—fellow dissidents—and many suggestions for recruiting additional ones. As I soon discovered, there were a good many more nonconformers ready and waiting than I at first appreciated, enough to add up to several solid critical examinations of many parts of the now standardized image of the Indian in North America. And the protagonist in that dominant narrative structure, I soon understood, is only one variant of an older, more inclusive image, the invented Native or Primitive (see Kuper 1988).

Recruiting capable, willing, sufficiently bold authors produced further unanticipated insights into the substance and defenses of the standard story about Indians. I had passing difficulty communicating the concept of *The Invented Indian* to a few, I found. Although this narrative structure has been preeminent for a good many years, I learned that some long time contributors to it still think of themselves as radical deconstructionists not orthodox conformers. Two essay plans and drafts I received were simply more of the same stuff—Tales Told About Victims. I believed that their battle had been won. Nonetheless, some scholars still dedicate themselves to correcting older, negative stereotypes about the Ignoble Savage—by substituting newer, positive ones, of the Noble Savage in modern garb, wearing a three-piece suit.

And several times I again carelessly strayed into that minefield. One potential author, for whose writings I had and have the utmost scholarly respect, at first responded enthusiastically and promised a solid essay for this book. Later, after sober reflection, the risks intruded into that individual's consciousness. The essay was withdrawn on the grounds that if it appeared in a book called *The Invented Indian* that researcher's own Indians would be greatly disturbed, blocking further studies of them. Another potential author, an equally well respected academician, responded expressing much interest but required that I provide certification that the other contributors were not "anti-Indian" or "racist." Declarations or protestations of loyalty and conformity, obviously, as well as fears of guilt by association, remain important to some anthropologists and historians involved with Indians.

One last example will illustrate how far such concerns can carry a few, and something more of the pattern of the minefield. Another potential contributor, who came well recommended despite weaker qualifications, at first also expressed enthusiasm about writing an essay for the book. Then came a nervous, late-night phone call from a fourth-party, a mutual acquaintance of ours prompted by the second-party, the potential author. The second-party had turned to some third-parties associated with the National Congress of American Indians, a major lobbying organization, to check out *my* allegiances. Although the reports were apparently not encouraging, the author, still tempted, wished to give me the benefit of the doubt but only after further inquiry, seeking declarations of my fidelity. Having been asked to do this, on the phone the third-party link in this net was apprehensive for having agreed to conduct an inquisition. I expect I added to my interlocutor's distress for having assumed this role with several reasonably polite remarks about "Red McCarthyism."

Whether I or the contributors to this book may be fairly characterized as "anti-Indian" or "racist," our readers may see for themselves. Such smears, I think, are no more than part of the sanctions protecting an orthodox politico-academic position. Lively, provocative, well-informed, thoroughly disciplined scholars willing to serve as intellectual dissidents would be a more accurate assessment of my colleagues, I believe. I have learned a great deal from and remain indebted to them for greatly improving my understanding. I anticipate that others not too strongly involved with or caught up by and committed to reinforcing the standard Indian story will find them equally informative and enlightening.

The Invented Indian is intended as an intelligent book about the conventional story most commonly told about the Indians of the United States and Canada. Necessarily, if in a subsidiary manner, it is also about alternative views of the changing nature of and relations between Indians and others, past and present. This book is designed as an alternative to and a corrective for a standard narrative now so deeply embedded in the American consciousness that its origins and purposes, its authenticity and validity, are rarely questioned in public, then only with some hazard. Altogether, there is no political aim to the essays in this book. Jointly, we are advocates of one thing: clear thinking, reason, solid evidence, relevant theoretical ideas. Thinking and writing about Indians, I believe, should not be conducted according to or rated by the standards used for press agents in a senatorial campaign, or those for an advertising agency.

The organization of the essays in this book is straightforward. Chapter 2 presents a compiled, annotated version of the dominant narrative account about the Indian. Chapters 3 through 8 each addresses at length one or more of the standard parts of this whole work of cultural fiction, specific invented traditions. Mostly these are of a type called "The Good Things the Indian Gave the Whiteman." An image of the original American as a protective sheltering woman, is one of these, as is the portrait of the hospitably generous Indian readily sharing his bounty with strangers. Among other "good things given," here critically examined, are models for the United States Constitution, for ecological sainthood, and for an egalitarian ethic. None of the authors of these first essays, like their insurgent companions in those that follow, is much interested solely in debunking or rapping scholarship that is shaky, politicized, or fallacious. Each reaches behind the popular fabrications to ask how they got invented, what functions they serve, for whose ends. Larger insights and lessons result from such disciplined, open-minded enquiries.

In chapters 9 through 12 somewhat broader issues are examined, recurrent themes involving the pattern of content and style in the parts of the dominant narrative, and questions of methodology and truth seeking. As David Henige shows in his critique of a striking example of the misuse of historical methodology, estimates of pre-Columbian native populations have been vastly inflated for apparently moralizing, not soundly scholarly purposes. Richard de Mille's essay, developed in concert with his pioneering efforts to expose the Don Juan hoax for what it was, lays out valuable standards for assessing the truth value of substantive representations of the Indian. The points de Mille makes about checking the authenticity and validity of such representations are applicable to questions raised in all other essays. Alice Kehoe's essay is a guide to one of the latest frenzies involving Indians, where "medicine men" and their imitators join urban witches and transplanted South Asian gurus in expanding American pop and do-it-yourself religiosity with primal minds and screams, only the most recent version of an ancient vision of the distant Alien as Natural Man. Readers of this section, except those especially interested in the anthropological mysteries of kinship studies, may find R.H. Barnes' essay the most difficult. But it deserves the closest attention, for Professor Barnes shows how, even for the purest of theoretical purposes, scholars can set off on an endless wild goose chase, constructing increasingly abstracted, barren models of aspects of Indian social life, representations based on faulty generalizations, for want of close attention to solid facts and a critical assessment of original sources. The Rise and Fall of the Omaha Kinship Type has never had the moral or political effects of the work of David Henige's "High Counters," and Barnes' essay is all the more important because of this, again showing that in science and scholarship clear thinking and method are more important than motive or the politicized use of scholarship.

The last five essays address comparative dimensions of the Invented Indian and fictions or traditions invented to present a usable image of this legendary being. From Anglo-Canada comes an assessment of the rhetorical excesses displayed by advocates of the Victimized Noble Savage. From south of that border arrives Stephen Feraca's feisty exposé of one of the more remarkable examples of institutional racism in American society, the inner workings of the Bureau of Indian Affairs. Important aspects of the Indian Before the Bar of Justice, and the dilemmas of citizens affected by court decisions regarding him, are discussed perceptively by Allan van Gestel. He is one the rarest of professional advocates, a scholarly attorney who defends the quarry, not the Indian. Crossing the Atlantic comes a wise assessment of Europe's Indians, imported and domestic, past and present, by Christian F. Feest, a scholar who knows both the European and the American varieties well, whether authentic or spurious. Lastly, from French-Canada comes our closing essay, Jean-Jacque Simard's five century wrap-up, a social and intellectual history of the Indian inhabiting the minds of Europeans and Americans, together with some nicely fused philosophical-sociological reflections about alternative futures for the real people who have been subjected to such extraordinary stereotyping for so long.

Up to the point of editing the final manuscript, it had not occurred to me how propitious the date of its publication might be—1990. This is just two years shy of 1992, the quincentenary of Christopher Columbus' first visit to the Americas. Already the first blasts have been fired in what soon will be two separate celebratory, public relations barrages timed to culminate in that year. From one side will come bursts advancing the prideful claims of Italian Americans, Spanish Americans, and others asserting European ancestries for having discovered and developed the Americas. To counter this offensive there will be heavy protective fire, from the defenders themselves—those claiming native American identity—as well as from their ardent allies. The heaviest caliber munition in the defenders' arsenal bears the label: The Massive Debts the Whiteman Owes the Indian. This weapon comes in several marks, including: I—The Good Things the Indian Has Given the Whiteman; and, II—The Bad Things the Whiteman Has Done to the Indian.

A preliminary salvo from Mark I has already landed, a book by anthropologist Jack Weatherford titled *Indian Givers* (1988). His title is a neat play on the ordinary slang meaning of this phrase, for the subject matter of the book is not what was given then taken back, but the enormous contributions of "the Indian" to world nutrition, capital formation, health, clothing, transportation, environmental ethics, institutions of representative democracy, and the like. If those touting this book are to be believed, Weatherford, who alludes to "some Creek Indian ancestry," set out on an 85,000-mile trek from Timbuktu to Tibet determined singlehandedly to illuminate "gigantic blind spots in the history of the Americas," a not unambitious solo voyage (Graham 1989). Whether the world's historians will cheer the results remains to be seen; but—Weatherford reports—from his Indian supporters he gets much applause and many gifts. Meanwhile, his fusillade has become that anthropological rarity, a best-seller. And plans are underway to retool this ordnance into larger caliber, a television epic, to be fired off at the primest of times—in 1992.

As the months pass, major national celebrations of this momentous event will be accompanied by counter-cultural media events endlessly replaying the victimization theme. Local and national Indian lobbyists, hobbyists, and their support groups will be out in force making the most of this opportunity to capture thirty seconds of prime time or half a column on the first page. There will be many grants awarded to Indians and faithful supporters for symposia and for the publication of pamphlets, more books, and docudramas. The *Indian Historian*, the *American Indian Culture and Research Journal*, the *Northeast Indian Quarterly*, and similar in-house publications will each devote one or more special issues to appropriately damning or glamorizing themes.[1] Vine Deloria will publish a book titled, *Columbus Was Red*. The *D'Arcy McNickle Center for Indian History* will organize a major series of symposia and publications about what Columbus and his progeny did to the Indians. However, the nomination of the Indian as *Time*'s person-of-the-year will be rejected, apologetically.

Indian delegations in great numbers will descend on Washington, Madrid, Moscow, the Vatican, other European capitals, and the headquarters of the United Nations with protests and demands. The United States Congress will respond with a concurrent resolution extolling the many crucial things Indians have freely donated to American civilization, reiterating its true faith and support of Indian self-determination and tribal sovereignty. Hundreds of American Indian newspapers and radio stations will feature specials on all these happenings. The arthritic American Indian Movement will rise again. There will be demonstrations at Plymouth Rock, in Philadelphia, and on Manhattan Island. Whether Indians will be successful in enlisting the aid and services of Greenpeace in providing a vessel loaded with wildflowers to be spread in the sea offshore of Guanahaní Island is still uncertain. But this pacific performance will be followed by an intercontinental Indian assault party which will land on Guanahaní's beaches, there to plant their flags and to repossess "these lands" in the name of the host nations of the Americas. And a massive intertribal delegation, in full regalia, thick with medicine men, will surely visit the Cathedral of Santo Domingo, to cast tobacco on the crypt and to chant prayers of forgiveness over the bones of the Admiral of the Ocean Sea, he who took the names "Christgiver" and "Colonizer."

I do not agree with Karl Marx that great events occur twice, first as tragedy, then as farce. These contrived happenings will not simply be political amusements—they are deadly serious twentieth century business. Indians have a good thing going for them, having long since mastered the fine arts of manipulating the mass media and public opinion to their own best advantage. My forecasts are safe bets in style and aim if not in exact form. They have ample, recent precedents. Even so minor event as a routine papal visit to Los Angeles, for instance, brought a hastily compiled "oral history" supposedly listing the "remembered" horrors of the Franciscan missions in Southern California, delivered to evoke the maximum of Catholic guilt (see Bahr 1989). And the serial celebrations of the United States' founding and Constitution over the past decade were each accompanied by counter-happenings staged by the Indian lobby.

Possibly, the maverick commentaries in *The Invented Indian* will be submerged by all this hullabaloo, which will be mostly aimed straight at Americans' brain stems, not their intellects. But we hope that readers will find illumination in the following pages, and ways of protecting themselves against being bamboozled.

Note

1. After this sentence was written, there arrived an announcement from the *Northeast Indian Quarterly* of its contribution to this counter-celebration, *Indian Corn of the Americas: Gift to the World*.

References

Bahr, Donald and Susan Fenger. 1989. "Indians and Missions: Homage and Debate with Rupert Costo and Jeanette Henry." *Journal of the Southwest* 31:298–329.

Bruner, Edward M. 1986. "Experience and its Expressions." In *The Anthropology of Experience*. Victor Turner and Edward M. Bruner, eds. Urbana, IL: University of Illinois Press. Pp. 3–30.

Clifton, James A. 1965. "The Southern Ute Tribe as a Fixed Membership Group." *Human Organization* 24:319–27.

———. 1976. "Fieldwork II: Applied Anthropology Among Wisconsin's Native Americans." In *The Study of Anthropology*. David E. Hunter and Phillip Whitten, eds. New York: Harper & Row.

———. 1977. *The Prairie People: Continuity and Change in Potawatomi Indian Culture, 1665–1965*. Lawrence, KS: Regents Press of Kansas.

———. 1984. *The Pokagons, 1683–1983: Catholic Potawatomi Indians of the St. Joseph River Valley*. Lanham, MD: University Press of America.

———. 1987. "The Political Rhetoric of Indian History." *Annals of Iowa* 49:126–35.

———. 1989. *Being and Becoming Indian: Biographical Studies of North American Frontiers*. Chicago, IL: Dorsey Press (Belmont CA: Wadsworth).

Dominguez, Virginia R. 1986. "The Marketing of Heritage." *American Ethnologist* 13:546–55.

Edmunds, R. David, ed. 1980. *Studies in Diversity: American Indian Leaders*. Lincoln, NE: University of Nebraska Press.

Graham, Keith. 1989. "Macalester Teacher Details American Indians' Impact."
Cox News Service. June 18. Menominie, MI: *Leader-Telegram*, P. 2F.

Henige, David. 1984. "Origin Traditions of American Racial Isolates: A Case
of Something Borrowed." *Appalachian Journal* 11:201–14.

Houghton, Richard H., III. 1986. "An Argument for Indian Status for Native
Hawaiians—The Discovery of A Lost Tribe." *American Indian Law Review*
14:1–55.

Joe, Jennie R., ed. 1986. "American Indian Policy and Cultural Values: Conflict
and Accommodation." Contemporary American Indian Issues Series, No.
6. American Indian Studies Center. Los Angeles: University of California.

Kamber, Peter Heinrich. 1989. "Timber and Termination: The Klamath Case."
European Review of Native American Studies 3:43–7.

Kopytoff, Igor. 1986 "The Cultural Biography of Things: Commoditization as
Process." In *The Social Life of Things: Commodities in Cultural Perspective.*
Arjun Appadurai, ed. New York: Cambridge University Press.

Kuper, Adam. 1988. *The Invention of Primitive Society: Transformations of an
Illusion.* New York: Routledge.

Landsman, Gail H. 1987. "Indian Activism and the Press." *Anthropological
Quarterly* 60:101–13.

———. 1988. *Sovereignty and Symbol: Indian/White Conflict at Ganienkeh.*
Albuquerque, NM: University of New Mexico Press.

Liberty, Margo, ed. 1978. *American Indian Intellectuals.* St. Paul, MN: West
Publishing Company.

Lippman, Walter. 1922. *Public Opinion.* London: Allen & Unwin.

Lurie, Nancy O. 1985. *North American Indian Lives.* Milwaukee, WI: Milwaukee Public Museum.

Paredes, J. Anthony. 1974. "The Emergence of Contemporary Eastern Creek
Indian Identity." In *Social and Cultural Identity: Problems of Persistence and
Change.* T.K. Fitzgerald, ed. Athens, GA: University of Georgia Press.

Porter, Frank, ed. 1986. *Strategies for Survival: American Indians in the Eastern
United States.* Westport, CT: Greenwood Press.

Prucha, Francis Paul. 1984. *The Great Father: The United States Government
and the American Indians.* 2 vols. Lincoln, NE: University of Nebraska Press.

Schultz, Terri. 1973. "Bamboozle Me Not at Wounded Knee." *Harper's Magazine* 246:46–8, 53–6.

Smith, Desmond. 1973. "Wounded Knee: the Media Coup d'Etat." June 25.
The Nation 216:806–9.

Stern, Theodore. 1966. *The Klamath Tribe: A People and Their Reservation.*
American Ethnological Society Monograph 41. Seattle, WA: University of
Washington Press.

Viola, Herman J. 1981. *Diplomats in Buckskin: A History of Indian Delegations
in Washington City.* Washington, DC: Smithsonian Institution Press.

Washburn, Wilcomb E., ed. 1988. *History of Indian-White Relations.* Handbook
of North American Indians, Vol. 4. Washington, DC: Smithsonian Institution.

Weatherford, Jack. 1988. *Indian Givers.* New York: Crown.

2

The Indian Story: A Cultural Fiction

James A. Clifton

After World War II the Indian again captured the hearts and imaginations of admiring, sometimes worshipful North Americans and Europeans. A much enlarged and radically revised edition of an older narrative account of the character and experiences of these native peoples appeared in this period. The storyline emerged in bits and pieces, each to be market-tested and further refined, eventually forming an orthodox version captivating the attention and sympathies of swelling, appreciative audiences.

Numerous authors have contributed to the development and enhancement of the modules and themes making up this stirring account. Many are living, some long dead. Many of its composers are identifiable—indeed, a few have achieved at least passing celebrity for their contributions—but others remain nameless or obscure. The story is embodied and transmitted across time and space by all available media: oral, print, the *tableau vivant*, still and mobile graphics, live theatrical, electronic.

The elements and keynote patterns of this narrative are borne to audiences through many genres in various ways. Among these styles of presentation are literary narratives such as novels, short stories, and poetry. These range from works intended as high culture to five dollar pulp dreadfuls of the horror fantasy, harlequinized romance, and frontier adventure varieties. Narrative chronicles of significant events and developments are another genre, many with all the trappings of professional historiography, others counterfeit. Case studies by anthropologists and their imitators about the cultures of native peoples, living and dead, real or entirely fictitious, are one more significant kind of exposition. Representations of "the Indian" which fit patterned expectations appear regularly in advertising campaigns, but similar notional portrayals are even more common in print and television journalism, as news items or in editorial pronouncements. Live, dramatized performances staged by suitably costumed soloists or troupes are another means of communicating the Indian story to mass audiences. Sometimes the latter are seasonally staged local spectacles purporting to be reconstitutions of important historical events. More often they are traveling amateur, semi-professional or professional enactments of culture, legend, and ceremonial carried over a established circuit to national and international audiences.

The authors, artists, managers, and actors who produce and present variants of this Indian narrative come from various social backgrounds. If they cannot or do not claim a native identity, they must face and deal with the problem of the plausibility of their representations. How did they come by the information and the interpretations they disclose? On the other hand, if they do assert Indianness, even if such an identity is merely hinted at, the question of believability is automatically blunted, even set aside entirely. Professed Indian performers, their audiences assume, are inherently, rightfully, fully possessed of the heritages they represent in public. There are no accepted esthetic or academic standards of criticism of such performances. In truth, critiques of them are not readily tolerated.

For those seen as not-Indian, the question of the authenticity of their portrayals is answered in several ways. Anthropologists accomplish this by remarking long periods of total immersion in participant observation of native peoples, and historians by citing exhaustive labor in archives and critical examination of documents. Print journalists double-check their hopefully authoritative sources, while in television news reports the issue scarcely arises: certitude is achieved by the pointing of a videorecorder at a happening. Writers of pulp novels or factitious reports regularly claim insider expertise gained during a period of intimate contact with well qualified traditional Indians, as do those clever actors who don costumes to conduct allegedly "Indian medicine" rites on behalf of the world-weary.

Performers or producers publicly recognized as genuine Indians, as noted, have much less of a problem with plausibility. However, both Indians and not-Indians presenting parts of the native story to others must cope with several complications in common. Whichever media or genre they use, when arranging an exhibition, a retelling of the established Indian story, neither can stray too far from what Edward M. Bruner calls the primary contemporary narrative structure that underlies such representations (Bruner 1986:12–20, 139–41). Performer and audience, also, are locked together by this dominant pattern of preferred expectations in style and substance. Yet audiences vary in wants and level of sophistication. Times and their pivotal urgencies also change, the demands of patrons of the paramount Indian narrative with them. So enhancements and elaborations of the storyline regularly appear.

The responses of one Hanay Geiogamah to a magazine writer epitomize many of these thoughts (Fenwick 1989). Creator of and impresario for the new *American Indian Dance Theatre*, he offered this complex image to his publicist: "a sense of family is a *sine qua non* for any Indian enterprise," adding, "There is a religious subtext to our production. The spiritual part of every aspect of Indian life is there." Hanay went on to stress traditional, intergenerational continuity, native community involvement in his troupe's productions, the "tension" between things sacred and ways theatrical, obtaining the consent of elders for revealing supernatural elements to other publics, and more in the same vein.

Until recently such an artist-entrepreneur, perhaps baptized as a person named William van der Bloomen, would have taken some such recognizably "Indian" name as Bill Swirling Thunder for a *nom de soiré*, implying an informal foot planted in two cultural worlds. Nowadays, with the theme of total return to native roots prevalent, adopting what for English-speaking audiences is a tongue-twisting "tribal" handle has become *de rigueur*. This new practice highlights the contrast between performer and audience, and increases the sense of authenticity. What's in a stage name? The most compelling public imago conceivable.

The rest of this sophisticated impresario's discourse is subtle but penetrable. It is mostly a replay, with refinements, of the earlier styles of announcements made at Powwow circuit performances, from which the most talented entertainers were selected for Geiogamah's *Dance Theatre*. Comments about "a *sine qua non*" and dramatic "tension" might not play well before audiences at a rural Kansas Labor Day performance; they do express just the right combination of slightly obsolescent *and* now trendy erudition to be appealing to those thronging the Kennedy Center and Albert Hall. The thematic constants in this dialogue, however, mark substantial continuity in the producer's expectations of the wants of all his troupe's patrons, past and present. "Ancient" traditions presented for the edification of not-Indian publics is but one of these. The sturdy, responsible subordination of an individual Indian—even a highly educated, much traveled Indian—to hearth and home community, the demurely reticent public revelation of formerly sacrosanct esoterica, are others. In the successes of the *American Indian Dance Theatre* before international audiences we may, perhaps, be witnessing a significant cultural uplifting. In earlier years Powwow dancing was staged by amateurs and semipros mainly as a diversion for rustics, later for middlebrows. Now the performers, reportedly, are beginning to captivate urban and elite audiences.

Such preliminaries aside, one feature of the dominant storyline about the Indian is arresting for its absence. The standard narrative is never presented as a whole, with all or even a large array of its parts stuck together in one place. Yet the historical and cultural pieces of it do fit together, implying and depending on one another. Presented singly or in partial combination, the events singled out, the strong metaphors, and the themes recurrently expressed rely on and have an inherent, dramatic relationship to one another. They form a larger, expressively cultural unity. This overall narrative about the Indian, moreover, has pronounced social, political, and economic implications. However powerfully stimulating it may be delivered piecemeal, the whole account is even more so. The complete story tells the traumatic experiences of the righteous Indian in North American history; but it also predicates and ratifies a special place for the Indian in modern North American moral orders and political systems.

An effort to compile at least an abridgement of the entire standard narrative is in order, for there comes a point when a simple listing of key words and themes will not do. However suggestive these may be, a full sense of the narrative's essential logic and plan are not thereby made explicit. Still, short of an encyclopedia, no such account can be anything more than a précis, listing the more common narrative elements in some reasonably coherent arrangement. The following paragraphs consist of an effort to spell out just such a digest. Each of the next fifteen chapters critically examines in detail one or more particular elements of some of those barely mentioned in this outline.

In the beginning, North America was motherland for between ten and thirty million truly humane beings. This dense population was organized into over two hundred separate, sovereign nations existing continuously—according to the unquestionable authority of their own traditional histories—from time immemorial. Each such sovereignty had its own government and exclusive national territory (Dobyns 1983 and 1987; Wilkinson 1987).[1] Although none of these indigenous nations understood or recognized the propriety of owning, buying, or selling land, they did claim and exercise the rightful privilege of occupying parts of it and using its fruits. This right, as hosts, they freely shared with their neighbors and visiting strangers, whom they treated generously as guests.

Mistakenly called Indians by the Whiteman who later invaded, defrauded them of, and despoiled their property and persons, these native peoples had no common name for themselves, nor any formal organization binding the separate nations together. Yet they were identified with one another as a genuine whole in an existential *communitas*. Each with its own language and special customs marking their unique identities, these nations lived in peace and harmony with one another.

Underneath these minor cultural differences, nonetheless, lay vitalizing commonalities, the heart and soul of the Indian. Each nation, for instance, defined its territory as a Holy Land (Dobyns 1987), and altogether they worshipfully personified their habitat as Mother Earth, existing in harmony with all her creatures. This "biological" or environmentalist ethic pervaded every aspect of the life of the Indian, for whom all things, all thoughts, all behavior, and all happenings were pervasively sacred. Animistic, purely spiritualistic, uncontaminated, these archaic nations existed in free-floating, ahistorical time, their beliefs and ways irreversible, insoluble, and—as others have but recently come to appreciate—ineradicable (Martin 1987: 3–34, 192–220).

These shared bonds of harmonious being were most conspicuous inside each Indian nation, within the daily and seasonal rounds of community life. There social living was marked by the great value placed on equality, tolerance, kindness, altruism, mutual affection, and respect. Interference in the freedom of every person to do what they pleased was unknown. Little children were treated with much regard as small-scale adults. Women enjoyed a position on a par with that of men. The enfeebled, incapacitated, and elderly were highly honored and their wants attended to. Gays were not only easily abided, they were specially recognized for their notable spirituality (Williams 1986).

Political power in these indigenous nations could not corrupt because it was so widely shared: important decisions were not made until full consensus spontaneously manifested itself, unprompted by anyone. Wealth could not be accumulated by any individual, group, or government because generous giving was the accepted rule. In fact, their economies were based on gratuitous reciprocal gift-exchange, not mean barter or profit-oriented selling. No man could be another's property. Even his labor could not be demanded or commanded by anyone. Freely given cooperation was the norm in all things political and economic, made possible because everyone owned all necessary means of production—tools, skills, access to raw materials. For all these reasons, the evils of political, economic, social, or gender inequality were unknown. Political hierarchy was incomprehensible to and incompatible with the Indian way, as was the drive to accumulate material things beyond the bare minimum required to satisfy the basic needs of everyday and seasonal life.

So, living spontaneously, joyously, in intimate, peaceful, stress-free relations with one another, close to and in harmony with the rhythms of the earth and its creatures, consuming natural foods, nearly free of disabling or deadly diseases, with extensive knowledge of nature's *materia medica*, their medicine men available to cure all ailments physical or mental, barring unforeseen accident the Indian lived to a ripe old age. Death came easily, recognized as but a natural step in the celestial cycle of all things, living or incorporeal. Following an elder's passing, the sanctified remains were laid in a consecrated place never thereafter to be desecrated, where memories of the ancestors were forever devoutly commemorated, their bones resting in peace.

This native North American way-of-being developed and was perfected primordially, existing over the ages with only minor changes, these merely refining the fundamental, archaic pattern. So ancient and ingrained, so inherently potent were these ways that they were carried and transmitted across the generations in the very life substance of every Indian, the blood that runs through their veins, almost impossible to weaken or repress, much less to extinguish. Yet an almost insurmountable threat of annihilation (of genocide) or, if not that, of cultural and group identity ruination (of assimilation) these native peoples faced unexpectedly, beginning just five centuries ago.

Until then unsuspected by the Indian, across a great geographic and cultural gulf, unknowably far to the East, there lived another variety of humankind, the Whiteman.[2] The Whiteman's values and ways were shockingly different from those of the Indian. Following his own ancient Judeo-Christian ethic, he was the greatest environmental sinner the world has ever known. Rather than to be worshiped, its resources husbanded, a life in harmony with it treasured, the earth for him was a thing, a physical asset to be ruthlessly exploited for his own crass materialistic gain. His fundamental ethic was secular, not sacred, for all the formal surface trappings of his artificial religiosity.

Finding his own lands and their resources inadequate to his ravenous greed, the Whiteman's destructively competitive craving for power and for the accumulation of wealth sent him forth to discover and capture the riches belonging to those inhabiting other parts of the globe. The Whiteman, overwhelmed by his own conceits, claimed these "New Worlds" as his own by right of "discovery" or "conquest." His blue bloods, who had previously dispossessed the exploited masses of his own nations, transported large numbers of them overseas, many millions into the lands of the Indian nations of North America. These new-found "others of the world" the Whiteman saw as peoples without history, with few rights except those subordinate to his own wants as their new masters, simply more helpless humans to be brutalized and overpowered for his own capitalistic gain. (Wolf 1982)

On the beaches and in the interior of North America the Indian at first peaceably and generously welcomed the Whiteman—as a respected guest sojourning in his ancient land. To these visitors the Indian selflessly gave much valuable knowledge and many of his even more valuable inventions and things: new food crops to feed his starving millions and to help develop the Whiteman's unproductive lands; unprecedented medicines to combat his terrible epidemic diseases; fresh, practical styles of clothing; previously unknown technologies; new kinds of raw materials and new sources for old ones for his expanding factories—all these the Indian freely gave, asking and receiving little in return. (Weatherford 1988)

The Indian even considerately gave the Whiteman bountiful places to live for his own pitiable pariahs—the deprived, the homeless, the banished, the disillusioned. These the Indian took in hand, teaching them the survival skills they needed in a strange land. The Whiteman, in his turn, looked on the Indian with racially prejudiced eyes. He called the Indian "Savage"; but in truth, as his own ruthlessly murderous behavior toward his host later amply demonstrated, it was the Whiteman who was the Savage. (Wrone and Nelson 1973)

However, the very best of the good things the Indian gave the Whiteman included a set of sterling ideals and values for proper social living. Following early experiences with Indians, reports about their estimable life-styles gradually filtered into the bigoted minds of these aliens, eventually producing radically new fashions of social thought. At first only a few of his philosophers, or an occasional legal theorist, for example, recognized the ultimate truths of the Indian way. These acknowledged the vast differences between the Indian's *communitas* and their own *dominium*, whereby power and wealth were held by a few at the expense of the many. Thus the Indian's ideals of liberty, human rights, representative democracy, and the sharing of power and property equally led first to fresh visions of new political styles for the Whiteman, eventually to shattering revolutions seeking their realization (Brandon 1986). One expression of this Indian political-economic gift was in the new United States, where the Iroquois Nations gave the Founders a model for their own constitution. (Barreiro 1988)

Many years later, only after the larger significance of the Indian way became more apparent to the Whiteman, did he begin accepting other parts of the Indian ethic. It was revealed to some, for instance, that God *is* Red (Deloria 1973). Disillusioned youth found in the stubborn Indian, refusing to dissolve in a Philistine melting-pot, the prototype for a genuinely meaningful countercultural identity (Brand 1988). Experiences with Indian spirituality began raising the consciousness of many when they gathered in sacred circles near ancient blessed power-points. And those frightened by their destruction of the habitat found in the Indian's environmental ethic, as expressed many years ago by the wise Chief Seattle, a secure, alternative global future. (Kaiser 1987)

The Whiteman did deliver to the Indian some things in return for the hospitality and the treasures given him. A few trinkets or pieces of silver in exchange for fraudulent "purchases" of valuable real estate was one such, in transactions the Indian could not comprehend, since the idea of selling strips of Mother Earth's tender flesh was quite beyond him. Servitude was another experience delivered the Indian, as the Whiteman sought profit from the labor of his body as well as from exploitation of his resources, or else imposed enslavement as punishment when some at long last rose up to rebel against the horrors inflicted on them. But this experiment failed, for no Indian could long survive as another man's chattel.

The Whiteman also tried to convert the Indian into a market for his surplus commodities, with little success, for the Indian's wants were limited and easily satisfied. Among the consumables the Whiteman forced down the Indian's throat was beverage alcohol, causing what many mistakenly have thought were grave social problems. As it happens, on later reexamination, it turns out that what once seemed to have been community and self-destroying chemical abuse by the Indian was really no more than a disguised social protest movement. (Lurie 1971)

The Whiteman also tried to bully the Indian into adopting new roles, accepting new customs, practicing new ways. Rape and the prostitution of Indian women were among these. The appointment of all-powerful, easily corrupted High Chiefs to do the Whiteman's bidding was another, as was widespread bribery. Numerous unthinkably barbarous customs the White-man intimidated the Indian into adopting, including their employment as Black and Indian slave hunters, and as mercenaries to fight the Whiteman's wars. Even the abominable practice of scalping the Whiteman introduced and compelled the Indian into practicing—rewarding him richly for slaughtering the Whiteman's enemies, Indian and White alike, and for delivering bloody trophies of the slaughter. (Axtell and Sturtevant 1980)

As the Whiteman's invasion of North America continued, other newly introduced evils only increased the plight of the suffering Indian. Spreading rapidly even before his explorers and settlers set foot on their lands were the Whiteman's killer plagues. These cataclysmic pandemics regularly wiped out whole communities and nations, massacring innocent victims by the untold millions, a holocaust that quickly reduced North America's native population by 95 percent, greatly easing the Whiteman's road into these conquered lands. (Thornton 1987)

Recognizing a useful thing when they saw it and convinced that the only good Indian was a dead Indian, in later years the Whiteman deliberately introduced germ warfare, seeking to accelerate the butchery—a Final Solution to the Indian problem. Discontent even with this improved rate of depopulation, later the Whiteman captured the few survivors, bound them in chains, and bulldozed them out of the remnants of their aboriginal Holy Lands, driving them westward like cattle along a Trail of Tears into the Great American Desert, hoping there they would soon languish and die unnoticed (Dobyns 1987:72). To these efforts at purging North America of the Indian, the Whiteman added military massacres, perpetrating innumerable My Lais in Indian Country. (Brown 1971)

In this massive, centuries-long campaign to totally stamp out the Indian in body and spirit, the Whiteman failed. In isolated regions—here a few individuals or families, there the fragments of communities or whole nations—some survivors somehow managed to endure, clinging tenaciously to their primordial identities, resolutely refusing to surrender what was most precious to them, their ethnic roots. Some did this directly under the "benevolent" paternalistic gaze of the Whiteman's governments which at last, once the Indian's resources had been despoiled, reluctantly agreed to preserve their few remaining bodies while laboring to "save"—to subvert—their unconquerable souls (Axtell 1985). More survived directly in the midst of the centers of Whiteman populations, even in metropolitan areas.

Some of the latter did so by adopting a cultural chameleon strategy, disguising themselves as Whitemen when heavily pressed to change their ways. Others accomplished the same end with a hideaway tactic, deliberately secreting themselves, remaining "undocumented," thus historyless and unidentifiable, avoiding contacts with domineering Whitemen who would have exposed and compelled them to do the unthinkable. In neither instance was the feigned Whiteness of the Indian even so much as skin deep. (Fogelson 1989:141–42)

Until recently, throughout these long centuries of forced conversions, the Indian survivor has often donned a thin veneer of Whiteness, but this was no more than superficial protective camouflage, a mere ploy used to safeguard their true inward Indianness.[3] The Indian was greatly aided in this cultural resistance movement by an intrinsic feature of his nature, one discounted if recognized at all by most Whitemen. His inherent Indianness is inevitably carried across the generations in his distinctively Indian blood. In fact, Indian blood has sufficient power to overwhelm even the results of many generations of interbreeding with Whitemen, compelling the original Indian's distant progeny to become, think, and act as a True Indian, producing an interesting biosocial phenomenon, the "cultural fullblood."

Therefore, however few they may be, and whatever the measure of their biological blanching or sociological compounding, even one or a scant few survivors of the bloodline of an aboriginal Indian nation served as hardy sociological rhizomes. These rootstalks awaited only proper nourishment and opportune conditions to regenerate, propagate, flourish, and perpetuate the ancient national life-ways.

Little by little, after World War II the conditions necessary for resuscitating this perennial intrinsic Indianness started appearing. More and more came out of hiding to doff their masks and take up their legitimate place as the heirs of North America's rightful, original owners. To many other thousands the long buried, unsuspected germ of their Indianness was revealed, and these started revitalizing their old nations. Other surviving Indian nations, beleaguered on small parcels of land, increased their recruiting of kin moved elsewhere and long lost track of. This "Indian renaissance" came about largely by the Indian's own efforts, with some modest help from a few kindly Whitemen and their institutions. (Leacock and Lurie 1971:418–80)

Among the most important of these institutions are the Indian treaty and the federal courts. Over the past thirty years, at long last, wise jurists have recognized the Indian treaty for what it was originally intended to be. When the United States began, they finally admitted, its founders saw that Indian nations were like all other nations on earth, sovereign peoples each owning its own territory. And so, when the Whiteman set out to steal Indian land, or to commit some other injustice, they negotiated treaties for such purposes. These Indian treaties, jurists now concede, have exactly the same standing as those negotiated with Germany or Japan. (Wrone 1987; Wilkinson 1987)

But at the time Indian treaties were negotiated there was a great difference in how the Whiteman and the Indian viewed them. Then, for the Whiteman, the treaty was little more than a scrap of paper, an instrument of temporary expediency which in later years could be easily discarded, ignored, or abrogated unilaterally. But for the Indian a totally different view prevailed. For him the treaty was a sacred pact, unalterable by any mortal, perpetual in its guarantees and provisions, a promise that the Whiteman would support and protect the Indian for as long as the grass grows and the waters flow. (Fogelson 1989:138, 142)

Today, impelled by idealistic attorneys, academics, and church people selflessly serving the Indian cause, this large truth has been accepted as the highest law of the land—moral and juridical. Among the most important of the sacrosanct guarantees the Whiteman offered the Indian in these old treaties were these: the Indian would forever be allowed to live unmolested and protected on the tiny reserved remnants of his national homelands. There, the Whiteman had irrevocably stipulated, the Indian would be allowed eternally to govern himself, living by his own chosen ways, separate and isolated from mainstream America, with his own special key to the federal treasury. These obligations, the Whiteman now came to understand and accept, are no more than the rents they must forever pay as unwelcome guests among the host nations of North America.

After many successes in the courts and in Congress, and after raising the public's consciousness about the Indian's important place in the history of North America and his vital contemporary role as mentor and model, the Indian is finally taking his proper place in modern American and Canadian societies. The Indian story, so long concealed by the Whiteman's shame or misshapen by his vanity, can now be proclaimed throughout these lands.

Compounding an abridgement of the contemporary Indian story like this must be followed by a disclaimer: it is only one of many possible variations. Anyone, scholarly authority or ordinary citizen, can quibble over its phrasing, examples, elements, code words, or emphasis. Indeed, most or all of these makings could be adjusted or replaced and others substituted without altering the fundamental, underlying prescription, or mitigating the rhetorical side-effects of a particular example.

The durable formula of the story—strong medicine, indeed—rests solidly on sharp contrasts, repetitive themes, standard motifs, a double standard of pervasively moral interpretation (Sheehan 1985), the suppression of logic and critical thinking, great selectivity of "evidence," and reliance on folk styles of explanation rather than scientific: one example of this being the use of popular biological-racial constructs such as the "myth of blood." In its several thousand year old historical origins this narrative framework is European, in its recent transformations Euroamerican; it was not indigenous to North America. An account those of European background once imparted exclusively to one another, it was later divulged to others of allegedly indigenous North American ancestry, where it was accepted as gospel. Now Whiteman and Indian regularly use this narrative framework in communicating with one another about themselves, and use it to think about and to deal with each other. It is in this sense, as Bruner suggests, that the narrative is endorsed, enhanced, and perpetuated by "co-conspirators," used by these accomplices as a "unit of power" (Bruner 1986:19–20). It certainly has this effect, by mystification.

The narrative's framework is composed of several parts, each of them subject to innumerable variations in expression and combination. Several timeworn themes recur, including: Victimizer versus Victim, Guilt Rampant versus Innocence Violated, Alien versus Indigene, Artificial versus Natural, Dominance versus Subordination. To further augment the effects of such already unadorned polar contrasts, a selected array of preferred, forceful code words are used, such as oppression, force, fraud, resistance, pluralism, colonialism, justice, and heritage. The dramatic play in the account commonly turns on invented speeches or dialogues presented as if they are verbatim records of words issuing from the mouths of real, historical figures. One of these imaginary actors often employed as a rhetorical foil is found in the much used Adario motif, which consists of a Wise Old Indian Uttering Marvelous Lessons for the Whiteman's Edification (Adams 1983:234–36). The aforementioned Chief Seattle is only one member of Adario's numerous tribe.

The elements of this narrative's framework aside, the content inserted into them to make up a retelling, in part or whole, is what stirs audiences the most. This content, which is to say the narrative as it is known to many millions, is effectively *factious*, also normatively *factitious*, and in substance largely if not fully *fictitious*, commonly two or all of these at the same time.

The narrations are factious because they serve to identify and set off as rigidly defined adversaries culturally constructed categories of humans—pseudo-species. Indeed, these accounts, in generating and perpetuating divisiveness, legitimize these categories in the minds of audiences, making them seem real, and the contests between people assigned to them meaningful. It is in this additional sense that the Indian and the Whiteman are inventions, used for contemporary purposes in the competition between interest groups for control of resources and for prestige.

Much water has flowed through that great gulf separating the real peoples of Europe and those of North America since Christopher Columbus first used the word *Indio* as a generic name for the latter. Following the custom of his time, because he thought himself east of the Indus River, he used the word in a purely *geographic* sense as a recognizable name for *all* the peoples of these continents indiscriminately. Today, nowhere in the Americas can "Indian" possibly have the same meaning of "all" inhabitants of an area. Five centuries of immigration from around the world, coupled with that many years of interaction, interbreeding, and social change transforming the original inhabitants biologically and culturally, make this usage impossible.

Presently, in North America, "Indian" has taken on a completely different, much-restricted meaning as a label for *some* inhabitants—a definable strata or identity group—in complex nation-states. In its broadest application, it is asserted as a personal or group identity marker for those who *claim* descent, however remote or partial, from one of North America's original inhabitants, whether such people are affiliated with a recognized Indian community or not. The ethnic semantics of "Indian" are straightforward. It is used, privately among themselves, by millions of individuals and families who are nominally identified as Whitemen, Black, or something else. It is from this large reservoir of potentials that many new, publicly proclaimed Indians regularly appear, presenting themselves to claim their rightful place and prerogatives as legitimate (that is, legal) Indians. Those otherwise readily identified as Black have grave difficulties in "passing" as Indians, however (Clifton 1989: 183–203); but for those formerly identified as Whitemen this is a much easier step (Clifton 1989:276–89). In the former instance, American rules for ascribing racial status nearly prohibit such a self-induced or externally encouraged transmutation of public identity. On the other hand, although the large Hispanic-American population could claim Indianness by virtue of the same cultural marker used by others in the United States, "Indian blood-quantum," exceedingly few do so.

Thus the Whiteman's main partners in fabricating versions of the Indian story come from those parts of North America's population that are, by modern definition, "Indians-by-blood," whether covert and potential or publicly certified as such by enrollment in a jurally defined nation/tribe. The standard Indian narrative is factious because in the minds of narrators and audiences it divides the whole population into adversarial groups and explains and justifies their opposition to one another. In the Indian story, the spirit of racial or ethnic separatism is manifested and flourishes most strongly. It is a political story, a "unit of power," because its melodramatic substance generates shame and guilt in the Whiteman, so promoting desires for restitution in and demands for reparations from him. It is political, as well, because decisions to certify "Indianness" for new candidates, individually or collectively, are decisions about allocating resources—prestige, prerogatives, land, and money. The greater the degree of guilt induced in the Whiteman, the larger the number of potentials legitimized as proper Indians, to serve as targets for the Whiteman's restitution fantasies and actions.

The elements of the narrative are factitious because they are fashioned and communicated, inadvertently or deliberately, to serve someone's ends, whether those of an individual engaged in face-to-face interaction or a group contending in a larger arena. This applies reciprocally, whether the creators and performers define themselves as Indians or Whitemen. The many advantages this tale gives the former in nation-states where public morality demands the utmost visible display of deference for the rights of those defined as underdogs is apparent. For them the orthodox Indian story is, unmistakably, a sturdy crowbar used to gain leverage in the play of interest-group politics. The Indian story so manipulated in recent decades has been extraordinarily influential, swinging legislative, executive, judicial, and public sentiment towards the Indian far and beyond their numbers as voting-blocs. For them the standard story brings large amounts of moral clout, not the power of the ballot-box or campaign contribution (Gross 1986).

Explaining the involvements and contributions of not-Indians in the development, enhancement, and replaying of this narrative structure is more complex. For a great many of them there is no accessible alternative. So pervasive a part of American popular culture has this story become, and so unrelieved in its expressions, that uncritical masses of a generation reared on *Custer Died For Your Sins*, *Bury My Heart At Wounded Knee*, and *Little Big Man* accept it as legitimate and authoritative. The force of fashionable orthodoxy is so great that publishing and other media enterprises, eying what scripts come to them on the one hand, what large audiences will eagerly accept on the other, hew to the line almost automatically. The standard narrative, additionally, forms the core of what the press and television journalism will accept as "hard" or "soft news" (Landsman 1988).

And academics, because of their own sentiments and preferred roles, readily identify or they are pressed to identify themselves as "Friends of the Indian," some out of idiosyncratic motives, others for ideological or pragmatic reasons. Many campus-bound and extra-mural intellectuals, of course, fancy themselves as critics of the establishment, and for such disgruntled commentators a properly constructed image of the Indian serves as a useful foil, just as centuries ago it did for Rousseau or the Baron La Hontan. Even the titles selected for recent scholarly books and essays commonly reveal dependency on the established phrases and forms of the standard narrative. Consider, as examples, *The Invasion of America: Indians, Colonialism, and the Cant of Conquest* (Jennings 1975); *Return of the Native: American Indian Political Resurgence* (Cornell 1988); *American Indian Holocaust and Survival* (Thornton 1987); *The Invasion Within* (Axtell 1985); and *Irredeemable America* (Sutton 1985). Although such volumes are draped with footnotes, statistical tables, and flow charts, a banal image of the invented Indian peeks through their rhetoric. In such academic jeremiads we rarely find a hint that what is resurgently irredeemable is the intellectual atrocity caused by modern cant. The partisan ends of such patrons of the Indian cause are served as well, if not better than those of allied client Indians themselves.

Starting with the assumption that the whole of the North American population can be easily divided into Indian and not-Indian, the conventional narrative in whole or substantial part is fictitious. It can be expressed as a wholly imagined representation of the past, or about present relationships and happenings, or versions of it may be severely distorted by fanciful imagery, selective reporting, hyperbole, and whatever other rhetorical devices are at hand. The aim of producers of the Indian narrative is not simply to inform or enlighten, but also to persuade—within the permissible confines of the narrative's structure. And above all else, the task of persuasion is greatly eased by sticking to a well-trodden path, one whose twists and turns are well known to audiences. Hence versions of the Indian story are mostly pieced together from borrowed hand-me-downs, with enough ruffles and flourishes sewn on to suggest innovativeness.

This last consideration suggests a problem associated with applying Richard de Mille's discussion of authenticity and validity to assessing the truth value of versions of the Indian narrative (see chapter 12). The power of orthodoxy is such as to encourage misperception and misconstruction, no matter how much actual first-hand observation is used to attest the materials used in fabricating a version of the story. Moreover, replicating large historical research or anthropological field studies is extraordinarily expensive and time-consuming, and such critical reappraisals are not nearly so well rewarded as fresh variations on an established theme. However, when such interpretations are reexamined against the original data, as David Henige reports in chapter 9, the results can be greatly illuminating and corrective. But they can also go unnoticed if their conclusions do not fit accepted styles of construction.

The question of a research report's validity, raised with respect to a particular account, say, of relations between some Indians and Whitemen, is equally thorny. But here the problem is of a different kind. De Mille addressed this question as regards reports where there were several bodies of substantial theoretical knowledge separate from the work of those who produce variations on the Indian story—pharmacological, zoological, neuropsychological, geographic. Against these bodies of knowledge the validity of particular research conclusions and interpretations can be checked.

Assessing the validity of versions of the conventional Indian narrative in this way is rarely attempted. On the contrary, their validity is ordinarily measured on a scale of conformity to the standard narrative structure. In this sense, so long as such depictions remain within the confines of agreeable orthodoxy they are—to all appearances—mutually self-validating. The terms of the narrative structure *are* the standard of proper truth. In few places where a part of the Indian story is rendered, as de Mille remarks for misbegotten hypotheses about the nature of physical or biological phenomena, is there a hard reality to rise up and strike down the careless or the over-conforming experimenter. Here the narrative structure, as a unit-of-power in its own right, is accepted and works as that hard reality. It is those who deviate from its normative tenets who are likely to be stricken.

To borrow Max Weber's thought, expressions of this basic framework "are not plowshares to loosen the soil of contemplative thought; they are swords against the enemies: such words are weapons" (1946:145). Sometimes legend, often allegory, not infrequently parable, frequently apocryphal anecdote, commonly dismal moral chronicle, the inventive versions of parts of the storyline are rarely anywhere near all that they pretend to be on the surface. But what of the whole? How can it be usefully characterized in a meaningful theoretical way? In the social sciences and history it is always useful to know what kind of a thing we are dealing with.

Viewing the thing as narrative structure or standard storyline has been useful, up to a point. However, this characterization does not distinguish a piece presented as a truthful account from one admittedly fictional, or instances of the latter disguised as the former. The authors of the following chapters are not reluctant about making just such a distinction, including several who use the everyday meaning of "myth" to express their judgment on the truth-value of the invented account they examine critically. Many other scholars use the word in just this sense, as does Leonard Thompson when he defines political myths as tales "told about the past to legitimize or discredit a regime," meaning the historical elements of an ideology (1985:1). However, the notion of "myth as ideological falsehood" conflicts with the second, technical meaning of myth, and in discourse of this order it is better to reserve the word for that special class of sacred narratives of anonymous authorship which explain the origins of the world and justify the arrangement of its features.

The accounts discussed here, however highly valued and strongly defended they may be, are not of that type. They are entirely mundane, lesser in scope, and the makers are usually identifiable. In the language of modern folklore studies, characterizing such accounts as mass or urban legends would be closer to the mark, but such narratives are commonly titillating amusements, and there is little that is diverting in the Indian storyline.

Some of the substantive nature, uses, and consequences of this narrative structure have been remarked. Recounting it promotes faction by factitious techniques in genres too often fictive. It is, above all else, in two distinct senses a "cover-story." It has achieved long running top-billing, and it obscures or suppresses other interpretations and conclusions. For this reason, it may be defined as a significant, multifaceted work of perfectly enchanting cultural fiction, one that is both believed by its impresarios and presented as believable to others. The aim of such a narrative is not to illuminate but to make converts.

The idea of cultural fiction has a respectable if discontinuous history in several disciplines. Its use in law as the "legal fiction" is discussed by Allan van Gestel in chapter 15. In anthropology, the fictive nature of many cultural elements and aspects of social organization have been long recognized and marked, as in the "genealogical fiction" and "fictive kinship" (Seymour-Smith 1986:116, 130). In history, it has been of special value in studying the origins of nationalism (Anderson 1983) and in the study of "invented traditions" (Hobsbawn and Ranger 1983). In sociology it is applied to understanding rural development projects (Goldman and Wilson 1984). And in political science there is long established precedent for viewing narratives created and presented for public consumption with the aim of concealing, mystifying, or obscuring the real nature of events and relationships as fictions (Lippman 1922: 10–14; Qualter 1985). Cultural fictions, then, are fabrications of pseudo-events and relationships, counterfeits of the past and present that suit someone's or some group's purposes in their dealings with others. In the following chapters, paraphrasing Herbert Spencer's experience, the authors may be seen assaulting a Brigade of Beautiful Fictions with a Gang of Brutal Facts and Ideas.

Notes

1. Only a few selected references for the more blatant, recent use of the code words, themes, and motifs assembled in this digest are given. The following fifteen chapters provide extensive references for many of these. A reasonably completed, critically annotated bibliography for a comprehensive glossary of these elements would require several volumes in its own right. The wording of the elements in this abridgement are mine, not necessarily the exact phrases used in the items cited or elsewhere. The soundness of this abridgement can be assessed by a reasonable amount of reading selected at random from titles about Indian-Whiteman relations published during the past ten years.
2. If readers feel I have overdrawn the adversarial relationship between these two monolithic, racially labeled entities with *The Whiteman* v. *The Indian*, I invite them, again, to browse through any of the multitude of recent publications written by professionally qualified academics, as well as by popular writers, church people, government organizations, and others, where this usage is nearly an unrelieved standard. In such contexts, readers must be wary, for in them "Whiteman" now means "not-Indian," by no means including only those of exclusively European ancestry, but African-Americans, Asian-Americans and others, as well. Nowadays "Indian" is not simply the logically balanced, reciprocal negative of the former; on the contrary, the terms of reference change for "Indian": it is the label for a ersatz subspecies,

a category of persons who publicly claim a native American ancestry, whatever their actual ancestries and heritages. (See Clifton 1989.)
3. For an excellent presentation, defense, and practical use of this "protective camouflage stratagem" notion, see Plaintiff's Post-Trial Brief, in *Keweenaw Bay Indian Community* v. *State of Michigan*, File No. M87–278–CA2. United States District Court for the Western District of Michigan. Northern Division (Lansing MI, 1989).

References

Adams, Percy G. 1983. *Travel Literature and the Evolution of the Novel*. Lexington, KY: University of Kentucky Press.

Anderson, Benedict. 1983. *Imagined Communities: Reflections on the Origin and Spread of Nationalism*. London: Verso Editions.

Axtell, James. 1985. *The Invasion Within: The Contest of Cultures in Colonial North America*. New York: Oxford.

Axtell, James and William C. Sturtevant. 1980. "The Unkindest Cut, or Who Invented Scalping?" *William and Mary Quarterly* 37:452–72.

Barreiro, Jose, ed. 1988. *Indian Roots of American Democracy*. Ithaca, NY: American Indian Program, Cornell University.

Brand, Stewart. 1988. "*Indians and the Counterculture, 1960s–1970s*." In Washburn 1988:570–72.

Brandon, William. 1986. *New World for Old: Reports from the New World and Their Effect on the Development of Social Thought in Europe, 1500–1800*. Athens, OH: Ohio University Press.

Brown, Dee. 1971. *Bury My Heart at Wounded Knee: An Indian History of the American West*. New York: Holt, Rinehart & Winston.

Bruner, Edward M. 1986. "Experience and its Expressions," and "Ethnography as Narrative." In *The Anthropology of Experience*. Victor Turner and Edward M. Bruner, eds. Urbana, IL: University of Illinois Press. Pp. 3–30, 139–55.

Clifton, James A., ed. 1989. *Being and Becoming Indian: Biographical Studies of North American Frontiers*. Chicago, IL: The Dorsey Press (Belmont, CA: Wadsworth Publishing Co.).

Cornell, Stephen. 1987. *Return of the Native: American Indian Political Resurgence*. New York: Oxford University Press.

Deloria, Vine, Jr. 1969. *Custer Died For Your Sins: An Indian Manifesto*. New York: Macmillan.

———. 1973. *God Is Red*. New York: Grossett and Dunlap

Dobyns, Henry F. 1983. *Their Numbers Become Thinned: Native American Population Dynamics in Eastern North America*. Knoxville, TN: University of Tennessee Press.

———. 1987. "Demographics of Native American History." In Martin 1987:67–74.

Fenwick, Henry. 1989. "An Ongoing Beat." *Modern Maturity* 32 (5):34–8.

Fogelson, Raymond D. 1989. "The Ethnohistory of Events and Nonevents." *Ethnohistory* 36:133–47.

Goldman, Robert and John Wilson. 1984. "The Selling of Rural America." *Rural Sociology* 48:585–606.

Gross, Emma R. 1986. "Setting the Agenda for American Indian Policy." In Joe 1986:47–63.

Hobsbawm, Eric and Terence Ranger, eds. 1983. *The Invention of Tradition.* Cambridge: Cambridge University Press.

Jennings, Francis. 1975. *The Invasion of America: Indians, Colonialism, and the Cant of Conquest.* Chapel Hill, NC: University of North Carolina Press.

Joe, Jennie R., ed. 1986. "American Indian Policy and Cultural Values: Conflict and Accomodation." Contemporary American Indian Issues Series, No. 6. American Indian Studies Center. Los Angeles: University of California.

Kaiser, Rudolph. 1987. "A Fifth Gospel, Almost," Chief Seattle's Speech(es): American Origins and European Reception. In *Indians and Europe: An Interdisciplinary Collection of Essays.* Christian F. Feest, ed. Aachen: Rader Verlag.

Landsman, Gail H. 1988. *Sovereignty and Symbol: Indian/White Conflict at Ganienkeh.* Albuquerque: University of New Mexico Press.

Leacock, Eleanor B. and Nancy O. Lurie, eds. 1971. *North American Indians in Historical Perspective.* New York: Random House.

Lippman, Walter. 1922. *Public Opinion.* London: Allen & Unwin

Lurie, Nancy O. 1971. "The World's Oldest On-Going Protest Demonstration: North American Indian Drinking Patterns." *Pacific Historical Review* 40:311–32.

Martin, Calvin. 1987. *The American Indian and the Problem of History.* New York: Oxford University Press.

Qualter, Terence H. 1985. *Opinion Control in the Democracies.* New York: St. Martin's Press.

Seymour-Smith, Charlotte. 1986. *Dictionary of Anthropology.* Boston: G.K. Hall & Co.

Sheehan, Bernard. 1985. "The Problem of Moral Judgments in History. *The South Atlantic Quarterly* 84:37–50.

Sutton, Imre, ed. 1985. *Irredeemable America: The Indians' Estate and Land Claims.* Albuquerque: University of New Mexico Press.

Thompson, Leonard. 1985. *The Political Mythology of Apartheid.* New Haven, CT: Yale University Press.

Thornton, Russell. 1988. *American Indian Holocaust and Survival: A Population History Since 1492.* Norman, OK: University of Oklahoma Press.

Washburn, Wilcomb E., ed. 1988. "History of Indian-White Relations." *Handbook of North American Indians, Vol. 4.* Washington, DC: Smithsonian Institution.

Weatherford, Jack. 1988. *Indian Giver.* New York: Crown.

Weber, Max. 1946. "Science as a Vocation." In *From Max Weber: Essays in Sociology.* H.H. Gerth and C.W. Mills, eds. New York: Oxford University Press.

Wilkinson, Charles F. 1987. *American Indians, Time, and the Law.* New Haven, CT: Yale University Press.

Williams, Walter L. 1986. *The Spirit and the Flesh: Sexual Diversity in American Indian Culture.* Boston: Beacon Press.

Williams, William A. 1974. *The Great Evasion.* Chicago: Quadrangle Books.

Wolf, Eric. 1982. *Europe and the People Without History.* Berkeley, CA: University of California Press.

Wrone, David R. 1987. "Indian Treaties and the Democratic Ideal." *Wisconsin Magazine of History* 70:83–106.
Wrone, David R., and R.S. Nelson, eds. 1973. *Who's The Savage? A Documentary History of the Mistreatment of the Native North Americans.* Greenwich, CT: Fawcett.

3

Pride and Prejudice: The Pocahontas Myth and the Pamunkey

Christian F. Feest

Late in 1607, when the Jamestown colony was plagued by a dangerous relationship between scanty food supplies and excessive factional strife, Captain John Smith ventured into Chickahominy Indian country to trade for corn. When exploring the country beyond their lands at the end of his foraging trip, he was apprehended by a sizable detachment of warriors of the Powhatan chiefdom as a suspect in the murder case of a Rappahannock Indian, who had been killed a few years earlier by an unidentified Englishman. Although Smith was cleared of this charge, he was taken before Powhatan at Pamunkey, tried, and (as far as he could make out) sentenced to death on more general grounds. Just as the tawny executioners readied themselves to knock out the Captain's brains, Pocahontas—Powhatan's favorite daughter (and cherished subject of later romantic biographers)—threw herself over the Captain's stocky body and thereby presumably saved his life (figure 3.1).

Later the noble teenager intervened repeatedly to extend economic aid and political advice to Smith and the fledgling colony. After Smith returned to England, Pocahontas disappeared from the colonists' view, and a moderately cold war ensued between the natives and these alien squatters. When, in 1613, Captain Samuel Argall had to go all the way to the Potomacs' territory to trade for corn, he encountered Pocahontas again. Seizing her as a hostage, Argall carried the young woman to Jamestown to extort peace from Powhatan. Pocahontas was soon moved to the settlement at Henrico where she was instructed in the doctrines of Christianity, to which she readily converted. The following year she eventually proved instrumental in mediating peace between her father's people and those of her newly acquired fiancé—John Rolfe, the pioneer of English tobacco cultivation in Virginia. This was a second marriage for both. Pocahontas (now Mrs. Rebecca Rolfe) gave birth to Thomas Rolfe in 1615, and a year later went to England with husband and son, where she was introduced to Queen Anne and unexpectedly met John Smith again. As she was preparing to return to Virginia in early 1617, Mrs. Rolfe—or Pocahontas—fell ill and died at Gravesend. The lasting power of images of this young woman and her associations with America's pioneer founders is evident in the title and jacket blurb of Leon Phillips' 1973 *First Lady of America: a Romanticized Biography of Pocahontas*, where she is touted for as being as "relevant today as she was in 1612 . . . a woman of enormous power and intellect" (compare Barbour 1970).

Many thousand pages of scholarly and literary writing have been devoted to the Pocahontas story. This is not the place to reevaluate the source materials or to argue the facts behind the tale. It is the myth itself, so dear to the American public, and its use by Powhatan's surviving children—the contemporary Indians of coastal Virginia—which deserves and will get a close scrutiny in this essay.

The Pocahontas-Smith-Rolfe story has all the distinctive features of an American origin myth. Of much significance is the era when what had been a colorful local story achieved nationwide popularity. Before the 1800s, Pocahontas and her role were little known outside Virginia. Thereafter the developing nation began to build and to catalog its own mythology, accounts of hero figures and basic values of America's beginning cast in epic form. Among these nationally favored tales was that of Pocahontas who, by repeatedly safeguarding the very existence of the first English colony on American soil, was drawn in an early image of Manifest Destiny. At the same time, likely of greater importance, Pocahontas was made to symbolize a virginal native America, for her representation was merged with the older Indian Queen and Indian Princess images. In mythic form, by saving Smith she legitimizes the Anglo-American presence in North America. By marrying Rolfe she conveys the aboriginals' title to the land to the English colonists and accepts a dependent status for native Americans. By her early death she makes room for Euroamerican expansion as all good Indians should do. For Virginians there were additional dimensions: her alleged contribution to her husband's experiments with tobacco cultivation helped to establish the basis for Virginia's economic prosperity, while through her son, Thomas, she infused the blood of native American "royalty" into the veins of the colonial elite.

During the eighteenth century, some thoughtful Virginians lamented that so few colonists had followed John Rolfe's example in marrying an Indian woman, because such unions would have established a better claim to the land. Extolling the benefits of native American-immigrant American conjugal ties, William Byrd II concluded: "Besides, the poor Indians would have had less reason to complain that the English took their lands, if they had received it by way of a marriage portion with their daughters" (Wright 1966:160). A few decades later, Peter Fontaine agreed that "if . . . we had taken Indian wives in the first place, it would have been some compensation for their lands . . . . We should [have] become the rightful heirs to their lands" (Maury 1872:350). Interestingly, these eighteenth-century sentiments conflicted with the existing laws of Virginia, which since 1691 had outlawed interracial marriage (Hening 1810–1823, 3:86–8). The nineteenth-century Pocahontas story, however, was obviously not concerned with the quantities of Indian woman-American male marriages: a single richly symbolic case served the explanatory purposes of myth-making much better.

The mythopoeic treatment of the Pocahontas-Rolfe episode confirmed later American intentions to include native peoples in their Melting Pot ideology and policies—to solve the Indian problem by fusing the latter's identity with their own. Nineteenth-century racial integrity laws in the South stressed this with a powerful jural distinction: the Indian might hope ultimately to become White; but the slightest touch of "Black blood" destined those so stigmatized to a perpetual Negro or Colored social category (Rountree 1986:179–80).

The actual experiences of the Algonquian tribes of coastal Virginia after the death of Pocahontas offer some striking contrasts to the sentiments embodied in the later Pocahontas myth (Feest 1978; and Rountree 1979). Recognizing that the peace brought about by Pocahontas would not keep the English colonists from their expansionist goals, the natives rose in 1622 in an attempt to rid themselves of the nail in their flesh. The English retaliated by declaring a war of extermination that lasted for ten years and continued on a lower level of intensity until 1644, when Powhatan's brother and heir, Opechancanough, launched a final, but unsuccessful counteroffensive. The peace agreement of 1646 at last relegated the native peoples to that dependent and tributary status which, although hoped for by the English colonists, had not automatically resulted from the Pocahontas-Rolfe marriage.

After 1646 the Algonquian peoples of Virginia were quickly becoming an insignificant factor both politically and militarily. As tribal populations rapidly decreased, reservation land was allotted to the tribes on a per capita basis, but even these small patches became increasingly subject to the encroachment of the rapidly growing populations of colonial neighbors. Military and political conquest had proved to be a much more effective means for obtaining possession of the country than either interracial marriage or the proposed Christianity-for-land deal which had figured so prominently in early promotional literature. In this respect, Pocahontas's conversion to Christianity remained an extremely uncommon case for many decades. No systematic missionary work was undertaken among the reservation groups, although their dependent status would have eased the labor of proselytizing them. Instead, Indian parents were encouraged to indenture their children as servants to English households, where they were to be reared in Christian civilization. In much idealized theory such children would eventually become integrated into English colonial society. But as a rule Indian children placed in English settlements only became separated and alienated from their natal communities. One serious consequence was that these young people lost the benefits associated with the status of "tribal Indian" as recognized by the colony (and later the state); they ended up dangerously close to the category labeled "free persons of color."

This came to pass in 1705, when legislation effectively placed the Indians of Virginia on the "colored" side of a system of biracial classification. Because of the tributary system, for some years those Indians who remained on the tiny reservations had the better of it. In this system the groups based on lands allotted them—the "tribes"—paid an annual tribute of arrows or game to the governor. This symbolic transaction brought in return continued recognition and, hopefully, the government's protection as well. This relationship, and the annual delivery of tribute to the governor of Virginia, continues to the present day (see figure 3.6). During the eighteenth century, trustees for the reservation communities or tribes were appointed by the legislature, who were to advise the tributaries, especially in matters relating to their lands. However, whatever their inclinations these appointed custodians had not the power to halt the steady shrinking of lands reserved for Indian occupation. Eventually, all such reservations disappeared, except the divided one today inhabited by descendents of the Pamunkey and Mattaponi.

This process was accompanied by a gradual loss of traditional Virginia Algonquian culture, which made it increasingly difficult for tribes and individuals visibly to signal their "Indian" identity. Bark-covered barrel-roofed houses gave way to wooden log and frame structures; traditional skin dresses were exchanged for cloth or cotton garments; native languages ceased to be used and were mostly forgotten by the early nineteenth century; and most Indians on and off the reservations became Baptists. English surnames became common during the late seventeenth century. One such was "Captain John West," the son of the "Queen of Pamunkey" at the time of Bacon's Rebellion, probably named after his natural father, Colonel John West of New Kent County. Others may have received their English names as indentured servants from their masters. The name Langston, for example, which is current to this day among the Pamunkey, is first documented as an Indian name (as well as that of a English landowner) as early as 1691. One of few long-surviving native crafts among the Pamunkey was pottery making, which was abandoned only in the 1890s. This lack of obvious identity markers made it next to impossible for the nonreservation populations to evade classification as "colored" by their Virginian neighbors (see Rountree 1986).

The complaint of William Byrd and Peter Fontaine that none had followed John Rolfe's example is not well founded. However, since such unions were disdained by elite Virginians, these couples and their offspring (or only the offspring if illegitimate like "Captain John West") usually ended up with their Indian not their Anglo-colonial kin. An early and well documented case is that of John Basse who in 1638 "Marrid Keziah Elizabeth Tucker, dafter of Robin the Elder of ye Nansimuns Kingdom, a Baptized Xtian, in Holy Matrimonie accdg to ye Canons of ye Church of England," though his brother Edward "departed from his Life among the Showanocks in Carolina" in 1696. John Basse became the ancestor of the Bass family among the Nansemond of Southside Virginia, who despite loss of their reservation have succeeded in retaining their identity until today (Bell 1961:11, 12). Other cases are less well documented, but the Bradbys among the Pamunkey and Chickahominy claim descent from a White man who married a Chickahominy woman at the time of the American Revolution. Similar claims are or were made by the Winns among the Chickahominy, the Byrd and Nelson families among the Rappahannock, and by the Newtons among the Potomac. Contrary to hopes raised by the model of Pocahontas, however, these marriages did not result in a general fusion of native Virginian and emigrant Virginian identities. In all these cases the White men chose to live with the Indians and raise their children as Indians.

Although denying the occurrence of such marriages, Virginians were quick to suspect a "blackening" of Indian blood through interbreeding with their African slaves in less formal unions. No doubt such consensual relations occurred, especially among the nonreservation groups, many of whom claimed to have been forced into such relationships by their masters so their children could become slaves. On the other hand, the groups with reservations quickly saw the danger to their legal status of marriages to Blacks. Hence such couples and their offspring were banned from tribal lands and probably joined nonreservation groups or the "free colored" segment of Virginia's population.

Pamunkey tribal law, amended as of 1887, leaves no doubt about their seriousness on this point. The first clause reads: "No Member of the Pamunkey Indian Tribe shall intermarry with any Nation except White or Indian under penalty of forfeiting their rights in Town." [1] On the whole, Virginia Algonquians succeeded well in meeting the specifications of "purity of blood" required by Virginia's race laws. After his first visit to the Pamunkey reservation, James Mooney commented, "I was surprised to find them so *Indian*, the Indian blood being probably nearly ¾, the rest white, with a strain of negro. Some would pass unquestioned in any western tribe" (Mooney 1899). To retain their rights and their identity as Indians they had to and did accept the common forms of White prejudice against their Black neighbors, though they were often themselves suspected to be mulattos hiding under veneer of Indianness.

In the absence of clearly visible cultural symbols of their Indian status and with pressures mounting to distinguish themselves from the Colored category after Reconstruction, Virginia Algonquians had to find ways to establish their separate identity. Certificates of Indian descent had been issued by local authorities during the eighteenth and early nineteenth centuries, but these were simply not enough (see, e.g., Bell 1961:15–16). Indian men wore their straight black hair to shoulder length both before and after the Civil War to proclaim their racial purity and their Indianness. And concerted efforts were made to attract Indians of federally recognized tribes to settle on the Virginian reservations, there to marry local Indians. Moreover, a group of Catawbas had lived with the Pamunkey some time after 1800 but had returned to South Carolina taking some Pamunkeys with them; and during the Civil War, a group of Chickahominies fled to Canada, one of them returning after the end of the war with an Ojibwa wife (Stern 1952:206).

Terrill Bradby, who served one term as chief of the Pamunkey during the 1890s, apparently actively pursued the promotion of immigration of non-Virginian Indians to the Virginia reservations. In 1893 the Pamunkey authorized Bradby to "visit the Indian Bureau in Washington and in all other Departments and Indian tribes, and also to visit the Columbian Exposition in Chicago," where he was made Honorary Assistant in the Department of Ethnology by Frederick Ward Putnam. The *Indian Journal* of Muskogee, Oklahoma, reported that the intention of the Pamunkey delegation to Chicago had been "to invite other civilized Indians to come and settle on their reservation and amalgamate with their tribe. The Pamunkeys have rich lands, are in prosperous circumstances, but they have entermarried for so long that the tribe is danger of extinction. The delegates took the precaution of obtaining from the government of Virginia a certificate to the effect that they were genuine Indians and had a secure tenure of their lands." [2]

According to information gathered by John Garland Pollard in 1893 and publicized more widely by the *Washington Evening Star* on 25 April 1894, their hopes were now concentrated upon the North Carolina Cherokees. "The Pamunkeys have a great deal of race pride," the *Evening Star* indicated, "They are very anxious to keep their blood free from further mingling with that of other races, and how to accomplish this purpose is a serious problem of theirs, inasmuch as they recognize the danger of too frequent marriage within the pale of consanguinity. To obviate this difficulty the chief men have been trying to devise a plan by which they may induce immigration from the Cherokees of North Carolina." [3] Already existing relationships between the Cherokee and the Pamunkey were brought to Bradby's attention only in 1899: "In the East Cherokee Tribe was found descendants of Mary Screechowl. She was originally from this tribe, though they had lost sight of her" (Anonymous 1899). But these attempts appear to have met with little success. It was not until the Chickahominy started to send their children to Bacone College in Oklahoma for higher education that members of other tribes occasionally married into Virginia Algonquian groups (Rountree 1972:88).

At about the same time—in the 1880s—the Pamunkey began to use the Pocahontas story to validate their Indian identity in the eyes and minds of their contemporaries: White, Black, and Red. This development should be seen as a profound emotional plea for a redefinition of their status in Virginia's race-class hierarchy. The Pocahontas story was of special value because it established a base for common ground between the Pamunkey and their neighbors, for the myth was long dear to other Virginians. But the Pamunkey drew different conclusions from the same mythic premises. Essentially, this process conformed to earlier Pamunkey practice—the adoption of broadly American criteria and symbols for defining their Indian identity. This tactic, the Pamunkey had learned, aided them in communicating their point of view.

The major vehicle used to transport the message to the public was a play reenacting Pocahontas's role in the salvation of Captain John Smith's life. This dramatic scene was more or less regularly performed between at least 1881 and 1915. It was probably intended as a reminder of the debt owed by Virginians to the Indians, of the old alliance between these peoples, and the fact that Powhatan's children were still alive— if not well—in Virginia. Our information on this pageant comes from a variety of sources. The earliest known photograph of Virginia Algonquians, for example, shows a Pamunkey troupe staging what is labeled as the "John Smith Play" at the Yorktown Centennial in 1881 (figure 3.2).

In this photograph John Smith is seated in the center of the picture, flanked by Pocahontas and Powhatan on his right and two Pamunkeys in American costumes on the left. Behind them one female and eight male Indians are dressed in fringed and partially beaded cloth shirts, with feather headdresses of a type widely used among Eastern tribes in the late nineteenth century (Dräger 1975). The figures are shown holding symbolic artifacts: bows, arrows, hafted stone axes, a multistemmed clay pipe of local manufacture, and a wooden ball-headed club. The club is of exactly the same type as that shown in the 1624 illustration of the episode (compare fig. 1). Other than these 1624 and 1881 visual representations of such ball-headed clubs, we have little evidence that such weapons were used by Virginia Algonquians. The Pamunkey and neighboring Indians may well have been copying older European print images of their dress and technology. In fact, during the 1920s, pioneer anthropologist Frank Speck obtained from the Pamunkey for museum collections a broken example of the same type of club, but he reported little about its recent use (Speck 1928:350). The club collected by Speck may possibly have been the one shown in the 1881 photograph, in use as a prop for the living historical tableau. Not to leave the Pamunkey empty-handed, this anthropologist later delivered Micmac clubs of a similar type to them. The clothing shown in the 1881 photograph are of a generic neo-Indian variety, and resemble stage costumes more than anything else. They are less fully beaded than examples dating from around 1900 and later (see figures 3.4 and 3.6). Moreover, we can assume that the idea of the play itself as well as some of the details shown were inspired by one of many Smith-Pocahontas plays written and performed by the citizens of Virginia during the nineteenth-century.

The 1881 performance was by no means the last, for an 1898 broadside advertising a performance that year gives both the real and stage names of the Pamunkey actors (figure 3.3). But in the later performance Pamunkey *dramatis personae* were joined by a powerful ally: next to the Smith-Pocahontas duo stands the figure of early nineteenth-century America's favorite pan-Indian hero, Tecumseh. And next to these four are several others whose stage names are not easily associated with historic figures. One such was "Deerfoot," played by Evans Bradby, a name that provides a tantalizing clue. This was the *nom de course* of Lewis Bennett (c. 1830–1895), a Seneca Indian athlete from Cattaraugus reservation in upstate New York, who had achieved celebrity status in

England in 1861–1862 when he competed and won against most English competitors in long-distance races. Although when in his own land Bennett "had dressed up in good store clothes without paint or polish," he pleased his British audiences by staging an Indian fashion show for their benefit. Photographs made during his sojourn in London indicate that at least one of his costumes closely resembled the Pamunkey fashions of 1881 (figure 3.5). It is not entirely clear where the Virginia Indians may have seen him compete, but it seems that after returning to the U.S., Deerfoot retained his track name, maybe his costume as well, and that he ran wherever opportunities offered themselves. Terrill Bradby may have met him at the Chicago World's Fair of 1893, but this was long after the original borrowing of his professional name, costume, and identity for the Pamunkey tableau (see Cumming 1981:51–62).

An item found under the headline "Pamunkeys Want a Sea Trip" in the *Washington Chronicle* of July 9, 1899, reports that tribal officials were planning to discuss their grievances with the governor of Virginia.

> One of the principal matters to be brought to Governor Tyler's attention will be the appeal of the tribe to have a suitable representation at the Paris Exposition. They want the State to give them financial aid to enable them to send over a creditable company to produce a play representing the saving of Cap. John Smith's life by Pocahontas. It is understood the cast of characters has already been selected. Among those who it is proposed will take part are Dead Shot Panther, Big Smoker, and Lone Trailer, all of whom occupy high official places in the councils of the tribe.[4]

A word of caution is in order—these "Indian names" were probably invented by the news writer to ridicule the Pamunkeys. In any event, the planned trip failed to receive Governor Tyler's financial support, who declared that Virginia had no authority in that matter. But the petition shows the desire of the Pamunkey to win recognition as Indians wherever possible.

In October 1899, anthropologist James Mooney of the Smithsonian Institution's Bureau of American Ethnology and photographer DeLancey Gill came to visit the Pamunkey reservation. The *Richmond Times* of December 3, 1899, printed a letter "from one of the most intelligent members of the tribe" (possibly Terrill Bradby) relating to Mooney's visit, who is described as having been sent "to hunt up a history of these people . . . . With him he had a photographer, who took pictures of ten families, also that of Powhatan and his warriors, which made an exceedingly fine looking picture. The picture was a representation of Pocahontas saving the life of Captain John Smith" (Anonymous 1899; see figure 3.4). This image shows the same cast as billed in 1898, except T.W. Langston, T.S. Dennis, and John Dennis were absent. So there was a Pocahontas with no Captain John Smith to save. Little Captola Cook, likely an apprentice Pocahontas, is also shown. Some of the costumes are of the same type as those worn in 1881 but others are much more extravagant. Bows, arrows, and a hafted stone axe are used, but the ball-headed club is missing.

By 1915 the play had become but one part of a larger "Forefathers' Festival" held each spring on the Pamunkey Reservation. A report in the *Cedar Rapids Gazette* reported that on this occasion the "tribe goes into the woods and re-enacts the story of Pocahontas and Captain John Smith. Some maiden of the tribe, probably today much like the princess of old, plays the leading part" (Anonymous 1916). But after 1915 there is no further indication that the Pocahontas-Smith play was performed again. Then, in the late 1930s and early 1940s some Pamunkeys, Chickahominies, and Mattaponis participated in an annual pageant staged on May 23, celebrating the anniversary of the first meeting between the English colonists and Powhatan (historically really "Little Powhatan," the head chief's son). This was sponsored by the Powhatan Hill Memorial Association, and in distinction to the earlier Pocahontas-Smith play it was organized by Whites with Indian participation. Of the acts billed for the 1898 program, only the Snake Dance (hallowed by its long distance association with the famous Hopi ceremony of the same name) apparently survived to 1940.[5]

There is other evidence, however, relating to the importance of the Pocahontas myth to the Virginia Algonquians. A missionary visiting Pamunkey in 1915 (almost three centuries too late) offered the following observation gathered in the Indians' houses. There he saw: "On the walls, a copy of the original picture of Mrs. John Rolfe number two, better known as the Princess Pocahontas, and perhaps an old time print of Capt. John Smith, a character even at this day revered by these Indians" (Gordon 1915:9). We may have doubts regarding the reasons for the alleged Indian sympathies for Smith, whose record as a friend of the Indians is—to say the least—equivocal. As part of the Pocahontas myth, however, his role was notably important to the Pamunkey. In contrast, if readers have not already noticed, conspicuously absent between 1881 and 1920 from all Pamunkey celebrations of the 1607 meeting and engagement was the figure of John Rolfe. This is especially noteworthy, for he had become their relative by marriage to Pocahontas. This relationship the Pamunkey certified later in the seventeenth century with the gift of a tract of land to Thomas Rolfe, which shows that this affinal tie was acknowledged by them as binding for some decades. Why the late nineteenth-century Pamunkey dropped his role in organizing and casting their pageant presents a puzzle. A useful interpretation is that the Pamunkey sense of their own history shifted with changes in their place in Virginia society. Their overriding concern in the late nineteenth century was to redefine their position—as Indians. Denying John Rolfe's role, and symbolically that of the numerous other later Englishmen who had married Pamunkey women, further reinforced their "racial purity" and the culturally redefined boundary between themselves and other Virginians.

That the Pamunkey (likely joined by other Virginia Algonquians) must have identified themselves with the Pocahontas-Smith play is shown by a change in naming patterns. Before 1880 given names tended to be of the ordinary Anglo-Christian variety. Then—abruptly—names from the play began to be given to children. George Major Cook, who took the part of "Cayatanita," named one of his daughters Pocahontas and one of his sons (who like his father became chief of the Pamunkey) Tecumseh Deerfoot. Among the Mattaponi we find Powhatan Major, and among Chickahominy children of this generation some were named Pocahontas and even Opechancanough, which was usually shortened to "O.P." (see Speck 1928).

Given the importance of the Pocahontas-Smith story and play for the Pamunkey around 1900, it seems odd that none of the anthropologists who did fieldwork among the Virginia tribes during the twentieth century paid any attention to it. There is no trace of it in the voluminous published and unpublished data collected by Frank G. Speck (whose major Pamunkey informant was George M. Cook) and his students. Tecumseh Deerfoot Cook, today in his eighties, could remember his father going with other Pamunkeys to Jamestown Festival Park around the time of the Jamestown Tricentennial in 1907 to perform some kind of play or dance, but he neither could remember what it was about, nor did he appreciate that his own name had come straight out of the script.

Though the Pocahontas-Smith pageant is no longer performed by the Pamunkey, the story continues to be important as a key symbol of their distinctive identity and their special relationship to American society. The myth lives on in a new art form. Pottery making was revived in 1932 when a pottery school was opened on the reservation with financial aid from the state of Virginia (figure 3.7). Brightly painted and glazed wares in this newly invented traditional style continue to be made by a few Pamunkey ladies of the older generation for sale to tourists. Some of these pots and plates are decorated with a kind of picture writing also of twentieth-century origin and itself an attempt to produce something that could be recognized as "Indian" by other Virginians.

The story most often told in these pictographs is that of Pocahontas and Captain John Smith. The Pamunkey translation (which once again stresses the aspects of friendship between Indians and Whites) reads as follows: "1. Indians 2. while hunting 3. discover 4. white man 5. standing 6. in shallow water 7. Indians 8. agree 9. to kill white man 10. at chief's seat 11. Indian maiden 12. disagrees with 13. Indian men 14. (and) makes no harm for 15. white man 16. but good wishes" (figures 3.8 and 3.9). In this manner, an event of no great world-historical significance lives on symbolically, perpetuated by the few surviving Pamunkey, used by them to fix their identity and to win the hearts and minds of Captain John Smith's children.

This essay is based in part on research done in 1972–1973 when I was a post-doctoral fellow at the Department of Anthropology, Smithsonian Institution, Washington, D.C. It is a somewhat revised version of the original in the European Review of Native American Studies *1 (1):5–12, 1987, where additional notes and full references may be found.*

Notes

1. See Pollard 1894:16; a more recent version of Pamunkey legal exclusion is cited by Rountree 1972:74.
2. *Indian Journal*, Muskogee, Eufaula, Indian Territory, August 3, 1893. A news clipping in Gatschet c. 1894–1900).
3. News clipping in Gatschet, c. 1894–1900; also see Pollard 1894:11.
4. News clipping in Gatschet, c. 1894–1900.
5. *Richmond Times-Newsleader* archives, Richmond, Virginia, clippings of May 20, 1937 and May, 4, 1940.

References

Anonymous. 1899. "Remnant of a Powerful Tribe." *Richmond Times*, December 3, 1899.
———. 1916. "Travelette—Indian Town." Reprinted from Cedar Rapids, IA *Gazette*. In *The Indian School Journal* 16:369.
Barbour, Phillip L. 1970. *Pocahantas and Her World: A Chronicle of America's First Settlement*. Boston: Houghton Mifflin Company.
Bell, Albert D. 1961. *Bass Families of the South* Rocky Mount, NC.
Cumming, John. 1981. *Runners and Walkers, a Nineteenth Century Sports Chronicle*. Chicago: Regnery Gateway
Dräger, Lother. 1975. "Federhauben bei Indianer des östlichen Nordamerika." *Jahrbuch des Museum für Völkerkunde Leipzig* 30:191–204.
Feest, Christian F. 1978. "Virginia Algonquians." In *Handbook of North American Indians—Northeast, Vol. 15*. Bruce Trigger, ed. Washington, DC: Smithsonian Institution. 253–70.
Gatschet, Albert S. 1894–1900. "Pamunkey Notebook." Manuscript 2197, National Anthropological Archives, Smithsonian Institution.

Gordon, Rev. Philip B. 1915. "The Remnants of Powhatan's Tribe." *The Indian Leader* 19:9–11.

Hening, William Waller, ed. 1809–1823. *Statutes at Large: Being a Collection of All the Laws of Virginia*. 13 volumes. Richmond-Philadelphia.

Maury, Ann, ed. 1872. *Memoirs of a Huguenot Family*. New York: G. P. Putnam.

Mooney, James. 1899. Letter to W. J. McGee, Savannah, Georgia, October 22, 1899. Bureau of American Ethnology Correspondence, National Anthroplogical Archives, Smithsonian Institution.

Phillips, Leon. 1973. *First Lady of America: a Romanticized Biography of Pocahontas*. Richmond, VA: Westover.

Pollard, John Garland. 1894. *The Pamunkey Indians of Virginia*. Bureau of American Ethnology, Bulletin 17. Washington, DC.

Rountree, Helen C. 1972. "Powhatan's Descendants in the Modern World." *The Chesopiean* 10 (3).

———. 1979. "The Indians of Virginia: The Third Race in a Biracial State." In *Southeastern Indians Since the Removal Era*. W. L. Williams, ed. Athens: University of Georgia Press. 27–48.

———. 1986 "Ethnicity among the 'Citizen' Indians of Tidewater Virginia 1800–1930." In *Strategies for Survival*. Frank W. Porter, ed. New York: Greenwood.

Smith, John. 1624. *The Generall Historie of Virginia, New-England, and the Summer Isles*. London.

Speck, Frank G. 1928. "Chapters on the Ethnology of the Powhatan Tribes of Virginia." *Indian Notes and Monographs* 1 (5).

Stern, Theodore. 1952. "Chickahominy: The Changing Culture of a Virginia Indian Community." *Proceedings of the American Philosophical Society* 96: 157–225.

Wright, Louis B., ed. 1966. *The Prose Works of William Byrd of Westover*. Cambridge: Harvard University Press.

FIGURE 3.1

Pocahontas saves the life of Captain John Smith. Part of an engraving by
Robert Vaughan for Smith (1624). Photo courtesy Library of Congress.

FIGURE 3.2

Pamunkey Indians dressed for performance of "John Smith Play" at Yorktown Centennial. Photo courtesy Virginia Historical Society.

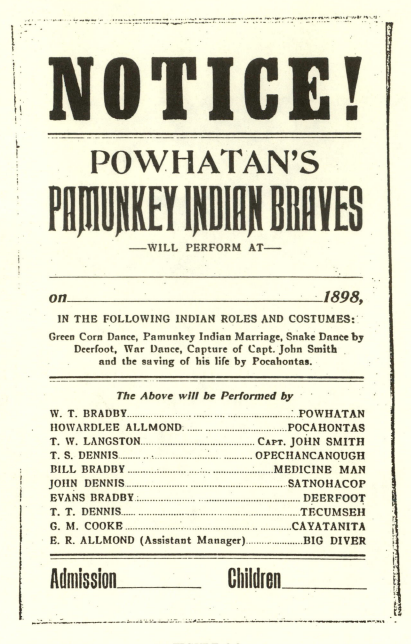

NOTICE!

POWHATAN'S
PAMUNKEY INDIAN BRAVES

—WILL PERFORM AT—

on_____1898,

IN THE FOLLOWING INDIAN ROLES AND COSTUMES:

Green Corn Dance, Pamunkey Indian Marriage, Snake Dance by
Deerfoot, War Dance, Capture of Capt. John Smith
and the saving of his life by Pocahontas.

The Above will be Performed by

W. T. BRADBY...POWHATAN
HOWARDLEE ALLMOND.............................POCAHONTAS
T. W. LANGSTON.....................................CAPT. JOHN SMITH
T. S. DENNIS..OPECHANCANOUGH
BILL BRADBY...MEDICINE MAN
JOHN DENNIS...SATNOHACOP
EVANS BRADBY..DEERFOOT
T. T. DENNIS..TECUMSEH
G. M. COOKE...CAYATANITA
E. R. ALLMOND (Assistant Manager)............BIG DIVER

Admission_____ Children_____

FIGURE 3.3

Handbill announcing the Pamunkey Indians' Pocahontas-Smith play.
Manuscript 4969. National Anthropological Archives, Smithsonian Institution.

FIGURE 3.4

"Deerfoot" (Lewis Bennett) in London, 1861. Photograph by George Newbold, London. Photo courtesy Museum of Mankind London.

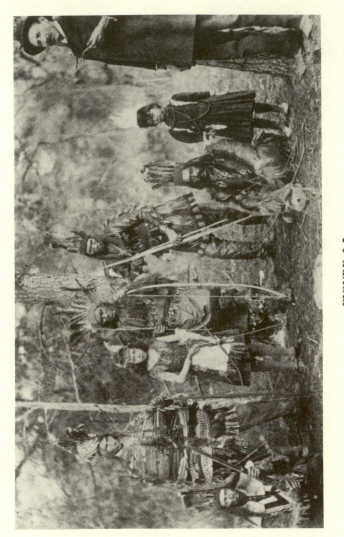

FIGURE 3.5

Pamunkey Indians dressed for the Pocahontas-Smith play, 1899. Left to right: William Bradby, J.T. Dennis, Howard Lee Allmond, William Terrill Bradby, T.T. Dennis, George M. Cook, Captola Cook, Rev. Alex E.R. Allmond. Photograph by DeLancey Gill. Photo courtesy National Anthropological Archives, Smithsonian Institution.

FIGURE 3.6

Pamunkey Indians paying annual tribute to the governor of Virginia, ca. 1930. Left to right: unidentified man, Dora Cook, George M. Cook, Gov. Harry Byrd, Pocahontas Cook, George Cook Jr., Jim Bradby, Tecumseh Deerfoot Cook. Photograph by Dementi Studio, Richmond. Author's collection.

FIGURE 3.7

Pottery school on the Pamunkey reservation, ca. 1932. Photograph by Dementi Studio, Richmond. Author's collection.

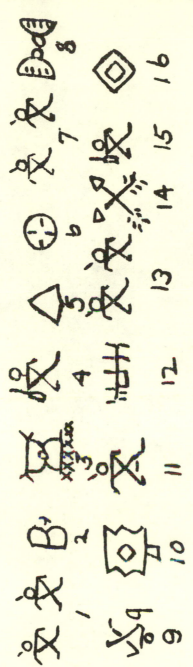

FIGURE 3.8

The pictographic story of Pocahontas and Captain John Smith, Pamunkey, ca. 1970. Mimeographed. Museum für Völkerkunde, Wien (Christian F. Feest collection).

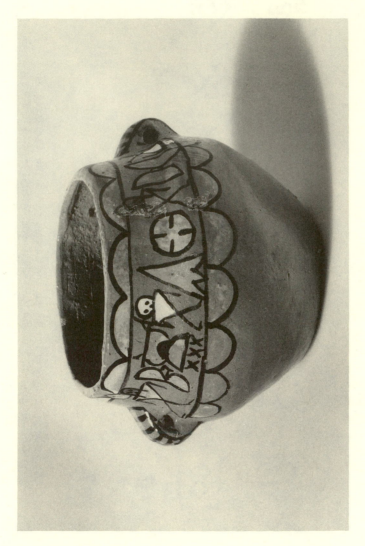

FIGURE 3.9

Pottery vessel with pictographic story of Captain John Smith and Pocahontas, by Daisy Bradby, Pamunkey, ca. 1970. Museum für Völkerkunde, Wien, cat. no. 154.194 (Christian F. Feest collection). Photograph by Fritz Mandl.

4

Squanto and the Pilgrims: On Planting Corn "in the manner of the Indians"

Lynn Ceci

On March 22, 1621, a New England native named Squanto strode into the Pilgrim's new settlement at Plymouth and offered the greeting, "Welcome Englishmen" (Mourt 1963:51; Hubbard 1848:58). According to Pilgrim William Bradford, that spring Squanto "directed them how to set their corn, wher to take fish, and to procure other comodities" (Bradford 1962:73), an act that gained him a prominent place in American history and folklore.

The Plymouth settlers, primarily artisans such as printers, weavers, watchmakers, and carpenters with little farming experience, readily accepted Squanto's advice. A letter written by E.W. (Edward Winslow?) from Plymouth on December 11, 1621 reports: "We set the last Spring some twentie Acres of *Indian* Corne, and sowed some six Acres of Barly & Pease, and according to the manner of the *Indians*, we manured our ground with Herings or rather Shadds, which we have in great abundance, and rake with great ease at our doores" (Mourt 1622:60; Mourt 1963:81).

Winslow's logical deduction that fish manuring was a "manner" of *all* Indians appears to be a syllogistic extension of Squanto's particular knowledge to Indians in general. It was written, it should be noted, before he or any other Pilgrim actually witnessed Indians planting anywhere. Indeed, by the spring of 1621, the cultivation practices of Squanto's own Algonquian tribe were no longer observable because of a recent plague; Squanto was then the "only native of Patuxet," the area the Pilgrims renamed Plymouth (Mourt 1963:55,61). When native planting was observed in the years following, reporters seemed surprised that Indians employed neither fish nor any other fertilizer.

Nonetheless, the original and, as I hope to demonstrate, unfounded conclusion that fish fertilizer was a "manner" of all Indians has long been accepted. It gained support in this century in 1916 when Clark Wissler proposed that the "aboriginal maize culture complex" included the trait of fertilizing with fish where available "everywhere in the Mississippi Valley and eastward" (1916:657–58). A year later he expanded his theory further by stating—still without evidence—that the method of "placing a fish in the maize hill" was "widely distributed in both continents" (Wissler 1937:23). Here, Wissler has apparently linked Squanto's local advice at Plymouth to coastal Peru, the only other confirmed location in the New World where the use of guano and fish fertilizer (actually fish *heads*) was demonstrably an indigenous practice (Mason 1964:139). In the decades following, the notion that American Indians in general knew about or used fish fertilizer became entrenched in anthropological and botanical literature.[1] It appears repeatedly in popular publications, often annexed to corn recipes (Fisher 1974:85; Sokolov 1974), and is reinforced annually when countless numbers of schoolchildren (including my own son and grandson) reenact Squanto's contribution to the Pilgrims in pageants celebrating America's first Thanksgiving. The figure of Squanto now stands immortalized in a diorama at the Plymouth National Wax Museum, where he is shown burying fish before the Pilgrims.

That the evidence for Indian fish fertilizer in North America is poor was first noted in 1880 by G. B. Goode (1880) who, citing the South American data, inferred agricultural fertilizers must be indigenous throughout the Americas. The first scholarly challenge appeared in Regina Flannery's 1939 research on coastal Algonquian culture traits. Unable to find ethnohistoric or ethnographic sources confirming the practice anywhere along the eastern seaboard she concluded, "The aboriginality of the trait is questionable" (1939:10). The second challenge came in 1957 when Erhard Rostlund discussed problems such as the seasonal availability of fish species in coastal zones, vagaries in the original citations, and the curious uniqueness of the practice. He concluded that the use of fish fertilizer was not a "common and widespread practice in any part of native North America" (1957:222).

In this essay I present new evidence from an ethnohistoric, anthropological, and archaeological perspective.[2] This evidence substantiates the conclusions of Flannery and Rostlund, and suggests further that Squanto learned about fish fertilizers in European settlements, not in those of his own or neighboring tribesmen.

Since Squanto's actions remain the single basis for the claim that use of fish fertilizers was a native practice, let us first examine the possible sources of Squanto's agronomical knowledge. His rather remarkable history, often uncited, indicates that he had ample opportunity to learn the European "manner" of planting, which included fertilizing with marine debris and cultivating the New World crop, maize.

In 1614, Captain Thomas Hunt, master of a vessel with Captain John Smith, kidnapped Squanto (and other Indians) and sold him into slavery at Málagá, Spain (Bradford 1962:73; Morison 1935:487). This may have been Squanto's second kidnapping experience because Gorges claimed in 1658, that Captain George Weymouth had kidnapped a "Tasquantum" before, in 1605 from Maine (Gorges 1837:50–51). However, this name or other variations thereof (Tisquantum) does not appear on crewmen Rosier's 1605 list of Indians (Tahanedo, Amoret, Skicowaros, Maneddo, Saffacomoit) Weymouth kidnapped that year in Maine (Rosier 1932:394). Since Gorges wrote his account fifty-three years after the event (and Maine was not Squanto's home), its accuracy is questionable (Burrage in Rosier 1932:394). Similarly, it is unclear whether the native "Tantum" brought from England to Cape Cod in 1615 by Captain John Smith (Morison 1935:487) was this same Indian, Squanto.

Somewhat better documentation indicates that Squanto was smuggled from Málagá after a few years by a captain of a ship belonging to the Guy Colony in Newfoundland; he was brought to a place (ironically) named "Cornhill" in London where he resided for about two years with John Slanie, treasurer of the Newfoundland Company (Mourt 1963:55). The "savage Tasquantum" was next sent to "The Cupids" settlement in Newfoundland (Prowse 1896:104) where he served Captain John Mason, "governour there for the undertakers of that plantation" (Anon. 1832:7). Captain Thomas Dermer next took Squanto with him back to England in 1618, then used this well-traveled Indian the following spring as pilot and guide along the stretch of coast between Monhegan and Virginia (Purchas 1906:129–33).

Squanto left ship at some point and returned to Patuxet prior to greeting the Pilgrims in clear English, one of at least three languages he then spoke (Prowse 1896:105). He quickly became advisor to the Pilgrims in provisioning and planting "corne," [3] "showing them both the maner how to set with it (in these old grounds) it would come to nothing, and . . . in the midle of Aprill they should store enough [fish] come up the brooke" (Bradford 1962:76). More critical to their survival, he also served as interpreter and guide, advising them on how to trade with local Indians for furs, especially the unfamiliar beaver that European ship captains would accept in exchange for supplies they badly needed. By November 1621 "2 hoggsheads of beaver and otter skins" exchanged for "trifling commodities" had been sent back to England (Bradford 1962:8). Squanto's advantageous dealings with the English led to jealousy among local Indians. He received desirable goods, for example, a "suite of cloathes, . . . a horsemans coate . . . [and] other things." And as a seasoned trader, he also "sought his owne ends . . . by putting the Indians in fear, and drawing gifts from them to enrich him selfe; making them believe he could stir up warr against whom he would . . . [and that the English] kept the plague buried in the ground, and could send it amongs whom they would." In late September 1622, Squanto "fell sick of an Indian feavor, bleeding much at ye nose and . . . dyed," after bequeathing his goods to English friends (Bradford 1962:83–85).

Thus, in the years immediately preceding his advice to the Pilgrims, Squanto had learned "foreign" ways by residing with Europeans in both the Old and New World. In Europe, use of fertilizer was a feature of farming technology since the Roman expansion, if not of the earlier Celtics (Vinogradoff 1904: 65; Curwen and Hatt 1953:68). The particular use of marine waste was famous since the medieval period in France, where the fertility of the zone in which it was employed earned it the name "gold belt." [4] Fish fertilizer (fish bones and rotted fish) was cited in a 1620 English publication, suggesting the practice was also known in England before Squanto—or the Pilgrims—departed for the New World (Rostlund 1957:223; Seebohm 1927:265). One might also note that Indian corn or maize had been cultivated in Spain since 1530, nearly a century before Squanto's arrival in Málagá; from there its cultivation with appropriate terracing and irrigation techniques quickly spread to several Mediterranean countries (Hamilton 1976:856–57; Masefield 1967:276; Sauer 1976:824).

Europeans creating gardens in the New World before 1621 may have also used fertilizer with their Old World seeds, for example, in New-foundland in 1583, the Cape Cod area in 1602 and 1603, and Maine in 1605, 1607, and 1614.[5] The 1605 and 1614 gardens in Maine were planted by crewmen of Weymouth and Smith, two possible contacts of Squanto. In the 1604–1607 French colony in Maine and Nova Scotia, established for trafficking with New England Indians, fertilizer usage was specified: the gardens were "improved" with "hogs' dung, or the sweepings of the kitchen, or the shells of fish" (Lescarbot 1907:247). So too the English used "manures" in 1611 and 1614 in the Virgina colony to the south (Purchas 1906:89,95).

A key location for Squanto was the John Guy and "Bristol's Hope" colonies located along "The Cupids" inlet[6] on Conception Bay, Newfoundland, where agriculture was practiced and domesticated animals kept since 1610 (Prowse 1896:98; Andrew 1934:305). In 1615, Guy was replaced by Captain John Mason (Stephen and Lee 1917:1313), Squanto's "governour." In his 1620 book entitled *A Briefe Discourse of the New-foundland*, Mason noted that "June has Capline a fish much resembling smeltes in forme and eating and such aboundance dry on shoare as to lade cartes." Looking to promote immigration, Mason continued with glowing accounts of the local harvests, attributing their success to the use of these fish as *manure*: "For one acre thereof be inclosed with the Creatures therein . . . would exceed one thousand acres of the best Pasture with the stock thereon which we have in England" (Dean 1887: 151). Newfoundlanders continue to rake up dead caplin to fertilize their gardens even today (Omohundro 1985).

Since Squanto served in the very settlement described by Mason, he most probably observed these same scenes of surplus fish advantageously converted to manure. Given this and the other opportunities to learn the value of fertilizer, I suggest the intelligent and enterprising Squanto acquired his knowledge from European examples. Then, on his 1621 visit to Plymouth, Squanto merely passed along the practical advice he knew to be successful from his most recent experience in European, *not* Indian, settlements.

The possibility that Squanto learned about fertilizer at his mother's knee is substantially reduced by the considerable negative evidence for the practice anywhere along the eastern coast of North America (compare Russell 1975:944). It is only in this zone that sufficient numbers of anadromous fish ascending the rivers to spawn would have been available in the critical spring corn-planting months. Corn was not grown by Indians along the western coast of North America (Wissler 1937:20).

Along the south Atlantic Coast from Florida to Virginia, sixteenth- and seventeenth-century French and English colonists described the native cultivation techniques; none mention the use of fertilizer (Rostlund 1957:224; Arber 1910:61–2). In Virginia, where corn planting and fish trapping by Algonquians were carefully detailed and illustrated, fertilizer use was emphatically denied: "The ground they never fatten with mucke, dounge, or any other thing, neither plow nor digge it as we in England" (Quinn 1955:341–42).

Further north, along the mid-Atlantic coast, the Dutch of New Netherlands (New Jersey to southern New England), also described native cultivation techniques. Again, the evidence for native fertilizers is negative, even in areas where fish were caught in great numbers each spring.[7] Adriaen Van der Donck claimed in 1653, after residing near Indians of the upper Hudson River Valley and coastal New York for eight years,

that he had "never seen land manured" by Indians and that "of manuring
. . . they know nothing" (Van der Donck 1968:30–1,96).

From New Netherlands north to the northernmost limit of maize
cultivation (Bennet 1955:370), except for two Pilgrim statements, it is
only the *English* who are identified as the users of fish fertilizer.[8] In
April 1622, the spring after the Pilgrims were warned that "it would
come to nothing" if they did not set seed with fish, visitor Richard
Whitbourne reported that an "incredible" abundance of herring-like
fish had been taken that month and used for "manure" (Arber 1910:781).
In 1627, Isaack DeRasieres, the Dutch Secretary at New Netherland,
also visited Plymouth and detailed how the English took 10,000 to 12,000
fish, carried them to their fields, and placed three or four in each cornhill
(Jameson 1909:111); his comments imply that he found the procedure
unusual and noteworthy, that is, unknown among Dutch or Indian cultivators elsewhere. In 1630, John Smith compared the fertile Virginia
soils with those of New England where the colonists stuck in a "herring
or two" with each corn plant (Arber 1910:952). In 1634, William Wood
reported how the English "manured their land with fishe," and that if
there was no "alewife-river" the English settlement suffered an "incon-
venience" (1634:12,34). Two years later, Edward Johnson, wrote that
"the Lord" provided the English in Concord with "great store of Fish
in the springtime, and especially Alewives . . . thousands of [which]
they used to put under their Indian Corne" (Jameson 1910:114).

Aside from the original 1621 claim, the single exception to these
accounts is John Winthrop's late 1678 comment: "Where the Ground
is bad or worn out, the Indians used to put two or three [Alewives]
under or adjacent to each Corn-hill" (1678:1065–66). The phrase "used
to put" like "manner of the *Indians*," it should be noted, represents a
conclusion rather than directly observed evidence; curiously, when the
younger Winthrop did observe natives planting in 1636, he reported that
they had "good corne without fish" (1863:515). Indeed, the absence of
a single line describing an Indian actually seen "planting" fish in any of
the reliable ethnohistoric sources seems nothing short of remarkable,
that is, *if* the practice was in fact current!

That Indians of New England did not farm as did the English instructed by Squanto earned them harsh criticism. One stern author wrote
in 1622, for example, "They are not industrious, neither have art, science, skill or faculty to use either the land or the commodities of it, but
all spoils, rots, and is marred for want of manuring" (Mourt 1963:
91–2). The reason Indians did not use fish fertilizer the biased Wood
believed was because they were "too lazie to catch fish" (1634:12).[9]

In short, the extant documentary evidence presents a consistent, uniform cultural pattern: no support for the use of any fertilizing agent as a "manner of the *Indians*" in the New England "homeland" of Squanto, among Algonquians and others along the Atlantic Coast, or in North America at large. Indeed, the failure to employ fertilizers even after years of exposure to European farming technology suggests some cultural "resistance" or, as we shall see, a better alternate strategy. Let us therefore examine the implications of planting corn with fish.

The type of Indian corn grown "throughout the eastern United States" in the prehistoric and early historic periods was a race of Northern Flint called *Maiz-de-Ocho* (*Zea mays* var., Galinat 1967:4; Yarnell 1964:23, 106, 148). This short eight-rowed race with dented kernels, adapted to northern growing conditions, arrived in New England about A.D. 1400 and was described in 1678 (Galinat 1985:277; Winthrop 1678:1065). Like its modern hybrid descendants, its productivity must have depended on a set of growing conditions such as soil type and fertility, total sunlight, length of the frost-free season, and moisture (Ceci 1979). The availability of particular nutrients, especially nitrogen, phosphorous, potassium, calcium, and lime (a neutralizer of the acid soils typical of coastal zones), directly affects corn's maturation rate and final size, hence its yields (Thompson and Kelly 1957:55–9; Follett et al. 1981:140,172–79).

Soils in which maize is planted, except naturally rich river alluvia, loess deposits, and old lakebeds, are annually depleted of critical nutrients. The resulting problem of lower yields is commonly resolved by either of two solutions: (1) *shifting cultivation*, move the planting to new still naturally fertile fields or older "fallowed," temporarily "rested" fields; or (2) *fertilizing*, restore the lost nutrients. The first solution was characteristic of earliest horticulturalists experimenting with cultigens and of later agriculturalists farming fields in marginally productive soil zones. Recent documentary and archaeological evidence indicates that this was also the practice of Indians cultivating maize races throughout the Eastern Woodlands including—counter to Wissler's claim—the Mississippi River Valley (Waselkov 1977:517). Indians planting maize along fertile riverbanks further west also "knew nothing of the value of manuring . . . " (Will and Hyde 1917:98).

In the interior Northeast, groups known as successful maize growers, for example, the Huron of southern Canada and Iroquois of New York, moved their settlements every eight to twelve years, in part because of soil depletion (Morgan 1901:251; Tooker 1964:42). Accordingly, northeastern archaeologists recognize the role of shifting cultivation and soil depletion when interpreting sites occupied by Indian corn cultivators; soil fertility appears to correlate with site location and duration, and may influence population size as well as the development of social, political, and economic complexity (White 1963: 4; Ceci 1982:15–16).

Shifting cultivation is also specifically reported for Algonquians in the Northeast. In 1605, Champlain noted that the Indians on Cape Cod left fields uncultivated in order to "let them lie fallow" (Biggar 1922: 351–52). Soils in the Plymouth area are "sandy, acid, easily leached . . . ill-suited to agriculture" (Rutman 1967:54). That native cultivators practiced fallowing in these poor soils may be inferred from the Pilgrims' own observations, in which they distinguished "formerly" planted corn ground from recent fields bearing "new stubble" (Mourt 1963:21–43). Fallowing was defined by Winthrop in 1636 for the Narragansett who had "good corne without fish" despite soils "farre worse" than Massachusetts: "they have every one 2 feilds, which after the first 2 yeares they lett one feild rest each yeare, & that kepes their ground continally in hart" (1863:515). In 1643, Roger Williams recorded two terms for "planting fields" among these natives, one meaning "worne out" field and the other "new ground" (Williams 1963:119); the distinction implies shifting cultivation. When Van der Donck recommended a site for maize, the New Netherland Indians responded: "It is but twenty years since we planted corn there, and now it is woods again" (1968:20).

The second solution for decreasing yields, the use of fertilizer, is thought to be historically a relatively late practice throughout the world, one associated with the establishment of permanent villages and fields (Curwen and Hatt 1953:68). Importantly, this technological advance is based on recognition of the cause and effect relationship between soil improvement and subsequent productivity, a process observable, for example, where domesticated animals are penned or organic waste accumulates. In North America, it should be noted, there were no penned domesticated fauna in pre-contact times for natives to observe, though the value of planting in old midden soils may have been recognized by some (Ceci 1984:67).

The most likely fertilizing agent American Indians might have used was the ashes created naturally wherever fields were cleared by burning. Yet documents raise doubts as to whether the specific value of ashes as a fertilizer—a modest source of phosphorous—was recognized or intended (Follett et al. 1981:73). In Virginia, for example, Indians burned "weedes, grasse, & old stubbes of corn stalkes" but neither dispersed the ash "heapes" to "better the grounde" or "set their corn where the ashes lie" (Quinn 1955:341–42). Further north, New Netherland Indians recognized that annual "bush burning" brought better grasses, but they, like those in New England, confined the burning to wild areas where they hoped to attract game and improve hunting (Van der Donck 1968:

20–1; Wood 1634:15). The concept of ash-improved growth, in short, was apparently not transferred to their gardens, and the beneficial effects of ashes on the soil were incidental.

The use of fish as fertilizer raises other more serious problems. First, as noted above, the seasonal availability and quantities needed restrict the practice to areas near the northeastern rivers where runs of alewife, shad, and herring species coincide with the mid-to-late April beginning of the frost-free season, the earliest time to plant corn (Rostlund 1957:222; Ceci 1978). Though collecting sufficient quantities was easy enough for natives or colonials, even without weirs (Josselyn 1833:273), it is the intensified labor afterward that suggests good reasons why the practice would not be attractive to any planter. Given cornhill spacings of six, five, four, three, and two and one-half feet apart (Jameson 1909:107,219; 1910:114; Van der Donck 1968: 31), the single acre would contain 1208, 1710, 2719, 4834, and 6961 cornhills respectively. If, as reported, two to four whole fish were placed in each hill, the single acre then required 2416 to 27,844 fish. That first planting of "twentie Acres of *Indian Corne*" in 1621 must have truly required the "great abundance" cited— 48,320 to 556,880 fish! A decade later, in 1632, New England farmers were said to fertilize 100 acres with 1000 to 3000 fish per acre (Weatherwax 1954:124), still great totals. If each fish weighed as little as one pound, then tons as well as quantities of fresh and rotting fish had to be gathered, transported to the fields, and buried one by one in each cornhill. The practice next generated the chore of guarding against night raiders attracted to the smelly fish in the fourteen-day rotting period, fauna such as wolf, bear, bobcat, raccoon, skunk, weasel, martin, fishers, and seagulls (Winslow 1832:101; Gould 1974).

And for all this labor, one must apply the critical test: was the effort worth it? There is first the news that despite their labors and "good increase in corn" (Mourt 1963:81) the Pilgrims starved in the first few years; they were "not well acquainted with the manner of Indian corne" and the planting—as we can see—was "arduous" (Bradford 1962: 84–7; Rutman 1967:10). In fact, their estimated rate of corn productivity, eighteen bushels per acre, was no greater than that for Indians *not* using fish, and less than the twenty bushels per acre raised in Plymouth County two centuries later *without* ground improvement (Rutman 1967:9,43; Dingley 1853:154). The properties of this fertilizer suggest reasons. Though processed fish *meal* well worked into the soil is an excellent source of nitrogen and phosphorous, unrefined fish scrap supplies only half the amount (Follett et al. 1981:73). Thomas Hutchinson suggests a related problem in his 1639 statement that three or four years of improving the ground "had exhausted the goodness of the soil

. . . . The common practice, of manuring with fish, left the land in a *worse* state than it would have been in if they had used no manure at all" (1936:85; emphasis mine). An explanation appears in a criticism made against the use of caplin in Newfoundland in the nineteenth-century: "The farmer, by using fish as a manure, enriches his pastures for a season, but impoverishes the ground rapidly . . . vast myriads of insects, grubs, and caterpillars are developed from the putrid soil, suddenly overenriched" (Omohundro 1985:22).

Thus as a cultural strategy, it is not difficult to understand why experienced and observant Indians might resist the practice of using fish to "improve" their crops in any period and why English farmers, in particular, abandoned the practice in favor of animal manures by about 1640 (Rutman 1967:17). From the native perspective, there was also the allocation of huge fish supplies into the ground during the hungriest season, the traditional lean spring (Van der Donck 1968:76; Bennet 1955:370). Records indicate instead that northeastern natives took the more predictable course of action by feasting on spring supplies of fresh protein and converting surplus fish into future food supplies by smoking or drying.[10] English farmers, in contrast, represent an alternate cultural strategy. The huge quantities obtained in one day—10,000 to 12,000 fish at "one tide" (Wood 1634:34; Jameson 1909:111)—must have resulted in surpluses far beyond the amount the Pilgrims could immediately consume or process by salting "against the winter"; such a surplus, perhaps grown spoiled and odoriferous, would then be used "for the ground" or even fed to the pigs (Wood 1634:34; Rutman 1967:48). That these farmers used fish as fertilizer only when or even *because* there was a surplus is suggested by both the Mason data from Newfoundland cited above and the New England comment, "the plenty of fish which they have for little or nothing, is better to be used, than cast away" (Wood 1634:12). If Indians were to resolve the problem of declining corn harvests, it seems unlikely that they would choose to gather thousands (and tons) of fish beyond their immediate needs and processing capabilities to reach that same point of surplus gathered by English settlers.

The tools and workforce needed to carry out this "solution" are additional considerations. While Indians possessed simple sacks, carrying baskets, crude stone, wood, bone or shell hoes, and wooden digging sticks,[11] the Pilgrim farmers had more efficient metal shovels, hoes, dung forks, and carts drawn by domesticated animals. Their metal plows, Indians observed, could "teare up more ground in a day, than their Clamme shels could scrape up in a month" (Rutman 1967:33,36; Wood 1634:78). Moreover, because the division of labor among northeastern

Indians reflected the value system of societies still largely dependent upon wild foods, the less prestigious planting chores were the work of females. They are consistently identified as those who "plant it, dress it, gather it, barne it, [and] beat . . . all their corne with hand" (Williams 1963:65).[12] The life of Indian women was thought "slavish" compared with European women because "they carry all their burdens, set and dress their corn, gather it in [about twenty-four to sixty bushels per family] . . . beat and make ready the corn to eat (Winslow 1832:96; Williams 1963:124). At estimated yields of eighteen bushels per acre, women working fields of 1.3 to 3.3 acres would have had to obtain, carry, and bury at least 3148 to 7973 fish—thousands more if cornhills were closer than six feet apart. Even if Indian males had recognized the value of the farming methods by male colonists and their indentured servants (Levermore 1912:826–31), they would not have easily changed their traditional roles to help with the heavy fieldwork fish fertilizer entailed. Planting was womens' work that would "compromise their dignity too much" and, as they realistically noted, the methods "require too much labor" (Jameson 1909:107; Van der Donck 1968:96; compare Ricciardelli 1963:309).

For settlers facing poor soils and yields, the reverse was the case: *less* labor was required to apply the abundant waste fish to their fields than to move the fields to other sites in the wilderness as did the Indians. Winslow implied this rationale in 1624 when he wrote: "Where men set with fish (as with us) it is easy so to do than to clear ground and set without some five or six years, and so begin anew"; but he added, perhaps a bit puzzled, that Indians in some places "set four years together without, and have as good corn or better than we have that set with them" (1832:101). In testing the Winthrop/Wissler claim, it is clear that decisions to fallow or fertilize must be evaluated as subsistence strategies, that is, specific programs designed to achieve desired levels of agricultural productivity in each ecological setting. These decisions, by natives or colonials, can only be understood within the social, political, economic, technological, and even ideological context of the whole cultural system in which and for which they were adaptive. Along with the availability of critical resources, each practice, like the Indians' seasonal "removes" (Williams 1963:74) to different locations are also settlement strategies. Therefore concepts of property ownership and community, "open" vs. "closed" land, and ease in moving and rebuilding settlements must also be considered. To invest so much labor and material in single cornfield plots implies being "anchored" (Bennett 1955:375) to real estate, a concept expected for Pilgrims seeking to possess new lands but not consistent with known native values. It also implies the establishment of habitation sites of long duration in the corn-planting era, from A.D. 1400–1600, that is, the presence of of archae-ological evidence for large deeply stratified permanent and well-populated village sites distributed in territories near the spring fish runs. This kind of evidence, like reports describing natives planting fish, is weak if not lacking the length of the New England and New Netherlands coastline.[13]

In fact, the many lines of evidence strongly suggest that the invention and use of fish fertilizer by northeastern Indians would have been mal-adaptive, a burdensome land-tethered chore of questionable value for improving corn yields. More adaptive, in fact, was the well documented fallowing technology, especially where beans were planted to "grow up with and against the maize" (Jameson 1909:107). In this way nitrogen became more available to the corn roots (through nitrogen fixation) and the weed area was reduced. The combined beans/corn diet is also higher in available protein and a balance of amino acids, so helps prevent deficiencies caused by corn alone. Given these strategies, might one not argue that the experienced Indians were *too wise* to adopt the onerous fish fertilizer "solution" taken by the early Pilgrims?

Data for the prehistoric and historic Iroquois suggest the kind of changes that would make fertilizer more adaptive for Indians. These occurred after the presence of traders and expanding colonial settle-ments had completely transformed the Indians' culture system and cul-tivation strategies. Scarce cultivable land and availability of European agricultural technology and staple foods are thought to have brought about permanent settlements (White 1963). Missionary pressure and acceptance of western values, life on reservations, and replacement of hunting by farming as prestigious male tasks are associated with the adoption of "white agriculture" centuries after contact (Ricciardelli 1963). Similar processual changes appear to have occurred among Algonquian farmers along the coast.

The belief that fish fertilizer originated among North American In-dians, and was communicated as such by Squanto to the Plymouth settlers, has achieved the status of an unquestioned legend and is there-fore difficult to challenge. Responses from my original study confirm both a worldwide interest[14] in the topic as well as the legend's cherished status in this country. Supporters outnumbered critics who, unexpect-edly, attacked my supposed "racist" motivations in portraying the In-dians as "lazy," "ignorant or incapable" of making technological ad-vances (Thomas 1975; personal communication; Warden 1975). One wrote, "After the harm we have done physically and culturally to the American Indian we are still relentlessly pursuing them but now . . .

on an intellectual level. Trying . . . to remove the American Indians from even our folklore is incredible" (LeBouton 1975, personal communication). Most painful of all were the comments of Mashpee Wampanoag spokeswoman, A.G. Bringham, who charged me with assuming Indians were incapable of surviving without Europeans and of being a non-Indian unable to understand Indian knowledge (Wassaja 1975).

I answered these charges in detail (Ceci 1975b), emphasizing that my cultural analysis of fish fertilizers should in no way be construed as any sort of slur on native capabilities—especially since the practice, in fact, appears to have been so maladaptive. The issue of whether I or any anthropologist can objectively assess the practices of a different ethnic group involves the classic emic-etic question—the different perspectives of knowledgeable participant insiders and that of scholarly outsiders. This question is best answered by the quality of scholarship, ideally, by combining information from "insiders" with expert native knowledge and the analysis of unbiased "outsiders" of scientific mind. Unfortunately, I know of no natives today with expertise in seventeenth-century Coastal Algonquian farming practices. Contrary to LeBouton's accusation, rather than trying to "remove American Indians from *our* folklore," I was trying to remove American folklore from scientific knowledge of American Indians.

That the fish fertilizer "manner of the *Indians*" was and remains so strongly defended despite the weak evidence raises questions about the "folklorification" process. Confabulated histories in several juvenile works make it clear that the Squanto figure is currently drawn as a "noble savage," a friendly, benign, almost childlike Indian who unhesitatingly shares native food, technology, and land with Europeans; he even welcomes their coming and suggests the Thanksgiving feast![15] This "invented" Squanto stands in contrast to the real, very interesting historical Squanto, an intriguing, enterprising survivor and culture-broker who facilitated the meshing of disparate cultures on a new frontier. More importantly, the invented Squanto *masks* the more threatening and numerous Indians of the frontier period who, objecting to the usurpation and "invasion" of their lands (Jennings 1975), attacked and killed settlers—a more accurate representation but a history too "uncomfortable" for popular American consumption.

The "noble savage" movement of the last century is rooted in romantic reconstructions of Indians (for example, *Hiawatha*) as uncorrupted natural beings—who were becoming extinct—in contrast to rising industrial and urban mobs. An Indian Head coin was struck in 1859 to commemorate their passing, and again (backed by the disappearing buffalo) in 1913–1938 (Yeoman 1987), the period when Wissler and others revitalized the Squanto/fish fertilizer story. Thanksgiving is also a nine-teenth-century invented tradition, a Protestant festival of Anglo-Saxon origins resurrected in 1863 by President Abraham Lincoln to promote a sense of national history and social cohesion in a country divided by Civil War and waves of new immigrants (Hobsbawm and Ranger 1983:279).

As folklore, then, the Squanto-fish fertilizer story contains elements that touch American national and religious values, as well as the feelings of guilt or anger many hold about true Indian history. For modern descendants of New England Indians, the hero Squanto-fish fertilizer story appears to lend strength to their "fragile traditions" (see Simmons 1985:52), especially since World War II when retribalization and land claims became important. This is also the period when the Squanto story entered juvenile literature. Thus to challenge any aspect of the popular story, for non-Indians and Indians alike, would seem "incredible" as the writer charged, if not an attack on personal beliefs.

Nevertheless, while Squanto was unquestionably an important historic figure and did contribute substantially to the Pilgrims' survival, the belief that fish fertilizer was a "manner of the *Indians*" because *Squanto knew about it* should be revised. The current evidence indicates that his advice at Plymouth is best viewed as a special example of culture contact dynamics, one in which a native culture-bearer conveyed a technological idea from one group of Europeans to another.

Notes

1. See for example, Mead 1921:409; Driver 1961:53; Weatherwax 1954: 124; Walden 1966:18; and Rutman 1967:9.
2. This essay is a revised and expanded version of an earlier work (Ceci 1975a, 1975b).
3. "*Corn*" etymologically refers to a "worn-down" particle or grain, and derives from the German *kern*, kernel (O.E.D.). Thus early documentary citations of "corne," without the modifier Indian or Guinea, may refer to "Wheate, Rye, Barlie, Oates, and Pease" (e.g., Dean 1887:149) rather than the New World grain maize (Arawak *maiz*).
4. "Cet amendement (débris de coquillages) . . . a beaucoup contribué, par las continuité immémoriale de son emploi, à créer tout le long des côtes de Bretagne une zone de quelques kilométres de profondeur . . . La fertilité de ce littoral lui a valu le nom traditionnel de 'ceinture dorée' " (Grand 1950:263). (This improvement [shellfish debris] . . . has contributed greatly, through the immemorial continuity of its use, to the creation of a zone of several kilometers' depth, the length of the Brittany coast . . . The fertility of this littoral has earned it the traditional name of "gold belt." [author's translation].)

5. See Haies 1938:284; Brereton 1966:6; Purchas 1906:326; Rosier 1932:365; Burrage in Rosier 1932, map facing 412; Smith 1836:113).
6. Recent archaeological fieldwork here has revealed early seventeenth-century foundations, ceramic sherds, and smoking pipes (R.A. Barakat 1978, personal communication).
7. See Van Wassener, deRasieres, Megapolensis, and DeVries in Jameson 1909:69, 72, 105, 107, 177, 206, 219, 333.
8. Some have interpreted Champlain's passage about Maine Indians planting maize with horseshoe crab shells (*signoc*) as evidence for the use of "fish" fertilizer. Careful reading of the original text, however, indicates that the shells were used as implements, not fertilizer, a function for which they would be poorly suited in their natural state (see Biggar 1922:327–28; Ceci 1982:21–2).
9. There is considerable archaeological, ethnohistoric, and ethnographic evidence for the trapping of large numbers of fish by northeastern Indians in various types of weirs and nets from the prehistoric Archaic period to the Historic.
10. See for example, Flannery 1939:178; Van der Donck 1968: 76; Williams 1963:138; Gookin 1806:150; Jameson 1909:177,222).
11. See for example, Flannery 1939:11–13; Jameson 1909:69,72,77,107,174, 222; Williams 1963:124; Winslow 1832:96.
12. See also, DeRasieres in Jameson 1909:107; Gookin 1806: 149; Higginson 1630:113; Van der Donck 1968:49; compare Ricciardelli 1963.
13. The weak archaeological evidence for large, prehistoric, corn-producing villages in Coastal New York was the problem that generated my original fish fertilizer research.
14. Letters and request for reprints came in from more than 50 academic departments, laboratories, and individuals in United States, Canada, South America, Europe, Africa, and Asia.
15. Surprising fictional details include: Squanto's birth in 1596; his gift of eels to a friend so the boy would not have to wear a dress; his fear of malevolent "witch doctors" and local Iroquois attacks; his "decision" since youth not to fight the whites and seek peace; his trading furs with Hunt and contentment with being kidnapped because Europeans were kind to him and taught him about European comforts; and finally how the always smiling Squanto taught the Pilgrims how to refine maple sugar (see chapter 5) and make chowder, cornbread and other foods for the Thanksgiving table (see Bulla 1954; Stevenson 1962; Weisgard 1967; Johnston 1972; Myers 1972; and the Squanto ditto-masters from the November Monthly Activity Units published by Continental Press, 1984).

References

Andrew, C. 1934. *The Colonial Period of American History*, Vol. 1. New Haven: Yale University Press.

Anon. 1832. "A Brief Relation of the Discovery and Plantation of New England." *Massachusetts Historical Society Collections* 9 (Series 2):1–25.

Arber, E., ed. 1910. *Travels and Works of Captain John Smith*. Edinburgh: J. Grant.

Bennet, M.K. 1955. "The Food Economy of the New England Indians 1605–1675." *Journal of Political Economy* 63:369–97.

Biggar, H.P., ed. 1922. *The Works of Samuel de Champlain*, Vol. 1. Toronto: Champlain Society.

Bradford, William. Wish, H., ed. 1962. *Of Plymouth Plantation*. New York: Capricorn Books.

Brereton, J. 1602. *Discoverie of the North Part of Virginia*. Londini: Geor. Bishop (Ann Arbor, MI: University Microfilms).

Bulla, C.R. 1954. *Squanto, Friend of the White Man*. New York: Thomas Y. Crowell.

Ceci, L. 1975a. "Fish Fertilizer: a Native North American Practice?" *Science* 188:26–30.

———. 1975b. "Letters." *Science* 189:946–50.

———. 1978. "Watchers of the Pleiades: Ethnoastronomy Among Native Cultivators in Northeastern North America." *Ethnohistory* 25:301–18.

———. 1979. "Maize Cultivation in Coastal New York: The Archaeological, Agronomical, and Documentary Evidence." *North American Archaeologist* 1:45–74.

———. 1982. "Method and Theory in Coastal New York Archaeology: Paradigms of Settlement Pattern." *North American Archaeologist* 3:5–36.

———. 1984. "Shell Midden Deposits as Coastal Resources." *World Archaeology* 16:62–74.

Curwen, E.C. and G. Hatt. 1953. *Plough and Pasture: The History of Farming*. New York: Collier Books.

Dean, J.W., ed. 1887. *Captain John Mason*. Boston: The Prince Society.

Dingley, I. 1853. "Report from Marshfield, Plymouth County Mass." In *Report of the Commissioner of Patents for the Year 1852, Part 2*. Agriculture Executive Document 65. Washington, D.C.

Douglas, George W. 1937. *The American Book of Days*. New York: H.W. Wilson Co.

Driver, H.E. 1961. *Indians of North America*. Chicago: University of Chicago Press.

Fisher, M.F.K. 1974. "How Victoria Set the American Table. *The New York Times Magazine* (September 15), 76–86.

Flannery, R. 1939. "An Analysis of Coastal Algonquian Culture." *Catholic University of America Anthropology Series 7*. Washington, D.C.

Follett, R.H., L.S. Murphy, and R.L. Donahue. 1981. *Fertilizers and Soil Amendments*. Englewood Cliffs, NJ: Prentice-Hall.

Galinat, W. C. 1967. "Plant Habit and the Adaptation of Corn." *University of Massachusetts Agricultural Experimental Station Bulletin 565*.

———. 1985. "Domestication and Diffusion of Maize." In *Prehistoric Food Production in North America*. R.I. Ford, ed. Museum of Anthropology, University of Michigan Anthropological Paper 75, 245–78.

Goode, G.B. 1880. "The Use of Agricultural Fertilizers by the American Indians and the Early English Colonists." *American Naturalist* 14:473–79.

Gould, J. 1974. "A Misreported Personality." *Christian Science Monitor* (March 28).

Gookin, D. 1806. "Historical Collection of the Indians in New England." *Massachusetts Historical Society Collections 1* (Series 1):141–227.

Gorges, F. 1837. "A Brief Narration of the Originall Undertakings of the Advancement of Plantation into the Parts of America [1658]." *Massachusetts Historical Society Collections 6* (Series 3):45–93.

Grand, R. 1950. *L'Agriculture au Moyen Age de las Fin de l'Empire Romain au XVIe Siècle*. Paris: E. DeBoccard, Ed.

Haies, E. 1938. "Sir Humphrey Gilbert's Voyage to Newfoundland." In *Voyages and Travels. The Harvard Classics 33*. E. Eliot, ed. New York: Collier, 263–98.

Hamilton, E.J. 1976. "What the New World Gave the Economy of the Old." In *First Images of America*. F. Chiappelli, ed. Berkeley: University of California Press, 853–84.

Higginson, F. 1955. "New England's Plantation [1630]." In *English Historical Documents*. D.C. Douglas, ed. New York: Oxford University Press, 107–14.

Hobsbawm, E. and T. Ranger, eds. 1983. *The Invention of Tradition*. Cambridge: Cambridge University Press.

Hubbard, W. 1848. "A General History of New England." *Massachusetts Historical Society Collections 5* (Series 2):1–768.

Hutchinson, T. 1936. *The History of the Colony and Province of Massachusett-Bay* [1764]. Cambridge: Harvard University Press.

Jameson, J.F., ed. 1909. *Narratives of New Netherland 1609–1664*. New York: Charles Scribner's Sons.

———. 1910. *Johnson's Wonder-Working Providence, 1628–1651*. New York: Barnes and Noble.

Jennings, F. 1975. *The Invasion of America: Indians, Colonization and the Cant of Conquest*. Chapel Hill: University of North Carolina Press.

Johnston, J. 1972. *The Indians and the Strangers*. New York: Dodd, Mead & Co.

Josselyn, J. 1833. "An Account of Two Voyages to New-England [1673]." *Massachusetts Historical Society Collections 3* (Series 3):211–354.

Lescarbot, M. 1907. *The History of New France. Vol. 3*. W.L. Grant, trans. Toronto: Champlain Society.

Levermore, C., ed. 1912. *Forerunners and Competitors of the Pilgrims and Puritans*. Vol. 2. Brooklyn, NY: New England Society.

Masefield, G.B. 1967. "Crops and Livestock." In *The Cambridge Economic History of Europe*, Vol. 5. E.E. Rich and C.H. Wilson, eds. London: Cambridge University Press, 275–301.

Mason, J.S. 1964. *The Ancient Civilizations of Peru*. Baltimore: Penguin.

Mead, C.W. 1921. "Indian Corn or Maize." *Natural History* 21:408–13.

Morgan, L.H. 1901. *League of the Ho-de-no-sau-nee or Iroquois* [1851]. New York: B. Franklin.

Morison, S.E. 1935. "Squanto." In *Dictionary of American Biography*. D. Malone, ed. New York: Charles Scribner's Sons.

Mourt, G. 1622. *A Relation or Journall of the Beginning and Proceedings of the English Plantation Setled at Plimouth in New England*. London (Ann Arbor: University Microfilms).

———. 1963. *A Journal of the Pilgrims at Plymouth, Mourt's Relation* [1622]. D.B. Heath, ed. New York: Corinth Books.

Myers, R.J. 1972. *Celebrations: The Complete Book of American Holidays*. Garden City, NY: Doubleday and Company.

Omohundro, J.T. 1985. "One Potato, Two Potato." *Natural History* 94:22–9.

Prowse, D.W. 1896. *A History of Newfoundland from the English, Colonial, and Foreign Records*. 2nd rev. ed. London: Eyre and Spotliswoode.

Purchas, S. 1906. *Purchas, His Pilgrimes* [1625], Vol. 19. Glasgow: J. MacLehose.

Quinn, D.B., ed. 1955. *The Roanoke Voyages, 1584–1590, 1*. London: Hakluyt Society Works 1 (Series 2).

Ricciardelli, A. 1963. "The Adoption of White Agriculture by the Oneida Indians." *Ethnohistory* 10:309–28.

Rosier, J. 1932. "A True Relation of the Voyage of Captaine George Waymouth, 1605." In *Early English and French Voyages, Chiefly from Hakluyt, 1534–1608*. H.S. Burrage, ed. New York: Charles Scribner's Sons, 353–94.

Rostlund, E. 1957. "The Evidence for the Use of Fish as Fertilizer in Aboriginal North America." *Journal of Geography* 56:222–28.

Russell, H. 1975. "Letters." *Science* 189:944–6.

Rutman, D. B. 1967. *Husbandmen of Plymouth*. Boston: Beacon Press.

Sauer, J.D. 1976. "Changing Perception and Exploitation of New World Plants in Europe," 1492–1800." In *First Images of America*. F. Chiappelli, ed. Berkeley: University of California Press. 813–32.

Seebohm, M.E. 1927. *The Evolution of the English Farm*. Cambridge, MA: Harvard University Press.

Simmons, W.S. 1985. "From Fakelore to Folklore: a Consideration of some Wampanoag Texts." *Man in the Northeast* 30:45–58.

Smith, J. 1836. *A Description of New England [1616]*. Massachusetts Historical Society Collections 6 (Series 3):95–140.

Sokolov, R. 1974. "The Ritual of Maize." *Natural History* 83:64–5.

Stephen, L. and S. Lee. 1917. "John Mason." In *The Dictionary of National Biography*, Vol. 12. Oxford: Oxford University Press.

Stevenson, A. 1962. *Squanto, Young Indian Hunter*. Indianapolis: Bobbs-Merrill.

Thompson, H. and W. Kelly. 1957. *Vegetable Crops*. 5th ed. New York: McGraw-Hill.

Tooker, E. 1964. *An Ethnography of the Huron Indians, 1615–1649*. Bureau of American Ethnology Bulletin 190.

Van der Donck, A. 1968. *A Description of New Netherlands* [1655]. T. O'Donnell, ed. Syracuse: Syracuse University Press.

Vinogradoff, P. 1904. *The Growth of the Manor*. London: Allen & Unwin.

Walden, H. 1966. *Native Inheritance: the Story of Corn in America*. New York: Harper & Row.

Warden, G.B. 1975. "Letters." *Science* 189:946.

Waselkov, G. 1977. "Prehistoric Agriculture in the Central Mississippi Valley." *Agricultural History* 51:513–19.

Wassaja. 1975. "Objections Voiced to a Newspaper Article in Boston." *Wassaja* 3 (4). The American Indian Historical Society.

Weatherwax, P. 1954. *Indian Corn in old America*. New York: Macmillan.

Weisgard, L. 1967. *The Plymouth Thanksgiving*. Garden City, NY: Doubleday.

White, M.E. 1963. "Settlement Pattern Change and the Development of Horticulture in the New York-Ontario Area." *Pennsylvania Archaeologist* 33:1–12.

Will, G.F. and G.E. Hyde. 1917. *Corn Among the Indians of the Upper Missouri.* Lincoln: University of Nebraska Press.

Williams, R. 1963. *The Complete Writings of Roger Williams.* J. H. Trumbull, ed. New York: Russell and Russell.

Winslow, E. 1832. *E. Winslow's Relation* [1624]. Massachusetts Historical Society Collections 9 (Series 2):74–104.

Winthrop, J. 1678. *The Description, Culture, and Use of Maiz.* Royal Society of London Philosophical Transactions 12 (142):1065–69.

Winthrop, J. 1678. *The Description, Culture, and Use of Maiz.* Royal Society of London Philosophical Transactions 12 (142):1065–69.

Winthrop, Jr., J. 1863. "Letter, &c., of John Winthrop, Jr., April 7, 1636." Massachusetts Historical Society Collection 6 (Series 4):514–5.

———. 1937. *The American Indian.* 3rd ed. New York: Oxford University Press.

Wood, W. 1634. *Neuu Englands Prospect.* London: Tho. Cotes, for John Bellamie (Washington, D.C.: Microcard Editions).

Yarnell, R.A. 1964. *Aboriginal Relationships between Culture and Plant Life in the Upper Great Lakes Region.* Museum of Anthropology, University of Michigan Anthropological Papers 23.

Yeoman, R.S. 1987. *A Guide Book of United States Coins for 1988.* 41st Revised Edition. Racine, WI: Western Publishing Company.

5

A Sweet Small Something: Maple Sugaring in the New World

Carol I. Mason

Americans know intuitively that maple sugar and maple syrup are among the things that spread from Indians to the rest of world culture after the discovery of the Americas by Europeans. In almost all books dealing with Indians for young readers, children learn that maple sugar was made before European contact (Gridley 1973; Franklin 1979; Poatgieter 1981); television cooks feature recipes made with this acknowledged Indian food (Smith 1987); and students of the maple products industry unhesitatingly ascribe the discovery of maple sugar to Indians (Nearing and Nearing 1970). Indians themselves claim to have discovered the process and taught it to Europeans (Keesing 1971). Indian priority in making maple sugar is so well-established a belief that even textbooks in North American ethnography routinely list maple sugaring as an aboriginal practice and include it in their general discussions of Indian life without particular comment (see, for example, Garbarino 1976). The Indian origin of maple sugaring is one of those things that everyone knows. How we know it and why we think it are questions hardly anyone ever asks: maple sugar and maple syrup are together a sweet small something that came from the Indians, in what way or how is quite beside the point.

Maple sugaring is such a minute part of the incredibly long and nutritionally potent list of New World contributions to the whole world's diet that it slips easily through the cracks of scholarly concern. It does not have either the modern economic importance or the obvious nutritional virtues of other pre-Columbian Indian foodstuffs. No one would range it next to corn or potatoes, beans or tomatoes and argue that it is in the same dietary league with these staples: sugar in any form is without redeeming value except insofar as it can provide calories where ordinary caloric intake is low or provide flavor to otherwise unpalatable foods. It is an active threat to health when it is responsible for dental caries and progressive tooth loss. Perhaps its relative unimportance has partially masked the search for the truth about its origins: does it really matter to know whether maple sugaring is truly indigenous to North America?

There are at least two reasons why puzzling over the origins of maple sugaring is not merely an exercise in historical trivia. One of these has to do with the place of American Indians in national life. Indians have not escaped being part of others' myths, whether on a large scale, as the bloodthirsty attackers of television wagon trains, or on more intimate ones as fathers of Thanksgiving, children of Mother Earth, or the original conservationists. These stories are part of a pattern, one seldom subject to scrutiny, and they ride along as the stuff of national self-image, influencing Indian self-conceptions as well as those of non-Indians and becoming new truths with spurious ancient roots. Philosophers have suggested that the unexamined life is not worth living, but the effects of the unexamined life for a single individual cannot be as great as the consequences for nations of unexamined national myths in action. Treatment of ethnic, racial, or religious groups may hinge upon the working out of myths, ancient or new-grown, and they need to be recognized, scrutinized, and "examined."

A second reason for concern with the small problem of maple sugar origins has to do with one of the major approaches of anthropology, the comparative method and what it can reveal about the workings of cultural evolution on a global scale. One of the most useful supports for the comparative method is accurate knowledge of the "Second Earth," the American continents so long separated from both Europe and Asia (Harris 1985). This American world, isolated for thousands of years from contact with the rest of world cultures, developed along its own lines and made its own way toward complex community life, towards agriculture and urban settlements, towards civilization. Using the data from these independent routes to complexity and comparing them to what happened elsewhere is a major tool for understanding possible causes for cultural development and relating outcomes to material and environmental factors affecting change (see, for example, Adams 1966 and Haas 1982). If what scholars are seeing in the New World and using in their testing of parallel phenomena is *not* the working out of indigenous patterns but the result of European contact after the 15th century, then their comparative efforts are seriously compromised. Western culture spread so fast and was so influential that the existence of "un-touched" societies, a pristine Second Earth, becomes suspect and the reconstruction of pre-European lifeways a much more daunting task (Wolf 1982). The problem of the origins of maple sugaring is a nicely bounded test case: was this practice, so widely "known" as an indigenous one, truly of American origin? Or might it have been introduced by Europeans? Being able to answer this question has a bearing on the anthropologists' grasp of the "Second Earth" and whether its realities are as they have been presented.

The pursuit of an answer to the "maple sugar question" is both a question of epistemology—how do we know what we know—and intellectual history, or how we have come to know what we know. In general, the *first* attempts to answer these questions depended heavily upon historical sources, the eye-witness accounts of European observers. The use of mutually supportive eye-witness testimony has to be the single most important body of corroborative evidence, but the eye-witness accounts do not speak for themselves. H.W. Henshaw (1890), the earliest anthropologist to consider the matter, cited Joutel's *Journal* of 1688, Lafitau's observations of 1724, Bossu's comments of 1756, Keating's description of 1825, Smith's statements of 1850 as well as comments by Lewis H. Morgan, Alexander Henry, John Tanner, and others. All of these mentioned maple sugaring as an Indian custom, and most considered Indian origins to be unquestioned. Henshaw was conscious that none of them was very early, but he thought that their near unanimity in supporting the Indian origins of maple sugaring and the fact that the comments themselves stretched over a very long time span were enough to "render reference to earlier authorities unnecessary" (Henshaw 1890:343). Another anthropologist, A.F. Chamberlain (1891), added the 1684 "Dr. Robinson to Mr. Ray" letter, so far the earliest mention of the maple sugar production process in English, a letter in which Indians are described as having been making sugar "for time out of mind" (381). In addition to historic accounts, both Henshaw and Chamberlain considered philological evidence very important in demonstrating the Indian origins of maple sugaring, a research route that needs to be pursued further, using more modern linguistic methods.

However, the strength of the Henshaw-Chamberlain approach to solving the maple sugaring question founders on two rocks. One of these is the sources they cite: none of them is early enough. The seventeenth century is much too late to trust eye-witness accounts; Indians already had nearly 200 years of contact with Europeans under their belts by the time Dr. Robinson wrote his famous letter to Mr. Ray in 1684. The other problem with the Henshaw-Chamberlain effort is more subtle and fits into how Indians were viewed by ordinary non-Indian Americans. When these two papers were published at the end of the nineteenth century, Indian life was not as well known to the general public, and the more romantic portrayal of Indians as "Noble Savages" was less widely accepted than interpretations of them as "blood-thirsty savages." Henshaw, in particular, took pains in his paper to point out the debts owned by "civilized" man to Indians and to establish in terms of dollars and cents just what value Indian discoveries have for modern civilization. In the context of the time, his paper was another attempt to redress a perceived imbalance and support more favorable press for Indians; he had a "hidden agenda" that favored Indians as having originated maple sugaring as part of their extended contributions to civilization, and evidence was not an important consideration.

In the late nineteenth century, then, Indians were allowed by scholars to be as enthusiastic users of maple sugar in prehistory as they wished, presumably reveling in its sweet taste, devouring it in great quantities (see Alexander Henry's account as analyzed in Quimby 1966), and undoubtedly laying up a legacy of dental problems for their old age. By the twentieth century, though, the scholarly community, looking at the *same* kind of data as Henshaw and Chamberlain, came to just the opposite conclusion. Evidently the felt need to defend Indians and celebrate their very real contributions to world culture was less pressing, and maple sugar was snatched from their prehistoric lips. The work done at this time was specifically directed at the earliest of the historic sources, and an exhaustive examination of the extant literature concluded that there is no evidence at all to support pre-European maple sugaring. Keesing, in his classic study of Menomini ethnohistory (1971), and Flannery, in her review of the early literature on Algonquin culture on the east coast (1939), both independently arrived at the same place in the same year: their replowing of the ethnohistorical field yielded an entirely different crop from some of the same seeds, and maple sugaring was seen as a post-European contact phenomenon. Any reexamination of the sources is very likely to come up with the same conclusions.[1]

Stepping outside the circle of the historic sources is one of the directions research into the origins of maple sugaring had to take, and one of the first attempts came about somewhat later than the work by Keesing and Flannery. This was the "argument from equipment." This point of view insisted that Indians could not have processed maple sugar without the metal kettles, metal spoons, and other paraphernalia brought by Europeans (Waugh 1916; Yarnell 1964). Indeed, the argument from equipment has this in its support: with the exception of birch-bark sap collectors, the "things" employed in the many descriptions of Indian maple sugaring are *all* European in origin. The familiar lithographs of Indians in the woods at sugaring time show them with their metal boiling kettles set directly over open fires, their steel axes at work shopping wood, and—most curious of all—their European-style wooden carrying yokes across their shoulders (see, for example, Schoolcraft 1851–1857 and Hoffman 1896). It is hard to find a body of "traditional" or even *old* maple sugaring equipment.

The argument from equipment, however, is seriously flawed. For one thing, it is based upon a model of maple sugar manufacture that would not have been present in prehistory: the eighteenth or nineteenth century commercial sugarbush camp. In these communal camps, Indians produced sugar in quantity for their own use *and* for sale, treating it as a commodity with a value over and above a single group's subsistence needs. The extent to which maple sugaring was a commercial operation among Indians at this time must not be underestimated: they produced it in quantities that are difficult to imagine, particularly as a single heap. For example, Hoffman cites a Leech Lake Chippewa group of 1500 persons whose maple sugar production in one year was recorded as 90 *tons* (1896:288). Given such a commercial redefinition of a possible aboriginal practice, it would not be surprising if the tools common among non-Indian producers, maximizing their own production as best they could, had come to be adopted by Indians in pursuit of the same goals. The argument from equipment is weakened by the simple insistence that Indians, like anyone else, were perfectly able to learn to use new tools, new techniques, new motor habits. They might simply have given up the less efficient, older tools and means of manufacture once they became sugar producers and entrepreneurs in the sugar trade themselves.

In the end, the argument from equipment is a spurious one, of interest only to eighteenth or nineteenth century sugar making. Whatever equipment was being used then was certainly European in origin and can hardly be useful to a discussion of possible prehistoric sugar making among Indians. Many simple techniques for concentrating at least small quantities of sap into syrup were within the reach of anyone who had a container of birchbark or, perhaps, of pottery. Syrup and eventually sugar production involves boiling, the standard means of concentrating liquids—whether syrups or soups—and it can be achieved in birchbark containers set over hot coals or less efficiently in clay pots heated with rocks; it is even possible to concentrate sap through the slow process of freezing and then removing the layers of ice as they form (see Holman and Egan 1985 for replication experiments).[2] If the goal is to make only a *little* syrup or a *little* sugar, then these methods may work well enough, although in the case of freezing, the authentic "maple" flavor does not seem to develop (see Henning 1965).

Combining a favorable reading of the argument from equipment with an exhaustive examination of the ethnohistorical sources, scholars were persuaded that the issue of maple sugaring in prehistory was settled and that maple sugaring could be removed from the list of "things that we got from the Indians." They reckoned, however, without the ingenuity and audacity of archaeologists hot on the trail of trying to understand the patterns of Indian subsistence in prehistory and not overly careful of what ethnohistorical toes they treaded upon in the process. Archaeologists had begun with a careful reading of previous work (see Quimby 1966; Fitting and Cleland 1969) and a properly agnostic attitude toward maple sugaring in prehistory. But with time their own pressing problems, especially those of trying to figure out how people actually lived in the western Great Lakes in Late Woodland times, began to convert some of them into true believers, ethnohistorical sources or not. In an impressive leap of faith, they pushed back into prehistory the pattern of *commercial* sugar production and began to "find" prehistoric maple sugaring stations in areas where historic people had been known to have produced maple sugar. The mere presence of historic maple sugaring seems to have been the principle stimulus for assuming that maple sugaring was practiced there in prehistory (see Pendergast 1974; Lovis 1978; Kingsley and Garland 1980; Holman 1984). Maple sugaring—in spite of the conclusions of ethnohistorians of the mid-twentieth century— suddenly appeared in the archaeological literature as simply another pattern of economic life in prehistory (Spence and Fox 1986).

The efforts of archaeologists to resuscitate Indian use of maple sugar in prehistory provoked still another assessment of the ethnohistorical sources (Mason 1985, 1986). The same literature that led to the original rejection of prehistoric historic maple sugaring in North America reconfirmed what Flannery, Keesing, and Henning had all insisted: the earliest historic accounts are not ambiguous at all; they do not—under *any* circumstances—refer to maple sugaring among American Indians at a date early enough to constitute historical proof. There is not a single eye-witness account in the critical stretch of time between Champlain in the first years of the seventeenth century and the earliest clear mention of maple sugaring late in that century (Schuette and Ihde 1946:95), a powerful silence that speaks volumes (Mason 1987). Almost anything could have happened in those years when "the people without history" confronted European culture for the first time (Wolf 1982).

A different approach picked up by archaeologists to support the presence of maple sugaring in prehistory is the "argument from availability."

In its simplest form it rests on a conviction that if a resource were there, surely people living in nature would have taken advantage of it. Henshaw (1890:342) considered the "great familiarity of the Indians with the natural edible products of America" to be a strong support to their having discovered it. After all, maple trees produced sap in prehistory as they do today; people living in close proximity to the trees and being "familiar" with them, would very likely have quickly learned to take advantage of this potentially important source of calories. Maple products have other virtues that might have attracted "natural man" to them: they are also a source of calcium, although whether people can drink enough syrup or eat enough sugar to make them an effective aid in protecting women from calcium depletion during infant feeding or osteoporosis after menopause is not yet clear (Holman and Egan 1985:69–70). On the basis of known patterns of life of hunters and gatherers, whose knowledge of and experience in a particular environment supports a model of use of whatever is there, the argument from availability seems reasonable. Yet, like necessity's being the mother of invention, it has its problems.

One of these is the fiction that maple sugar is a quintessentially American product, something that cannot be produced elsewhere. This would account for North American aboriginal people's having picked up on the presence of maple trees and to have produced sugar as a regular part of a hunter/gatherer diet while people elsewhere did not. The truth is, though, that many trees in many places produce a sweet sap and some have as potentially useful a sugar-producing role as the sugar maples of the New World, but nowhere did hunters and gatherers tap them to produce sugar. Even European trees will produce sugar and sweet syrup, but although the potential is there, a sugar industry from trees never arose in Europe. European hunters and gatherers and, later, farmers were presumably as knowledgeable as American Indians about the possibilities inherent in their own backyards, but they did not make sugar by tapping trees. Curiously enough, the record for the manufacture of sugar and syrup from trees is about as old in northern Europe as it is in the New World. There are records going back into the seventeenth century of northern Europeans' making their own sugar from the sap of trees (Henning 1965:13–14). It has even been proposed that Swedish immigrants introduced the process into the Americas (Henning 1965:20), but the coincidence of sugaring's arising in two places at the same time has an easier explanation than enterprising Swedes or world-wandering American Indians. It has more to do with new patterns of consumption, low cost of production, difficulties in transportation and the vagaries of trade. Commercial production in Europe of sugar from the tree sap occurred as late as the nineteenth century (Deerr 1950), but it faltered and failed owing to the undoubted fact that by then other sources of sugar were far cheaper.

The archaeological leap into the maple sugar problem highlights a difficulty with so much of ethnohistoric research: it is bounded by a single kind of evidence, the documentary one. Whatever the virtues of such work, breaking out of its circle and obtaining independent confirmation from a different kind of evidence should be a major line of attack. Once archaeologists made the assumption that maple sugaring was prehistoric, they were faced with the practical problem of how to distinguish maple sugaring camps in the ground. Their efforts in this direction constitute the first real steps to identify the possible archaeological remains of sugar camps independent of historic documents. Loftus (1977) suggested on the basis of excavation of a known *historic* site that one characteristic of *prehistoric* sites might be low levels of food refuse bcause people ate sugar and dried meat at the camps and left no animal or fish bones behind. Other possible traits might be the presence of extensive hearth areas resulting from long term boiling; small, impermanent storage buildings; and whatever fragments of maple sugaring equipment as might have survived. The excavators of the prehistoric DeBoer site in Michigan followed this lead, speculating that a maple sugaring camp might also have an unbalanced sex ratio, since women did most of this work, plus a large number of potsherds relative to other kinds of equipment, indicating sap collection and not as much hunting or fishing (Kingsley and Garland 1980). Holman (1984) accepted these in-the-ground indicators, but after trying to stone boil sap in a clay pot, she abandoned the use of large numbers of potsherds as a possible sign that maple sugaring might have been done on the premises (Holman and Egan 1985). Using clay pots was simply too inefficient to be an effective means of production.

All of the archaeological efforts to "find" prehistoric maple sugaring sites are limited by the same problems that beset the ethnohistoric sources: how can independent testing procedures verify or not verify the conclusions drawn from the documents? In the form of archaeological evidence, at least two further tests can be attempted. Sugar residues leave a telltale chemical trace behind them; since the only sugar that could have been in the hands of Indians before Columbus would have been maple sugar, any identifiable sugar residue would support prehistoric sugar use (Holman: personal communication). A second possible line of investigation is to judge the beginning of maple sugaring by assessing the dental health of Indian populations, both historic and prehistoric (Kelley, Barrett, and Saunders 1987). In the maple sugaring country, this would mean examining the teeth of hunters and gatherers rather than farmers in order to avoid confusion when dealing with a diet rich in corn and hence in carbohydrates not derived from maple sugar. Dental caries rates across the historic boundary would be especially significant (Holman and Mason n.d.) since they could be expected to go up when people began to use sugar in quantity.

The promise of archaeological verification for problems of this kind is too often still but a promise, and the ethnohistorical conclusions continue to stand as a powerful corrective for precipitate flights of fancy. But there is one other tool that can be brought to bear on the whole issue, a tool that should be part of the standard equipment of ethnohistorians: how does the phenomenon under discussion fit into the general course of world history? It is commonplace to consider the fur trade, for example, in the context of supply and demand for beaver hair in the European hat business or the political activities of Indians in terms of the competition of France and Britain in the New World. But what of maple sugar? Does its development in the seventeenth century, its expansion into a commercial activity in the eighteenth and nineteenth occur in a vacuum? Or can it be understood and in a way "revealed" through its ties with what was going on elsewhere? It turns out that maple sugaring and the maple sugar industry make enormous good sense when considered within a broader historical framework: it may not even be necessary to belabor the historic sources further or struggle to dig up archaeological techniques for identifying maple sugaring sites. The road to understanding may reach beyond the borders of North America and even beyond the Second Earth into the Old World itself.

In the seventeenth century, maple sugaring was not alone as a high calorie, low nutrient addition to the human diet. It was a small part of the rapid spread of sugar into the human—and especially, the European—diet, fueled by the natural attraction sweetness has for human beings and the development of sugar production as a money-making activity on a large scale (see Mintz 1985; Wolf 1982; Deerr 1949 and 1950). Sweet foodstuffs in general, sugar in particular, have been around for a long time; human populations probably enjoyed honey in the Paleolithic, and the process for making sugar from cane was neither difficult nor abstruse. However, sweetness was a tiny portion of the human diet, a thing to be used sparingly as a condiment, taken as medicine, employed as a preservative, or enjoyed as a treat or on special occasions; it was not food in the ordinary, everyday sense of a repeated, regular source of nutrition. The American Indian pattern of supra-consumption, of eating pounds and pounds of it is peculiar; what it resembles most of all is the similar reaction Europeans had when they themselves were first introduced to sugar on a grand scale (see Mintz 1985).

The basic, archaic technique for making sugar from the liquids taken from plants—before the invention of refining—was "boiling down the juice to a solid mass, allowing the magma of crystals and molasses to drain and recrystallizing the product" (Deerr 1950:449). This simple process was recorded as early as A.D. 375, but it did not initiate a world-wide sugar industry: the technology was simple but hardly amenable to production on a large scale at that time. Furthermore, a market had not been created for sugar in quantity, the European social system was not structured for mass consumption habits, and a slave-based labor force in cane-producing areas was unavailable. It was not yet worth anyone's while to mass produce it, and even by A.D. 1000, sugar was a rarity (Mintz 1985).

Things changed by the fifteenth century as markets developed and sugar in quantity reached more and more people. The island of Madiera became one of the important sugar centers (Deerr 1949), by 1456 producing tons and tons for the European market. By 1480, the Canaries had a local sugar industry and became an important source for sugar experts who could be moved from there to wherever sugar production was possible. With the discovery of the New World, sugar production was on the minds of the discoverers very early; Columbus himself brought sugar experts from the Canaries to the New World, clearly with an eye to expanding what was already seen as a potentially lucrative industry (Mintz 1985). By the early sixteenth century, Hispaniola was exporting sugar to Europe, and as slaves became the pre-eminent labor force "in sugar," production spread rapidly. By 1548 sugar was being produced on a large scale commercial basis: by 1576, local figures mention between 675 and 950 tons from Brazil alone (Deerr 1949:100–01).

What this meant for Europeans was a vastly expanded role for sugar in their diet. Beginning with the privileged classes, sugar consumption spread throughout the social order, perhaps replacing more nutritious foods and serving as an easy source for empty calories (Mintz 1985:177). No one needs to persuade people to like sugar; its attraction may begin before birth, and it is hard to do without once taste has been habituated to it. For those who sell sugar, it is an ideal substance: people do not like to do without; the sugar itself is eaten and consumers always have to buy more; and its shelf life is excellent. And unlike other very attractive, addictive substances, it does not interfere with the working life of working people. By the time Europeans began to immigrate to the Americas, they were avid sugar consumers, and they saw it as a proper part of an ordinary human diet.

The Europeans who came to North America liked sugar perhaps more than others—they were mainly English, and the marketing of sugar in that country reached unimaginable proportions in a very short time (Mintz 1985). The same English consumers who managed to put away 10,000 tons in 1730 were eating 150,000 tons only 70 years later (Henning 1965:12). When New England was settled, a source for sugar was one of the necessities of life, not something that people were wiling to do without. Where it was to come *from*, of course, was a difficult matter, considering the intricacies of international trade, the problems in taxation, the cost of transportation, and a myriad of other little vexations. Sugar transshipped from the Caribbean or from Brazil was very expensive to begin with; the additional costs of overland travel brought the price sufficiently high as to force complaints from colonists unwilling or unable to foot the bill. Relief from the high cost of cane sugar came about through a series of steps that, taken together, leave a trail of evidence from the sugar works in Brazil to the doorsteps of thrifty New Englanders.

The first calamity for European sugar users was the destruction of the very lucrative Portuguese sugar trade in Brazil by the Dutch (Deerr 1949:104–7). The ruin of the Brazilian trade was accomplished by 1635, well over 100 years after the effective start of commercial sugar production there. Those who knew the sugar business and wanted to continue supplying the growing market in Europe shifted operations to the West Indies, the "sugar islands," where many different national groups attempted to make their fortunes on the sweet tooth of Europe by exploiting the horrors of the African slave trade (Sheridan 1974). By the end of the first half of the seventeenth century, Martinique, Barbados and other islands had successful sugar industries, all of them jumping into the vacuum left by the ruin of the industry in Brazil (see Deerr 1949; Mintz 1985).

The ruin of the trade from Brazil and the great demand for sugar in Europe left New Englanders to satisfy their own sweet tooth either by paying the exorbitant price of imported sugar or developing a substitute themselves. At this point the nature of capitalism came to their rescue. The sugar trade was so profitable and was so nicely enriching both planters and the mother countries that the larger sugar producers, often with the help of home governments, were able to squeeze out the smaller shareholders and establish monopolies with more relaxed competition. The smaller shareholders were "forced" out (Deerr 1949:160), and there were no alternative ways for them to live on the islands. They had to emigrate, carrying in their heads everything they knew about sugar manufacture. Around 1200 of these failed small shareholders are documented as being resident in New England between 1643 and 1647 (Deerr 1949:160). These people had the expertise for sugar production, and they knew that sugar could be made from the juices of plants; some of the earliest comments about sugar in the New World come from natural historians inquiring about and experimenting with saps that might, like cane, be induced to give a sweet substance when heated and reduced (Schuette and Schuette 1939). And it is from New England in 1664 that the very first known reference to maple sugar comes, a comment by Robert Boyle citing the governor of "Masathusets" as his authority for a practice carried out in that "great and populous" colony, but Boyle never once mentioned Indians (Schuette and Ihde 1946:95).

The history of maple sugaring in the New England area is predominantly one of non-Indian producers. Their great demand for a source for sweetness, the influx of an enormous number of technically expert producers, and the high price of imported sugar were a potent combination for the development of maple sugaring as an industry. Prior to this time, the only recorded use for the maple tree was for its wood or for its untreated sap, a refreshing drink to some, a cure for stomach disorders for others (Schuette and Schuette 1939; Schuette and Ihde 1946). After this time, it becomes the standard source for sugar in the region, made not by Indians selling their native products but by thrifty farmers unwilling to do without sugar and even more unwilling to pay the high prices for imported cane sugar. The extent of the maple sugar industry in colonial New England was sufficiently great that, by the eighteenth century, sugar was being produced as a matter of course by every farmer, to the tune of between 600 and 1500 pounds per year each, more than enough for family use (Schuette and Ihde 1946:106, 112–13, 187) with surplus production sufficient to provision places as populous as the city of Boston. Maple sugar production quickly became a *major* part of the New England economy.

The presence of maple sugaring on the periphery of the development of sugar as a commodity with a world market is too much of a coincidence to suppose them to be unrelated events. Bringing the one into the orbit of the other and appreciating the circumstances of profit-making, cost-benefit, and the other appurtenances of a market economy certainly reinforces a picture of their mutual dependence. Maple sugaring is what happened when a demand for sugar existed in an area where cane could not grow, and people turned expertise and ingenuity toward the nearest equivalent vegetable source (Mason n.d.). Indians, when they were first described as maple sugar makers, were part of this entrepreneurial complex: small capitalists producing for themselves, at least partly responding to the demands of consumers, whose decisions to use or not use maple sugar were in turn based on sugar supplies elsewhere in the world.

Why maple sugaring should *ever* have been identified as a pre-Columbian Indian practice is a mystery. Scholarly examination of historic sources has over and over again demonstrated an absence of acceptable documentation for aboriginal maple sugaring during the critical early years of contact. It is not that available sources are equivocal or confusing; there simply are none. Archaeology has yet to provide confirmation of the practice from any sites in the area where maple sugaring might have been assumed to have been actively pursued. In addition, the curious spectacle of prehistoric Indian foragers and farmers making intensive use of what is an almost useless food files in the face of data pointing to the generally well-balanced and nutritious diet of aboriginal hunter-gatherers and horticulturists, no matter what their environment happens to be. American Indians in the Northeast would stand as a conspicuous exception to this pattern if they were in fact consuming sugar in prehistory.

There is no good reason to attribute sugar making to Indians other than the irrelevant fact that they lived with maple trees for a long time and were "likely" to have observed sap running. In European eyes, given the possibilities, Indians *had* to have been perceptive enough to have figured out that desirable, omnipresent, addictive, and entirely unnecessary sugar could be made from maple sap. Only in European eyes could sugar have been acknowledged as a virtue; perhaps attributing sugar to human beings living "in nature" made its consumption seem natural also. The Indian as aboriginal sugar maker is a projection of the state of dietary affairs in seventeenth-century England, a clearly ethnocentric interpretation of what constitutes an appropriate human diet.

Notes

1. See Henning 1965, Mason, 1985, 1986; but see also Pendergast 1982 and Holman 1986 and Mason's rejoinder 1987.
2. Replication experiments involve trying to duplicate the technology used by prehistoric people and to understand what was involved in production; artifacts and patterns in the ground can then be interpreted in the light of what has been learned.

References

Adams, Robert M. 1965. *The Evolution of Urban Society*. Chicago: Aldine Publishing Company.

Chamberlain, A.F. 1891. "Maple Sugar and the Indians." *American Anthropologist* 4:381–83.

Deerr, Noel. 1949/1950. *The History of Sugar*. 2 Vols. London: Chapman and Hall.

Fitting, James E. and Charles E. Cleland. 1969. "Late Prehistoric Settlement Patterns in the Upper Great Lakes." *Ethnohistory* 16:289–302.

Flannery, Regina. 1939. "An Analysis of Coastal Algonquian Culture." *The Catholic University of America Anthropological Series* 7.

Franklin, Paula. 1979. *Indians of North America: The Eight Culture Areas and How Their Inhabitants Lived Before the Coming of Whites*. New York: David McKay Company.

Garbarino, Merwyn S. 1976. *Native American Heritage*. Boston: Little, Brown and Company.

Gridley, Marion. 1973. *Indian Tribes of America*. Northbrook, IL: Hubbard Press.

Haas, Jonathan. 1982. *The Evolution of the Prehistoric State*. New York: Columbia University Press.

Harris, Marvin. 1985. *Culture, People, and Nature*. 4th ed. New York: Harper & Row.

Henning, Darrell Davis. 1965. "The Origins and History of the Maple Products Industry." Master's Thesis, State University of New York, College of Oneonta, Cooperstown.

Henshaw, H.W. 1890. "Indian Origins of Maple Sugar." *American Anthropologist* 3:341–51.

Hoffman, Walter J. 1896. "The Menomini Indians." *Bureau of American Ethnology 14th Annual Report*. Washington: Government Printing Office.

Holman, Margaret B. 1984. "The Identification of Late Woodland Maple Sugaring Sites in the Upper Great Lakes." *Midcontinental Journal of Archaeology* 9:63–90.

———. 1986. "Historic Documents and Prehistoric Sugaring: A Matter of Context." *Midcontinental Journal of Archaeology* 11:125–31.

Holman, Margaret B. and Kathryn Egan. 1985. "Processing Maple Sap with Prehistoric Techniques." *Journal of Ethnobiology* 5:61–75.

Holman, Margaret B. and Carol I. Mason. N.d. "Breaking the Circle: Independent Physical Techniques for Testing Ethnohistorical Conclusions About Indian Origins of Maple Sugaring."

Keesing, Felix M. 1971. *The Menomini Indians of Wisconsin*. New York: Johnson Reprint Corporation (originally published in 1939).

Kelley, Marc A., T. Gail Barrett, and Sandra D. Saunders. 1987. "Diet, Dental Disease, and Transition in Northeastern Native Americans." *Man in the Northeast* 33:113–25.

Kingsley, Robert G. and Elizabeth B. Garland. 1980. "The DeBoer Site: A Late Allegan Phase Site in Allegan County, Michigan." *Michigan Archaeologist* 26:3–44.

Loftus, Michael K. 1977. "A Late Historic Period Chippewa Sugar Maple Camp." *The Wisconsin Archaeologist* 58:71–6.

Lovis, William A. 1978. "A Numerical Taxonomic Analysis of Changing Woodland Site Location on an Interior Lake Chain." *Michigan Academician* 11:39–48.

Mason, Carol I. 1985. "Prehistoric Maple Sugaring Sites?" *Midcontinental Journal of Archaeology* 10:149–51.

————. 1986. "Maple Sugaring: A Sticky Subject." *North American Archaeology* 7:209–303.

————. 1987. "Maple Sugaring Again; or the Dog That Did Nothing in the Night." *Canadian Journal of Archaeology* 11:99–107.

————. N.d. *Indians, Maple Sugaring, and the Spread of Market Economies.* N.p.

Mintz, Sydney. 1985. *Sweetness and Power.* New York: Viking Press.

Nearing, Helen and Scott Nearing. 1970. *The Maple Sugar Book.* New York: Schocken Books.

Pendergst, James F. 1974. "The Sugarbush Site: A Possible Iroquoian Maple Sugar Camp." *Ontario Archaeology* 13:31–61.

————. 1982. "The Origin of Maple Sugar." *Syllogeus* 36. National Museums of Canada.

Poatgieter, Hermina. 1981. *Indian Legacy: Native American Influences on World Life and Culture.* New York: Julian Messner.

Quimby, George I. 1966. *Indian Culture and European Trade Goods.* Madison: University of Wisconsin Press.

Schoolcraft, Henry R. 1851–1857. *Historical and Statistical Information Respecting the History, Condition, and Prospects of the Indian Tribes of the United States.* Philadelphia: Lippincott, Grambo.

Schuette, H.A. and A.J. Ihde. 1946. "Maple Sugar: A Bibliography of Early Records II." Transactions of the Wisconsin Academy of Sciences Arts and Letters 38:89–184.

Schuette, H.A. and Sybil C. Schuette. 1939. "Maple Sugar: A Bibliography of Early Records." Transactions of the Wisconsin Academy of Sciences, Arts, and Letters 29:209–36.

Sheridan, Richard B. 1974. *Sugar and Slavery.* Baltimore: Johns Hopkins University Press.

Smith, Jeff. 1987. *The Frugal Gourmet Cooks American.* New York: William Morrow and Company.

Spence, Michael and William A. Fox. 1986. "The Early Woodland Occupations of Southern Ontario." In *Early Woodland Archaeology.* Kenneth B. Farnsworth and Thomas E. Emerson, eds. Kampsville, IL: Center for American Archaeology Press.

Waugh, F.W. 1916. "Iroquois Foods and Food Preparation." *Geological Survey of Canada* Memoir 86, No. 12.

Wolf, Eric R. 1982. *Europe and the People Without History.* Berkeley: University of California Press.

Yarnell, Richard A. 1964. *Aboriginal Relationships Between Culture and Plant Life in the Upper Great Lakes Region.* Museum of Anthropology, University of Michigan, Anthropological Papers 23.

6

The United States Constitution and the Iroquois League

Elisabeth Tooker

Four hundred years ago perhaps, the five Iroquois nations united in a confederacy, their tradition states, to establish peace among themselves. The effort proved successful, and in the years that followed the League of the Iroquois rose to a place of preeminent power in the Northeast, a position it lost when some two hundred years ago another confederacy, that of the thirteen colonies, was formed and achieved ascendancy in the area.

That two such remarkable confederacies arose in the same geographic region has suggested to some that there might be a connection between them, that the founding fathers of the new nation, the United States, fashioned its political institutions after those of the older Iroquois League. That such may have been the case has been noted by a number of writers. The distinguished anthropologist Clark Wissler was one, writing in 1940: "There is some historical evidence that knowledge of the league influenced the colonies in their first efforts to form a confederacy and later to write a constitution" (Wissler 1940:112). The historian Paul A. W. Wallace is another, stating that the Iroquois League "provided a model for, and an incentive to, the transformation of the thirteen colonies into the United States of America" (Wallace 1946:3).

More recently this subject has been given more extensive consideration in two books: *The Iroquois and the Founding of the American Nation* by Donald A. Grinde and *Forgotten Founders* by Bruce E. Johansen. Both attempt to chronicle, in Grinde's (1977:xii) words, "the role of the Iroquois in forming a part of the political basis for the new American nation." Both conclude it was of significance: Grinde (1977:133) finds that "the formation of the United States was influenced by Iroquois political and philosophical traditions" and Johansen (1982:xii) that the Iroquois "played a key role in the ideological birth of the United States."

The bicentennial of the Constitution has witnessed a still wider dissemination of this conclusion, long prevalent among the Iroquois, as fact (see, for example, Wilson 1960:47; Johansen 1982:xi–xii). It has been mentioned at various conferences held during the year and in articles appearing in various newspapers, including the *New York Times*. Calls have been made to include the subject in school curricula, and the United States Senate has been asked to recognize Iroquois contributions to the Constitution.[1]

The idea, however, figures not at all in the standard histories of the Constitution nor in the documents on which they rest. Research over the past several decades has revealed that the sources of thought embodied in the Constitution are more varied and its history more complex than had previously been suspected, and there has been something of a revolution in this regard. But of all the influences that have been uncovered and assessed in recent years, none points to an Indian one.

The question thus becomes: Is the influence of the American Indians, particularly the Iroquois, on the United States Constitution a "story that has lain largely forgotten, scattered around dusty archives, for more than two centuries" as Johansen (1982:xvi) asserts? Have historians, deceived by their own narrow cultural perspectives, failed to acknowledge that Indians, so often regarded as "primitive savages," could contribute to "civilization"? And should John Locke be demoted as honorary founding father of the United States and Deganawida and Hiawatha, legendary founders of the Iroquois League, be promoted in his place? Or are the statements that the United States Constitution is patterned on Iroquois political ideas a myth, which through repetition has taken on the aura of truth? And if the latter, when did the myth begin and how did it develop?

At least, it is the intent of the following to explore these issues through an examination of such evidence, both that contained in the historical documents and in the ethnographic accounts, as is presently available, as well as to treat the related issue of how the League functioned in the seventeenth and eighteenth centuries.

The Documentary Evidence

Embedded in the various statements respecting the influence of the Iroquois form of government on the later American one are two quite distinct ideas.[2] One derives from the popular notion that the Indians generally had a democratic form of government. It claims that those great American political ideas—freedom and democracy, among others—that so deeply inform the American experience were unknown to Westerners and that the colonists espoused them only after their arrival in the New World—and then only after they had learned them from the Indians.

If not a conclusion mentioned in the great treatises on government, it is one that has been given expression in the literature, albeit not in that usually read by historians. An example is an explanation of the origin, history, and purposes of the Improved Order of Red Men, a fraternal organization that traces its origin back to the Sons of Liberty of Revolutionary days:

> The early patriots who founded the old Sons of Liberty in Colonial times, never knew what real American liberty was, they having lived under kings all of their lives, and having no vote or voice in some of the most important matters pertaining to their own government. Their first vision of real freedom was caught from the wild savages, who roamed the forest at will rejoicing in the unrestained [sic] occupation of this great new world; who selected their own Sachems and forms of religious worship; and who made their own laws and tribal regulations, which were few and simple, and only such as were suited to primitive tribal life, while the white men, who came here, were continually followed up and hampered by unreasonable laws and regulations, imposed by a distant king and his local appointees, were denied the right of a trial by jury, and were burdened by unjust taxes. They began to chafe under their thralldom, which finally resulted in the "Boston Tea Party," the Declaration of Independence, and the War of the Revolution.
>
> The children of the forest, having furnished the first inspiration of true liberty, and whose paint and feathers were used to escape detection by British sympathizers, it was but natural that the name of the old Sons of Liberty should be changed so as to suggest the true cause of its origin, thereby giving honor to whom honor was due, hence—"The Improved Order of Red Men." Its principle is the teaching of Patriotism, Love of Country and allegiance to the Flag and Constitution and Obedience to the Law. (Sheehan 1937:4)

Another example is an article in the *American Scholar*, written by the eminent student of Federal Indian law, Felix S. Cohen. Cohen observed that "what is distinctive about America is Indian, through and through" (Cohen 1952:178) and, among other things, that

> [I]t is out of a rich Indian democratic tradition that the distinctive political ideas of American life emerged. Universal suffrage for women as well as for men, the pattern of states within a state that we call federalism, the habit of treating chiefs as servants of the people instead of as their masters, the insistence that the community must respect the diversity of men and the

diversity of their dreams—all these things were part of the American way of life before Columbus landed. (Cohen 1952:179–80)

The second type of statement points not to the influence of Indian political ideals in general but rather quite specifically to that of the Iroquois League. It is this confederacy, such writers contend, that provided the model for the American federal union.

Three passages in the eighteenth-century documents would seem to give some confirmation for this conclusion, and since they are the only ones that have been offered in support of it, they merit close consideration. One is a passage in a letter by Benjamin Franklin. The letter was published anonymously as a kind of appendix to a pamphlet written also anonymously by Archibald Kennedy published by James Parker in 1751 and republished in London the following year. In "The Importance of Gaining and Preserving the Friendship of the Indians to the British Interest, Considered" Kennedy proposed various measures to preserve the goodwill of the Indians, a matter of great importance at the time. Among other things, Kennedy viewed a union of the colonies (not a new idea) as necessary. As he expressed it:

Whenever the Collonies think fit to joint [such a union], *Indian* Affairs will wear quite another aspect. The very Name of such a Confederacy will greatly encourage our *Indians*, and strike terror into the *French*; and be a Means to prevent their unsupportable Incroachments, which they daily make with Impunity and Insult And this is what they have long dreaded. (Kennedy 1751:18)

Franklin concurred, observing that

a voluntary Union entered into by the Colonies themselves, I think, would be preferable to one impos'd by Parliament; for it would be perhaps not much more difficult to procure, and more easy to alter and improve, as Circumstances should require, and Experience direct.

In a now often-quoted passage, Franklin added that

it would be a very strange Thing, if six Nations of ignorant Savages should be capable of forming a Scheme for such a Union, and be able to execute it in such a Manner, as that it has subsisted [for] Ages, and appears indissoluble; and yet a like Union should be impracticable for ten or a Dozen Colonies, to whom it is more necessary, and must be more advantageous; and who cannot be supposed to want an equal Understanding of their Interest. (Labaree 1961:118–19)

A second often-cited passage is contained in a speech by Canasatego, an Onondaga chief and spokesman for the Iroquois, at a treaty conference held in Lancaster in 1744 attended by representatives from Pennsylvania, Maryland, and Virginia. After years of uneasy peace, war had again broken out between England and France; the colonists used the treaty conference, called for another purpose, to seek the aid of the Iroquois in what in America came to be called King George's War.

The proceedings of this conference were published that same year by Benjamin Franklin.[3] They included Canasatego's speech on the final day of the conference, and Canasatego's observation in that speech:

> We have one Thing further to say, and that is, We heartily recommend Union and a good Agreement between you our Brethren. Never disagree, but preserve a strict Friendship for one another, and thereby you, as well as we, will become the stronger.

> Our wise Forefathers established Union and Amity between the *Five Nations*; this has made us formidable; this has given us great Weight and Authority with our neighbouring Nations.

> We are a powerful Confederacy; and, by your observing the same Methods our wise Forefathers have taken, you will acquire fresh Strength and Power; therefore whatever befalls you, never fall out one with another. (Van Doren and Boyd 1938:78)

Just how much the representatives of the colonies took Canasatego's advice to heart is uncertain. In his reply to this portion of Cannassateego's speech, Lieutenant Governor George Thomas only observed:

> We obliged to you for recommending Peace and good Agreement amongst ourselves. We are all Subjects, as well as you, of the Great King beyond the Water; and, in Duty to his Majesty, and from the good Affection we bear to each other, as well as from a Regard in our own Interest, we shall always be inclined to live in Friendship. (Van Doren and Boyd 1938:78)

Nonetheless, Canasatego's statement, having made it way into print, was noticed by patriots. At least the commissioners of Indian Affairs mentioned it in a meeting with the Six Nations at Albany in August 1775:

> Brethren,
>
> Our business with you, besides rekindling the ancient council-fire, and renewing the covenant, and brightening up every link of the chain, is, in the first place, to inform you of the advice that was given about thirty years ago, by your wise forefathers, in a great council which they held at Lancaster, in Pennsylvania, when Cannassateego spoke to us, the white people, in these very words.

"Brethren, we, the Six Nations, heartily recommend union and a good agreement between you, our brethren. Never disagree, but pre serve a strict friendship for one another, and thereby you as well as we will become the stronger. Our wise forefathers established union and amity between the Five Nations. This has made us formidable; this has given us great weight and authority with our neighboring nations. We are a powerful confederacy; and if you observe the same methods our wise forefathers have taken, you will acquire fresh strength and power. Therefore, whatever befalls you, never fall out with one another."

These were the words of Canasatego.

Brothers,

Our forefathers rejoiced to hear Cannassateego speak these words. They sunk deep into their hearts. The advice was good; it was kind. They said to one another, "The Six Nations are a wise people. Let us hearken to them, and take their counsel, and teach our children to follow it. Our old men have done so. They have frequently taken a single arrow, and said, Children, see how easy it is broken. Then they have taken and tied twelve arrows together with a strong string or cord, and our strongest men could not break them. See, said they, this is what the Six Nations mean. Divided, a single man may destroy you; united, you are a match for the whole world." We thank the Great God that we are all united; that we have a strong confederacy, composed of twelve provinces, New Hampshire, etc. These provinces have lighted a great council-fire at Philadelphia, and have sent sixty-five counsellors to speak and act in the name of the whole, and consult for the common good of the people, and of you, our brethren of the Six Nations, and your allies. (Commissioners of the Twelve United Colonies 1836:83–4)

The Ethnographic Evidence

Considered together these statements confirm what is already well known: at least some whites and some Indians in the eighteenth century realized the advantages of confederation. None, however, go beyond the observation that the Iroquois tribes had successfully confederated before the colonies did.

Left unanswered is the question: How much did the founding fathers actually know about Iroquois political ideas and the Iroquois form of government? Were they actually influenced by Iroquois ideas respecting proper forms of governance or merely their image of what these ideas were? There can be little question that William Brandon is correct in observing, "the effect of the Indian world on the changing American soul, [is] most easily seen in *the influence of the image of* the American Indian on European notions of liberty" (Brandon 1965:24; emphasis added). But does this mean, as Johansen misquotes Brandon, that "the effect of the Indian world on the changing American soul, [is] most easily seen in *the influence of* the American Indian on European notions of liberty" (Johansen 1982:16; emphasis added)?

To answer these questions, to properly understand what Iroquois political ideas were, we ought to have discussion of them by the Indians themselves in their own language. These we do not have.[4] We do have records of the treaty councils held between whites and Indians. But these meetings were of a diplomatic character, hardly concerned with philosophical questions regarding the proper nature of political relationships between men.

What we do have now are ethnographic data on the Iroquois form of governance. Thus, although we cannot answer the question What abstract political ideas did the Indians possess and consequently what influence might they have had on colonial Americans? we can treat another: Did the founding fathers get any ideas about form of governance from the Iroquois?

Just how much the eighteenth-century colonists also knew about the Iroquois system of governance—other than the fact that the Iroquois had a confederacy—is uncertain. Some, such as Sir William Johnson, who had extensive political dealings with the Iroquois, may have known something, as perhaps did also some interpreters. Little of this information, however, made its way into print; most of what was written about the Iroquois in the seventeenth and eighteenth centuries concerned the effect of the Iroquois League on political affairs in the region that they so dominated—wars, treaty councils, and the like—not how they governed themselves.

Not until Lewis H. Morgan made it a special subject of study and published his findings did an account of the Iroquois form of government become available. In the early 1840s, Morgan joined a secret society called the Gordian Knot whose members shortly after decided "to cut the knot," as they said, and reorganize it as "an Indian society" modeled after the Iroquois League. Finding no information on the "structure of the League"—as Morgan later termed it—in the available literature, they turned to the Iroquois themselves, interviewing them on the form of governance they had adopted at the time of confederation. The results of this research were published by Morgan (who had done much of the fieldwork) in 1847 in a series of articles in the *American Review* and again in 1851 in *The League of the Ho-de-no-sau-nee, or Iroquois*.

Subsequent ethnographic work has substantiated Morgan's findings.[5] Briefly summarized, they are as follows: The government of the Iroquois League was vested in a council of fifty chiefs,[6] often termed "sachems" in the literature to distinguish them from other kinds of chiefs. Each sachem chief held his right to sit on the League council by virtue of having been given the name of his predecessor, in effect, by receiving a name-title. This title was in some sense hereditary. Each of the fifty name-titles belonged to a particular clan in a particular tribe. Thus, for example, when the sachem chief who held the name-title Skanyotaiyo' ("Handsome Lake") died, his successor—"raised up," as the Iroquois say, at a condolence ceremony—had to be of the Turtle clan of the Seneca tribe since the name Skanyotaiyo' belonged to the Seneca Turtle clan.

The system was not a truly representative or elected one. Although each tribe had chiefs on the council, their numbers were unequal. The Mohawks and Oneidas had nine each, the Onondagas fourteen, the Cayugas ten, and the Senecas eight—an inequality that did not reflect population size; the Senecas were by far the largest tribe, said sometimes to equal the population of the other four tribes combined. Nor did every clan have a sachem name-title. Some Onondaga, Cayuga, and Seneca clans had none. Not even within the clan was the position purely elective. The successor to a League chief was chosen by the "clan mother," the senior woman of the clan—or perhaps more accurately, the senior woman of the lineage in which the name was held—in consultation with other women of her clan.[7] And as the clans were matrilineal (each Iroquois gets his or her clan affiliation from his or her mother, who in turn received her clan affiliation from her mother), a League chief was not succeeded by his son, but rather often by his brother or nephew.

Decisions of the League council required unanimous consent for adoption. In theory, each sachem chief held veto power. In practice, the sachems attempted to find a solution to each question through extended discussion. In these deliberations, the Mohawks and Senecas sat on one side of the council fire; the Oneidas and Cayugas on the other side and facing them; and the Onondagas, the "firekeepers" of the League, on a third side. As they were the firekeepers, the Onondagas were charged with the responsibility of presenting the matter to be discussed and, after the sachems of each tribe had agreed among themselves and with the sachems of other tribes, of announcing the decision, thus confirming and proclaiming it.

Even cursorily considered, there is little in this system of governance the founding fathers might have been expected to copy.[8] It is doubtful, for example, that the delegates to the Constitutional Convention meeting during the legendary long, hot Philadelphia summer of 1787 would have proposed a system under which only their relatives could become members of Congress, and a system under which each legislator was chosen by a close female relative of the previous holder of the office.

Nor does it seem likely—even if John Adams had heeded his wife's admonition to "remember the ladies"—that if such a hereditary system had been adopted the Constitutional Convention would have opted for matrilineal inheritance of office, which by its very nature excludes a son from succeeding to his father's position.

It also seems unlikely that the delegates at that convention would have approved a system requiring unanimous agreement on any bill to be passed. Even small states fearful that larger states might gain too much power if representation was solely proportional to population might well have been more fearful about giving veto power to other small states—even if the largest state had the fewest delegates, as was the case in the Iroquois League. Nor does it seem likely that the Constitutional Convention would have decided that only Pennsylvania—most centrally located of the thirteen colonies (as Onondaga was the most centrally located of the Iroquois tribes)—could bring matters before the legislative body.

The Development of a Myth

The evidence presently available, then, offers little support for the notion that the framers of the Constitution borrowed from the Iroquois ideas respecting the proper form of government, ideas that were, in fact, radically different from those familiar in Western civilization that were subsequently incorporated into the Constitution. The question is, then, if there is virtually no evidence that the framers borrowed from the Iroquois, how did the contrary come to be supposed in the popular mind?

In some sense, it is an attempt to reconcile two contradictory ideas: that the Indians of the New World had no form of government and that they did. Colonial officials may not have been aware of the details of the internal political organization of the various Indian nations with whom they dealt, but they knew they were dealing with peoples who had governments. Some Indians somewhere in the New World may not have, but those they knew had. They also well knew that if they were to successfully treat with them, they would have to follow Indian, not white, protocol at these international conferences with them.

Others, however, held a contrary view. Some political philosophers, for example, believed that the Indians lived in a "state of nature" (a condition characterized by lack of government), not in a "state of society" (one that does have a government). Undoubtedly the most influential, but by no means only, of those holding this view was John Locke. He thus observed that "in the beginning all the world was Amer-

ica" (Locke 1690: chapter 5); "if Josephus Acosta's word may be taken
. . . in many parts of America there was no government at all" (Locke:
chapter 8).

It mattered little to Locke's argument, however, whether the Indians
actually had government or not. If Indians were not found to be living
in a "state of nature"—what Locke also argued was a state of perfect
freedom and liberty—but in a "state of society," his conclusions would
not be invalidated. For Locke was performing a kind of "thought experiment," and if the Indians were not living in a "state of nature,"
others were. As he observed, "since all princes and rulers of independent
governments all through the world, are in a state of nature, it is plain
the world never was, nor ever will be, without numbers of men in that
state" (Locke: chapter 2).

Although Indians may have mattered little to Locke, they were important to the colonists. Living on the borders of white settlement, they
posed a constant threat, a matter complicated by the economic dependence of a number of whites on trade with the Indians. The French
were also a threat; the contest in North America became a struggle
between France and its Indian allies and England and its Indian allies
for control of this trade and of the continent.

It did not escape notice that if the colonies could unite on a policy,
they might more successfully prosecute any war with France and its
Indian allies (or for that matter any Indians) that might break out. A
number of suggestions were made for such a union, although, as Andrews (1938:413) has remarked, they "were little more than armchair
proposals, which never reached the state of definite and precise formulation." It is undoubtedly no accident, then, that Kennedy advocated
such a union in 1751 as an aid in meeting the Indian and French en-
croachments and no accident that Franklin concurred. Nor may it be
an accident that the Albany Plan of Union was proposed on the eve of
the French and Indian (Seven Years') War and at a conference called
to treat with the Indians.

Canasatego may well have had a similar idea in mind. At the time,
war between France and England had just broken out, and he could
not help but be concerned about the outcome. What Canasatego may
have been saying was, "If you want us to aid you in this latest conflict
with France, you had best get your act together. If we are going to help
you, we don't want to have to deal with a bunch of squabbling colonies,
as we have had to do in the past. Do as we have done and establish
peace and goodwill among yourselves first. Then you'll be better able
to prosecute this war."

When the conflict between France and England finally ended in English victory and the surrender of New France to the British Crown, the colonies no longer needed the Indian support they earlier had. They could entertain—in a way they could not have earlier—independence from England. But once independence had been achieved, they faced something of a crisis of identity.

No longer part of England, Americans could not look to British history for a sense of national identity. Of necessity, they had to forge one of their own, constructed of events on this continent, not those of the Old World. Indians were a part of that history, and so not unexpectedly the new nation turned to the Indian for symbols.

It was a process that had begun even before independence was won. To cite one example: members of the secret revolutionary society the Sons of Liberty, organized in Maryland in the 1760s and then in other colonies, regarded themselves as being under the patronage of the Indian chief Tamina (Tammany). May 12 was chosen as St. Tamina's day, often celebrated with a military salute—the firing of guns—and Indian war dances. It became popular with both citizens and soldiers and was observed by the army from the time of the Revolution to just before the War of 1812 (Stevens 1907:239–42, 323–24). And as every schoolchild "knows" (or at least once knew), it was Sons of Liberty dressed as Mohawk Indians who threw the tea into the harbor at the Boston Tea Party.

For the previous century and a half, life in the New World had been regarded as being freer than life in the Old. After independence it was just a short step to suppose that this liberty was of the same sort that the Indians had earlier enjoyed in Locke's "state of nature," and only another short step to suppose that white Americans had learned of "real freedom" from their red predecessors.

In one variation of this idea, Americans—it was believed—were destined to raise up on the continent a new government, one superior to that of the Indian but based on the same principles. And it is this kind of notion that underlay the formation of the "Grand Order of the Iroquois." Morgan and the others who founded this society believed they were establishing a society based on "Indian principles," a "New Confederacy of the Iroquois" that would replace the old one of the Indians, which was dying. They were in error. Within a half dozen years the "New" Confederacy itself had died. It was the "Old" that lived on.

Although there is no evidence that Morgan believed that white Americans had obtained their political ideals from the Iroquois, he may have inadvertently contributed to the belief's development. The Iroquois had long before earned the epithet "The Romans of the West" (Clinton 1812:9), partly for "their martial spirit and rage for conquest" (ibid.:16;

cf. Colden 1747:4), partly perhaps also for their oratorical skill. The Iroquois, Morgan (1851:3) declared, "achieved for themselves a more remarkable civil organization, and acquired a higher degree of influence, than any other race of Indian lineage, except those of Mexico and Peru." Morgan's account of the League's organization may not have been studied, but many recalled that Morgan believed the Iroquois had a remarkable political organization.

By the end of the nineteenth century the idea that "the formation of the United States was influenced by Iroquois political and philosophical traditions" and that the Iroquois "played a key role in the ideological birth of the United States" was in place. At least that seems indicated in William E. Griffis's observation:

> How far the various attempts of the red man to combine in federal union for common strength or defence, and especially those in the stable political edifice in New York, were potent in aiding the formation of the American Commonwealth, is an interesting question worthy of careful study. That it was not without direct influence upon the minds of those constructive statesmen like Franklin, Hamilton, Madison, Monroe, who came so numerously from States nearest the Long House, and most familiar with Iroquois politics, cannot be denied. The men of the English-speaking colonies which had been peopled from continental and insular Europe, were inheritors of classic culture. They naturally read the precedents furnished by Greece and Rome; but they were also powerfully affected by the living realities of the federal republics of Holland and Switzerland, as well as in the aristocratic republic of Venice, while in the one nearest England many of them were educated. It is not too much to affirm, however, that the power of this great example at home, on the soil and under the eyes, was as great in moulding opinion and consolidating thought in favour of a federal union of States, as were the distant exemplars of the ancient world, or in modern Europe. Though we give him no credit, and spurn the idea of political indebtedness to the red man, with almost the same intolerant fierceness that some of the latter-day New England Puritans deny obligations to the Dutch Republic that sheltered and educated their fathers, yet our government is in a measure copied from that of the forest republicans, whose political edifice and conquests shaped the history and civilization of this continent [Griffis 1891:53–54].

The idea is also indicated in Herbert M. Lloyd's (1901:147) statement that the League's "influence has been most strongly felt in our political constitution and in our history as colonies and nation" and in the passage that Lloyd prefaces with a quotation from Morgan's (1881) *Houses and House-Life of the American Aborigines*:

> "It is worthy of remembrance that the Iroquois commended to our forefathers a union of colonies similar to their own as early as 1755. They saw in the common interests and common speech of the several colonies the elements

for a confederation, which was as far as their vision was able to penetrate." (*Houses* 1881:32)

On the other hand Franklin's plan of union, which was the begin ning of our own federal republic, was directly inspired by the wisdom, durability, and inherent strength which he had observed in the Iroquois constitution. Under the Articles of Confederation we managed our af fairs for a dozen years very much on the Iroquois plan, and it must be confessed were not quite as apt in execution and in administrative wisdom as our barbarian predecessors.

When the colonies became the United States, the Iroquois recognized the similarity of the League to their own, and gave to the new nation the name of The Thirteen Fires. (Lloyd 1901:204)

The closing decades of the nineteenth century also witnessed the identification of the letter in the Kennedy pamphlet "The Importance of Gaining and Preserving the Friendship of the Indians to the British Interest, Considered" as being from the pen of Franklin. In publishing this letter in his *Complete Works of Benjamin Franklin*, John Bigelow (1887:217n) noted:

The editor is happy to acknowledge his obligations to Professor Edward Eggleston to calling his attention to this letter, which that gentlemen found in the Harvard College Library. "I think," says Professor Eggleston, in a letter to the editor, "the pamphlet is anonymous, but I have a minute that the author is Archibald Kennedy. The first edition, N.Y., 1751, and the letter I believe to be Franklin's was dated at Philadelphia and addressed to the printer of the first edition—Parker."

Eggleton's surmise has been given subsequent confirmation by discovery of contemporary evidence of Franklin's authorship (Labaree 1961:117).

In this century if not before, some Indians noted that certain ideas later adopted by whites had been incorporated into Iroquois political life. For example, Arthur C. Parker, a grandnephew of Morgan's in terpreter and collaborator Ely S. Parker, found "the right of popular nomination, the right of recall and of woman suffrage, all flourishing in the old America of the Red Man and centuries before it became the clamor of the new America of the white invader" (Parker 1916:11). A dozen years later, William B. Newell, a Caughnawaga Mohawk, averred that the Iroquois Confederacy "was the first democracy of the modern age. From its principles of equality, liberty, and fraternity [have] de veloped our great republics" (Newell 1928:19).

Circumstantial evidence, however, suggests it is the ideas of another Iroquois, J. N. B. Hewitt, that are recalled in many recent statements asserting that the Iroquois League provided a model for the United States Constitution. They are contained in a Smithsonian press release dated March 26, 1936.[11] It reports that Hewitt has found "a direct chain of evidence linking the basic document of the American Government [the Constitution]" to Canasatego and his speech at the 1744 Lancaster treaty conference and that "the evidence seems strongly in favor of an Iroquois origin for the American system of government."

Hewitt, a Tuscarora Indian, had been in the employ of the Bureau of American Ethnology since the 1880s. Undoubtedly it was Hewitt's conclusion that Matthew W. Stirling, director of the Bureau, was referring to when he wrote, "There is reason to believe that the framers of our Constitution were inspired in some degree by the League of the Five Nations" (Stirling 1937:552). It is also likely that Wissler was referring to Hewitt's observations when he wrote, "There is some historical evidence that knowledge of the league [of the Iroquois] influenced the colonies in their first efforts to form a confederacy and later to write a constitution" (Wissler 1940:112).

The idea received further support in 1946 when Paul A. W. Wallace published *The White Roots of Peace*, a retelling of the Iroquois tradition of the founding of their League with allusions to its similarity to the United Nations, the latter echoing Hewitt's (1920:527) earlier comparison to the League of Nations. Wallace introduces his subject thus:

This is the story of the founding at Onondaga (Syracuse, N.Y.), some time about the middle of the fifteenth century, of the United Nations of the Iroquois, the famous Indian confederacy that provided a model for, and an incentive to, the transformation of the thirteen colonies into the United States of America. (Wallace 1946:3)

He then repeats Franklin's observation in his letter of 1751, and, having noted that the Iroquois "were the greatest Indian power on the American continent," states:

It was not by force alone that the Iroquois held this vast region under their Peace. It was by statesmanship, by a profound understanding of the principles of peace itself. They knew that any real peace must be based on justice and a healthy reasonableness. They knew also that peace will endure only if men recognize the sovereignty of a common law and are prepared to back that law with force—not chiefly for the purpose of punishing those who have disturbed the peace, but rather for the purpose of preventing such disturbance by letting all men know, in advance of any contingency, that the law will certainly prevail. (Wallace 1946:3)

In the following years, a number of statements similar to Wissler's and Wallace's appeared. In chronological order these include Underhill's (1953:83, 94) statements that "some have even thought it [what

Underhill terms 'a Woodland League of Nations'] gave suggestions to the American Constitution (Lee, Franklin, Jefferson, and Washington were quite familiar with the League)" and that the Iroquois system "has been suggested as a model for the United States Constitution"; Hallowell's (1957:232) that "It has even been said that information about the organization and operation of the League of the Iroquois, which Franklin picked up at various Indian councils, suggested to him the pattern for a United States of America"; Reaman's (1967:xiv, cf. 24) that the Iroquois furnished "the prototype for the Constitution of the United States—it is said that Jefferson used the Iroquois Confederacy as a basis—and [their] Confederacy has many of the aspects of our present-day United Nations"; Marriott and Rachlin's (1968:33) that "Its organization became one of the models for the United States Constitution"; Farb's (1968:98) that "some historians believe that it was one of the models on which the Constitution of the new United States of America was based"; and Eckert's (1969: 624 n. 21) that "Knowledge of the League's success, it is believed, strongly influenced the Colonies in their own initial efforts to form a union and later to write a constitution."

None of these writers refers specifically to Hewitt or to the evidence he thought supported his conclusions. Hewitt published no scholarly paper on the subject that could be cited (he died in 1937, a year after Thomas Henry wrote the press release), but men such as Stirling and Wissler could be expected to know of Hewitt's idea through conversation if not the press release itself.

This paucity of information may be the reason behind accretions to the myth. Hewitt had rejected the idea that the Iroquois League had influenced the Albany Plan of Union, but Lloyd had earlier asserted it had. The Albany Plan of Union was added to the legend. There followed a change of date respecting when Franklin had made the statement popularized by Wallace: some (e.g., Cohen 1952:184; Eckert 1969:258; *New York Times* 1987) assumed Franklin made it at the Albany conference, not three years earlier in a publication that surely would have gone unnoticed by most if it had not been identified as Franklin's a hundred years ago, well over a hundred years after Franklin wrote it.

Yet perhaps there is a lesson to be learned from this tale of scholarly misapprehension. In white interpretations of Indians there has been a persistent theme, as Berkhofer (1978:25–26) has reminded us, of "conceiving of Indians in terms of their deficiencies according to White ideals rather than in terms of their own various cultures . . . to describe Indian life in terms of its lack of White ways rather than . . . positively from within the framework of the specific culture under consideration." Some recent interpretations of Indian cultures and history have turned this "negative prototype" on its head, asserting that, indeed, Indians did hold white ideals and, in the case discussed here, even that whites got them from the Indian. But as laudable as this might at first glance seem, such a positive stereotype exhibits not only as little fundamental understanding and appreciation of Indian cultures as a negative one, but also little understanding of Western culture. We owe our fellow residents on the continent better.

This abridged essay is reprinted with permission from *Ethnohistory* 35(4) 1988. Copyright © 1988 by the American Society for Ethnohistory. Interested readers may consult the original for sections on the structure and spirit and the evolution of the Iroquois league, and for a true copy of the original 1936 Smithsonian press release.

James Axtell kindly read an earlier version of this paper and offered many valuable suggestions, some of which have been incorporated. I am also indebted to William N. Fenton, William C. Sturtevant, and James A. Clifton for comments, and to William Cox of the Smithsonian Institution Archives for locating a copy of the 1936 press release and providing me with information on Thomas R. Henry's association with the Smithsonian.

Notes

1. The relevant sections of Senate Concurrent Resolution 76 are:
    Whereas, the original framers of the Constitution, including most notably, George Washington and Benjamin Franklin, are known to have greatly admired the concepts, principles, and governmental practices of the Six Nations of the Iroquois Confederacy; and,
    Whereas the Confederation of the original thirteen colonies into one Republic was explicitly modeled upon the Iroquois Confederacy as were many of the democratic principles which were incorporated into the Constitution itself . . . .
    Resolved by the Senate (the House of Representatives concurring), That:
    (1) The Congress, on the occasion of the 200th Anniversary of the signing of the United States Constitution, acknowledges the historical debt which this Republic of the United States of America owes to the Iroquois Confederacy and other Indian Nations for their demonstration of enlightened, democratic principles of government and their example of a free association of independent Indian nations (United States Congress 1987).
    The proceedings of the conference on "The Iroquois Great Law of Peace and the United States Constitution" held at Cornell University in September 1987 have been published under the title *Indian Roots of American Democracy* (Barreiro 1988).
2. For references to statements specifically referring to the influence of the Iroquois League on United States political institutions I have relied heavily on Johansen's (1982:8–20) survey. I attempt here no consideration of all the questionable interpretations of the data such authors as Johansen and

Grinde make, or of the larger issues such handling of the material pose respecting the doing of historical studies.

3. These proceedings of the Lancaster treaty conference are also published in Colden (1747:sec. 2, 87–152) and in Provincial Council of Pennsylvania 1851:698–740. The journal of the secretary of the Maryland commissioners has also been published (Marshe 1801).

In the light of later events it might be suspected that Franklin invented the part of Canasatego's speech here quoted and inserted it into the proceedings of the Lancaster conference he published. I think not. Franklin was a well-known hoaxer, and in fact Canasatego appears in two of his fabrications (Aldridge 1950; Adams 1976). But in printing this (and other treaties) Franklin was not just publishing something that might entertain the populace but the official record of the conference. It does strain the imagination to suppose that Franklin's usual sure political sense should have abandoned him in this instance and have caused him to risk the ire of those present at the conference—not only the commissioners from Virginia and Maryland but also the lieutenant governor of Pennsylvania and Richard Peters, the provincial secretary (who attested to the copy Franklin printed)— by tampering with it in a manner that would only come to have significance many years later. Internal evidence—Governor Thomas's reply and the content of this reply—also indicate that it is not Franklin's invention.

The overriding matter of concern in 1744, of course, was not independence but a better policy in respect to Indian affairs—as is evident in the opinions of Kennedy and Franklin quoted above. Since the issue was Indian policy, not independence, if Franklin had written it, it would have been interpreted in that context. Nor should it be forgotten that it was the war with France and its Indian allies that was on the minds of the colonists in 1744—scarcely a time to entertain thoughts of separation from England.

It also should not be forgotten that at the time the colonists viewed themselves as British subjects. As is evident in the Albany Plan of Union, union of the colonies was viewed as a kind of confederation under the Crown: the Albany plan proposed that the Crown appoint a "President-General" and that the colonies elect members of a "Grand Council." Some may have been thinking of independence at that time, but merely a union of colonies under the Crown would not achieve that purpose. Only after the success of the Revolution could the various earlier plans of union be seen as forerunners of the federal union. Jameson's (1920:15–16) observation on a comparable claim—that of Dutch influence on the Constitution—is perhaps relevant here:

> There have been a few who have even gone so far as to declare with great emphasis that our federal system and our habit of the written constitution, since the English did not have them, must have come to us from the Dutch. It is true that the seven Dutch provinces in 1620 were a confederation, and that that confederation had a written constitution. But surely there is a natural history of federal governments, wherein we see the operation of similar causes producing similar results, without the need of resorting to the hypothesis of imitation.

4. It might seem that Parker's (1916) *The Constitution of the Five Nations* is such a document. But neither the Newhouse version or the chiefs' version (earlier published by Duncan Campbell Scott, 1912) printed in this volume

discusses political ideas in the abstract. Further, the Newhouse version, the one most frequently cited, is seriously flawed and was rejected on several occasions by the chiefs' council (see especially Fenton 1968 and Weaver 1984). Both versions are essentially codifications of the tradition of the founding of the Iroquois League and of the political organization of the League.

5. For references that confirm Morgan's account as well as a more detailed summary of the structure of the League see Tooker 1978.

The key to the structure of the League is the Roll Call of the Chiefs, and it was Morgan's discovery of that Roll Call while on his first field trip to the Tonawanda Seneca Reservation in the fall of 1845 that opened to him an understanding of how that structure worked. Subsequent to Morgan's study and independent of it, others have published this list of chiefs. These vary slightly from one another, but in no significant respect, and it is for this reason, in part, that ethnographers are inclined to trust Morgan's account and not to view other, later ones as a mere copy of it.

The fifty name-titles on the Roll Call of the Chiefs are the fifty positions, that is, seats, on the League council. And since these same seats are listed on the Roll Calls of both Iroquois now living in New York State and those now living in Canada, they almost certainly existed before these two Iroquois groups separated in 1784.

6. Sometimes said to be forty-eight or forty-nine, because one sachemship is not filled and two others are regarded by some to be a single sachemship. The past tense is used here for convenience only; something of the League still continues to function. The term *clan* is used here in its technical anthropological sense.

7. The clan mother could also "dehorn" a chief (take away his symbolic horns of office) by taking away his name and giving it to another man. This power of some Iroquois women has contributed to the notion that Iroquois society was a "matriarchy." But is should be noted that women did not have the right to speak in council, and therefore could not participate directly in the decision-making process.

8. There is a similar lack of resemblance between the forms of government contained in the Albany Plan of Union (see note 3) and in the Articles of Confederation to that of the Iroquois League.

9. It is somewhat curious that Richter, who otherwise tends to dismiss the nineteenth- and twentieth-century ethnographic accounts, should choose to give so much weight to the Condolence ceremony. It is clear, I believe, that in the seventeenth and eighteenth centuries the Condolence ceremony was a kind of swearing-in or installation ceremony for new members of the League council. Before the business of the council could be taken up it was necessary to know what men were to replace those who had died since the last meeting; this was accomplished at the Condolence ceremony, customarily the first order of business of the League council. By Morgan's time, the League council had far less business to transact than it earlier had, and it seems to have met infrequently if at all. The Iroquois, however, felt it necessary to have such sachem chiefs in place, and consequently continued to raise them up. (Reports on the proceedings of three such Condolence councils—those held in 1845, 1847, and 1848—are preserved in the Morgan papers in the University of Rochester Library; see, for example, Tooker

1989.) This practice has continued in the twentieth century, and for reason. The councils governing the Onondaga and the Tonawanda Seneca reservations are composed of their respective tribes' sachem chiefs and these chiefs' subchiefs, necessitating the continued performance of the Condolence ceremony. By default the Condolence ceremony has become the principal business of the League and is sometimes so reported in the ethnographic literature. (On the Six Nations Reserve in Canada a League council separate from that in the United States served as the governing body of the reserve until 1924, and the Condolence ceremony served as the installation ceremony for these chiefs.)

Richter, I suspect, was led to this dubious conclusion—that the Grand Council of the League existed merely to preserve the "Great Peace" through the forms of the Condolence ritual, a ritual that includes the "ceremonial Words of Condolence and exchanges of ritual gifts" (now the latter involves only the passing and return of a set of strings of wampum)—by a failure to grasp the reality of unanimity in Indian political life, not only in the seventeenth and eighteenth centuries, but also today among some Indians, including some Iroquois. He is thus led to contend that previous students of the Iroquois League have confounded "two related but distinct phenomena": what he terms the "League"—"a cultural and ritual institution" that "is undeniably old, relatively unchanging, and very much alive to the present day"—with what he terms the "Confederacy"—"a political and diplomatic entity" that "virtually ceased to exist" during the American Revolution (Richter 1987:11–12).

The Condolence ceremony, however, is not held now for merely ritual or cultural reasons involving the "Great Peace" as Richter supposes, but for practical political ones. League chiefs are still raised up either because they constitute the governing council of a reservation (as they do on the Onondaga and the Tonawanda Seneca reservations and as they did until 1924 on the Six Nations Reserve) or because some faction wishes to reestablish the League council as a legitimate governing body. And if the League as "a political and diplomatic entity" seems to have "virtually ceased to exist" during the War of Independence, it is because after that war the political situation changed. After the Revolution, the Iroquois found themselves divided, roughly half in the United States and half in Canada, each with its own set of League chiefs, facing two militarily superior powers, the Americans in the United States and the British in Canada. To the degree that the Iroquois could no longer control events in the Northeast, coordinated activities of the Iroquois became superfluous and councils involving all the Iroquois of little consequence. Among those Iroquois who remained in their own homelands, now within the territorial limits of the United States, each nation continued to decide matters of interest to the nation, most notably sale of their lands; over time it became largely the right of each reservation to decide matters of interest to those "belonging"—as the Iroquois say—to that reservation.

10. I have more fully discussed some aspects of this question in Tooker 1981.
11. As William N. Fenton has suggested to me, this press release was undoubtedly written by Thomas R. Henry, who was press writer for the Smithsonian Institution and concurrently science writer for the Washington *Evening Star*. At the time, Henry wrote a thrice-weekly science column for the *Star*, but

this press release was neither mentioned in his column nor published by the *Star*, although Henry later quoted extensively from it in his book *Wilderness Messiah: The Story of Hiawatha and the Iroquois* (Henry 1955:226–28). See the Appendix in the full version of this essay in *Ethnohistory* for the Smithsonian press release.

References

Adams, Percy C. 1976. "Benjamin Franklin and the Travel-Writing Tradition." In *The Oldest Revolutionary: Essays on Benjamin Franklin*. J.A. Leo Lemay, ed. Philadelphia: University of Pennsylvania Press, 33–50.

Aldridge, Alfred Owen. 1950. "Franklin's Deistical Indians." *Proceedings of the American Philosophical Society* 90:398–410.

Andrews, Charles M. 1938. *The Colonial Period of American History*. Vol. 4, England's Commercial and Colonial Policy. New Haven, CT: Yale University Press.

Barreiro, Jose, ed. 1988. *Indian Roots of American Democracy*. Ithaca, NY: Northeast Indian Quarterly.

Beauchamp, W. M. 1886. "Permanency of Iroquois Clans and Sachemship." *American Antiquarian and Oriental Journal* 8:82–91.

Berkhofer, Robert F., Jr. 1978. *The White Man's Indian*. New York: Random House.

Bigelow, John, comp. and ed. 1887. *The Complete Works of Benjamin Franklin*. Vol. 2. New York: G. P. Putnam's Sons.

Brandon, William. 1965. "American Indians and American History." *American West* 2(2):14–25, 91–93.

Clinton, De Witt. 1812. *Discourse Delivered Before the New-York Historical Society, at Their Anniversary Meeting, 6th December, 1811*. New York: James Eastburn.

Cohen, Felix S. 1952. "Americanizing the White Man." *American Scholar* 21: 177–91.

Colden, Cadwallader. 1747. *The History of the Five Indian Nations of Canada*. London: T. Osborne.

Commissioners of the Twelve United Colonies. 1836. "Journal of the Treaty Held at Albany, in August, 1775." Collections of the Massachusetts Historical Society, 3d ser., 5:75–84.

Eckert, Allan W. 1969. *Wilderness Empire*. Boston: Little, Brown.

Farb, Peter. 1968. *Man's Rise to Civilization*. New York: E. P. Dutton.

Fenton, William N. 1968. Introduction. In *Parker on the Iroquois*. William N. Fenton, ed. 1–47. Syracuse, NY: Syracuse University Press.

Griffis, William E. 1891. *Sir William Johnson and the Six Nations*. New York: Dodd, Mead.

Grinde, Donald A., Jr. 1977. *The Iroquois and the Founding of the American Nation*. San Francisco: Indian Historical Press.

Hallowell, A. Irving. 1957. "The Backwash of the Frontier: The Impact of the Indian in American Culture." In *The Frontier in Perspective*. Walker D. Wyman and Clifton B. Kroeber, eds. Madison: University of Wisconsin Press, 229–58.

Henry, Thomas R. 1955. *Wilderness Messiah: The Story of Hiawatha and the Iroquois*. New York: William Sloane Associates.

Hewitt, J. N. B. 1920. *A Constitutional League of Peace in the Stone Age of*

America: The League of the Iroquois and Its Constitution. Annual Report of the Smithsonian Institution for 1918, 527–45.

Jameson, John Franklin. 1920. *The Arrival of the Pilgrims*. Providence, RI: Brown University.

Johansen, Bruce E. 1982. *Forgotten Founders*. Ipswich, MA: Gambit.

Kennedy, Archibald. 1751. *The Importance of Gaining and Preserving the Friendship of the Indians to the British Interest, Considered*. New York: James Parker; London: E. Cave, 1752.

Labaree, Leonard W., ed. 1961. *The Papers of Benjamin Franklin*. Vol. 4. New Haven, CT: Yale University Press.

Lloyd, Herbert M. 1901. Appendix. In *League of the Ho-de-no-sau-nee or Iroquois*, by Lewis H. Morgan. Herbert M. Lloyd, ed. Vol. 2. 143–312. New York: Dodd, Mead.

Locke, John. 1690. *Second Treatise of Government*. London.

Marriott, Alice, and Carol K. Rachlin. 1968. *American Indian Mythology*. New York: Thomas Y. Crowell.

Marshe, Witham. 1801. "Witham Marshe's Journal of the Treaty Held with the Six Nations by the Commissioners of Maryland, and Other Provinces, at Lancaster, in Pennsylvania, June, 1744." *Collections of the Massachusetts Historical Society*, 1st ser., 7:171–201.

Morgan, Lewis H. 1847. "Letters on the Iroquois." *American Review* 5: 177–90, 242–57, 447–61; 6:477–90, 626–33.

———. 1851. *The League of the Ho-dé-no-sau-nee, or Iroquois*. Rochester, NY: Sage and Brother.

———. 1881. *Houses and House-Life of the American Aborigines*. Contributions to North American Ethnology 4. Washington: U.S. Geological and Geographical Survey of the Rocky Mountain Region.

New York Times. 1987. "Iroquois Constitution: A Forerunner to Colonists [*sic*] Democratic Principles." *New York Times*, June 28.

Newell, William B. 1928. "Indian Contributions to Modern Civilization." *36th Annual Archaeological Report, Being Part of Appendix to the Report of the Minister of Education, Ontario*. 18–26. Toronto.

Parker, Arthur C. 1916. *The Constitution of the Five Nations*. New York State Museum Bulletin 184. Albany.

Provincial Council of Pennsylvania. 1851. *Minutes of the Provincial Council of Pennsylvania* 4.

Reaman, G. Elmore. 1967. *The Trail of the Iroquois Indians: How the Iroquois Saved Canada for the British Empire*. New York: Barnes and Noble.

Richter, Daniel K. 1987. "Ordeals of the Longhouse: The Five Nations in Early American History." In *Beyond the Covenant Chain: The Iroquois and Their Neighbors in Indian North America, 1600–1800*. Daniel K. Richter and James H. Merrell, eds. 11–27. Syracuse, NY: Syracuse University Press.

Schoolcraft, Henry R. 1847. *Notes on the Iroquois*. Albany, NY: Erastus E. Pease.

Scott, Duncan Campbell. 1912. "Traditional History of the Confederacy of the Six Nations." *Proceedings and Transactions of the Royal Society of Canada (for 1911)*, 3d ser., 5(2):195–246.

Sheehan, Edward J., comp. 1937. *225th Anniversary Program, Old Fort Hunter and Queen Chapel at Fort Hunter, N.Y., Sept. 12, 1937*. St. Johnsville, NY: Press of the Enterprise and News.

Stevens, Albert C. 1907. *The Cyclopaedia of Fraternities.* Rev. ed. New York: E. B. Treat.

Stirling, Matthew W. 1937. "American's First Settlers, the Indians." *National Geographic Magazine* 72:535–96.

Tooker, Elisabeth. 1978. "The League of the Iroquois: Its History, Politics, and Rituals." In *Handbook of North American Indians.* William C. Sturtevant, gen. ed. Vol. 15, Northeast. Bruce G. Trigger, ed. Washington: Smithsonian Press, 418–41.

———. 1981. "Eighteenth Century Political Affairs and the Iroquois League. In *The Iroquois in the American Revolution: 1976 Conference Proceedings.* Rochester Museum and Science Center Research Records 14:1–12.

———. 1989. "On the Development of the Handsome Lake Religion." *Proceedings of the American Philosophical Society* 133:35–50.

Underhill, Ruth Murray. 1953. *Red Man's America: A History of the Indians in the United States.* Chicago: University of Chicago Press.

United States Congress. 1987. *Congressional Record, 100th Congress, 1st Session.* Vol. 133, no. 140, S 12214.

Van Doren, Carl, and Julian P. Boyd, eds. 1938. *Indian Treaties Printed by Benjamin Franklin, 1735–1762.* Philadelphia: Historical Society of Pennsylvania.

Wallace, Paul A. W. 1946. *The White Roots of Peace.* Philadelphia: University of Pennsylvania Press.

Weaver, Sally M. 1984. "Seth Newhouse and the Grand River Confederacy." In *Extending the Rafters: Interdisciplinary Approaches to Iroquoian Studies.* Michael K. Foster, Jack Campisi, and Marianne Mithun, eds. Albany: State University of New York Press. 165–82.

Wilson, Edmund. 1960. *Apologies to the Iroquois.* New York: Farrar, Straus and Cudahy.

Wissler, Clark. 1940. *Indians of the United States.* Garden City, NY: Doubleday, Doran.

7

Mother Earth: An American Myth

Sam Gill

Once the world was all water, and God lived alone; he was lonesome, he had no place to put his foot; so he scratched the sand up from the bottom, and made the land and he made rocks, and he made trees, and he made man, and the man was winged and could go anywhere. The man was lonesome, and God made a woman. They ate fish from the water, and God made the deer and other animals, and he sent the man to hunt, and told the woman to cook the meat and to dress the skins. Many more men and women grew up, and they lived on the banks of the great river whose waters were full of salmon. The mountains contained much game, and there were buffalo on the plains. There were so many people that the stronger ones sometimes oppressed the weak and drove them from the best fisheries, which they claimed as their own. They fought, and nearly all were killed, and their bones are to be seen in the sand hills yet. God was very angry and he took away their wings and commanded that the lands and fisheries should be common to all who lived upon them. That they were never to be marked off or divided, but that the people should enjoy the fruits that God planted in the land and the animals that lived upon it, and the fishes in the water. God said he was the father, and the earth was the mother of mankind; that nature was the law; that the animals and fish and plants obeyed nature, and that man only was sinful. This is the old law. (MacMurray 1887:247–48)

This story was told in the late nineteenth century by a Sahaptin speaking native American named Smohalla who lived in the state of Washington. He did not recognize the territory in which he lived by the name "Washington." Neither did he recognize the rights to the land that

Americans of European ancestry claimed—as they occupied his land, forcing him to live as an outlaw. Nor would he have recognized the word *myth* by which his story of the creation and history of his world would be called by them. The word *myth* has long been a problem for me in my study of native American cultures. I dare not tell native Americans that I consider their stories to be myths, for they know that in standard English usage myth denotes the fictitious, the unscientific, the false. Native Americans do not want their stories to be thought of as false, nor do they appreciate others claiming that their beliefs are unfounded. In recognition of and respect for Smohalla and many other native Americans, I have tried to use the word *myth* sparingly, if at all. When I attempt to use it, I find myself spending more time and effort clarifying and defending what I mean than I do using the word in service to the study and appreciation of stories like the one told by Smohalla. I find the word *story* acceptable. It can be used along with descriptive adjectives to clarify story type. Though often misleading, the use of the word *myth* persists.

Myth has a European etymology, rooted in the Greek *muthos* meaning "word" or "speech" about the gods and supernaturals. The classic Greek stories, as well as the ancient and sacred stories of the peoples of Asia, Africa, Melanesia, and the Americas, have been most commonly designated as myths by Westerners. The term *myth* may have a variety of meanings: it may be thought of as a true story or as foundational underpinning of a society. Yet, the use of the word nearly always conveys a qualitative, even emotional, judgment. For many, referring to a story as a myth often bestows a special quality upon it—a spirituality, a primordiality, even a romanticism.

Curiously, we contemporary Westerners have difficulty using the term *myth* in a positive sense when referring to anything in our own culture. When applied to our own culture, the attributes of myth tend to invert. We seek to dispel our myths and to chastise those among us who believe in myths as being not of this age. Should a contemporary Westerner believe in myths, he or she is charged with harboring a naive romanticism for the ancient past or indulging in a curious folk wisdom based on unscientific premises, or holding outright fallacious beliefs.

Since those whose stories we call myths do not seem to care for the term, I am curious as to why Westerners persist in using it. Perhaps the study of myth might best be focused upon those who use it—American and European writers, who reflect and influence Western culture to a significant degree.

In this essay I will examine a lineage of Western writers who have considered the Mother Earth figure as a native American goddess. From their writing a story of Mother Earth emerges, a story attributed to native Americans but actually created by the writers themselves.

The story of Mother Earth begins almost concurrently with the story told by Smohalla in 1885, and a remarkable connection exists between the two. According to Smohalla's story, "God said he was the father, and the earth was the mother of mankind," but he went on to say,

> Those who cut up the lands or sign papers for lands will be defrauded of their rights, and will be punished by God's anger . . .

> It is not a good law that would take my people away from me to make them sin against the laws of God. You ask me to plough the ground? Shall I take a knife and tear my mother's bosom? Then when I die she will not take me to her bosom to rest.

> You ask me to dig for stone! Shall I dig under her skin for her bones? Then when I die I can not enter her body to be born again.

> You ask me to cut grass and make hay and sell it, and be rich like white men, but how dare I cut off my mother's hair?

> It is a bad law and my people shall not obey it. I want my people to stay with me here. All the dead men will come to life again; their spirits will come to their bodies again. We must wait here, in the homes of our fathers, and be ready to meet them in the bosom of our mother. (MacMurray 1887: 247–8)

This statement attributed to Smohalla has been often and widely quoted. Moreover, it has served as the principal example scholars have used to demonstrate the native American belief in the goddess Mother Earth. We may begin our analysis of the story of Mother Earth with an excerpt from the writings of Edward B. Tylor, sometimes credited as the father of modern anthropology. In his classic book *Primitive Culture*, published in London in 1873, Tylor proclaimed that: "The idea of the Earth as a mother is more simple and obvious, and no doubt for that reason more common in the world, than the idea of the Heaven as a father. Among the native races of America the Earth-mother is one of the great personages of mythology" (Tylor 1873: volume 1, 326). However, Tylor cited only three insignificant examples of its uses. These citations are therefore of little consequence in reporting major beliefs of native Americans.

Within a decade, Hubert Bancroft, undoubtedly influenced by Tylor, affirmed the same view in his American publication *The Native Races* (1882). He wrote, "It seems long ago and often to have come into men's minds that the over-arching heaven or something there and the all-producing earth are, as it were a father and mother to all living creatures" (Bancroft 1882:volume 3, 121).

Tylor's and Bancroft's views of the ancient motherhood of the earth received a fuller and more concrete expression in Smohalla's later statement in 1885. Shortly after he recited his story, two ethnologists, Albert Gatschet and James Mooney, who were studying the cultures of the Washington-Oregon area, used Smohalla's statement to exemplify a Mother Earth theology they believed to be common to all native Americans. These were the first of many such uses of Smohalla's statement.

In 1890, Albert S. Gatschet, in an ethnography of the Klamath of southern Oregon, waxed poetic on the native belief in the earth as mother.

> Among all nations of the world we find the idea, which is real as well as poetical, that the Earth is our common mother. "She is dealing out her bountiful gifts to her children, the human beings, without envy or restraint, in the shape of corn, fruits, and esculent roots. Her eyes are the lakes and ponds disseminated over the green surface of the plains, her breasts are the hills and hillocks; and the rivulets and brooks irrigating the valleys are the milk flowing from her breasts." [Gatschet did not indicate the source of this quotation.]
>
> The Indian Smúxale [Smohalla] at Priest Rapids, on Middle Columbia River, and his numerous followers, called the "Dreamers," from the implicit faith these Sahaptin sectarians place in dreams, dissuade their adherents from tilling the ground, as the white man does; "for it is a sin to wound or cut, tear up or scratch our common mother by agricultural pursuits; she will revenge herself on the whites and on the Indians following their example by opening her bosom and engulfing such malefactors by their misdeeds." [Again, no source of the quotation is given.]
>
> The Earth is regarded by these Indians as a mysterious, shadowy power of incalculable energies and influences, rather mischievous and wicked than beneficial to mankind. The Indians ascribe anger and other passions to it, but never personify it in clearer outlines than the ancients did their 'Epa or Tellus. (Gatschet 1890:xci–xcii)

Although Gatschet's comments on the Indian belief in Mother Earth have had minimal popular effect because they have remained hidden away in a little-read book, they almost certainly influenced James Mooney, who in 1896, just six years later, published a major study, "The Ghost Dance Religion and the Sioux Outbreak of 1890." His work became a widely read classic. In it Mooney not only quoted Smohalla's statement as a chapter epigraph, but he used the statement to exemplify the idea that:

> The earth is the mother of all created things lies at the base, not only of the Smohalla religion, but of the theology of the Indian tribes generally and of primitive races all over the world. . . . In the Indian mind the corn, fruits,

and edible roots are the gifts which the earth-mother gives freely to her children. Lakes and ponds are her eyes, hills are her breasts, and streams are the milk flowing from her breasts. Earthquakes and underground noises are signs of her displeasure at the wrongdoings of her children. Especially are the malarial fevers, which often followed extensive disturbance of the surface by excavation or otherwise, held to be direct punishment for the crime of lacerating her bosom. (Mooney 1896:721)

Mooney's quotation of Smohalla and his romantically colorful description of the Mother Earth theology, which he declared to be common to "primitive races all over the world," stimulated the explosion of literature about Mother Earth that began at the turn of the century and has yet to subside.

Such eminent scholars and well-known authors as Andrew Lang, Albrecht Dieterich, Sir James George Frazer, George B. Grinnell, and Hartley Burr Alexander held the view that Mother Earth is one of the great deities of native Americans. Yet only a few examples from tribal cultures in North America were cited as evidence for the statements made by these writers. None of these citations was as significant as nor has had the influence of the statement attributed to Smohalla. By the middle of the twentieth century, the statement had come to be a favorite used by the late eminent historian of religion, Mircea Eliade, in his discussion of Mother Earth. In his classic *Patterns of Comparative Religion* (1958), Eliade uses the Smohalla source to exemplify Mother Earth as she exists in the history of religions.

Before becoming a mother goddess, or divinity of fertility, the earth presented itself to men as a Mother, *Tellus Mater*. The later growth of agricultural cults, forming a gradually clearer and clearer notion of a Great Goddess of vegetation and harvesting, finally destroyed all trace of the Earth-Mother. In Greece, the place of Gaia was taken by Demeter. However, certain ancient ethnological documents reveal relics of the old worship of the Earth-Mother. Smohalla, an Indian prophet of the Umatilla tribe, forbade his followers to dig the earth, for, he said, it is a sin to wound or cut, tear or scratch our common mother by the labours of farming. "You ask me to plough the ground? [completing the famous statement]" . . . Such a mystical devotion to the Earth-Mother is not an isolated instance. (Eliade 1958:245–6)

In Eliade's view, Mother Earth is an ancient goddess, preexisting the rise of mother goddesses and fertility goddesses who replaced her during the rise of agricultural cults. Smohalla's statement, found in "ancient ethnological documents," is understood by Eliade as a relic of this "old worship." Although when he quotes Smohalla in his discussion of "Mother Earth and the Cosmic Hierogamies" in his book *Myths, Dreams and*

Mysteries, Eliade recognizes the recentness of the statement, he still maintains that the concept came from the very distant past.

> Those words [of Smohalla] were spoken not more than half a century ago. But they come to us from very distant ages. The emotion that we feel when we hear them is our response to what they evoke with their wonderful freshness and spontaneity—the primordial image of the Earth-Mother. It is an image that we find everywhere in the world, in countless forms and varieties. (Eliade 1957:155)

In the most recent generation in this literary lineage, the latest dependence on Smohalla's statement comes from the noted Swedish authority on native American religions, Åke Hultkrantz. His views of Mother Earth appear in his book (1979) and an essay on the native North American Goddess herself (1983). Hultkrantz understands Mother Earth to be a deity of great antiquity. He writes:

> It is an indisputable fact that the concept of the earth goddess has grown strongest among the cultivating peoples. . . . Her origins may have been in the old hunting culture which ranged all through America until about 2000 B.C. and was maintained by many tribes until the last decades of the nineteenth century. Far away from agricultural peoples lived, in the state of Washington, those Sahaptin Indians whose chief in the 1880s was the dreamer Smohalla. [Hultkrantz quotes the famed statement here.] As elsewhere, the earth deity is here represented as animatistic, at one with her substratum and yet an intimately experienced personal being. Many hunting tribes in North America manifest the same primitive belief in "our mother," "Mother Earth." (Hultkrantz 1979:54)

Even in this bare outline of writings on Mother Earth we find evidence of a highly interesting story. For even though Smohalla's remarks clearly speak to a specific crisis experienced by native peoples in that region during the last half of the nineteenth century, they have been used again and again to document not only the religious beliefs of Smohalla, the theology of the Wanapum and other Sahaptin speakers, and the peoples native to North America or all of the Americas, but of "primitive" peoples the world over. Moreover, the statement has been used to document beliefs not only during Smohalla's lifetime but of hunting peoples some millenia ago. The resulting Mother Earth story is therefore truly an Amazing Story.

Although Tylor stated that "among the native races of America the Earth-mother is one of the great personages of mythology," the Mother Earth story that seems most mythic is the one Europeans and Americans have created in their writings based on a statement attributed to Smohalla. Let me briefly tell this European-American Mother Earth story.

Long, long ago there were hunting peoples who ranged throughout the world. Some of them lived in that landscape we now know as the Americas. Being peoples of so long ago, at such an early stage of development, they were very primitive. Their material cultures were undeveloped as were their mental capacities. Because of the simplicity of their minds they could not yet comprehend the complex idea of the heaven as a father, they could only conceive of the simpler idea of the earth as a mother. They could recognize parts of her body in the landscape in which they walked. The hills and hillocks were her breasts, the rivulets and brooks were the milk flowing from her breasts. The ponds and lakes were her eyes. From her body she gave people their nourishment: roots, fruits, and plants. She took people back into her body upon their deaths.

As time went on some of these peoples developed more advanced cultures, though compared to us they remained primitive; and eventually the idea dawned that the sky was a father and they came to realize that the sky, as father, and the earth, as a mother, came together as progenitors of all life.

Much, much later, though still long, long ago, as some of these people continued to develop, they finally discovered agriculture and agricultural cults arose among them. With this development the earth mother was replaced by fertility goddesses and mother goddesses who were separate from the earth itself.

Some of these ideas were known to our ancient ancestors who lived in Greece and wrote them down. These writings have been passed down to us. In this way our ancient ancestors provided us with an understanding of all of the forms that cultures and religions take as they are developing. We are now in the fullest and most advanced stage of development.

Since those archaic times many peoples and cultures developed as we have, but some did not. They remained primitive while we became civilized. Even today there are primitive people who speak to us of the beliefs of the archaic peoples of millenia ago. Just a century ago, shortly after Washington became a state in North America, a man there spoke of the belief in Mother Earth as it existed among ancient hunters. His name was Smohalla.

This story is amazing in several respects. During the last 100 years it has gradually developed in the writings of some of our most eminent scholars, specialists in the study of culture. Smohalla's single statement provides almost the only cited evidence on which to base the story. Most remarkably, the story is not about native American beliefs at all; it is not even about native Americans. If it were, a great many more native American examples from their cultures would be present. Standard academic procedure used to document the presence of a trait among any culture or culture group requires the exhaustive analysis of the available data. In the case of the study of Mother Earth as one of the great goddesses in the mythology of North America, this clearly was not done by any one of these writers in the lineage outlined above. The questions that comes most immediately to mind are: Do these writers' views about Mother Earth accurately represent native American beliefs? What were these scholars really writing about? A little reflection on these writings and especially on the use made of the Smohalla's alleged statement suggests that historical and ethnographic accuracy were largely irrelevant to the Mother Earth story and in fact would lead us away from what is important about it. We must consider both the Mother Earth story as it emerged through European and American writings and the one told by Smohalla as myths. This must be so because, curiously, both versions are stories told about the Other.

At the time Smohalla told his story, he was one of only a few hundred native Americans in the Washington-Oregon area still holding out against American plans to confine Indians to reservations. Throughout Smohalla's lifetime there had been pressures to radically transform native ways of life. Early in the nineteenth century trappers and missionaries came into the area. Their success encouraged settlers to seek land in the Pacific Northwest. By midcentury, the U.S. government procured treaties that effectively removed the Indians from lands and resources almost desirable to them. Statehood for Washington and Oregon followed. Reservation lands were reduced so that gold mining, lumbering, farming, and ranching could expand. Any real hope held by the native peoples that they might retain their traditional way of life was destroyed when Chief Joseph was captured in 1877. Nonetheless, Smohalla and his followers persisted in attempting to live according to the old ways. They dreamed of the time when the Americans would be destroyed and past ways could be restored to the Indians. Smohalla and his followers practiced a ritual born of and shaped by this crisis. They met in a churchlike building and included obvious Christian ritual elements in their meetings. The story he told in 1885 must be viewed against this historical backdrop.

Smohalla's story tells of the creation of a world by a god who, in his loneliness, scratched sand from the bottom of the water that covered the world. From this sand he made the land. This god created human beings and furnished the world abundantly with plants, animals, and fish. He gave humans wings so they could travel wherever they liked. But many people came to inhabit the land, and the stronger oppressed the weaker. They drove the weaker from favorite lands and fisheries, killing almost all of them. This angered the god and "he took away their wings and commanded that the lands and fisheries should be common to all who lived upon them. That they were never to be marked off or divided."

Though this story is set in the time of creation, it is clearly a story about the oppression that Smohalla and the Indians suffered at the hands of American settlers and government authorities. It directly reflects the situation at the time of the storytelling. Not only does it make their oppression meaningful by incorporating it into the story of creation, but it also offers the hope that, as in the story, God will eventually punish the oppressors and command that the lands and fisheries be common to all.

The European-American story of Mother Earth must also be seen in its historical and cultural context. Beginning as early as the first voyage of Columbus in 1492, the European-Christian world faced constant challenges to its most basic beliefs concerning the shape and extent of the world and nature of humankind. Since the middle of the nineteenth century, with the rise of anthropology and comparative studies of culture and religion, thinkers and writers have been challenged to comprehend patterns, themes, and ideas that would enable them not only to understand the hundreds of newly emerging or discovered cultures but also to interpret them in Western terms.

Smohalla lived in a world collapsing from the unwelcome presence of others. Europeans and Americans, in their turn, found their conceptions and knowledge of the world threatened by their encounters with strange and exotic peoples who were unlike themselves.

The story of Mother Earth as told by Europeans and Americans is a story of the development of human religiosity and culture. It is a story of the evolution of religious structures and forms, a story enriched by the patterns and categories derived from Western antiquity. It is a story of society's growth from the simple to the complex, from the primitive to the civilized, from a nonliterate to a literate culture. It is a story in which native Americans, by virtue of the statement made by Smohalla in 1885, could be placed at a very early stage of cultural and religious development. The story of Mother Earth helps resolve the crises of Western worldview by providing it a basis on which to incorporate the worldview of these Others.

Surprisingly, when the two stories are compared, they share more than might at first be expected. Both stories respond to a situation of encountering some "others" (see chapter 17). Both expand and develop an existing view of the world so that those others might be understood in such a way as to make the relationship with them meaningful, if not manageable. Both respond creatively to an encounter characterized by dominance and oppression. It is clear that both stories serve the most basic needs of the story creators and·tellers. And it is clear that both articulate foundational values—unquestionable assumptions and perspectives that underlie all that is seen and done.

According to these observations I would suggest that myth should be thought of as the story on which truth is based, rather than thinking of myth as a true story. Myths are stories that articulate that which is itself not subject to verification or validation. This is a logical definition of myth, positing that in questions of truth there must be some base on which truth-judgments are made (see chapter 12). If one could isolate that base, it would necessarily not be subject to a demand for validation. For if it were, another unquestionable base would have to be posited. If this base for truth is called *myth*, we could not ask if myth was a true story. We would assume rather that myth is the foundation on which truth is based. Given this view of myth, we may understand why myths are set in the primordium. This kind of story has nothing to do with the historical past. The temporal setting of "in the beginning" or "long, long ago" marks the mythic quality of the story—the quality of articulating that which is beyond question most fundamental.

It is commonly thought that myths provide for humans a vehicle by which they may return to the paradisiacal conditions of primordiality, to be refreshed in the pristine conditions of the newly created. Perhaps a complement to this view is to understand that myths function as a means by which human beings can articulate that which is most fundamental to them through the revision and re-creation of their stories, a kind of eternal renewal. Rather than returning to the primordial era of creation, the condition of primordiality may be carried along through history firmly grounding that which, in the present, is deemed by a people to be most fundamental, to be beyond doubt. Myth thereby serves as creative means of effectively responding to crises and change while maintaining tradition and identity. The word *return* suggests a connection between the primordial setting, which is essentially a mythic marker in a narrative, and history—a return in time to the beginning, a reversal or annihilation of history. I do not think history is reversed or destroyed in myth; rather the experiences of history are digested and recreated through the ongoing mythic process of producing newly vitalized articulations of that which is most fundamental to any people.

It is because of mythic qualities that the validity of neither story we have considered is subject to question. Smohalla's story has obvious Christian influence and is clearly shaped, if not wholly formed, to meet the crisis situation being experienced. But it would be senseless to argue that the story could not possibly be correct in its assertion about the creation, because it can be historically documented that the story was formulated in the nineteenth century. From the point of view of Smohalla and his followers, this story articulates the grounds upon which they can in a crisis retain any meaning in life, which means that their very lives depend upon the story.

Likewise, in terms of the Mother Earth story that emerges from European and American writings, although our first question is whether or not they are historically and ethnographically accurate, it is in one sense an inappropriate question. Were these writings primarily scholarly in character, the question would be appropriate, but they are mythic. To even suggest that Mother Earth might not have existed in the religious traditions of native Americans or other tribal peoples throughout the world constitutes heresy. It challenges the very foundations of one of our important beliefs of the world. For Westerners, Mother Earth is not a hypothesis: She is a figure whose existence, structure, and character is the basis on which many of the disparate and diffuse cultures cohere meaningfully. She is of our myth; she is primordial; and her story is not subject to questions of historical or ethnographic accuracy.

While it is clear that those writers who created the theology of Mother Earth had no ill intent toward native Americans (indeed, there is abundant evidence that the opposite was often true), they nonetheless participated in what can only be termed a logic of dominance and conquest. Native Americans have been forced to participate in this same logic. This may seem harsh, but the fact cannot be ignored.

In the story told by Smohalla, the message of dominance is clear. The story was told in the midst of a history of oppression and is about oppression. The Indians are oppressed, and Americans are the oppressors.

In the European-American story of Mother Earth the logic of dominance appears under the rubric of the dichotomy between primitive and civilized. Here the theme of dominance may be more subtle, but it is also more sinister.

Each taken in the context of its own historical background, both stories show the creativity not only of human, but of the genre and process I am identifying as myth. These stories not only share a common history, they have a common landscape and characters. The characters are not fictitious imaginings, but living human beings. Seen in this light, this logic of dominance, oppression, and conquest is not confined to the innocence of interesting stories idly told. Rather, these stories, especially the European-American Mother Earth story, articulate unquestionable principles and assumptions that have been fundamental to a long history of U.S. government policy towards Indians (characterized at best as paternalism), to a long history of missionization (that denied the religious freedom of native Americans), and to the military and legal enforcement of the removal of native Americans from the lands they occupied when they first came under American jurisdiction. This mythology has articulated the categories and theories that have also shaped the academic study of native Americans. It must be acknowledged that a logic of domination and conquest has motivated and shaped even this supposedly detached and objective study.

This last point is conclusively demonstrated by Anne Doueihi in her article "Trickster: On Inhabiting the Space Between Discourse and Story" (1984). She focuses on a century of academic study of native American stories in which the protagonist is a trickster, a fool, a buffoon. These stories include Coyote (popularized in the "Coyote and Roadrunner" cartoon), Raven, Raccoon, Spider, and many others. For a century, Western scholarship has posited a common figure as appearing in all of these stories. They called this figure Trickster. The intellectual problem has been to explain how Trickster can be both wise and foolish; a player of malicious tricks as well as a hero; the epitome of rudeness, yet considered sacred. The following is Doueihi's startling conclusion to a review of twentieth century scholarship on the Trickster:

> The traditional discourse about Trickster is a discourse which reflects a cultural bias; by imposing on Indian culture its own frame of concern, Western culture turns the discourse about Trickster into a discourse by Western culture about Western culture, with Trickster serving only in a nominal function so that the discussion may begin. This is a form of domination and repression of which any discourse about any "Other" must be guilty unless that discourse is self-questioning, that is, unless it involves a questioning of the very language it itself uses and a questioning of the discourse of which that language is a part. (Doueihi 1984:297)

Mother Earth and Trickster both owe their existence to a logic of conquest and dominance; they are characters in a mythology of dominance, in "a discourse by Western culture about Western culture." In a sense, so too does the modern use of the word *myth*, for in its principal use as a category by which to understand the Other and in our tendency to characterize myth as archaic, it participates in the logic of domination. The advice of Doueihi is well put. In a modern pluralist world, a world obviously shaped by the logic of conquest and dominance, it is essential that the language used in discourse about every Other be analyzed. The word *myth* has become increasingly important to this discourse, and, in many of its uses and implications, it has not escaped the logic of dominance. Western scholars and writers, in their study of myth and in their creation of such figures as Trickster and Mother Earth, have been creating their own mythology. Yet they have steadfastly refused to apply the category "myth" to their own work.

Perhaps the simplest way to avoid the logic of conquest and dominance is to apply the categories usually reserved for dealing with Others also to the task of understanding ourselves. This is what I have attempted to do, both in the way I have suggested the term *myth* be understood and in viewing as myth a lineage of Western writings on the figure Mother Earth.

Now, throwing caution to the wind, risking serious emotional reprisals, knowingly committing the act of heresy, I ask the question: Were the European and American writers correct in a historical and ethnographic sense? There are many rich and wonderful female figures known in native American stories. Some are related to the earth, but most are not. Almost none are understood as the earth personified, and those who approach this do not have a developed story tradition or ritual presence. This should not be surprising, since there were hundreds of distinct native peoples in North America, each with a different language, religion, and culture. How could anyone expect to find a goddess common to all in such diversity?

While in terms of the story of Mother Earth this observation is insignificant, it is important to show conclusively that Mother Earth in North America is of the mythology created by Westerners, not a historical and ethnographic reality to native North Americans. But upon applying the term *myth* to our own mentors, some complex questions arise. These scholars have been authoritative because they were believed to have acquired their knowledge of Others through careful observation, and to have based their conclusions on plentiful and carefully documented sources. What is shown in the case of Mother Earth is that no North American evidence exists. Mother Earth emerges not from ethnographic documentation but from an imaginative construction. What scholars have been writing about was not the Other at all, but about their own views of human history.

As a result, the general populace and contemporary Indians, as well as scholars, now accepts without question Mother Earth as a historical and ethnographic fact in native North America and throughout the world. This raises the most fundamental questions about what constitutes responsible scholarship. What is the difference between scholarship and mythmaking, between fact and fiction? Is there a connection between some styles of scholarship and writing, some ways of seeing the Other, and oppressive political and economic perspectives? Is not the formulation of self-expression in the guise of stating knowledge about some Other a powerful form of dominating them? Is this activity not somehow participating in the political, social, and economic oppression of the Other while being understood as objective observations motivated only by a humanistic interest?

A final issue is perhaps most remarkable. Among native Americans today there is much evidence in a deep and abiding belief in a figure they identify by the name Mother Earth. She is often paired with Father Sky, the Great Spirit, or the Creator. Examination of the history of this figure shows that she arose in the process of the formation of the pan-Indian or pantribal alliance among native Americans who, in this century, have increasingly forged a common identity in the face of a common experience of oppression and loss. As the Indian peoples lost the land base on which their various group identities depended, the Mother Earth figure grew in importance among them.

What seems to have happened is that the oppressed native Americans have appropriated the mythology of the oppressors. Indians acquired what they knew to be expected of them, a belief in a figure known as Mother Earth. But, as often happens with the oppressed, the Indians transformed the Mother Earth concept through their own creative mythic processes to articulate for them what was most fundamental; that has been the survival of their separate identity as Indians even without tribal lands, without continuing political institutions or shared images and meanings, and without traditional languages.

Mother Earth arose among Western writers so that native Americans could be understood and somehow likened to European-Americans. By identifying Mother Earth as a major figure in Indian mythology, these writers were able to place native Americans in a schema of the evolution of cultures and religions in which those representatives of Western civilization stood at the top. In contrast, Indians in recent decades have, through their appropriation of Mother Earth, attached to her the qualities that articulate distinctively "Indian" in contrast and clearly superior to "white" American, attributes. Indians are of the earth (specifically of the American soil); they care for and nurture Mother Earth, who in turn cares for and nurtures them. They do not plow or mine, tear, waste, or desecrate the earth as they see "white" Americans doing. Thus Mother Earth helps Indians retain their identity, their pride and dignity. By holding Mother Earth as their goddess, native Americans have articulated what is most distinctively Indian, and they have done so by appropriating and transforming the myth of their oppressors.

Mother Earth, as she currently exists in Indian religions, is primordial, a creator, a nurturer, a bona fide goddess in every sense of the word, even though we may understand that historically her origins are not only very recent, but doubtless owe much to the mythic views of Westerners on Mother Earth.

References

Bancroft, Hubert Howe. 1882. *The Native Races* [of the Pacific States]. 5 vols. San Francisco: A. L. Bancroft. First published 1874–75.

Doueihi, Anne. 1984. "Trickster: On Inhabiting the Space Between Discourse and Story." *Soundings: An Interdisciplinary Journal* 67:283–311.

Eliade, Mircea. 1957. *Myths, Dreams, and Mysteries*. New York: Harper & Row.

————. 1958. *Patterns of Comparative Religion*. Cleveland and New York: World.

Gatschet, Albert S. 1890. *The Klamath Indians of Southwest Oregon*. Contributions to North American Ethnology, Vol. 2, Pts. 1 and 2. Washington, D.C.: Government Printing Office.

Hultkrantz, Åke. 1979. *The Religions of the American Indians*. Berkeley: University of California Press.

————. 1983. "The Religion of the Goddess in North America." In *The Book of the Goddess Past and Present: An Introduction to Her Religion*. C. Olson, ed. New York: Crossroads.

MacMurray, J. W. 1887. "The 'Dreamers' of the Columbia River Valley, In Washington Territory," *Transactions of the Albany Institute*. 241–48.

Mooney, James. 1896. *The Ghost Dance Religion and the Sioux Outbreak of 1890*. Fourteenth Annual Report of the Bureau of Ethnology, 1892–1893. Washington, D.C.: Government Printing Office.

Tylor, Edward B. 1873. *Culture: Researches into the Development of, Philosophy, Religion, Language, Art and Custom*. 2 vols. London: John Murray.

8

Liberty, Equality, Fraternity: Was the Indian Really Egalitarian?

Leland Donald

> *I am as free as nature first made man,*
> *Ere the base laws of servitude began,*
> *When wild in woods the noble savage ran.*
> —*John Dryden The Conquest of Grenada* 1664

The Noble Savage is one of the key ideas of the European Enlightenment, important in the development of political theory and influential in shaping European perspectives towards the indigenous peoples they found inhabiting the many lands "discovered" during the Age of Exploration. In dialectical fashion, while ideas about the noble savage affected European attitudes toward the native inhabitants of North America, in their turn early travelers', missionaries' and settlers' accounts of these native peoples influenced the development of the concept of the Noble Savage.[1]

A classic example of this process can be found in the works of Louis-Armand de Lom d'Arce, Baron de Lahontan (1666–1715), whose travel books were popular around the turn of the eighteenth century. Between 1703 and 1760, for example, his *New Voyages to North-America* appeared in numerous French, English, Dutch, and German editions. Lahontan both reflected the ideas of the Enlightenment and, as a much-traveled eyewitness, influenced European ideas about the New World and its inhabitants. Thus he vividly describes Indian life "Ere the base laws of servitude began":

The *Savages* are utter Strangers to distinctions of Property, for what belongs to one is equally anothers . . . Money is in use with none of them but those that are Christians . . . The others will not touch or so much as look upon Silver, but give it the odious Name of the *French Serpent*. They'll tell you that amongst us the People Murder, Plunder, Defame, and betray one another, for Money, that the Husbands make Merchandise of their Wives, and the Mothers of their Daughters, for the Lucre of that Metal. They think it unaccountable that one Man should have more than another, and that the Rich should have more Respect than the Poor. In short, they say, the name of savages which we bestow upon them would fit our selves better . . . 'Tis vain to remonstrate to them how useful the Distinction of Property is for the support of a Society: They make a Jest of what's to be said on that Head. In fine, they neither Quarrel nor Fight, nor Slander one another. They scoff at Arts and Sciences, and laugh at the difference of Degrees which is observ'd with us. They brand us for Slaves, and call us miserable Souls, whose Life is not worth having, alleging, That we degrade our selves in subjecting our selves to one Man who possesses the whole Power, and is bound by no Law but his own Will . . . Besides, they value themselves above any thing that you can imagine, and this is the reason they always give for't, *That one's as much Master as another, and since Men are all made of the same Clay there should be no Distinction or Superiority among them.* (1905:420–1)[2]

Later in this book, Lahontan contrived a long dialogue between himself, pretending to defend European civilization, and a literary antithesis—a probably fictional Huron whom he named Adario. The following statement, Lahontan's thoughts presented as coming from Adario's mouth, continues the preceding themes:

We are resolv'd to have no Laws, for since the World was a World our ancestors liv'd happily without 'em. In fine, as I intimated before, the Word *Laws* does not signify just and reasonable things as you use it, for the Rich make a Jest of 'em, and 'tis only the poor wretches that pay any regard to 'em. But, pray, let's look into these Laws, or reasonable things, as you call 'em. For these Fifty Years, the Governors of *Canada* have still alleged that we are subject to the Laws of their great Captain. We content our selves in denying all manner of Dependance, excepting that upon the Great Spirit, as being born free and joint Brethren, who are all equally Masters: Whereas you are all Slaves to one Man . . . In earnest, my dear Brother, I'm sorry for thee from the bottom of my soul. Take my advice, and turn *Huron*; for I see plainly a vast difference between thy Condition and mine. I am Master of my own body, I have the absolute disposal of my self, I do what I please, I am the first and the last of my Nation, I fear no Man, and I depend only upon the Great Spirit: Whereas thy Body, as well as thy Soul, are doom'd to a dependance upon thy great Captain; thy Vice-Roy disposes of thee; thou hast not the liberty of doing what thou hast a mind to . . . and thou dependest upon an infinity of Persons whose Places have rais'd 'em above thee. Is it true, or not? . . . Ah! my dear Brother, thou seest plainly that I am in the right of it; and yet thou choosest rather to be a *French* slave than a free *Huron*. (1905:553–5)

Lahontan had spent some years traveling and living among the natives of northeastern North America, but clearly he was less interested in accurate description of the customs of those he met than in making invidious comparisons, in constructing a Noble Savage and using him as commentator on life in Europe. Others who traveled to North America tried to communicate what they witnessed but many wrote their accounts so as to use the native as foils, either to criticize or to justify conditions in Europe (as did most of the intellectuals who stayed at home rehashing the accounts of travelers).[3]

In this manner the image of a free, liberty loving Indian, unfettered by laws and enjoying a society unmarked by social, economic or political inequalities, became a favorite figure in European thought.

By the middle of the nineteenth century, the foundations were being laid for what became twentieth-century social science, including anthropology. Authentic descriptions of Indian societies then began to have value in their own right. But these descriptions also served speculative social theory, by then mainly full blown reconstructions of "stages" of social evolution. Although by the nineteenth century there was an enormous amount of information on various native societies in explorers', settlers' and missionaries' accounts, the first systematic descriptive study of an Indian group was not published until 1851, when Lewis Henry Morgan published *League of the Iroquois*, "the first scientific account of an Indian tribe." Morgan had interviewed and observed the Iroquois of upper New York state and his book is based on this research, but echoes of the Noble Savage and the use of the nature of Indian society to criticize the contemporary scene are in his writing, combined with new scientific goals and interests. This can be clearly seen in the following passage from Morgan's later, highly influential theoretical work, *Ancient Society*, published in 1877:

> Property and office were the foundations upon which aristocracy planted itself.

> Whether this principle shall live or die has been one of the great problems with which modern society has been engaged through the intervening periods. As a question between equal rights and unequal laws, between the rights of wealth, of rank and of official position, and the power of justice and intelligence, there can be little doubt of the ultimate result. Although several thousand years have passed away without the overthrow of privileged classes, excepting in the United States, their burdensome character upon society has been demonstrated.

> Since the advent of civilization, the outgrowth of property has been so immense, its forms so diversified, its uses so expanding and its management so intelligent in the interests of its owners, that it has become, on the part of the people, an unmanageable power. The human mind stands bewildered in

the presence of its own creation. The time will come, nevertheless, when human intelligence will rise to the mastery over property, and define the relations of the state to the property it protects, as well as the obligations and the limits of the rights of its owners. The interests of society are paramount to individual interests, and the two must be brought into just and harmonious relations. A mere property career is not the final destiny of mankind, if progress is to be the law of the future as it has been of the past. The time which has passed away since civilization began is but a fragment of the past duration of man's existence; and but a fragment of the ages yet to come. The dissolution of society bids fair to become the termination of a career of which property is the end and aim; because such a career contains the elements of self-destruction. Democracy in government, brotherhood in society, equality in rights and privileges, and universal education, foreshadow the next higher plane of society to which experience, intelligence and knowledge are steadily tending. It will be a revival, in a higher form, of the liberty, equality and fraternity of the ancient gentes. (1964:466–67)

This passage is full of echoes of Lahontan and other Enlightenment writers. There is the criticism of property and its consequences, of authority, of aristocratic rule, and also a strong reprise of the Noble Savage in "the liberty, equality and fraternity of the ancient gentes." Now, we would say clan instead of gentes, but here in Morgan's evolutionary speculations are Lahontan's liberty-loving Indian organized into fraternal groups, bands of brothers, and sisters (the Iroquois were matrilineal and Morgan well understood this). Like Lahontan, Morgan's Noble Savage did not need kings, aristocrats, privilege or property to lead the good life. But now the image is based on a "scientific" account of Indian culture.

Morgan worked with many other Indian groups, although with none nearly so intensively as the Iroquois. Nonetheless, he viewed all Indians (and all others at "their level" of social evolution) through Iroquois-colored glasses. While Morgan's Iroquois ethnography has been supplemented, but never surpassed, his particular scheme of social evolution is no longer accepted as valid. Because Morgan had many successors, the New York Iroquois have remained a dominant influence on the image of the American Indian, both scholarly and popular. Although recent popular images are dominated visually by the movie version of plains Indians—feather headdresses, horses and tepees—still the social characteristics of this popular image remain Morganian: fierce, proud, liberty loving warriors fighting for an independent, egalitarian way of life. The scholarly view takes into account far more detail, drawn from over a century of study that has ranged over the entire continent. Yet when scholars summarize, Morgan's images of the Iroquois peek out from behind the curtain of generalizations. Many examples could be produced, all presenting the same general interpretations: in political terms, the indigenous societies of North America all lacked the state and were varieties of "tribal" societies. They tended to be egalitarian, lacking social or economic inequities, except for those based on age or gender.[4]

All the world's societies probably had and have at least minimal inequality based on age and perhaps gender as well. Thus the status of the sexes and generations are certainly the most widespread bases for allocating resources, power, and prestige, especially so in those societies lacking the centralized political institutions known as the state. Moreover, there are (or were) societies which do not have inequalities *other* than those based on gender and age; and such societies (inside and outside native North America) are often labeled as egalitarian! Readers sensitive to age or gender discrimination may sense there is something a bit odd about this, but I will accept the convention here because I wish to concentrate on inequalities other than those involving sex or generation.

Even a casual reading of the world ethnographic record will reveal considerable variation among the planet's societies (past and present) in what I shall call "structured social inequality." In many instances members of a society recognize and accept that some of their fellows have greater advantages with respect to access to some or many of the things important to the local version of the good life. This advantage is usually based on some culturally constructed attribute of an individual or of some category to which such fortunate individuals belong. Especially where these groups of individuals contain all ages and both genders, and where superior status can be successfully transmitted from generation to generation, and especially if some of the advantages of the superior include better access to the resources necessary for life itself, then that society is not egalitarian.

My aim in this essay is not to show that there were no genuinely egalitarian societies—in the classic, conventional sense—in native North America. Surely there were. But there were also many that were not. Numerous indigenous societies were in fact highly stratified, containing groups and categories of people who were seriously disadvantaged when compared to others. Space limitations prevent a systematic region by region survey. A discussion of two culture areas where "Liberty, Equality, Fraternity (and Sorority)" were absent except for the favored will have to do. After a discussion of these two areas—the Southeast and the Northwest Coast, plus one particularly important case from elsewhere—I will conclude by briefly considering why inequality among traditional native societies has been ignored or obscured and suggest why it is important not to disregard it.

In 1775 James Adair published *The History of the American Indians*, meaning the Indians he knew reasonably well, "those Nations adjoining to the Mississippi, East and West Florida, Georgia, South and North Carolina, and Virginia." Based on at least thirty-four years of experience as trader with Indian communities of this region, Adair's book is a major source for eighteenth-century Southeastern ethnography. This observant merchant was so struck by what he saw as the lack of hierarchy among southeastern Indians of his time that he dismissed older reports of class differentiation and political centralization among them. He went even farther than this, denying political hierarchy among all other American Indians—going so far as to deny the possible existence of the state among even the Aztecs of Mexico or the Inca of Peru. "The emperor [Montezuma]," concluded Adair,

> who they [the Spanish] pretend bore such universal arbitrary sway, is raised by their pens, from the usual rank of a war chieftain, to his imperial greatness: But despotic power is death to their [Indian] ears, as it is destructive of their darling liberty . . . they have no name for a subject, but say, "the people." In order to carry on the self-flattering warromance . . . [the Spanish] began the epocha of that great fictitious empire, in the time of the ambitious and formidable Montezuma, that their handful of heaven-favoured popish saints might have the more honour in destroying it: had they described it of a long continuance, they forsaw that the world would detect the fallacy, as soon as they learned the language of the pretended empire; correspondent to which, our own great Emperor Powhatan of Virginia, was [that way] soon dethroned . . . Our Indians urge with a great deal of vehemence, that as every one is promoted only by public virtue, and has his equals in civil and martial affairs, those Spanish books that have mentioned red emperors, and great empires in America, ought to be burnt in some of the remaining old years accursed fire. (1968:211)

Adair's experiences, which convinced him that the Native inhabitants of the Southeast were classic examples of the egalitarian, liberty-loving Indian, and his hatred of his Spanish rivals and Catholics generally, were not unusual for his time. One more of the many similar characterizations of southeastern Indians must suffice:

> The [Cherokee] are an odd Kind of People, as there is no law nor Subjection amongst them. They can't be compelled to do any Thing nor oblige them to embrace any party except they Please. The very lowest of them thinks himself as great and as high as any of the Rest . . . everyone of them must be courted for their Friendship with some kind of Feeling and made much of" [Captain Raymond Demere, July 30, 1757, quoted in Gearing 1962:38–9].

Adair was almost certainly right that early explorers and settlers often spoke of Indian "kings" in situations where the European terminology and its implications were most inappropriate: Powhatan (of Pocahontas fame, see chapter 3) was not a "monarch" in the seventeenth-century European sense. But Adair was clearly wrong about the Inca and the Aztec, neither of whom he knew first-hand. Was he also wrong about at least some of the native peoples of the Southeast? Were some of their societies organized in ways that cannot reasonably be called egalitarian? We can answer both these questions with a fairly clear yes. And we can do so with two independent kinds of evidence: the first archaeological, the second historic.

Social inequality rarely leaves unambiguous evidence for the archaeologist to uncover. Yet we have considerable archaeological evidence from Southeastern sites to suggest that at various times and places some of the region's prehistoric communities contained socially stratified populations. This evidence indicates that, long before Columbus, some communities were divided so that certain groups within them had greater access to wealth, resources, and marks of privilege than did others.

Some of the most useful evidence pointing to this conclusion can be found in burials. Not uncommonly in archaeological sites we discover that some individuals have had buried with them a fairly rich array of artifacts, often of the kind that can be reasonably interpreted as markers of power, wealth, or prestige, while other individuals have few or even no fancy artifacts in their graves. Though a deceased individual might be entitled to such marks of superiority because of unusual personal accomplishments marking a distinctive career, the rich funeral goods of others were present because they belonged to a social group which entitled them to such signs of superiority. If "rich" burials are found for all ages and both genders, while "poor" burials are also found across age and gender categories, this can be interpreted as evidence that posh graves are a hereditary right rather than an earned privilege. This is not the only interpretation of such finds, but where such differentiation in death is accompanied by other probable indicators of stratification, we have good grounds for ruling out an egalitarian society, even if we cannot be certain of just what kind of social inequalities were present.

Much of just this kind of evidence is present in the Southeast.[5] Indeed, some archaeologists are convinced that structured social inequality characterized several Southeastern communities as early as the late Archaic period, as many as 3000 years ago (Muller 1983:383–84).[6] One recent overview of Southeastern prehistory gives a picture of the waxing and waning of complex, inegalitarian societies in various parts of the region from the Archaic period until late prehistoric times, about 1500 A.D.

(Muller 1983). Such evidence suggests there was probably a decline in social complexity and hence in inequality just before European intrusions into the region. So sixteenth century and later European observers like Adair would have seen less inequality than they would have had they arrived a century or two earlier. And European contact itself, both directly (conquest) and indirectly (disease), almost certainly contributed to a breakdown and a break up of larger native Southeastern polities. Thus even very early in the contact period, European observers were describing societies that were coping with and reacting to the damaging effects of culture contact.

In at least one Southeastern case *both* archaeological *and* ethnohistoric evidence exhibits social inequality: the Calusa of southern Florida. John Goggin and William Sturtevant (1964) assembled much evidence that points explicitly to stratification among these people. They summarize this evidence as follows:

> [Calusa] society was stratified, with at least two classes (possibly hereditary) in addition to some slaves. Several individual statuses of high rank existed, which apparently had greater access than the rest of the population to at least some economic resources, which possessed sociopolitical authority, and which had distinctive ceremonial duties and privileges. (1964:208)[7]

Important here is the suggestion that the elite class had superior access to resources, for this is the classic marker of a stratified or nonegalitarian society (Fried 1967:186–87). Documentary sources suggest that other indigenous Southeastern societies were stratified, but I will mention only the best-known, most clear-cut example.

The Natchez, who lived along a short stretch of the lower Mississippi River, are known to us from descriptions and comments by nearby French settlers during the period 1700 to 1731. They were destroyed by the French about 1730, although a few survivors fled to the neighboring Chickasaw. French sources reveal an elaborate, even intricate system of social, religious, and political hierarchy. The ethnologist John Swanton used these sources to reconstruct a version of their social system which he first published in 1911. He described a system of two social "classes," with the upper class being further divided into three ranked groups. Translating from the French, he labeled the three upper classes (in order of superiority) as "Suns," "Nobles," and "Honored People," and the lower-class as "Stinkards." Swanton's reconstruction included a tangled set of marriage and status inheritance rules whose interpretation and reinterpretation has produced a steady stream of commentaries ever since.[8]

Whatever reconstruction of Natchez marriage and status inheritance rules one accepts, however, clearly they had at least two social classes. Members of these two strata experienced not only markedly different prestige and conditions of life (upper-class women, for example, had more extensive body tattooing than did lower-class women), but the upper-class also monopolized political power and almost certainly had superior access to economic resources. In addition, within the upper-class the ruling descent group (the Suns) enjoyed power and privileges considerably greater than that of other upper-class groups. Whatever the details, no one could call early eighteenth-century Natchez society egalitarian.

In summary, the archaeological evidence strongly suggests a long history of social stratification and privilege in southeastern societies and there is strong ethnohistoric evidence for at least two stratified societies at the time of contact (the Calusa and Natchez). Careful research would almost certainly produce evidence of more nonegalitarian societies in the prehistoric and early historic Southeast. The standard notion that Southeastern societies were generally egalitarian results from overlooking the possibility of variation, not paying sufficient attention to the Natchez and Calusa cases, not recognizing the destruction of traditional institutions throughout the Southeast quickly after European contact, and the widespread acceptance of the assumptions of the "egalitarian Indian" model.

At the opposite, northwestern corner of the continent we find many native societies on which no one could force-fit the Noble Savage image of liberty, equality, and fraternity. The Northwest Coast culture area includes the Alaska panhandle, the coastal strip of British Columbia and Washington and, for some scholars, the sea coasts of Oregon and northern California as well. No one with even a modest familiarity with the peoples of this region could call them egalitarian. Competition for social position, prestige seeking, and striving for higher rank and honors are all perennial themes in ethnographic descriptions of Northwest Coast peoples. Despite many published descriptions of traditional Northwest Coast social life, knowledge of their deeply and intensively stratified communities has had little influence on the "the Indian's" egalitarian image (sayings such as "low man on the totem pole" notwithstanding). Indeed, the popular stereotype of the egalitarian Indian may well have contributed to the curiously narrow view of inequality that anthropologists have taken when writing about Northwest Coast social systems.

Although there was (and is) variation between the societies of the Northwest Coast, in terms of inequality all followed a basic pattern. The typical community in the region had the following form: (1) Members of a named local community resided together during the winter;[9] (2)

the winter village consisted of several kinship groups, whose members lived together in one or more large wooden plank houses; and, (3) the community contained persons belonging to each of three (unequal) ranked strata that can be called *Titleholders*, *Commoners*, and *Slaves*.

Titleholders dominated their communities; they were the wealthy and successful who staged the famous potlatches.[10] In many communities, in addition to being members of a distinct social strata, Titleholders were organized into a ranked hierarchy among themselves. Commoners, in contrast, were full members of the same extended kin groups as Titleholders but lacked titles and did not command the respect, prestige, or economic clout of their superiors. Slaves represented an even more extreme contrast of inequality: they were the *property* of either kin groups or individual Titleholders. Slaves were economically exploited and could be exchanged for other goods. They might be given away at ceremonies; and, in an ultimate display of power over powerlessness, slaves could be killed to enhance the prestige of a Titleholder or kin group. Slaves, in their origins, were prisoners of war. Being forcibly removed from their villages, their kin ties were ruptured by capture and they had no kinship rights in the communities where they were held in bondage.[11]

This view of Northwest Coast stratification is somewhat controversial. While all of the fuller ethnographic accounts mention slaves, they are treated as economically unimportant and are not usually taken into consideration in analyses of the culture area. It is also unusual to recognize a division of the "free" population into two strata. Most students of the region claim that there was a gradation of rank that included all non-slaves. In Helen Codere's phrase there was "rank without class" on the Northwest Coast (1957).

I will deal briefly with the position of slaves and then turn to the question of divisions within the free population. Downplaying the economic importance of Northwest coast slaves is an old tradition that continues even today: "the slave, who had little or no economic value" (Hodge 1981:407). This doctrine began with Franz Boas, the dominant figure in American anthropology in the first half of this century, whose major ethnographic work was done on the Northwest Coast, especially among the southern Kwakiutl. Boas published several thousand pages of Kwakiutl ethnography. In his account of southern Kwakiutl social organization that Codere has declared "definitive," Boas does not mention slavery at all (1966:37–67). Indeed, in the summary volume, *Kwakiutl Ethnography*, edited by Codere, there is no index entry for "slave" or "slavery."

Boas' most important (and virtually only) statement about southern Kwakiutl slavery appeared in his first major book about these people:

> So far we have considered the clan as a unit. The individuals composing the clan do not form, however, a homogenous mass, but differ in rank. All the tribes of the Pacific Coast are divided into a nobility, common people, and slaves. The last of these may be left out of consideration, as they do not form part and parcel of the clan, but are captives made in war, or purchases, and may change ownership as any other piece of property. (1897:338)

The irony is that, while originating the pattern of ignoring or downplaying Northwest Coast slavery, Boas's early statement is accurate — as far as it goes. If one wishes to analyze the internal composition of a kin group, slaves may indeed be "left out of consideration" for they are the property of — not members of — such free groups. But it is easy to demonstrate the economic importance of slaves for many of the area's communities and to show that there were too many of them to ignore and still claim a thorough understanding of societies in the region.

The range of economic tasks performed by slaves was wide: they collected firewood, fetched water, gathered berries, fished, hunted, preserved food, prepared food, acted as domestic servants, paddled canoes, cared for their owner's children, delivered messages, carried burdens, pulled snow sleds, ran errands and acted as servants on ceremonial occasions. This labor was important both for the contribution it made to production (in procuring and preserving food) and in freeing owners to pursue the more prestigious activities of Titleholders. In addition, slaves were economically important as items of value in the extensive trade networks found throughout the area. Finally, although quantitative data are poor, the numbers of slaves were not inconsequential: in some communities slaves probably made up at least 20 and at times, perhaps, up to 30 percent of the population.[12]

The traditional view, which essentially overlooks slavery as a significant institution in Northwest Coast societies, thus ignores one of the most critical things we should remember about them — that they practiced, in an important way, the institution that carries inequality in human affairs to its greatest extreme. One might as well write a history of the antebellum South omitting mention of slaves there on the grounds that they were not members of plantation-owning families.[13]

The following summary by Harold Driver represents the orthodox view of anthropologists about rank among non-slaves on the Northwest Coast:

In respect to differences in rank of freemen, all anthropologists agree that most freemen were carefully ranked from highest to lowest according to wealth and heredity. The two always went hand in hand because the most valuable kinds of property were inherited. Freemen were carefully scaled according to rank at potlatch feasts in four ways: they were seated, served, and given presents to take home in order of rank, and the value of the present was correlated with the order of rank . . . Because the same persons attended many potlatches every year, this carefully calibrated order of rank was confirmed publicly again and again. (1961:389)

Driver goes on to write that in all probability the ranking of individuals was fairly stable before contact times, with only occasional shifts in position by particularly lucky or unlucky individuals. After European contact, however, mobility in rank supposedly was greatly increased. One reason for such increased upward mobility was increased economic activities, which made it easier for individuals to accumulate wealth; and a second reason was drastic population decline (largely due to newly introduced diseases), which created relatively more openings for fewer competitors. Driver goes on to note that there is some controversy as to whether or not there are or are not "social classes" among those he calls "freemen." He puts the controversy down to confusion about variation from village to village. Within some communities all freemen seem to have had some sort of title, within other communities there were clearly "nobles"—who held titles, and commoners—who did not (1961:389–90).

There are considerable difficulties with this conventional interpretation of Driver and others. In the first place, to my knowledge no one has ever attempted to demonstrate the actual existence of a rank order of all the non-slaves in a community in any concrete case except for Boas' southern Kwakiutl. Many other communities are known to have had ranked titles associated with potlatching (among other things), and the assumption has been that these must have worked much like the southern Kwakiutl system. However, a careful reading of the ethnographic accounts of other Northwest Coast groups fails to reveal good evidence (often *any* evidence) for an overall Kwakiutl style rank order. And, as Driver acknowledges, there is good evidence for a two-part division of non-slaves in many Northwest Coast communities.

For example, Verne Ray noted that for almost all Northwest Coast groups there is a name in the indigenous language for the commoner group. Thirteen of seventeen of the groups represented on Drucker's Culture Element Distribution List for the northern and central parts of the culture area have such a named class of commoners; and other ethnographic sources also indicate the near universal presence of commoners as a named social group (1956:165).[14] In his short paper Ray made a vigorous case for the presence of distinct social classes on the Northwest Coast (1956).

Ray was promptly slapped down by the defenders of Boasian orthodoxy, by Robert Lowie, for instance, who had never researched anywhere in the culture area (1956), and by Helen Codere, who had worked mainly with Boas' southern Kwakiutl materials. In contrast, most of Ray's ethnographic studies were in the southern part of the culture area. Shortly after the Ray-Lowie-Codere exchange, Wayne Suttles examined the possibility of social classes among the Coast Salish, who live south of the Kwakiutl along the Gulf of Georgia and Puget Sound. He concluded that these peoples had distinct social classes. He did suggest, however, that the free "lower class" was quite small and relatively unimportant and he accepted Codere's non-class view of the southern Kwakiutl as correct (1958). The rank without class view of Northwest Coast society in this fashion prevailed.

But Codere's view of an integrated overall ranking of non-slave southern Kwakiutl and a lack of a two class division of non-slaves can also be challenged. Even Boas himself, in the quote above, described southern Kwakiutl society and the other societies of the Pacific Coast as "divided into a nobility, common people, and slaves." Codere would dismiss this and other similar statements of Boas in favor of what she considers his later (1920) "definitive" view of the southern Kwakiutl as "classless." For her the following paragraph represented Boas' mature and final position on the subject:

> It seems to me that the conditions among the Kwakiutl and the Nootka must have been quite similar insofar as a sharp line between the nobility and the common people did not exist. In one Kwakiutl tale, it is even stated that the youngest of five brothers "was not taken care of by his father and was like a slave or a dog". (1940:361, cited in Codere 1957:482)

We should note that Boas' comments concerned a dictated text, not a set of observations of the actual workings of Kwakiutl society. And if we examine the full narrative he cites (Boas 1921:1097), several interesting points emerge. In Kwakiutl society, according to their oral traditions, titles and other property were transmitted by the rule of primogeniture (the eldest inheriting first and most). And the youngest of the five brothers in this story was treated badly, not because he was the youngest, but because he was the *fifth* child. Only the first four of a Titleholder's children could properly inherit titles and thus rank.[15] The use of the number four here is a reminder of another important point often overlooked in discussions of southern Kwakiutl—rank had a sacred quality, it represented power (religious or spiritual as well as social and economic) and it did not devolve without limitations to a person's heirs. A man had only so much of the stuff associated with rank that he could transmit to his offspring. When that was done (and the limit was four partitions) his other children could receive no sacred inheritance from him. Such unfortunate offspring were still a man's children and were remained members of his kin group, but from a Titleholder's perspective they were like dogs or slaves—*this great was the distinction between Kwakiutl titleholder and commoner*.[16]

Why does late nineteenth-century ethnographic data appear to support the notion that the southern Kwakiutl had rank without class? There are at least two reasons. First, as noted by Harold Driver and many others, immediately after contact there was a precipitant decline in the population of all Northwest Coast groups, including the Kwakiutl. Suddenly there were more titles than persons to fill them, so nearly all nonslaves could become Titleholders. Second, Boas' interpretations were biased by the fact that he obtained his information largely from Titleholders and thereby reflected their views of Kwakiutl institutions (see Kroeber 1956:151).

In summary, traditional Northwest Coast societies were the antithesis of the egalitarianism that dominates the orthodox image of the native societies of North America. This is true in two specially important ways. First, these societies practiced slavery, not in a casual or minor way but as a major feature of their political and economic activities; and, second, the nonslave part of the population was divided into two major social strata, one of which—Titleholders—had numerous material, political, and spiritual advantages, which the the Commoners were denied.

East and north of the Northwest Coast's inegalitarian societies lived groups of Athapaskan speaking peoples. At the time of first contact with Europeans these hunting-gathering populations of interior Alaska, the Yukon region, and northern British Columbia exemplified the features of egalitarian values and institutions thought to be distinctive of "band-level" peoples who forage for their subsistence.

In this interior region resources available for exploitation by hunting are scanty and dispersed, so the presence of small traditional societies here is not surprising. Both the Noble Savage image and anthropological theory about low productivity hunter gatherers predict egalitarian social systems for the area. Yet we now have good evidence that at least one cluster of societies in this region was far from egalitarian. Because of the careful ethnographic and ethnohistoric research of Dominique Legros we can now see that among the Tutchone in the southeast Yukon social inequality was significant and prominent.[17]

Legros's reconstruction of Tutchone social life begins in the mid-nineteenth century. At that time, he notes, Tutchone society was "still free from any significant and direct Euroamerican economic, political, and cultural meddling" (1985:38). The Tutchone then had the simplest of subsistence technologies. This included traps and deadfalls used to take land mammals, and nets and weirs used to capture their most predictable and abundant resource, salmon. Such subsistence techniques supported a population of about 1,100 people, divided into some seventy localized "resource exploitation groups." Obviously these seventy groups on average were small: a third consisted of a single nuclear family, and another third probably contained no more than two such. Fewer than a dozen of these groups were—by Tutchone standards—large, containing ten or so nuclear families.

Interestingly for foraging peoples, the Tutchone were matrilineal, and they were organized as strictly exogamous matrilineal moieties—socially defined halves named Raven and Wolf. Within each moiety the taboo on marriage, even on any potential sexual encounter, was strictly enforced. However, marriage and sexual relations were possible between Ravens and Wolves—members of opposite moieties—irrespective of generation or genetic closeness. For example, a Raven man could marry or engage in sex with his father's mother or brother's daughter because they were in the opposite moiety, therefore, by Tutchone reckoning, not closely related.

Though they were members of different moieties, Father/Daughter marriage and sex were not much favored, though Legros has recorded some cases of Father/Daughter marriages that were allowed to stand. The preferred form of marriage was with a bilateral cross-cousin.[18] These technical details of Tutchone kinship and marriage must be emphasized because such forms of marriage are generally associated with simple, egalitarian societies (Levi-Strauss 1969). Nonetheless, what Legros has shown is that not only was inequality important among the Tutchone, but that those who dominated others did so in part by successfully manipulating the culturally ideal practice of bilateral cross-cousin marriage!

Tutchone society was divided into three ranked strata: the "rich," the "poor," and the "slaves." Rich families made up about 15 percent of the whole population. Rich families formed the core of the ten or so largest local resource exploitation groups; they controlled the best resource sites[19]; and they monopolized trade with the Tlingit of the Northwest Coast culture area to the south. Poor families comprised about 75 percent of the population. They were either attached to a rich leader's group or lived in very small groups (one or two nuclear families) in the poorer resource areas. Legros calls the former the "dependent poor" and the latter the "autonomous poor." Finally, slaves made up about 10 percent of the population. Not surprisingly, all slaves belonged to rich Tutchone.

The rich dominated and exploited both poor and slave. Although there was a little social mobility, rich status was largely inherited, so that the rich were able to pass their advantages on to their children. The lesson of this case is that even in conditions that seem ideal for the presence of the classic egalitarian Indian society, it is possible for marked inequalities to emerge. As Legros says:

> The Tutchone case demonstrates that socioeconomic inequalities may be present among hunter-gatherers even in one of the harshest environments in the world. Tutchone population density was one of the lowest known anywhere, and its spatial distribution was characteristic of the simplest societies of hunters and gatherers. Their production techniques, their products, and the goods they exchanged had nothing exceptional. Yet, they were divided into socioeconomic strata. A few rich families monopolized the best extraction sites and access to extra-local trade, and defended their monopoly through the use of naked force. Moreover, these families used the resources they had appropriated to further exploit poor families, going so far as to make some poor individuals their slaves in the full sense of the word. (1985:62)

These examples and the discussion show that many traditional native American societies simply do not fit the conventional image of egalitarian tribal peoples, a representation that has long dominated both anthropology and popular thought about Indians. The contrary illustrations used come largely from two areas of the continent, but other cases from different regions could be used as well, as in the Upper Mississippi Valley and in the Northeastern Woodlands culture areas. However, there is no need to over-react and claim that equality existed in no Indian society. Certainly, many native American societies fit the egalitarian model. My conclusion is straightforward and broader. If we deliberately set aside the dominant stereotype and carefully examine historical and ethnographic facts about Indian societies on an explicit equality/ inequality scale, we find a great deal more variation in aboriginal North America than is usually recognized.

Why, then, has the Baron Lahontan's egalitarian image of the Noble Savage persisted? Why has the evidence of inequality been ignored, overlooked or played down? There are at least three major sets of reasons. The first is the outcome of systematic methodological—especially an ahistorical and non-contextual—bias. The second represents the persistent influence of the Noble Savage tradition and its modern progeny. The third comes from a weak, underdeveloped theory of inequality. And these are now augmented by the recent rise of the native rights movements as a significant political force. These elements are not mutually exclusive. On the contrary they have often interacted with one another; but we can now look at each in turn.

The methodological and ahistorical bias was rampant in the time of the earliest proper ethnographers—of Lewis Henry Morgan's mid-nineteenth century generation—more so among the earliest keen observers of Indians during the seventeenth and eighteenth centuries. By the time even the latter came on the scene as witnesses all native North American societies had experienced and were undergoing dramatic social and cultural change. There had been substantial declines in population, for instance, and native populations had been displaced from vital resource bases, reshuffled, and combined. Moreover, Euroamerican expansion and settlement had meant an end to their political-economic independence.

For the more complex, and the more stratified, native societies this usually meant devolution, a breakdown of older institutions into smaller units of living and production. One of the more important aspects of this devolution was a leveling of social, political, and economic differences. By Lahontan's and James Adair's times, the native peoples they knew first-hand had come to share a new political status; while by Morgan's time they were sharing their poverty in common.[20] Until recently most ethnographers have given little attention to available historical material when describing native cultures. Similarly, they have not taken into disciplined consideration the larger contemporary social and economic context in which their own research was conducted. Instead, they have assumed that what they found in the memories of living informants was a secure basis for describing "traditional society," little influenced by past or present political and economic currents, or the informants' own position in their communities. The effects of drastic social change and devolution as likely influences on their informants' accounts and perspective were scarcely considered. However, as the interdisciplinary field of ethnohistory has developed and better use is made of the often rich historical record, many older views of aspects of native life have had to be revised. Faulty generalizations about the egalitarian Indian are obviously among these.

As we have seen, the durable Noble Savage image has remained a standard stereotype—a cliché that represents the eternal Indian. So powerful has this cliché been that many supposedly objective observers were overly prone to seeing egalitarian, liberty-loving Indians, free of the vices of property and class distinction where the opposite often was true. Morgan's career exemplifies this. His early interest in native peoples was that of a devoted, practicing Indian hobbyist. Only later did he work out the beginnings of a scientific approach to studies of native cultures. And when he did his earlier assumptions carried over into his evolutionary model and his interpretations. So his studies of the New York Iroquois and his comparative researches reported in *Ancient Society* gave a seemingly "scientific" boost to the image of the Noble Savage.

Morgan, and a good many other scholars who followed in his tracks, never purged their thinking of the images fashioned by the Baron Lahontan and other Euroamericans born of the Enlightenment. For them the Indian remained a foil on which they impaled the faults of their own "civilization," imperfections as defined by themselves, fitting the forms of alienation characteristic of their times. Just as Enlightenment thinkers were opponents of absolutist monarchies, Morgan was an American democrat opposed to aristocracy. Moreover, as Elisabeth Tooker points out in chapter 6, Morgan thought and wrote in an era when American intellectuals were determined to construct a history of their nation as separate from that of Europe as possible. Significantly, images of Indians untrammeled by restrictions on their liberty, by inequities in their societies, and by conflict in their relationships became part of that invented tradition. Though he lived in a different era, like Lahontan before him Morgan used distorted depictions of native American social and political forms to contrast the idyllic way of life of the Savage with the corrupt, degraded life of those who enjoyed the finest benefits of Civilization.[21]

In the century following Morgan's pioneering studies, anthropological theorists have not displayed a strong interest in structured social inequality, particularly so among those societies once called "primitive," that is, those classified as bands and tribes. Almost all treatments of political, social, and economic hierarchy have been limited to centralized states, which is to say those commonly classified as "civilized." That states are divided like layer-cakes and shaped like pyramids with the icing of both power *and* wealth concentrated at the peak has become an anthropological truism.

Implicit in this assumption has been the belief that economic inequality and the state are invariably and inseparably linked. As ideal types opposite to the "the state" anthropologists have cast generalized portraits of "the tribe": the state is stratified, the tribe egalitarian. That this conviction is an inheritance from the Enlightenment's own Noble Savage tradition should be obvious. If centralized political authority and economic inequity are strongly linked, where hierarchies of power are absent we would not expect to find wide differences in access to and ownership of resources either. This unquestioned conventional view has predisposed anthropologists to expect no significant structured social inequalities in native American societies. Why not? Because in North America, at least during the historic era, we find exceedingly little political hierarchy and only weak political authority in any traditional society. In short, the state was probably absent in Native North America and even weak political authority of the chiefdom type was relatively rare. Thus the misleading logical leap: no native American societies could have been other than egalitarian.

Could the same factors with respect to the "state in native America" be operating as we found with respect to "inequality in native America"? This is an empirical question, an issue of careful definition and then factual inquiry. Interestingly enough, the answer is probably no. As we have seen, there is ample evidence of *social* stratification in some indigenous North American societies. But it is difficult to make a good case for centralized political *institutions* anywhere among historic native peoples there. Political authority seems to have been fairly weak everywhere on the continent.

To take but one example, the legitimate power of the so-called "chiefs" on the Northwest Coast was so weak and circumscribed that, as Drucker has argued, actors playing such roles had little authority over people outside their own kin group, even among *non-kin within* their own community. Even less so did their power reach *beyond* the local community (Drucker 1983). This is why I have preferred to label such roles Titleholders rather than "chiefs." Both the ethnographic and ethnohistoric evidence support Drucker on this point, just as it does not confirm his conclusions with respect to social stratification. The hypothesis which defines a necessary universal link between the political state and economic stratification is wrong. The cultures of Native North America supply ample examples which falsify it.

Unfortunately, in anthropological studies of Indians this theory has been largely implicit and applied automatically, rather than being made explicit and tested. Rather than rethinking and revising the theory, anthropologists have generally ignored the data. This tendency has been strongly reinforced by the vitality of the Noble Savage image in Europe (see chapter 16), in Canada, and in the United States (see chapters 7, 10, and 17). Wherever the Indian is evoked today, a descendent of Lahontan's Adario emerges as a powerful figure on the political and philosophical agendas of anyone concerned with modern problems about liberty, equality, and fraternity, just as he was a vital and useful image in the minds of eighteenth-century European Enlightenment thinkers. And today, with native Americans achieving positions of much greater cultural and political influence than formerly, some of them are as apt to take and play the part of Noble Savages as are journalists, novelists, film-makers, and politicians to replay the image.

Whatever one's political perspective, it is necessary to recognize the risks of false images, however old and popular, much less false consciousness based on false images, however old and popular. This is why recognition of inequality in some native American societies is important. This is as true for ordinary citizens interested in alternative models of social living as it is for academics, who need to get their theories and facts straight. Not only must we recognize what actually was true of traditional Indian societies in all their varieties, but we need to uncouple marked social and economic inequality from the peculiar institutions of the state, with its centralization of political power. There is an important practical as well as a theoretical lesson in the Tutchone case. Great economic and social inequality and the exploitation of human beings by other human beings can arise under the most unpromising political and environmental circumstances, with no Priest-King, Emperor or Czar, not even a popularly elected President or Prime Minister, or even a Bureaucrat present to take the blame.

Notes

1. When Dryden first coined the phrase "Noble Savage" in this epic, his reference was to the Moor, Almanzor's opposition to the Spanish during the reconquest. However, the Noble Savage was soon found populating the Americas and other more remote, recently discovered parts of the world. For an introduction to the literature about images of the Indian in European thought, see Marshall and Williams 1982 and Dickason 1984. See also chapters 16 and 17.
2. Italics and capitalization in original.
3. So popular did this literary contrivance become and remain that it has been named "the Adario motif." The Adario figure consists of an fictionalized Indian, preferably a wise old Indian, who declaims at length on the failings of Euroamericans. For a discussion of the Adario motif, see Adams 1976 and 1983:234–36. It has been suggested that Lahontan's Adario was based on a real Huron leader named Kondiaronk. If this is the case, Kondiaronk's known career is in sharp contrast to Lahontan's philosophical Noble Savage. For a factual account see William Fenton's article on Kondiaronk in the *Dictionary of Canadian Biography*.
4. See, for example, the address of a recent president of the *American Society for Ethnohistory*, who declared that, "The native societies of North America were small-scale units characterized by considerable internal equality, self-reliance, and individual consent as a prerequisite for the implementation of public policy" (Trigger 1986:255).
5. For late prehistoric times see the papers by Brown, Larson, and Peebles in Brown 1971.
6. The Archaic ended about 700 B.C.

7. The most recent discussion of the Calusa case, which combines a thorough review of the ethnohistorical data with recent archaeological research, is in essential agreement with Goggin and Sturtevant's interpretation of the evidence for Calusa social inequality (see Marquardt 1988).

8. Swanton 1911; see White, Murdock and Scaglon 1971 for a good discussion of the technical problems involving Swanton's interpretation; see Hudson 1976, especially pages 206–10, for a more accessible account of Natchez class organization.

9. At other seasons, winter village communities were usually dispersed, with members residing at various resource exploitation sites.

10. Ceremonial feasts at which much property was given away to other Title-holders, usually to validate a claim to a title or "name."

11. For documentation of this summary see Donald 1983 and 1984, and sources cited therein.

12. See Donald 1983, Mitchell and Donald 1985 for details and documentation.

13. Ignoring the implications of the presence of slavery in societies otherwise interesting or admirable is rather common in Western culture. Standard views of the ancient Greeks as the founders of Western civilization, inventors of democracy and so on, is only one example. Greek "democracy" sprang up in a society dependent on slave labor (see Finley 1973).

14. Ray's use of Drucker as a source to support the presence of a class division among non-slaves in the culture area is important because Drucker is one of the most important proponents of the "rank without class" position. Drucker's 1939 essay contains his most detailed discussion of the topic, although his position did not change in later publications.

15. Four was a sacred number to the Kwakiutl, and most other native American groups.

16. While southern Kwakiutl descent groups (house groups) all contained both Titleholders and Commoners, in some other Northwest Coast societies (such as Haida or Tlingit) some households were exclusively Titleholder and others Commoner.

17. My account is based entirely on his work; see Legros 1982 and 1985.

18. From a woman's perspective, a man who is simultaneously her father's sister's son and her mother's brother's son is a bilateral cross-cousin.

19. The salmon fishing stations, the sources of native copper, the best beaver hunting areas, and so on.

20. Historians commonly call such results of processes of sociopolitical devolution "the dependency syndrome" (see White 1983:xv–xix).

21. We should not jump to the conclusion that this contrast was all romantic nonsense or merely a result of an excess of political rhetoric. During the colonial and early national periods, many frontier folk were forcibly abducted by Indians and adopted into native societies. Not uncommonly, years later—when offered repatriation—some of these "White Savages" flatly refused, preferring to remain with their Indian families and communities (Axtell 1981). A similar process of ethnic mobility continues today but on a voluntary basis, with numerous formerly "Whites" and "Blacks" assuming "Indian" identities, as discussed in chapters 1, 3 and 14. Also see Clifton 1988: chapters 1, 2, 6, 8, and 12.

References

Adair, James. 1968. *The History of the American Indians*. New York: Johnson Reprint Corporation. [Originally published 1775.]

Adams, Percy G. 1976. "Benjamin Franklin and the Travel Writing Tradition." In *The Oldest Revolutionary: Essays on Benjamin Franklin*. J. A. L. Lemay, ed. 33–50. Philadelphia: The University of Pennsylvania Press.

———. 1983. *Travel Literature and the Evolution of the Novel*. Lexington, KY: University of Kentucky Press.

Axtell, James. 1981. *The European and the Indian: Essays in the Ethnohistory of Colonial North America*. New York: Oxford University Press.

Boas, Franz. 1897. "The Social Organization and Secret Societies of the Kwakiutl Indians." In *Report of the U.S. National Museum for 1895*. Washington: Government Printing Office.

———. 1921. *Kwakiutl Ethnology*. United States Bureau of American Ethnology, Thirty-Fifth Annual Report, Parts 1 and 2.

———. 1940. "The Social Organization of the Kwakiutl." In *Race, Language and Culture*. New York: The Free Press.

———. 1966. *Kwakiutl Ethnography*. Helen Codere, ed. Chicago: University of Chicago Press.

Brown, James A., ed. 1971. "Approaches to the Social Dimensions of Mortuary Practices." *Memoirs of the Society for American Archaeology*, no. 25.

Clifton, James A., ed. 1988. *Being and Becoming Indian: Biographic Studies of North American Frontiers*. Chicago: Dorsey Press.

Codere, Helen. 1957. "Kwakiutl Society: Rank Without Class." *American Anthropologist* 59:473–84.

Dickason, Olive Patricia. 1984. *The Myth of the Savage and the Beginnings of French Colonialism in the Americas*. Edmonton: University of Alberta Press.

Donald, Leland. 1983. "Was Nuu-chah-nulth-aht (Nootka) Society Based on Slave Labor?" In *The Development of Political Organization in Native North America*. Elisabeth Tooker, ed. 1979 Proceedings of The American Ethnological Society.

———. 1984. "The Slave Trade on the Northwest Coast of North America." *Research in Economic Anthropology* 6:121–58.

Driver, Harold E. 1961. *Indians of North America*. Chicago: University of Chicago Press.

Drucker, Phillip. 1939. "Rank, Wealth and Kinship in Northwest Coast Society." *American Anthropologist* 41:55–64.

———. 1983. "Ecology and Political Organization on the Northwest Coast of America." In *The Development of Political Organization in Native North America*. Elisabeth Tooker, ed. 1979 Proceedings of The American Ethnological Society.

Dryden, John. 1664. *The Conquest of Granada*.

Fenton, William N. 1969. "Kondiaronk." *Dictionary of Canadian Biography* 2:320–23.

Finley, Moses. 1973. " Was Greek Civilization Based on Slave Labor?" In *The Slave Economies* 1. Eugene D. Genovese, ed. New York: John Wiley and Sons.

Fried, Morton. 1967. *The Evolution of Political Society*. New York: Random House.

Gearing, Fred. 1962. "Priests and Warriors: Social Structures for Cherokee Politics in the 18th Century." *American Anthropological Association Memoir*, 93.

Goggin, John M. and William C. Sturtevant. 1964. "The Calusa: A Stratified, Nonagricultural Society." In *Explorations in Cultural Anthropology*. Ward H. Goodenough, ed. New York: McGraw-Hill.

Hodge, William. 1981. *The First Americans, Then and Now*. New York: Holt, Rinehart and Winston.

Hudson, Charles. 1976. *The Southeastern Indians*. Knoxville: University of Tennessee Press.

Kroeber, A.L. 1956. "The Place of Boas in Anthropology." *American Anthropologist* 58:151–59.

Legros, Dominique. 1982. "Reflexions sur l'origine des inegalites social a partir du cas de Athapaskan tutchone." *Culture* 2(3):65–84.

———. 1985. "Wealth, Poverty, and Slavery Among 19th-Century Tutchone Athapaskans." *Research in Economic Anthropolgy* 7:37–64.

Lévi-Strauss, Claude. 1969. *The Elementary Structures of Kinship*. Boston: Beacon Press.

Lom d'Arce, Louis-Armand de, Baron de Lahontan. 1905. *New Voyages to North-America*. Rueben Gold Thwaites, ed. Chicago: A.C.McClurg & Co. [original edition 1703].

Lowie, Robert H. 1956. "Boas Once More." *American Anthropologist* 58: 159–64.

Marquart, William H. 1988. "Politics and Production Among the Calussa of South Florida." In *Hunters and Gatherers I: History, Evolution, and Social Change*. T. Ingold, D. Riches, and J. Woodburn, eds. Oxford: Berg.

Marshall, P.J. and Glyndwr Williams. 1982. *The Great Map of Mankind: British Perceptions of the World in the Age of Enlightenment*. London: J.M. Dent & Sons.

Mitchell, Donald and Leland Donald. 1985. "Some Economic Aspects of Tlingit, Haida and Tshimshian Slavery." *Research in Economic Anthropology* 7: 19–35.

Morgan, Lewis Henry. 1964. *Ancient Society*. Leslie White, ed. Cambridge: Harvard University Press [originally published 1877].

Muller, Jon. 1983. "The Southeast." In *Ancient North Americans*. Jesse D. Jennings, ed. San Francisco: W.H.Freeman and Co.

Ray, Verne F. 1956. "Rejoinder." *American Anthropologist* 58:164–70.

Suttles, Wayne. 1958. "Private Knowledge, Morality, and Social Classes Among the Coast Salish." *American Anthropologist* 60:497–506.

Swanton, John R. 1911. *Indian Tribes of the Lower Mississippi Valley and Adjacent Coast of the Gulf of Mexico*. Bureau of American Ethnology Bulletin, no. 43.

Trigger, Bruce G. 1986. "Ethnohistory: The Unfinished Edifice." *Ethnohistory* 33:253–67.

White, Douglas R., George P. Murdock, and Richard Saglion. 1971. "Natchez Class and Rank Reconsidered." *Ethnology* 10:369–88.

White, Richard. 1983. *The Roots of Dependency: Subsistence, Environment, and Social Change among the Choctaws, Pawnees, and Navajos*. Lincoln: University of Nebraska Press.

9

Their Numbers Become Thick: Native American Historical Demography as Expiation

David Henige

To kill an error is as good a service as, and sometimes even better than, the establishing a new truth or fact. (Darwin 1903, 2:422)

Recently a devotee of J.R.R. Tolkien's Middle-Earth cycle bethought himself to estimate the size of the elf population there (Losack 1987). Unfortunately, it appears that no formal count of these creatures survives, forcing the author to extrapolate from certain figures cited in his sources, particularly the reported size of various elf military detachments. In addition he calculated average generations and "typical" family size, adding and deducting various elements of elf society arbitrarily. In the end he determined that at its height the elf population reached one million and then began to decline precipitately.

Sound far-fetched? Not to anyone familiar with recent studies of the contact population of the New World. In this essay I will show that much of this work has chosen to base itself on sources that are not very different from the Tolkien canon and has adopted methods uncannily similar to those used to estimate the elf population of Middle-Earth.

[The Credulous Man] finds most delight in believing strange things, and the stranger they are, the easier they pass with him; but he never regards those that are plain and feasible, for every man can believe such [Butler 1970:265].

The size of the aboriginal population of the Americas was the object of guessing games almost from the Discovery itself, and enjoyed a considerable vogue in the latter part of the eighteenth century (Gerbi 1973: 50–120; Commager and Giordanetti 1967). Still, no earlier interest was as sustained or as extensive as that shown during the past forty years or so. This modern movement was initiated in the 1940s by the so-called Berkeley School—Lesley B. Simpson, Sherburne F. Cook, and Woodrow W. Borah (with Carl O. Sauer as godfather)—and has continued ever since. This work has been extensive, undoubtedly impresses at first sight, and has been extremely influential both within the field of historical demography and in the larger scholarly world.[1]

The systematic distortion of the historical record gained momentum with the Berkeley School and it too continues unabated. At first, the conclusions of the High Counters (as I shall term them) were fairly modest and relied largely on the evidence in the early writings on the conquest of Mexico (and later of Peru, Hispaniola, and Central America). But as their estimates began to spiral dizzily upwards from two million in central Mexico to twenty-five million for the same area, other materials were conscripted into the study, particularly tribute records (for want of a better term) from the pre-Conquest period. Today it is routine for the high counters to advance figures for the entire New World that range upwards of one hundred million, with North America's portion of the whole growing ever greater, and with no end in sight for the spiraling increases.[2]

The High Counters were able to raise their estimate twelvefold in large part because they abandoned sound historical method, which ordains that *all* relevant sources be sought out and studied critically, both textually and contextually; that accepting and rejecting sources be done explicitly; that dissenting points of view be recognized and also dealt with explicity; that sources be cited fully and honestly; and that conclusions be framed as cautiously as the evidence requires. Under these rules of evidence, such statements as "in the absence of any contrary evidence" (Cook and Borah 1971–79, 3:152) become inadmissible when no such evidence can possibly exist. As we will have occasion to notice, though, the High Counters have not conspicuously followed any of these rules, perhaps realizing that to do so would severely hamstring their flights of fancy.

The High Counters have written thousands of pages, and here I can deal only with limited aspects of that production. On the assumption that extraordinary claims require extraordinary evidence, I will concentrate on the High Counters' use of written post-conquest sources and will generally confine my discussion to the works of Simpson, Cook, and Borah, as well as to Henry Dobyns, for this seems to be the direct line of descent of the baton. The presuppositions and techniques behind the High Counters' use of *pre*-conquest materials have been criticized briefly by Henige (1978b) and more extensively by Zambardino (1980).

Along the way, the Berkeley School, like most movements, came to resemble an echo chamber—self-congratulating, self-validating, and exclusionary.[3] Its members have no doubt that they are on the side of the angels and do not expect their views to be nourished by disagreement. Quite the contrary; dissent is not entertained, and critics necessarily speak only from ignorance and want of skill. After all,

> [a] complex and most bewildering series of calculations and adjustments is necessary to make allowance for such matters [how to multiply, how to add]; the calculations and adjustments in turn must be based upon close study of the society, the administrative system, and the circumstances of the making of the count or assessment. It is no wonder that people unacquainted with such techniques or with the methods of historical verification [*sic*] are tempted to dismiss all such studies as mere legerdemain. (Borah 1976:26)

Borah expatiated at some length in this vein, speaking of "the application in full of very elaborate and exacting techniques of verification" and "painstaking reading" of the sources. Finally, in an outburst of irrepressible modesty, he concluded by confessing that the whole enterprise of the High Counters has been firmly anchored in the lofty standards of textual analysis established by the Bollandists and Maurists (Borah 1976:24–25, 33).

All these statements have an unedifying whiff of divine-right-to-be-right pronouncements by a prophet declaiming arcane knowledge vouchafed him by a preternatural being, and the last amounts to a piece of preposterous, if unintended, self-parody. For the High Counters, textual criticism consists in seeking out and then justifying belief in, and *only* in, the very highest numbers in the sources.[4] But at least, as I will argue here, Borah in fact well christened the techniques of the High Counters: "mere legerdemain."

> Know for the truth that in the army there were 300 giants, 163,000 infantry all armed with the skins of hobgoblins, 3,400 men at arms, 3,600 double cannons and arquebusiers without number; 94,000 pioneers, 450,000 prostitutes. . . . (Rabelais 1965:137)

The High Counters often turn for comfort to warrior counts—early estimates of Indian armed forces. The reason is simple enough—such estimates very frequently make their appearance in the historical record. Interpreting warrior counts involves two issues: what proportion of the general population do they represent; and how accurate are they? Comment on the first I defer for the moment. About the second a great deal might be said, far more than is possible here. The technique of the High Counters is occasionally to notice briefly criticisms of warrior counts, peremptorily dismiss them, and hasten to assure readers that they find the counts persuasive. High Counters tend to find them so reasonable in fact that they have no compunction in accepting *any* estimate of Indian armies as reasonably accurate (Henige 1986a:703–8). But they prefer the larger estimates. In the process the High Counters repeatedly grant eyewitness estimates privileged status, though on what grounds can hardly be imagined. Virtually all the several hundred examples of inflated warrior counts from other times and places of which I am aware entered the historical record by way of participants, and there are no reasons to accord eyewitness testimony any more credibility than we might give any other military estimates (e.g., Hollingsworth 1969:227–32).

The Spanish began by having trouble estimating even the small numbers of Guanches in the Canaries—estimates of the population of Gran Canaria ranged from 6,000 to 60,000 (Fernández-Armesto 1982:10–11). For Hispaniola the difficulties only increased (Henige 1978a). In turn, with regard to Mexico, the problems were fewer only than the estimates themselves. Unlike most other students of the subject, the High Counters lend eager ears to these numbers, which are usually in the hundreds of thousands. Those who do not actually regard them as underestimates (e.g., Dobyns 1966:407–8) claim to find them "a faithful and exact portrayal" and "eminently reasonable." (Cook and Simpson 1948:23; Cook and Borah, 1971–1979, 1:9). In doing so they never wonder how the estimates were made, either physically or psychologically, which is remarkable in light of both the wide range of discrepancy and particularly in view of the fact that the Spanish chroniclers believed they were recounting the springing to life of the marvelous deeds in the chivalric romances of the time (Leonard 1949; Weckmann 1984:117–223; Fernández-Armesto (1982:208–2ll).

A single example must do here to suggest the dimensions of the problem, but it is an extraordinarily apt one. In one of his numerous estimates of the formidable forces that he must (and did) overcome, Cortés asserted that the enemy numbered "more than 149,000" men. This curious statement forces us to believe that the number was also under 150,000; in other words, Cortés was effectively claiming to be able to estimate within 0.6 percent the size of an army he had never seen before! How was he able to accomplish this miraculous feat? Had the enemy conveniently arrayed itself in formations of exactly 1000, or maybe 149, or even 74.5 each? Or perhaps Cortés merely counted arms and legs and divided by four? Or did the enemy commander carelessly leave behind a roster of men on active duty at that very moment? All possible alternatives? Of course. Any of them attractive? Of course not. Have the High Counters suggested any other possibilities? Not at all. Whence this peculiar number then? Like all the numbers in his dispatches, Cortés offered it on a take-it-or-leave-it basis. But then the High Counters require only the number, not its explanation.

Such numbers of course are no more than metaphors for "a lot," but then "a lot" is not multipliable and affords no basis for extrapolative flights of fancy into the millions (Blázquez Garbajosa 1985). Cortés' estimates were nothing more than one brief tableau in a tapestry reaching back to the time of Ramses II of Egypt and forward to the Iran-Iraq conflict or United States Football League crowd estimates.

To return to the first question posed above—the relationship of army size to population size—we need to know more about the circumstances than we do in this case. Elsewhere Cook (1973:13) had the answer for the New England Indians. Their armies were about one-quarter of the entire population—certainly a reasonable enough figure under most circumstances. But here, it seems, we have the stirrings of a problem. The estimates of army sizes in Mexico, however inflated, are still far too low to serve the High Counters' cause very well. Even if we accept every one of these at face value and we further accept that no Indians were counted twice (or more often), the numbers of Indian soldiers would be less than one twenty-fifth of the population eventually posited for the area by the High Counters.

This embarrassing state of affairs arises because, while the High Counters were increasing their estimates for central Mexico from some two million in 1946 (Cook 1946:98) to over twenty-five million scarcely fifteen years later (Borah and Cook 1963), the warrior counts in the record stubbornly remained the same. To what extent this has given the High Counters pause is anyone's guess since they never discuss their sources critically. But, while they have never publicly disowned reliance on warrior counts, it is not without interest that Cook and Borah (1966:231) eventually decided that maybe, after all, "such materials must be considered of low order of credibility" or were even . . . "unreliable" (Borah 1976:26; cf. Dobyns 1966:407–408).

Our own judgment is, that in his eagerness to make discoveries, our author has done what nearly everybody is sure to do under similar circumstances. He has opened both his eyes and his mouth a little too wide, and swallowed a great deal more than he has sufficiently tasted. (Anonymous 1969:485)

The High Counters (Cook and Simpson 1948:18–22; Cook and Borah 1971–1979, 1:12–13) also rely heavily on baptismal figures to give their estimates respectability—they are the only sources actually to include the magic term "millions." These figures (not records, I emphasize) are embedded in the histories of the Christianization of Mexico written by Toribio de Benavente (better known as Motolinía), Jeronimo de Mendieta, and Juan de Torquemada. As always, the High Counters try hard (e.g., Cook and Borah 1971–1979, 1:12) to convince us that each of these sources constitutes independent corroboration of the others. They do not. Mendieta relied heavily on Motolinía, and Torquemada on both Motolinía and Mendieta (Alcina Franch 1973:267–270; Lopez-Portilla 1979:309–12).

Motolinía began the process by offering several conflicting figures. At one point (Motolinía 1941:118) he estimated that "more than four million" Indians had been baptized between 1521 and 1536. Then, only a few passages later (1941:120–21), he looked again at his information and broke it down "in two ways." First he estimated (1941:120–21) that "about five million" Indians had been baptized "by [Franciscan] friars" and named several, together with the numbers (all well rounded) each allegedly baptized. He then looked at the distribution "by towns and provinces." Dividing New Spain into four regions, he found that, oddly enough, in each of them "more than one million" Indians had been baptized. For good measure, he added that, since the figures for this regional breakdown had been gathered, another half million baptisms had taken place, bringing the two calculations into closer alignment. Then—and this is distinctly odd, to be sure—Motolinía seemed to forget that his last two sets of figures actually duplicated each other, and promptly concluded (1941:121) that "more than nine million" Indians had been baptized.

To explain this the High Counters assure us that Motolinía "thought the [regional] figures too conservative" and so promptly doubled them (Cook and Simpson 1948:20–21; Cook and Borah 1971–1979, 1:12). Again, this is not the case. Motolinía prefaced his statement of nine million with "therefore" ("por manera que") indicating that in his mind—erroneously—that figure emanated directly from his earlier calculations and not from any doubts.

When his turn came, Mendieta (1870:275) unlike the High Counters was not taken in by Motolinía's shaky arithmetic. He noted that Motolinía had stated that "about five million" Indians had been baptized by 1536, and added that by 1540 another million had been added to the total, but provided no details.

Writing much later, and basing himself explicity on Motolinía and Mendieta, Torquemada (1977, 5:237) had some strange things to say. He cited Motolinía's regional figures almost *verbatim*, but claimed that they covered the period from 1524 to 1540. In other words, by reporting the same numbers but for a different span of years, Torquemada in effect claimed either that there had been no baptisms between 1521 and 1524 or none between 1536 and 1540! Then he added another touch of his own (Torquemada 1977, 5:237): the Franciscans had baptized "another two million . . . in other [but unnamed] provinces and towns." In this way he "corroborated" Mendieta's total of six million.

All in all, this comedy of errors is quite an unconvincing *modus operandi*. Clearly enough, despite his claims of "actual counts," Motolinía had no such thing at his disposal. In his turn Torquemada's tortuous efforts to bring various figures into harmony led him to offer self-contradictory claims. Interestingly, though, however slavishly he followed Motolinía's procedures, Torquemada was no more inclined than Mendieta to accept Motolinía's figure of nine million. On the other hand, the High Counters (Cook and Borah 1971–1979, 1:12–13) profess to see "nothing improbable" in even that high figure.

The arithmetical skills exhibited by Motolinía and his followers are not likely to impress skeptics, but Henry Dobyns is no skeptic. As an indication of the vast numbers of Indians available for baptism, Dobyns (1966:405) approvingly cited several cases where Motolinía justified his high figures (even Motolinía seems to have doubted them!) by providing examples of hard working friars baptizing everyone in sight. Motolinía (1941:126) related one case where two priests baptized 14,200 Indians in five days, or one Indian per priest per minute for the entire five days. For Dobyns this "rings true." Dobyns is even willing (Dobyns 1966:405) to credit that a single priest could have baptized 14,000 Indians in a single day—one baptism every six seconds non-stop! Motolinía himself made no greater claim than that a single hardy priest had baptized 10,000 Indians one busy day, or a more leisurely pace of one baptism every 8.5 seconds. Putting his predecessors to shame, Dobyns concluded (1966:405) in a whirlwind of extrapolative energy that "sixty priests would [*sic*] have baptized 2,184,000 Indians annually." The mind boggles.

But enough of this. We could ask how many times some Indians were baptized or why the missionaries' estimates were always so vaguely rounded off to the nearest million or why (or whether) the missionaries believed what they wrote, but there seems little point to that. In the context of the times, of themselves, and of the procedures they describe, the baptismal figures do not abide scrutiny. They are, more than anything else, paeans to the power of the Holy Spirit and, as such, useful indicators only of the mental world in which the missionaries operated.[5]

But if it is difficult to understand the High Counters' credulity, it is even harder to explain their constant massaging of the baptism figures. As they stand in the historical record, these figures are, quite like the warrior counts, an embarrassment to the High Counters' own figures, which actually serve to indict the missionaries for inefficiency. But this is only the last of several puzzling features that beset recent use of baptismal figures by the High Counters.[6]

> It [Oz] has nine thousand, and fifty-four buildings, in which lived fifty-seven thousand three hundred and eighteen people. (Baum 1910:29)

In addition to estimating numbers of living persons the Spanish were fond of estimating numbers of dwellings and even the number of skulls they encountered. Since neither houses nor skulls move about while being counted, we might expect that discrepancies in estimating them would be few and minor. Surprisingly (not surprisingly?) this proves not to be the case. In a passage that mixes misleading statements with an unconscious candor more characteristic of the earlier than the later work of the High Counters, Cook and Simpson (1948:31) addressed the problem with respect to Tenochtotlán:

> Firmly embedded in the historical literature is the statement that the city contained 60,000 houses, which would imply a population of 300,000. This estimate first appears in Gómara . . . No explicit statement of the sort, however, is contained in the letters of Cortés, the True History of Bernal Díaz, the narrative of the Anonymous Conqueror, or in Andrés de Tapia.

Cook and Simpson then went on to cite two seventeenth-century estimates, one that Tenochtotlán contained 80,000 houses in 1519, the other 120,000.

What are we to make of this? Surely a statement that appears in *no* primary source can hardly be described as "firmly" embedded in the historical literature." Nor are we told just what constitutes "the historical literature" in question, only what does not. Cook and Simpson fail to cite a single source besides Gómara in which the figure 60,000 appears.

Cook and Simpson then proceed to discuss various (and varying) estimates of the population of towns contiguous to Tenochtotlán, reducing or increasing these figures at will in order to produce a figure they deem acceptable, all without a single demonstrably accurate datum. Their effort in this respect highlights one difficulty in interpreting dwelling counts: the identity of that which is being counted. As Cook and Simpson note (but only to further their own calculations), the cities around the lake of Texcoco form a conurbation in which it is extremely difficult to distinguish city 'boundaries' when estimating, so we cannot assume that each chronicler was defining "Tenochtotlán" or "Texcoco" or any other place name in consistent fashion. The same applies for other parts of Mexico, where it is often impossible to know whether a reference is to a town or its region. When in doubt, the High Counters have been wont to accept the highest count and then apply it to the smallest possible unit, thereby ensuring the extrapolation of the highest possible number.[7]

The High Counters have not attempted a comprehensive canvass of dwelling estimates; presumably such a study would only turn up further unwelcome discrepancies.[8] What does seem clear is that when estimates agree with each other, one of them is textually dependent on the other, rendering the agreement meaningless.

In turn, in his study of Timucuan population, Dobyns is not averse to squeezing all he can—and then some—some from the less than a handful of estimates of Timucuan town sizes that are available (Henige 1986a:707, 715). In fact Dobyns (1983:209) goes so far as to take a single estimate of a single village to extrapolate the size of the entire Timucuan population. In general the practice is becoming more widespread, even when it involves accepting a single observation or one (or the average) of several discrepant estimates and then conjecturing about the average number of persons per dwelling, average dwellings per town, average towns per polity, etc.

Something must be said about such averaging, a technique which of course is commonplace in historical demography as a means of "reconciling" ranges of figures. To the extent that the figures involved are known to be accurate, averaging has a place—must have a place. But for the New World, averaging merely replaces several unknowns with another unknown and at the same time suppresses the reality of discrepant estimates. The notion that averages are really a species of Golden Mean (e.g., Cook and Simpson 1948:30–34) is nonsensical. No figure in a range may be correct, or the entire range may be too high or too low. In these circumstances averaging is just an expedient to mask the notionality of the numbers being averaged.

Finally, we must bear in mind that the Spanish habit of estimating dwellings in urban settings was in a long-established tradition, a tradition that also had a long-standing history of being inaccurate. Whether we turn to European estimates of their own cities or their estimates of the cities of alien societies or other peoples' estimates of European cities, we find consistent patterns of over estimation and hyperbole; the estimates are victims of culture contact.[9]

> Let us estimate the number of cannibals at a minimum, say 4,000. Say that each one ate one person a month; and we arrive at a total of 48,000 persons eaten during one year . . . If to this we add those killed in battle, drowned, starved to death, devoured by wild beasts . . . we arrive at a population of [two million] [Ellenberger 1912:225].

The theme of human sacrifice also figured prominently in the accounts of the chroniclers, whether secular or clerical. How could it not, when it provided the strongest possible rationale for the conquest of Mexico? Oddly, though, there are only two estimates (Cook 1946:88–89) of the numbers of skulls in the pyramids that purportedly dotted the landscape of Mexico in 1519. Bernal Díaz provided the first. Cook (1946:88) quoted him as writing of one town: "there were piles of human skulls so regularly arranged that one could count them, and I estimated them at more than one hundred thousand." Actually, Bernal (Díaz del Castillo 1982:116) was slightly more cautious than this, saying only that "it appeared to me that there were more than one hundred thousand skulls." If they were as easily calculable as Bernal said they were, why did he not do so? And was it not thoughtful of the Indians to have accumulated such a nice round number of skulls just in time for the Spanish to count them? The other, and slightly more notorious, estimate is that Andrés de Tapia (Tapia 1866:583) made of the rack of skulls in the main temple in Tenochtotlán. Tapia arrived at a figure of 136,000 skulls and the High Counters (Cook 1946:88–89; Cook and Borah 1971–1979, 1:11–12; Borah:231–232) have had no trouble at all in accepting this. In doing this they overlook at least one early demonstration (García 1902:xiii) that Tapia's estimate was impossibly high. Still, the beguiling character of large numbers is nowhere more graphically illustrated, and the Tapia count has also led to no end of silliness by cultural materialists (Harner 1977; Harris 1977:107–110; compare Price 1978 and Sahlins 1978) hoping to show that the Aztecs were so driven by a protein deficiency that they dined on their fellows in exceedingly large helpings.

In criticizing the cultural materialists Ortiz de Montellano (1983) points out (in contradiction to Cook, who could "see no reason for not accepting their figures at face value") that in the circumstances it is only surprising that no more than two exaggerated accounts have come down to us.[10] Cook and Borah (1966:232), though, think of these estimates as "sober and serious." If the High Counters had familiarized themselves with other reactions of Europeans to real and alleged practices of human sacrifice in the non-European world, perhaps they might have reconsidered.[11]

> When you write again, cite fairly the Records and Authorities you make use of, and endeavour to find out the genuine and just sense of them; and abuse not, nor trouble the World by currupting them with false, partial, factious, and opinionative Glosses [Brady 1684:325].

A trait shared widely among the High Counters is the unscholarly practice of heaping praise on each other while ignoring or dismissing uncongenial sources and unwelcome criticism. Thus the detailed on-site inspections of Alonso de Zorita are stigmatized (Cook and Borah 1960:13) as "partisan" because Zorita observed that the *encomenderos* tended to overstate the number of Indians under their control, whereas the High Counters much prefer to see these numbers as undercounts.

But perhaps the most interesting example of the ostrich at work is the High Counters' treatment of Bernal Díaz del Castillo. As the author of one of the most extended accounts of the conquest of Mexico and adjacent areas, Bernal must at all costs be shown to be embraced by those intent on ascribing high populations to the area. No problem. Cook and Simpson (1948:23; cf. Cook and Borah 1971–1979, 1:23) are more than happy to credit Bernal's account as being "full of firsthand observation which supplements the statements of Cortés to an extraordinary degree" and go on to claim that "the testimony of two such experienced witnesses must be accepted . . . as probably coming fairly close to the truth." To drive the point all the way home, they go on (Cook and Simpson 1948:23) to assert that "the size of Indian armies . . . as stated throughout [*sic*] the accounts of Cortés and Bernal Díaz, corresponds with the values given for the preceding decades by native historians."

This sounds promising; but wait, why do we then find that Bernal's testimony is used rather sparingly by the High Counters? After being cited for one set of figures (Cook and Simpson 1948:24)—which were only one-third as large as those Cortés cited for the same incident— Bernal virtually disappears from the writings of the High Counters, to reappear (Cook and Borah 1971–1979, 1:11) only as a kind of ancillary witness to the din created by the large crowds in the marketplace of Tenochtotlán. The reason for this erratic treatment becomes apparent as soon as we look at what Bernal really said. We then find that he is not the comfortable bedfellow of Cortés or Gómara that the High Counters imply. Nor would he likely have welcomed their brief if warm embrace.

In fact Bernal was scathingly critical of Gómara's account of the conquest and so, by inference, of Cortés' version, and his numbers are always very much smaller.[12] More to the point, Bernal was repeatedly critical of one particular aspect of Gómara's account, his propensity for

. . . high numbers. Early in his narrative Bernal (Díaz del Castillo 1982:34) charged that Gómara's version of things was "very much contrary" to what really happened, especially when he wrote of "great cities and such large numbers of their inhabitants" and that Gómara would just as soon write "eight thousand" as "eight." Eventually, tiring of criticizing Gómara at every juncture, Bernal offered a final portmanteau critique. There he was intent on pointing out that Gómara was wrong to attribute to Cortés alone things that his whole force had accomplished. Once again, he castigated Gómara (1982:296) for his habit of exaggerating numbers:

> This chronicler says that so many thousands of Indians encountered us on the expedition and such high numbers have no rhyme or reason. And he also speaks of cities and towns and villages in which were so many thousands of houses, when there was not a fifth part of them . . . He would as soon write one [or eight] thousand as eighty thousand. By this boasting he believes that his history will be pleasing to those who hear it, by not saying what really happened.[13]

These are strange words indeed from someone whom the High Counters represent as "supplementing to an extraordinary degree" the very historian whom he criticized so severely.

Bernal Díaz's fate at the hands of the High Counters exemplifies, but scarcely exhausts, their penchant for tendentious selection and characterization of the materials they choose to use and abuse. There can be no doubt that the High Counters were quite aware of Bernal's true feelings about the size of the population of central Mexico. Since they could not afford to ignore him altogether, they distorted his views beyond recognition with heavy-handed artfulness. Despite their efforts, Bernal remains a Banquo at their feast, a hovering presence that can be ignored but not exorcised.

The original is unfaithful to the translation. (Borges 1974:732)

No one would deny that translating is an art that can abide no timeless or straightforward rules, but there are general principles under translators ordinarily operate. The most important of these, but one of which the High Counters seem not to be aware, enjoins that any translation reflect the general linguistic usage of the time, as well as that of the author. Another axiom of translating, which the High Counters seem to understand more thoroughly, is that even the slightest twist in the interpretation of a word or phrase can have significant ripple effects.

With this in mind I would like to examine several instances of translations that do not bear scrutiny well.

As I have noted elsewhere (Henige 1978a:220n), Cook and Borah (1971–1979, 1:378) saw fit to translate Columbus' phrase "mayor que," which he used to compare the *size* of Hispaniola with that of England, as "more populous." Since they were far more interested in numbers of people than in numbers of square miles, they found this a handy way to suggest that Columbus had discerned a population in Hispaniola exceeding that in England. Columbus was wrong in thinking that Hispaniola was larger than England, and Cook and Borah were just as wrong in suggesting that Columbus was referring to people. The degree of calculation in each error is best left to the imagination. In his litany of baptism statistics Motolinía (1971:108) referred to one of his regions as "pueblos de la Mar del Sur." This is rather ambiguous, but not so ambiguous as to justify translating it as "South Sea coast," which was exactly what Cook and Simpson (1948:20) decided was most appropriate. Certainly it was useful for their own argument because it allowed them to claim that Motolinía excluded "most of Oaxaca, parts of Guerrero, and much of Michoacán," forcing them to add 3.9 million to the totals they had devised from Motolinía's figures (Cook and Simpson 1948:22). In their haste to aggregate, they neglected to mention that Torquemada, who followed Motolinía very closely, rendered (Torquemada 1977, 5:237) Motolinía's phrase as "Michoacán and Matltzinco, which is the valley of Toluca, with their provinces," thereby including at least Michoacán in Motolinía's totals.

Recognizing a useful tactic, Henry Dobyns has proved to be the equal of the Berkeley School in the art of Mystical Translation. In fact, in his *Their Number Become Thinned*, he has managed to surpass them in the sustained application of the rule that a little mistranslation can go a long way.[14] But Dobyns' record is longer than this. In his attempt to calculate the ratio of depopulation for the entire New World Dobyns treated the reader to several examples of this tactic. For instance, he asserted (Dobyns 1966:405) that in 1609 a Spanish soldier "saw a total of sixteen million baptisms . . . recorded in a Franciscan convent at Xochimilco." This conjures up an image of huge registers filling room after room with substantiable details of Indian baptisms—certainly a source to be reckoned with by those who would doubt the wisdom of believing in the calculating ability of Motolinía and others. But this was not quite what Dobyns' source said. Quiros stated (Fernández de Quiros 1609 and 1866:507) that he "saw written in a convent . . . that the friars alone baptized sixteen million Indians."

"Recorded" and "written" are not synonyms. Recording is a specialized form of writing and implies (as Dobyns must have known) a certain procedure of registering data in detail and/or on the spot.[15] Quiros may have seen register after register, but all he said was that he had seen something written to the effect that sixteen million Indians had been baptized. It would be possible but pointless to chronicle the further adventures of the High Counters in the land of translating, but a systematic campaign to deploy mistranslations as a means to persuade doubters is evident. It betokens a contempt for both their sources and their readers.

> I have shown in many instances, how partial you have been in your Citations, taking some fragments, or parcels of Sentences, or sometimes a short Sentence you thought might serve your turn, and always leaving what you could not but know would have destroyed your Notion or Argument [Brady 1684:325].

The High Counters' practice of the genteel art of decontextualization brings to mind Ronald Reagan's question: "Where is the rest of me?" Reading a citation or quotation in the writings of the High Counters is sometimes reminiscent of perusing a movie ad or a blurb for a best-seller—it really isn't all there. Even the ellipses are missing . . . As far as I can tell, Henry Dobyns is in a class by himself as far as wrenching materials from any context but his own preconceptions. Already in 1966 Dobyns (1966:405) cited Motolinía's nine million baptisms without indicating that Motolinía had offered other, lower, figures as well. By eliminating Motolinía's self-contradictions Dobyns presumably hoped to make this excessively high figure more appealing by masquerading it as Motolinía's only guess.

In his study of the Timucuan Indians and beyond, Dobyns suffers from what might be called *hambre*-phobia; that is, he goes to great lengths to expunge any mention of hunger in his allusions to the historical record. This aversion seem to be in aid of thrusting onto center stage the notion of epidemics (discussed below) as the chief cause of depopulation. At any rate, whenever the sources specify hunger as the sole or as a contributing factor, Dobyns eliminates it (Henige 1986b), often adding a phrase that makes it appear as though disease was actually cited when it was not.

No example of the High Counters' studied indifference to textual integrity is more outrageous than their handling of Las Casas' estimates of the contact population of Hispaniola. In all, Las Casas made no fewer than twelve of these (Henige 1978a:222–25). Five times he estimated that there had been about one million Indians, another six times that there had been about three million, and once that there had been "many" millions. But if Las Casas was confused, the High Counters seem not to have noticed it. Not one of them (Borah 1964:379; Cook and Borah 1971–1979, 1:376, 386, 393; Borah 1976:14) mentions the figure of one million, including Cook and Borah's extended discussion of the sources for estimating that population.[16]

How can this be? It seems that the High Counters simply stop looking when they find the figures they want. If they discover these before they canvass an entire body of literature, so much the better. If they discover other, lower, figures along the way, no matter either; these are simply ignored. Which of these decidedly non-Bollandist alternatives this case represents is unclear. It might be sheer laziness since the lower figures generally appear in the earlier and less accessible writings of Las Casas. On the other hand, the figure of one million also appears in his *Historia de las Indias*, which Cook and Borah duly cite—for the three million figure.

More than any other discursive strategy, the High Counters' penchant for treating texts as a chaos of broken atoms constantly allows them to appear to be startled by their own proofs. In this strategy they invoke the conventions of a 'scientific' style, according to which the disinterested scholar finds himself confronted with findings that impose themselves by their sheer inner cogency, quite independently of, if not in outright contradiction to, the scholar's own working hypothesis. Nothing could be further from the truth.

> In Larynx and Pharynx, two cities as large as Rouen or Nantes . . . there died of plague more than twenty two hundred and sixty thousand and sixteen people within the last eight days [Rabelais 1965:172].

The High Counters acknowledge Las Casas as their ideological ancestor, but events of late might have caused them some ambivalence in that regard. They must still admire the abandon with which he threw impossibly high numbers around. On the other hand, as their own estimates continue to escalate, they might well be dissatisfied with the causes to which Las Casas attributed Indian depopulation. Virtually without exception he ascribed it to hunger, to Spanish abuses of the *encomienda* system, and to their astonishing feats of slaughter in battle.

These reasons seemed to satisfy Las Casas but the High Counters have recently discovered their philosophers' stone which enables them to reconcile both the low numbers described in the actual counts and the extraordinarily high numbers they posit as having existed just a few years earlier. This *deus ex machina* is disease—disease introduced by the Europeans, presumably from the moment Columbus set foot on

Guanahani. Yet somehow Las Casas was oblivious to all this, even while claiming eyewitness status to the death of millions of Indians in Hispaniola and elsewhere (Henige 1978a:222–225). The High Counters never tell us how this could be, beyond disingenuously claiming that Las Casas "was merely the earliest and best-known commentator upon the biological [sic] plight of the Indian" (Dobyns 1966:412; cf. Dobyns 1983:24).

Of course the High Counters were not the first to notice the effects of the newly introduced diseases on the Indians, but they are among the first to claim (e.g., Dobyns 1983:34–35) both that the pre-conquest New World was virtually free of any infectious diseases at all and (e.g., Dobyns 1973:295–296) that most of the post-conquest mortality occurred very early and well beyond the purview of any recorded observation. Thus, according to Dobyns (1983:13, 217) the smallpox epidemic that struck the West Indies and Mexico (and possibly Central America) between 1518 and 1524 also "swept through all [sic] of the most densely populated portions of the Americas" and probably had a mortality rate of 50 percent or more. *Voilá*, before any Europeans could start counting Indians, at least half of them had already died! Las Casas, Cortés, and others not only were not exaggerating, they could only have been seriously underestimating the extent and speed of the depopulation.

There is no denying that from the standpoint of the High Counters this is truly a marvelous argument. Certainly no one holding this point of view can ever be refuted. One does not even need to produce any evidence—the argument *presumes* the absence of it as part of its own logic! Doubters might doubt, but they can do no more, and doubt is, we would all concede, rather like sticks and stones. As a result, this convenient doctrine appears on its way to becoming a new orthodoxy, at least with respect to North America. Under its terms, there is no figure that is too high; infer a sufficient number and variety of epidemics within a sufficient period of time (as Dobyns 1983:254–270 does for Florida) and any finite number can easily be reduced to any small number.

Unfortunately for the cause of the High Counters, Dobyns has not done an effective job in dealing with the evidence he adduces for such disease "episodes" (Henige 1986b) and he would best have left it entirely aside, leaving his case firmly entrenched in the domain of the Possible without attempting to whisk it to the land of the Real. Other attempts to interpret the historical record as suggesting earlier and wider-ranging epidemics have not been particularly successful either. In most cases the sources simply do not allow this—and willing meanings to resisting texts or drawing conclusions from their silence ("in the absence of any evidence to the contrary . . .") are hardly acceptable substitutes.

It is all too easy to confuse the possible with the probable, or even with the real, particularly when in hot pursuit of a desired conclusion. Doing so as part of testing hypotheses is legitimate, in fact inescapable, historical method. But adopting it as standard operating procedure without the slightest effort at devil's advocacy is unacceptable. For the moment—and apparently for all time—the notion that newly introduced infectious diseases quick assumed epidemic (or "pandemic") proportions throughout the New World is, by its very nature, detached from any evidence. Accepting it is solely a matter of belief, an odd posture for the High Counters, who relish (as we see from Borah's quote cited above) in claiming a certain "statistical" luster status for their work. In the meantime the study of the effects of well-documented disease episodes in specific contexts, while contributing to our knowledge of historical epidemiology, can have little effect on Native American historical demography beyond suggesting slightly higher population levels, a matter of saying something like X +, which is hardly ever enlightening.[17]

> Whether it is the truth of history or fiction matters not, because the example is not supplied for its own sake, but for its significance [John Bromyard, quoted in Owst 1933:155].

What accounts for the phenomena discussed in this paper? Why is there at this moment an increased and sustained interest in the contact population of the New World supported by a slapdash and intuitive method of operation that ensures that only unsuspected—and indemonstrable—high population levels are "found" (a word the High Counters often use to describe their 'success')? Two attitudes predominate in the writings of the High Counters: a palpable sense of self-evident truth value and a belief that all questions have answers rather than, as would be more circumspect in the circumstances, that all answers have questions.

In referring to criticisms of Las Casas' free use of large numbers, one commentator recently had this to say: "Such an approach has something repulsive about it . . . It would like to prove Las Casas a liar but let the murderers go scot-free because they killed only 8, 5, or 3 million Indians instead of 20 million. That is the way the *National Zeitung* protects the German facists, claiming that not 6 million Jews were killed but at most 5 (Enzensberger 1974:13)." This is probably an extreme *expression* of this point of view, but not necessarily an extreme *sentiment* in the field of contact demography about the unquestioned accuracy of congenial texts. Many of the High Counters, especially those writing today, seem to see their work as having many of the trappings of a morality play. We see this in much of Dobyns' work (e.g., Dobyns 1966:395–396; Dobyns 1973:292–294; Dobyns 1983), which fairly exudes with moral indignation. Not content with referring to DeSoto's men as "Spaniards" or "soldiers" or even "invaders," he prefers the harsher term "marauders." And of course these "marauders" were armed, wittingly or unwittingly, with an entire arsenal of biological weapons. By this angle of vision, 'enlightened' scholars are to foster this image by inflating the number of victims that resulted—and keep inflating it until the specter of genocide appears. In effect, in "counting" millions of Indians they deliver a moral judgment, minus the evidence to support it (Borah 1976:19–20).

Rather paradoxically, the other main tenet of the High Counters is the belief that any number can serve as a proxy and render the unknowable knowable, the uncertain certain. This is to be accomplished by pressing into service techniques that will demonstrate that the size of at least part of the contact population can be measured and the measurement tested. Such procedures can then be encoded and extrapolated from one part of this universe to all others. The uncritical acceptance of Dobyns' crypto-scientific 20:1 depopulation ratio is simply the most obvious manifestation of the view that, given time and technique, modern man can turn the silences of history into the facts of history.[18] In this mode of thinking the very lack of information becomes a force in its own right, giving unbridled rein to ingenuity cast adrift.

Does disagreeing with this belief *necessarily* mean that there were not about (or even exactly) 25.2 million Indians in central Mexico in 1519? Or even one hundred million in all of the New World? Not at all. Is it *likely* that there were? Not at all. This latter view, prompted by common sense and enjoined by the available evidence, is only reinforced by the persistent but misguided efforts of the High Counters and particularly by the irredeemably damaging effects of their nonchalant attitude towards that evidence.

Close analysis of the materials used by the High Counters awaits the extended effort it will require and this obliges us to withhold final judgment of the value and the validity of the uses to which the High Counters have put them.[19] In the meantime, to judge from the skill with which they have deployed the post-conquest data they have used, it is difficult to imagine that they have managed to treat pre-conquest materials any more responsibly (Zambarino 1980). Consequently, any interim judgment can only be that the very methods of the High Counters *require* us to reject their conclusions.

A final point remains to be made. Some readers may well wonder whether it is necessary to devote so much attention to appraising critically the methods of the High Counters. Does this particular dead horse really need to be flogged? Surely they condemn themselves by their own irresponsibility? Sadly, this is not true, or at least far from entirely true. As I suggested in opening this paper, the sedulously cultivated illusion of the High Counters has been, and continues to be, influential, to the point where the techniques they have developed—and their attitude towards sources—have sprouted clones in Africa (Henige 1986c) and Australia (Butlin 1983), in both cases spawned by the same fatal combination of the lack of evidence and the apparent need for expiation.[20] Why this should be so is perhaps not for historians to surmise, but certainly historians have an obligation to test *any* set of arguments, if only to lend them credibility. In this case at least the High Counters, with their unerring propensity for the improbable, badly fail that test.

Notes

1. Without going into detail here, let me mention works by W.H. McNeill, Ladurie, and others, which attempt to provide a unifying framework for world history and in doing so feature disease prominently. See as well Crosby 1986; Hopkins 1983.
2. A recent survey of these estimates is Thornton (1988:22–32). Thornton inclines toward believing in larger contact populations but offers no estimate of his own and is not uncritical of the work of the high counters. Stuart (1987 45–46) mentions the contact population only in passing, also offers no estimate, and credits Dobyns, apparently without irony, with a "reassessment of the sources."
3. For instance, Dobyns 1976 did not manage to cite a single work critical of the High Counters, thereby belying its sub-title, ceasing to be a work of reference, and becoming a propaganda tool. It is an uncommon man who can glimpse the possibility of conducting a vendetta in a bibliography.
4. It is revealing that in seeking to demonstrate what he meant by Bollan distlike textual analysis, Borah argued against accepting the *lowest* estimate of the contact population of Tenochtotlán.
5. On this matter see, among many others, Phelan 1956 and Weckmann 1984.
6. As at least Torquemada (1977, 5:238) had the grace to notice, there were early criticisms of Motolinía's claims. Already Gomara (López de Gomara 1943, 2:281–282) found them hard to believe. To my knowledge none of the High Counters have pointed this out, ignoring Gomara in this instance just as they ignore Bernal Díaz del Castillo in so many other cases (for which see below).
7. For examples of this in their use of post-conquest sources see Slicher van Bath 1978.
8. The dwelling count ploy reaches a crescendo in Cook and Borah 1971–1979, 2:25–38, concerning Yucatan.
9. Innumerable examples could be cited; for starters see Russell 1958.

10. For further criticism of the protein hypothesis see Conrad and Demarest 1984:166–70.
11. For accounts of similarly exaggerated estimates of human sacrifice in India and west Africa and for identical cultural reasons see Davies 1984:220–22; Graham 1965; Igbafe 1979:40–49, 70–72.
12. E.g., Marcus 1977:199–201.
13. In one of the surviving manuscripts Bernal used "1,000," in another "8,000."
14. For details see Henige 1986b.
15. Cook and Borah (1971–1979, 1:388) emulated Dobyns' twist here, translating "se alcanza" as "may be found in the records" when "alcanzar" simply means to "find" or "glean," without implying the existence of any records.
16. In fact, with his usual consummate misreading of the sources, Dobyns (1973:293) asserts that Las Casas estimated the aboriginal population of Hispaniola at four million, as well as that the only other "materially lower" figure was that of a "polemicist" (to the High Counters of course Las Casas was not a polemicist!) who was contemporary with Las Casas. Neither claim is true.
17. For a good overview of this issue see Joralemon 1982.
18. This roseate view is typified in Borah's criticism of Angel Rosenblat's work (Borah 1968:476) because it suggested that "scholars can disagree endlessly about which source is reliable, which ought to be discarded, which interpretation of the text is correct, and so on."
19. For a detailed critique of the High Counters' high conversion factors for tribute records see Rosenblat 1967:25–71 and Slicher van Bath 1978, to which—need I say it?—the High Counters have never responded in kind. Also see Doybns, Snow, Lamphear, and Henige 1989.
20. In a recent study of the contact population of Hawaii, Stannard (1989) has embraced the premises and methods of the High Counters, and with them the same brand of scattershot arithmetic, tendentious reliance on dubious comparative material, and studied indifference to critical literature in the field.

References

Alcina Franch, José. 1973. "Juan de Torquemada." *Handbook of Middle American Indians* 13:256–75.
Anonymous. 1869. "The Later Life of De Foe." *British Quarterly Review* 50: 483–519.
Baum, L. Frank. 1910. *The Emerald City of Oz*. Chicago: Reilly & Britton.
Blázquez Garbajosa, Adrián. 1985. "Las 'Cartas de Relación de la Conquista de Mexico': Política, Psicología y Literatura." *Bulletin Hispanique* 87:5–46.
Borah, Woodrow W. 1964. "America as Model: The Demographic Impact of European Expansion Upon the Non-European World." *In Actos y Memorias del XXXV Congreso International de Americanistas* (Mexico, 1962), 3: 389–97. Mexico City: Instituto Nacional de Antropología.
———. 1968. Review of Angel Rosenblat, "La población de América en 1492." *Hispanic American Historical Review* 48:475–77.
———. 1976. "The Historical Demography of Aboriginal and Colonial America: An Attempt at Perspective." In *The Native Population of the Americas in*

1492. William M. Denevan, ed. 13–34. Madison: University of Wisconsin Press.

Borah, Woodrow W. and Sherburne F. Cook. 1963. "The Aboriginal Population of Central Mexico on the Eve of the Spanish Conquest." *Ibero-Americana* 45. Berkeley: University of California.

Borges, Jorge Luis. 1974. *Obras completas*. Buenos Aires: Emece Editores.

Brady, Robert. 1684. *Introduction to the Old English History*. London.

Butler, Samuel. 1970. *Characters*. Charles W. Daves, ed. Cleveland: Case Western Reserve University.

Butlin, N.G. 1983. *Our Original Aggression. Aboriginal Populations of Southeastern Australia, 1788–1850*. Sydney: Allen & Unwin.

Commager, Henry Steele and Elmo Giordanetti. 1967. *Was America a Mistake? An Eighteenth-Century Controversy*. New York: Harper & Row.

Conrad, Geoffrey W. and Arthur A. Demarest. 1984. *Religion and Empire: The Dynamics of Aztec and Inca Expansionism*. Cambridge: Cambridge University.

Cook, Sherburne F. 1946. "Human Sacrifice and Warfare as Factors in the Demography of Pre-Columbian Mexico." *Human Biology* 18:81–102.

———. 1948. "The Population of Central Mexico in the Sixteenth Century." *Ibero American* 31. Berkeley: University of California Press.

———. 1973. "Interracial Warfare and Population Decline Among the New England Indians." *Ethnohistory* 20:1–24.

Cook, Sherburne F. and Lesley B. Simpson. 1948. "The Population of Central Mexico in the Sixteenth Century." *Ibero-Americana* 31. Berkeley: University of California Press.

Cook, Sherburne F. and Woodrow W. Borah. 1960. "The Indian Population of Central Mexico, 1531–1610." *Ibero-Americana* 44. Berkeley: University of California Press.

———. 1966. "On the Credibility of Contemporary Testimony on the Population of Mexico in the Sixteenth Century." In *Summa Anthropologica. Homenaje a Roberto Weitlaner*. 229–39. Mexico City: Instituto Nacional de Antropologia e Historia.

———. 1971–1979. *Essays in Population History: Mexico and the Caribbean*. 3 vols. Berkeley: University of California Press.

Cortés, Hernán. 1958. *Reluciónes de Hernan Cortés a Carlos V sobre la invasion de Anáhuac*. Eulalia Guzmán, ed. Mexico City: Libros Anáhuac.

Crosby, Alfred W. 1986. *Ecological Imperialism. The Biological Expansion of Europe, 900–1900*. Cambridge: Cambridge University.

Darwin, Charles. 1903. *More Letters of Charles Darwin*. Francis Darwin, ed. 2 vols. New York: D. Appleton & Co.

Davies, Nigel. 1984. "Human Sacrifice in the Old World and the New: Some Similarities and Differences." In *Ritual Human Sacrifice in Mesoamerica*. Elizabeth H. Boone, ed. 211–26. Washington: Dumbarton Oaks Research Library.

Díaz del Castillo, Bernal. 1982. *Historia verdadera de la conquista de la Nueva España*. Carmelo Sáenz de Santa Maria, ed. Madrid: Instituto Gonzalo Fernández de Oviedo.

Dobyns, Henry F. 1966. "Estimating Aboriginal American Population: An Appraisal of Techniques with a New Hemispheric Estimate." *Current Anthropology* 7:395–416, 440–44.

————. 1973. "Review of Cook & Borah, Essays in Population History, I. Hispanic." *American Historical Review* 53:292–96.

————. 1976. *Native American Historical Demography: A Critical Bibliography.* Chicago: Newberry Library.

————. 1983. *Their Number Become Thinned: Native American Population Dynamics in Eastern North America.* Knoxville: University of Tennessee.

Dobyns, Henry F., Dean R. Snow, Kim M. Lamphear, and David Henige. 1989. "Commentary on Native American Demography." *Ethnohistory* 36: 285–307.

Ellenberger, D.F. 1912. *History of the Basutos, Ancient and Modern.* J.C. Macgregor, ed. London: Caxton.

Enzensberger, Hans M. 1974. Introduction in Bartolomé de las Casa, *The Devastation of the Indies: A Brief Account.* New York: Seabury Press.

Fernández-Armesto, Felipe. 1982. *The Canary Islands After the Conquest.* Oxford: Oxford University.

Fernández de Quirós, Pedro. 1609/1866. " Memorial dado a S.M. por el capitán Pedro Fernán dez de Quirós. In *Colección de Documentos ineditos relativos al descubrimiento, conquista y organización de la antiguas posesiones españolos de América y Océania.* Madrid.

García, Genaro. 1902. *Dos antigos relaciones de la Florida.* Mexico City: Aguilar

Gerbi, Antonello. 1973. *The Dispute of the New World: The History of a Polemic, 1750–1900.* Pittsburgh, PA: University of Pittsburgh.

Graham, James D. 1965. "The Slave Trade, Depopulation, and Human Sacrifice in Benin History." *Cahiers d'etudes africaines* 5:317–34.

Harner, Michael. 1977. "The Ecological Basis for Aztec Sacrifice." *American Ethnologist* 4:114–35.

Harris, Marvin. 1977. *Cannibals and Kings.* New York: Random House.

Henige, David. 1978a. "On the Contact Population of Hispaniola: History as Higher Mathematics." *Hispanic American Historical Review* 58:217–37.

————. 1978b. "Response to Rudolph Zambardino." *Hispanic American Historical Review* 58:707–12.

————. 1986a. "If Pigs Could Fly: Timucuan Population and Native American Historical Demography." *Journal of Interdisciplinary History* 16:701–20.

————. 1986b. "Primary Source by Primary Source? On the Role of Epidemics in New World Depopulation." *Ethnohistory* 33:293–312.

————. 1986c. "Measuring the Immeasurable: The Slave Trade, West African Population, and the Pyrrhonist Critic." *Journal of African History* 27: 295–313.

Hollingsworth, T.H. 1969. *Historical Demography.* London: Hodder and Stoughton.

Hopkins, Donald R. 1983. *Princes and Peasants: Smallpox in History.* Chicago: University of Chicago Press.

Igbafe, Philip A. 1979. *Benin under British Administration.* London: Longman.

Joralemon, Donald. 1982. "New World Depopulation and the Case of Disease." *Journal of Anthropological Research* 38:108–27.

León-Portilla, Miguel. 1979. "New Light on the Sources of Torquemada's *Monarquía Indiana.*" *The Americas* 35:287–316.

Leonard, Irving A. 1948. *Books of the Brave.* Cambridge: Harvard University Press.

López de Gomara, Francisco. 1943. *Historia de la Conquista de Mexico*. Joaquín Ramírez Cabañas, ed. 2 vols. Mexico City: Editorial Pedro Robledo.

Losack, Tom. 1987. "The Kindreds, Houses, and Population of the Elves During the First Age." *Mythlore* 51:34–8, 56.

Marcus, Raymond. 1977. " La conquête de Cholula: conflit d'interpretations." *Ibero-Amerikanische Archiv* 3:193–213.

Mendieta, Jeronimo de. 1870. *Historia Ecclesiastica Indiana*. Joaquín García Icazbalceta, ed. Mexico City: Antigua Libreria.

Motolinía, Toribio de Benavente. 1941. *Historia de los Indios de la Nueva España*. Mexico City: Chavez Hayhoe.

————. 1971. *Memoriales o libro de las cosas de la Nueva España y de los naturales de ella*. Edmundo O'Gorman, ed. Mexico City: Universidad Autonoma Nacional de Mexico.

Ortiz de Montellano, Bernard R. 1983. "Counting Skulls: Comments on the Aztec Cannibalism Theory of Harner-Harris." *American Anthropologist* 85:403–06.

Owst, Gerald R. 1933. *Literature and Pulpit in Medieval England*. Cambridge: Cambridge University Press.

Phelan, John L. 1956. *The Millennial Kingdom of the Franciscans in the New World*. Berkeley: University of California Press.

Price, Barbara J. 1978." Demystification, Enriddlement, and Aztec Cannibalism: A Materialist Rejoinder to Harner." *American Ethnologist* 5:98–115.

Rabelais, François. 1965. *Pantagruel*. V.L. Saulnier, ed. Geneva: Droz.

Rosenblat, Angel. 1967. *La población de América en 1492*. Mexico City: Colégio de México.

Russell, Josiah C. 1958. *Late Ancient and Medieval Population*. Philadelphia: American Philosophical Society.

Sahlins, Marshall. 1978. "Culture as Protein and Profit." *New York Times Review of Books* (23 Jan):45–49.

Slicher van Bath, B.H. 1978. "The Calculation of the Population of New Spain, Especially for the Period Before 1570." *Boletin de Estudios Latino-Americanos y del Caribe* 24:67–95.

Stannard, David E. 1989. *Before the Horror: The Population of Hawai'i on the Eve of Western Contact*. Honolulu: University of Hawaii, Social Science Research Institute.

Stuart, Paul. 1987. *Nations Within a Nation: Historical Statistics of American Indians*. Westport, CT: Greenwood Press.

Tapia, Andrés de. 1866. "Relación hecha el Señor Andres de Tapia sobre la con quista de Mexico." In *Colección de Documentos para la Historia de Mexico* 2:554–94. Joaquín García Icazbalceta, ed. Mexico City: J.M. Andrade.

Thornton, Russell. 1988. *American Indian Holocaust and Survival: A Population History Since 1492*. Norman: University of Oklahoma Press.

Torquemada, Juan de. 1977. *Monarquía Indiana*. 5 vols. Mexico City: Universidad Autónoma Nacional de Mexico.

Weckmann, Luis. 1984 *La herencia medieval de México*. 2 vols. Mexico City: Colégio de México.

Zambardino, Rudolph A. 1980. "Mexico's Population in the Sixteenth Century: Demographic Anomaly or Mathematical Illusion?" *Journal of Interdisciplinary History* 11:1–27.

10

Primal Gaia: Primitivists and Plastic Medicine Men

Alice B. Kehoe

I first saw Adolf Hungry Wolf at the 1972 Kainai Days powwow on the Blood Indian reserve in Alberta. Dancing with rapt intensity, he wore black longjohns under his impressive ground-trailing tailfeathers bustle, and his two black braids looked like a wig (among the Blackfoot, men wear *three* braids, women two). In one hand, he carried a toma-hawk, as if he were an illustration in one of Karl May's German fantasies about Indians (see Honour 1975:242–43). Adolf Hungry Wolf stuck out like a sore thumb at the Blood powwow. He was dancing in the beginning of the afternoon, when only children and a few old people go into the arena. His attempt to cover up his North European paleness with black cloth added a stark darkness to the brilliant colors of others' dyed turkey feathers and rayon dresses. And most of all, his tense concentration on his dancing contrasted with everyone else's relaxed, happy appearance.

Adolf Hungry Wolf, born Adolf Gutohrlein, felt a strong attraction to nature and the American Indians even as a boy in his native Germany. Immigrating with his parents to the United States, Adolf grew up in postwar California to be a counterculture flower child. Like many of his generation, he and his woman came as pilgrims to a mountain valley, building a log cabin, keeping goats. From ethnographies and craft books, he cobbled together paperbacks on Indians to bring in a little cash. Typical of popular writers on Indian spirituality, he sprinkled capital letters with great liberality: "Good Medicine is a Way to live in Harmony with Nature . . . following the Path of the Sacred Circle . . . in the Light of Today" (Hungry Wolf 1973:4). More sincere than many purveyors of the Way to Live, Adolf looked for a guru in a genuine Indian community, the Blood reserve in southern Alberta, Canada. His efforts met with limited success: he did find a couple of elderly men who let him try to apprentice himself to learn the ways of the Blood (a Blackfoot group), and he did marry a young woman, Beverly, from one of the reserve families, who became his collaborator in retelling Blackfoot culture. The time came, however, when Adolf (Gutohrlein) Hungry Wolf's intrusions became too troublesome, and he found himself outcast from the reserve. This odyssey he recounts in *Shadows of the Buffalo* (1983).

Thousands of Americans and Europeans believe, as Adolf Gutohrlein had, that American Indians retain a primordial wisdom that could heal our troubled world. American Indians are supposed to be *Naturvölker* (natural peoples), in contrast to the civilized nations alienated from Nature. Personified as Mother Earth (see chapter 7), Nature is the embodiment of life and thus the hope of a future. She may be called Gaia (from Ge, as in *ge*ology), the living goddess; heedless greedy civilized men rape her, tearing ores from her womb and crops from her bosom. *Naturvölker* respect her, taking only what she freely and lovingly offers, wild foods and regenerating materials. Her gifts to her human children include medicines, so among the *Naturvölker* are "medicine men" (and women) with knowledge infinitely older and truer than that of graduates of accredited medical colleges. From this supposition, a number of practitioners of "Indian" medicine and spiritualism have gained comfortable livings.

The belief that there exist founts of true goodness and knowledge among savage peoples can be traced back to the earliest documents of Western thought, Homer's *Iliad* (c. 700 B.C. [Fontaine 1986:118]) and the *Europa* of Ephorus in the early fourth-century B.C. (Lovejoy and Boas 1965:288). In a magisterial survey, Lovejoy and Boas called this idealization "cultural primitivism . . . the discontent of the civilized with civilization." That discontent gives rise to "one of the strangest, most potent and most persistent factors in Western thought—the use of the term 'nature' to express the standard of human values, the identification of the good with that which is 'natural' " (1965:7, 11–12).

These authors point out that the Scythians were to the Classical Greeks what North American Indians have become to modern writers—repositories of virtues lost in urban societies. Strabo claimed, in the first century B.C., "our mode of life has caused the deterioration of nearly all peoples, introducing among them softness and the love of pleasure and evil arts and greed in its myriad forms" (translated by Lovejoy and Boas 1965:289–90). Åke Hultkrantz, professor of comparative religion at the University of Stockholm, follows Strabo when he claims that a problem "of modern western life is our inability to lead authentic lives" (Vecsey 1981:xii). Hultkrantz, like young Adolf Hungry Wolf, was from boyhood attracted to "the romantic image of Indians as lovers of nature, as people at harmony with their world . . . the mysteries of American Indian life" (Vecsey 1981:x). Encouraged as a student by his professor in the department where he himself then taught, Hultkrantz pursued field research from 1948 to 1958 among the Shoshoni on the Wind River Reservation in Wyoming. Through his university position, Hultkrantz has supervised graduate students studying American Indian religions, teaching them his classical Western primitivist premise.

In an oft cited essay, anthropologist Edward Sapir distinguished "genuine" from "spurious" culture (1956). Sapir, like Hultkrantz and Hungry Wolf, supposed that American Indians enjoyed real satisfactions in their daily lives, "authentic" lives of "genuine" culture. Like Karl Marx, Max Weber, and Emile Durkheim, however, Sapir was decrying the construction of a spectator society in which the mass of Americans control neither the activities of their daily employment nor the enactment of art and ritual, now reserved for professionals. Hultkrantz and Hungry Wolf have no real interest in analyzing or understanding European and Euro-American culture. Convinced of its "inauthenticity," they define for themselves the mission of bringing their "knowledge" of American Indian spirituality to the peoples of modern Europe and America.

They are not alone. By a curious twist of logic, hundreds of thousands of Europeans and Americans, alienated by our culture pushing us toward mere passive existence, do not strive simply to engage themselves more in direct production and performance. Instead, they look to representations of non-Western cultures for "authentic" experiences. To gain "genuine" culture, they seek instruction in non-Western spiritual exercises, Asian or American Indian. Historian Calvin Martin embraces and expresses this quest succinctly: "These people [American Indians] key their speculative philosophies to an overarching and undergirding biological system. The biological focus bequeaths to its adherents and practitioners a profoundly different set of . . . key and fundamental questions of human existence" (1987:8). Both the scholarly work of professionals like Hultkrantz and Martin and the popular books of Hungry Wolf and his ilk assume an immense difference, a Great Gulf between "these peoples" and the rest of us.

Nature is life, culture is artificiality—this assumption becomes the primal vision. The authentic life is not merely that in which one retains a sense of control, in which a "captain of industry" can, as Sapir noted, enjoy genuine culture: the authentic life must be lived close to nature, away from artificiality. Modern American Indians are seen as "natural people" because their reservations are rural and there they live largely free of the encumbrances of machines. That these conditions are due to political acts of the dominant society is ignored. Reservation Indians are outside Euro-American cities and thereby, ergo, they must live "authentic" lives infused with spiritual meaning.

When Pope John Paul II was scheduled to fly into Fort Simpson, North West Territory, in 1987 to meet with Indian leaders, reporters were "as usual searching for mystical explanations from the Indian people. . . . What did it mean when the pope's plane couldn't land in 1984? He had to cancel his trip. No, I mean, why did it happen? It was too foggy . . . [S]earching for significance to the early morning rain, [a reporter] asked a young Dene man, what did they call it? The young man paused, looked skyward, and then said, 'We call it the 20-per-cent-chance-of-rain rain' " (Johnson 1988:17). The amused correspondent from the Indian-published bimonthly had seen it before, the unshakable conviction that Indians represent Harmony with Nature, the Spiritual Way.

The Primal Mind, published in 1981 by Jamake Highwater and soon made into a television film, quickly became a best-selling gospel of the primitivist concept of a primordial and therefore true religion among a "natural people," American Indians. Exactly who Jamake Highwater is has been subject to controversy. He claims to be Blackfoot and also Cherokee;[1] he admits to having been a choreographer in San Francisco under the name J. Marks; he denies being a Greek-American film-maker from Toledo, Ohio, named Gregory J. Markopoulos. Whatever he once was, Highwater is a talented popular writer whose assertion of American Indian identity has lent credibility to his representation of Indian religion as "primal vision."

The central place of the visionary experience in "American Indian" religion was popularized long before Highwater in *Black Elk Speaks* by John Neihardt, poet laureate of Nebraska. The focus of *Black Elk Speaks* is a magnificent vision the old man remembered from his boyhood, a revelation that he believed empowered him to cure and to lead. In his old age, Black Elk regretted failing to live faithfully according to his vision. Unknown to Neihardt, he had been employed for decades as a catechist for the Catholic Indian mission (Castro 1983:94; DeMallie 1984). Seizing the opportunity presented by John Neihardt's efforts to obtain details to enliven his own epic *Cycle of the West*, Nick Black Elk engaged the poet to inscribe and present the message of his boyhood vision to the world. The lyrical beauty of Neihardt's version of what Black Elk spoke carried the book to an eventual huge popularity.

An admirer of *Black Elk Speaks*, Joseph Epes Brown, later made a pilgrimage to Pine Ridge Reservation to see the visionary. To his delight, the aged Nick Black Elk had more to give the reading public. Brown, one of Hultkrantz's students, assisted the Lakota former Catholic catechist to codify Oglala rituals and beliefs into seven sacraments unified by the pipe as central symbol (Brown 1953). This was clearly an effort by the old visionary, aided by scholar Brown, to make Oglala religion over into a straightforward alternative to the Catholicism he had formerly taught. The effort succeeded; the one-to-one correspondence between crucifix and pipe, Christ and White Buffalo Woman, sacrament to sacrament, produced an easy transfer of allegiance from Christianity to "Indian religion." Unquestionably this syncretism has been instrumental in establishing Black Elk's version of Oglala supernaturalism as *the* Indian religion, just as nineteenth-century Lakota costume has become *the* Indian dress. But Black Elk's vision, and Black Elk's religion, were never presented as primordial. "Primal vision" is a step—no, a leap—beyond anything Black Elk spoke.

It was Joseph Epes Brown, not Black Elk, who vaulted from Oglala concepts to traditional *Western* cultural primitivism. As Brown expressed it, "American Indian religions represent pre-eminent examples of primal religious traditions that have been present in the Americas for some thirty to sixty thousand years. Fundamental elements common to the primal nature of those traditions . . . survive into the present among Indian cultures of the Americas" (1982:1). These seemingly authoritative statements by a professor of religious studies begin with the premise that contemporary North American Indian religions incorporate "elements" unchanged for thirty to sixty millennia. Many archaeologists would insist that except for an undated carved llama pelvis from a late Pleistocene stratum at Tequixquiac in the Valley of Mexico, the scanty imperishable remnants of human habitation in Pleistocene America, securely dated only to about 12,000 B.C., cannot by any stretch of analogy be interpreted to signify religious concepts (Kehoe 1981:chapter 1). Brown's enterprise is built upon an unverified and probably unverifiable premise.

Brown spells out "fundamental and universal characteristic[s] of Native American cultures, as *indeed of all primal or primitive cultures*" (1982:x; emphasis added). He goes on to write that,

> "religion" . . . is not a separate category of activity or experience [but] is in complex interrelationships with all aspects of the peoples' life-ways. [S]hared principles underlie sacred concepts that are specific to each of nature's manifestations and also to what could be called sacred geography. [I]n addition, a special understanding of language in which words constitute distinct units of sacred power. [S]acred forms extend to architectural styles so that each

dwelling . . . is an image of the cosmos [Brown 1982:x]. Mysticism, in its
original and thus deepest sense, is an experiential reality within Native American spiritual traditions. (Brown 1982:111; emphasis added)

"Primal religion," such as Brown describes, is nothing more than
Euro-American cultural primitivism. It has been an integral part of that
nineteenth-century evolutionism popularized by Herbert Spencer and
Lewis Henry Morgan, and accepted by John Wesley Powell, founder
of the Smithsonian Institution's Bureau of American Ethnology (Kehoe
1985). Closely allied to the assumption of the persistence of an unchanged primal culture among American Indians was the invention of
an unbridgeable difference between Indians and Europeans. Powell wrote
in his Annual Report, published in 1896, of "a difference so profound
that few civilized men ever comprehend the mental workings of the
uncivilized man, while it is doubtful whether any uncivilized man ever
comprehends the mentation of his cultured brother" (Powell 1896:
xxiii-xxiv).[2]

These twin chimeras of primal persistence and radically contrasting
"mentations" fostered policies that still bedevil American Indians. Ben
Reifel, Brulé Sioux on his mother's side, Harvard Ph.D., congressman
from South Dakota, in 1967 remembered the assumptions behind the
Indian Reorganization Act of 1934:

> Mr. [John] Collier [Commissioner, Bureau of Indian Affairs, 1933–1945]
> had the feeling, and I've heard him say that the Indians are in the vanguard
> of this world-wide loop back into the land . . . About 1928, and with the
> Merriam survey, [the B.I.A.] began to bring in professionally qualified peo-
> ple—more doctors, more nurses, more teachers—and the New Deal sort of
> built right on this. One of the misfortunes among the Indians, I feel person-
> ally, was the part where education was concerned. That the cause of this
> whole national feeling of reversion to the land, and that the Indians were in
> the vanguard, leadership in the Indian education was . . . goats brought in,
> little projects where the little kids would work with chickens or rabbits and
> gardens, and they tended to be losing sight of learning to read and write and
> to figure. (Reifel 1971:125–6)

Collier's notion of an ideal Indian education reflected the influence of
John Dewey. Even more, Collier's programs for American Indians
stemmed directly from long-standing conventions of cultural primitivism, views reinforced by his association with the wealthy art patron
Mabel Dodge Luhan, herself seeking authenticity living beside Taos
pueblo (Kelly 1983:52, 118–20).

In 1974, when Gary Snyder received a Pulitzer Prize for his poems
and essays in *Turtle Island*, the loop back into the American land that

Collier had envisioned received its widest acceptance. An anthropology major from Reed College in Oregon, Snyder developed a sophisticated ecological orientation that borrows images from Indian sources, archival and contemporary (Castro 1983:chapter 6). "Turtle Island" is a phrase drawn from Siouan cosmology describing the earth resting on the backs of a pair of primeval turtles, and the phrase also resonates to the common collocation of turtles with the countryside and natural bodies of water. Snyder is convinced that—as a poet—he shares an openness to primal experiences with those Indians who like himself have avoided the appurtenances of Euro-American urban culture. Primitivism to Snyder is a practical option, a design for living that can be chosen by anyone, whatever their cultural heritage.

In contrast to Snyder, Joseph Epes Brown seems to consider American Indians the sole repositories of authentic religiosity: "[B]y taking the pains to learn what one can from Native American traditions one who as yet is unaffiliated with *a* true tradition will be aided in knowing what a tradition is in all its complexity, depth, and richness of cultural expressions" (Brown 1982:113; his emphasis). Why this could not be achieved by taking instruction in Roman Catholicism, Greek or Russian Orthodoxy, or German Lutheranism, Brown does not explain. His privileging of American Indian traditions as "true" above all others shares in a trend that has become highly profitable to many more charismatic and entrepreneurial than Professor Brown.

"Plastic Medicine Men," an Austrian Friends-Of-The-Indian group calls them, the gaggle of pay-up-front impresarios and conductors of "American Indian" spiritual exercises. The notion that the *Naturvölker* know the secrets of health is part of cultural primitivism (Lovejoy and Boas 1965:155). Around 1860, "Indian doctors" were listed among medical practitioners in the Washington, D.C., city directory (Moldow 1987:13), and others like them could be found in many American settings. Then as now, the claim that one has studied the healing art with Indians seemed sufficient to attract clients. There has been a significant change, however. Through the nineteenth and into the early twentieth-century, practitioners of "Indian" medicine dispensed herbal potions, ointments, oils, and other "simples," natural medications used to treat specific bodily ailments. But in this last quarter of the twentieth century, "Indian medicine men" have concentrated on mental disquiet and spiritual malaise. Today, because these "medicine men" are believed to combine spiritual insight and "natural" medicines, as opposed to licensed medical doctors who are said to be coldly rational, followers of "Indian" practitioners revere them as spiritual gurus as much as healers.

One of the best established and most popular "medicine men" is Sun

Bear, who told an interviewer that he is a Chippewa from White Earth Reservation, Minnesota (Shorris 1971:130–133). Sun Bear spent his first twenty years there but left to sell real estate in North Dakota, worked in Hollywood as an actor and "technical advisor," and has been married twice, each time to a non-Indian. In 1970 he was employed seeking grants and loans for businesses on Indian reservations, and he also published an Indian lore magazine. By the 1980s, he had privately developed an enterprise called the Bear Tribe, an outlet for the sale of packaged Indian rituals and easy-to-read books on Indian spirituality. Sun Bear named himself Chief of the Bear Tribe Medicine Society, "a group of people striving daily to relearn their proper relationship with the Earth Mother, the Great Spirit, and all their relations in the mineral, plant, animal and human kingdoms . . . a tribe of teachers responsible for sharing . . . lessons of harmony" (Sun Bear 1970:book cover).

Joseph Bruchac, himself an Indian, in 1983 attended one of the Bear Tribe's Medicine Wheel Gatherings. Hundreds of others attended, too, paying $100 each for three days of events, camping, and six meals. The Medicine Wheel itself was a large circle of stones laid out near the lake in a Catskills summer camp. The idea of a potent "Medicine Wheel" entered pop Indian spirituality through Hyemeyohsts Storm's much criticized *Seven Arrows*, where it is said to be "the very Way of Life of the People" (1972:l). Storm, who is flatly called "non-Indian" by Michael Castro (1983:155), in his turn seems to have lifted the medicine wheel from George Bird Grinnell's classic ethnographic study of the nineteenth-century Cheyenne. However, Grinnell unmistakably describes these "wheels" as a minor item in Cheyenne life, little wooden hoops used primarily in a game of skill (1972 II:296). Storm creatively embellished this older Cheyenne practice, converting the medicine wheel into a symbolic figure constructed of pebbles, perhaps borrowing that form from the boulder construction marked on Wyoming road maps as the Big Horn Medicine Wheel.[3]

This practice of spiritual license continues. Participants in Sun Bear's 1983 "East Coast Gathering," for instance, were invited to place a small tobacco offering and their own "personal stones" within the camp wheel. They could steam themselves in the sweat lodge, puff on the communal pipe, and take part in the Child Blessing and the Give-Away. Wait, there was more! All attending could broaden their experience through "Traditional East Indian Fire Ceremony at the Medicine Wheel" and a "Conscious Movement exercise at the Social Hall with Vyasananda." There were, of course, free periods available for purchasing Sun Bear's *Earth Astrology*, bear claws, tobacco, and sage, healing crystals, and cassette tapes of sacred songs.

Bruchac, the eyewitness commentator, raises a profound issue when he comments (1983:21), "you could make up new rituals as you went along, just as long as you were sincere" (1983:21). Ongoing revelation through personal visions has been integral to Plains Indian religious practices, but it is counteracted by the custom of a recognized older religious leader "straightening out" (interpreting) a younger person's vision.[4] American Indian religious leaders strongly rooted in Indian communities usually discuss innovations with others in their own and neighboring communities before adopting them. This submission to collegial evaluation is missing in the usually quite standardized fêtes conducted by touring pop medicine persons for the enlightenment of their American clientele.

Rolling Thunder is another peripatetic medicine man, in the business as long as Sun Bear. In a book on psychic healing, he is described in his Nevada home, "sitting underneath a stuffed eagle," identified earlier in this same account as "his totem bird" (Krippner and Villoldo 1986:9, 6). Can Rolling Thunder really possess supernatural power so great that he can sit calmly beneath so blasphemous a sight as an eagle "totem" stuffed and hung upon a living-room wall? Most of Rolling Thunder's clientele seem to be from California, where he is frequently encountered (Boyd 1974). Said to be a Shoshoni, Rolling Thunder at sunrise purveys a standard pipe offering to the Four Winds (apparently omitting the other two sacred directions of traditional Indians, zenith and nadir). For Americans who have had disease-causing feathers and stones magically shot into their innards, he also delivers a sucking-doctor shamanic healing routine (similar to that amply described in anthropological publications and films such as *Pomo Shaman*). Rolling Thunder's wife is named—What did you expect?—Spotted Fawn.

Wallace Black Elk is genuinely Lakota, though (when pinned down) not related to Nick Black Elk of the Pine Ridge Oglala (Cameron 1985:32). Wallace, like Sun Bear, is well known to the avocational Indians of Europe (see chapter 16). He toured the continent in 1983 accompanied by an anthropologist, William S. Lyon, and in 1986 he joined Lyon in advertising seminars on Indian shamanism featuring an "enactment over a five-day period of the Lakota *inipi* ('sweat-lodge') purification ceremony." Lyon promises Wallace will also perform "routine shamanic duties such as shamanic healing via the 'sacred-pipe,' precognitive experiences, the leading of traditional ceremonies, and other such normal shamanic activities" (Lyon 1986). Wallace must compete with another trading on the fame of Black Elk, Hilda Neihardt Petri, daughter of the Prairie Poet Laureate, Black Elk's amanuensis. Petri had accompanied her father and sister to Pine Ridge in 1931, and transcribed for her father what Nick Black Elk *spoke* in 1944 for Neihardt's second book with him. She now is advertised as "one of the last living links with the traditional Indian culture" and she will retail her memories in a "po-etically haunting and spiritually enriching" narration from her father's works. Hilda's customers can use the most modern forms of commu-nication to reach out and touch her, by dialing (918) 747–POET to reserve a presentation of "the natural culture and profound wisdom of the American Indians" (Handy 1985).

A variant of the plastic medicine man is the Indian artist-healer. John Redtail Freesoul is one such. He claims to be "Cheyenne-Arapahoe," and like Sun Bear he heads an "inter-tribal medicine society," in this case, the Redtail Hawk Medicine Society. Freesoul and his ex-wife, "Riverwoman," identified as Cherokee, carve and sell pipes and "my Northern Plains style of southwestern fetish which I call 'spirit fetishes' " (Freesoul 1986:199). The Redtail Hawk Medicine Society is described by its "sacred pipeholder" Freesoul as a "warrior society . . . organized by Nantan Lupan and James Bluewolf . . . in 1974 . . . fulfill[ing a] Hopi prophecy that new clans and societies shall emerge as part of a larger revival and purification of the Red Road" (Freesoul 1986: 105–106). This entrepreneur's own clan is also "intertribal, one of the changes in tradition as a result of the Indian unity movement of the 1960s" (Freesoul 1986:143). From astrology, Freesoul borrows animal, vegetable, mineral, and time-of-day associations—totems, he calls them (1986:58–59). His "totems" were originally the grizzly, the mullein plant (appropriately, a European import), jet (a coal-like mineral), and sun-set, a set supposedly inherent in persons born in autumn. As he broad-ened his experiences, he acquired additional "totems"—"the golden eagle, the redtail hawk," and "phases of Grandmother Moon." To cap his pilgrimage, Freesoul has been born again in Jesus Christ—Praise the Lord! (Freesoul 1986:chapter 16).

On the shelves of bookstores catering to New Age devotees are a dozen competitors of Freesoul's all-in-one handbook. According to the introductory pages of another, Eagle Walking Turtle (otherwise known as Gary McClain) has "the natural Choctaw sadness that was his heritage by birth, yet there was also an Irish wisdom and laughing acceptance" (Hausman 1987:9). The jacket of McClain's book—which consists of a series of paintings accompanying excerpts from *Black Elk Speaks*— describes it as "a universal, salvific message that transcends politics, governments, and religions. It is the medicine way on how to achieve peace, harmony, and the healing and cleansing of ourselves and the earth."

The earth-cleansing theme is a favorite of the New Age questers.

British chemist James E. Lovelock, for example, pictures our planet as basically a self-regulating feedback system "which seeks an optimal physical and chemical environment for life on this planet" (1979:11). Adopting the suggestion of novelist William Golding, Lovelock bestowed upon his system the Greek name "Gaia." Though he carefully referred to his Gaia as a scientific hypothesis, Lovelock tends to slip into anthropomorphisms, as when he writes that his system "seeks" optimization. He opened the door to cultural primitivism when he explained, "The Gaia hypothesis is for those who like to walk or simply stand and stare, to wonder about the Earth and the life it bears, and to speculate about the consequences of our own presence here. It is an alternative to that pessimistic view which sees nature as a primitive force to be subdued and conquered" (1979:12).

Gaia has been developing into the central icon of a New Age cult with primitivist overtones. She is merged into Mother Earth, also described as a Global Brain (Russell 1983), a "living organism with a lattice of geometric lines—energy fields—running through it" (Paulson 1987). Like others of his vocation, Rolling Thunder echoed the theme, "earth is a living organism" (Krippner and Villoldo:6). Plastic medicine men fit easily into New Age workshops such as one advertised for October 17, 1987, where between the hours of 9 A.M. and 5 P.M., for only $30 including lunch, refreshments, and materials, seekers could learn about the "Gaia Hypothesis, Mayan Calendar, Global Brain Theory, Power Points, Polar Shift, Transpersonal Psychology, Esoteric Teachings, Native American Spirituality, Planetary Grid System [the 'energy fields'], End Times Theology, Age of Aquarius, and the Matriarchal Principle," all "Converging Perspectives on the Coming Transformation" (Paulson 1987).

The "Matriarchal Principle," related of course to Gaia and Mother Earth, pulls in yet another audience: women and the men who love them. The size of that flock created bestsellers for Lynn Andrews, who describes herself as a "warrioress of the rainbow . . . a bridge between the two distinct worlds of the primal mind and white consciousness" (Andrews 1985:xi). She began producing such wisdom in 1981 with *Medicine Woman*, opening with a quote from her "Cree" guru, Agnes Whistling Elk:

There are no medicine men, without medicine women. A medicine man is given power by a woman, and it has always been that way. A medicine man stands in the place of the dog. He is merely an instrument of woman . . . Woman is the ultimate . . . Mother Earth belongs to woman, not man. She carries the void. (Andrews 1981:i)

What red-blooded American female could resist such promise of primal power? Especially so when on the next page we are in Los Angeles at a trendy gallery opening, then on to a party in a Bel Air mansion with a French maid declaring Mademoiselle's "black silk crepe kimono" to be "magnifique!" Who should be at this party but Hyemeyohsts Storm (if it were Carlos Castaneda, the reader might be tipped off too easily. See chapter 12).[5] Storm directs our heroine to "the Cree Reserve north of Crowley, Manitoba" to find Agnes Whistling Elk, "a heyoka, as they call some medicine women" (Andrews 1981:17).

There is a town in California called Crowley; there is none by that name in Manitoba. Andrews rents a car at Winnipeg Airport and thirty minutes later is "out in the Canadian tundra," not the plain prairie ordinary people find a half hour's drive from Winnipeg (1981:21). When she arrives at the hamlet of "Crowley," Andrews must first inquire for Whistling Elk's friend Ruby Plenty Chiefs. Ruby, she is told, used to live nearby "up on Black Mesa," an odd name for any place close enough to the flatlands around Brandon, Manitoba, for shopping (1981:179). Ruby, and the other Indians on the reserve at "Crowley," call Andrews *wasichu*, the Lakota—not Cree—word for Euroamericans, with spelling following Neihardt's in *Black Elk Speaks*. *Heyoka* is another Lakota word; it refers to persons who have been chosen by the Thunder Beings to communicate blessing through performing the ritual of that name (DeMallie 1987:36–37). Why a rural Manitoba woman from a Algonquian Cree community would go through a Siouan ritual, and why these Cree would use a language foreign to them, Andrews never explains. Possibly Ruby and Agnes are really Dakota Sioux, who in fact have several reserves around Brandon, and possibly Andrews has never become aware of the substantial differences between Cree and Sioux?

Nit-picking will never deter readers from the excitement of Andrews' apprenticeship to medicine power, power she desperately needs, we find out, because she is pursued by the evil Red Dog (a man, of course). One chapter ends with Agnes saying, "I hope you don't die. Now, young lady, you will have to face the passions of Red Dog" (1981:148). Happily, fifty-two pages later "Red Dog was shriveling up and growing old . . . the eerie light was gone, and all that was left was an ancient white-haired man." In the Epilogue, Agnes orders Andrews to go back to Beverly Hills, to "write a book and give away what you have learned. Then you may come back to me" (1981:204).

Whether she *gave* away what she learned might be debated. But come back she did—with a book nearly every year. *Flight of the Seventh Moon* (1984), declared on the flyleaf to be "a true story," describes Andrews' hard-won initiation into the secret Sisterhood of the Shields. Here we learn of forty-four medicine women with magical Women's Shields (also called mandalas! 1984:xii). Andrews may have drawn inspiration from Storm's imaginative paragraphs about Twelve Sacred Shields: "Over the Earth there are Twelve Great Tribes. Two of these Peoples are the Indian Peoples. The Other Ten are the Other Peoples of the Earth. These Twelve Peoples are the Sacred Shields" (1972:8–10). Storm once again may have been dipping into and expanding on Grinnell's classic study of the Cheyenne, this time from that serious scholar's sober description of Cheyenne shields (1972 I:187–202). But Grinnell explicitly indicates that only "men of years and discretion" owned shields with spiritual power (1972 I:188).[6]

Jaguar Woman in 1985 continued Andrews' mind-boggling adventures in Indian country. This saga starts with our heroine mushing along behind a dogteam toward her guru's cabin, apparently relocated from southern to northern Manitoba. Once there, she steps outdoors and has a vision of a Butterfly Woman with a crystal sword. The scene shifts, to Andrews' impulsive trip to Yucatán, where Agnes awaits her in the hut of a Mayan medicine woman. For good measure, there's a medicine wheel thrown in (1985:119). In *Star Woman* (1986), Andrews rides Arion, the "magnificent white stallion" of every young girl's dreams. Subsequently, in *Crystal Woman* (1987), the loyal reader finds Andrews and her guru Agnes in a Land-Rover bumping along toward an Aborigine camp near Ayers Rock in "primeval" Australia. There a native Australian medicine woman guides them to the secret women's village, where magic is performed with crystals (compare Bell 1980:244). Always, the women's nemesis Red Dog lurks around; every Andrews book is a bodice-ripper, a Harlequin Romance liberally laced with inflammatory feminist rhetoric plus pop-Zen enigmas galore.

Calmer by far than Andrews, a Peacekeeper rather than a Warrioress, is she who calls herself Dhyani Ywahoo, the twenty-seventh generation of the Ywahoo lineage of the "traditional Etowah Band of the Eastern Tsalagi (Cherokee)." Dhyani works out of her Sunray Meditation Society, "a *gadugi* (society) affiliated with Igidotsoiyi Tsalagi Gadugi of the Etowah Band" (1987:xi), located not in the Cherokees' native North Carolina, but in Vermont. "Until 1979," Ywahoo informs unsuspecting readers, "it was illegal in the United States for Native Americans to practice their traditional religions," (1987:l), immediately establishing her tenuous hold on simple facts. Ywahoo's lineage began, she states, with "the Pale One" whose "teachings flourished throughout the Americas" (1987:2).[7] Her Pale One "rekindled the holy fire and renewed the original instructions encoded within the Crystal Ark, that most sacred crystal that ever sings out harmony's beauteous note . . . The duties of each Ywahoo are to care for the Crystal Ark . . . and the crystal-activating sound formulas and rituals" (1987:2–3). There were, of course, "twelve original tribes . . . the people were the dream children of the angels, their dreaming arising with the primordial sound" (1987:10) which, be it known, "is sung by the quartz crystal . . . it vibrates at 786,000 pulses per millisecond . . . the axis of the universe" (1987:33).[8] "Christ energy is symbolized by the ruby" (1987:251), "the shape of the quartz crystal, its hexagonal structure, is the double triangle or the Star of David" (1987:253). Join in, all ye nations! or as Ywahoo says, in the Lakota phrase we read in *Black Elk Speaks*, "all my relations" (1987:7).

The publication of Ywahoo's book was timed to a momentous event announced by the New Age's favorite art historian, José Argüelles. "The new cycle of thirteen heavens began August 30, 1987, thirteen days after Fifth World ended" (Ywahoo 1987:7). Argüelles calls it the Mayan Factor: the Tzolkin of the Maya, "More than a calendar," we are informed, "the Mayan Harmonic Module . . . evokes . . . the I Ching for Hexagram 49 . . . the phenomenon that I have come to understand as a galactic master-code" (1987:20–21). Argüelles' earlier books were densely packed with references to scholarly figures such as Johann Winckelmann, Odilon Redon, and his dissertation subject, Charles Henry, a student of the psychology of perception. By 1975, Argüelles realized "the split in favor of the left cerebral hemisphere . . . was overtly to come in . . . 1519 when the mental condition of the human race slipped out of balance . . . [into] the Fifth Sun, the Sun of Movement' (1975:14). "The balance maintained by the 'transformative visionaries' is nothing less than a dialog between the two hemispheres" (1975:15). So through two applications of the word "hemisphere," conflict between East and West on the planet merges with conflict between art and cold rationality in the brain, all to be healed beginning August 16, 1987, as Argüelles reads the Mayan calendar (or was it August 30?).

The Indian-published periodical *Daybreak* reported an interview with a Guatemalan Maya, Don Miguel Ajpu, in which the writer mentioned to Don Miguel the "harmonic convergence."

> He said at first he was soundly perplexed . . . Coming back, he . . . said . . . "it is only a mental construction he [Argüelles] made up. Dozens have speculated in this way, but they don't really know our reality, our ceremonies, our ancestor stories, our languages . . . the convergence message, this time, tell the world, it wasn't from us" (Ismaelillo 1987:20).

From "Indian doctors" in antebellum Washington to art historians prophesying the healing of the world, the purported wisdom of American Indians is invoked to allay the malaise of civilization. The "Indians," or their disciples, who proffer the desired wisdom are curiously remote from actual Indian communities.

With no change in the basic thinking, "Indian" has replaced the Classical "Scythian" as the label for the fabled *Naturvölker*. Cultural primitivism, constructed as the opposition to civilization with its discontents, has been part of Western culture for close to three thousand years. This fiction is picked up by credulous scholars and by common charlatans, by neo-romantic writers and by earnest counterculture pilgrims. Borrowing from and serving one another, poets and plastic medicine men earn a living from the hoary tradition of ascribing virtue to nature. The tradition will not die. Its invented Indians are eternally reincarnated Scythians from the primal Gaia of the Western imagination.

Notes

1. For comments on Highwater's pedigree, see *Akwesasne Notes* 16(4):10–12; 17(6):5. The Cherokee are one of the most favored tribal identities assumed by aspirant marginal "Indians." An identity as Cherokee and Blackfoot was also elected by Sylvester Long, the tragic "Chief Buffalo Child Long Lance," who was born as a Black in North Carolina (Smith 1983 and 1988).
2. Ironically, Powell's conjectures were published in the same volume with James Mooney's masterpiece of field observation and reasoning, *The Ghost Dance Religion* (see Kehoe 1988).
3. See Kehoe and Kehoe 1979 for a discussion of the boulder constructions called medicine wheels.
4. For an example of this practice, see the description of the elder, Black Road, counseling the young Black Elk at the end of chapter XII, *Black Elk Speaks* (Neihardt 1932).
5. For more on that equally prolific primitivist, Castaneda, see Richard De Mille's essay, chapter 11 in this volume; also Needham 1985:chapter 9; and Zolla 1981.
6. Incidentally, Grinnell also refers to a Cheyenne named Whistling Elk (1972 I:196–197). Andrews may have borrowed Agnes's name from the same source.
7. By "the Pale One" Ywahoo is apparently referring to the Aztecs' Quetzalcoatl. Exactly where she got this is not cited, but for an example see Hansen 1963.
8. During the early nineteenth century a much-favored explanation of the origins of American Indians was that they were the Lost Tribes of Israel.

References

Andrews, Lynn V. 1981. *Medicine Woman*. San Francisco: Harper & Row.
———. 1984. *Flight of the Seventh Moon*. San Francisco: Harper & Row.
———. 1985. *Jaguar Woman*. San Francisco: Harper & Row.
———. 1986. *Star Woman*. New York: Warner Books.
———. 1987. *Crystal Woman: The Sisterhood of the Dreamtime*. New York: Warner Books.

Argüelles, José A. 1975. *The Transformative Vision*. Boulder: Shambhala.
————. 1987. *The Mayan Factor: Path Beyond Technology*. Santa Fe: Bear & Co.
Bell, Diane. 1980. "Desert Politics: Choices in the 'Marriage Market.' " In *Women and Colonization*. Mona Etienne and Eleanor Leacock, eds. New York: Praeger. 239–69.
Boyd, Doug. 1974. *Rolling Thunder*. New York: Random House.
Brown, Joseph Epes. 1953. *The Sacred Pipe*. Norman: University of Oklahoma Press.
————. 1982. *The Spiritual Legacy of the American Indian*. New York: Crossroad.
Bruchac, Joseph. 1983. "Spinning the Medicine Wheel: The Bear Tribe in the Catskills." *Akwesasne Notes* 15(5):20–22.
Cameron, Charles. 1985. "Creature Spirits Everywhere About Us: A Voice of the Black Elk Nation." In *The Human/Animal Connection*. Randall L. Eaton, ed. Incline Village, NV: Carnivore Research Institute, Sierra Nevada College. 30–36.
Castro, Michael. 1983. *Interpreting the Indian*. Albuquerque: University of New Mexico Press.
DeMallie, Raymond J. 1984. *The Sixth Grandfather*. Lincoln: University of Nebraska Press.
————. 1987. "Lakota Belief and Ritual in the Nineteenth Century." In *Sioux Indian Religion: Tradition and Innovation*. Raymond J. DeMallie and Douglas R. Parks, eds. Norman: University of Oklahoma Press. 25–43.
Freesoul, John Redtail. 1986. *Breath of the Invisible: The Way of the Pipe*. Wheaton, IL: The Theosophical Publishing House.
Grinnell, George Bird. 1972. *The Cheyenne Indians*. Lincoln: University of Nebraska Press. (First edition, 1923.)
Handy, Bob. 1985. *Flyer for "Flaming Rainbow."* Tulsa, OK: Flowering Tree Productions.
Hansen, L. Taylor. 1963. *He Walked the Americas*. Amherst, WI: Amherst Press.
Hausman, Gerald. 1987. "Introduction." In *Keepers of the Fire*, by Eagle Walking Turtle (Gary McClain). Santa Fe: Bear and Company, 9–10.
Highwater, Jamake. 1981. *The Primal Mind: Vision and Reality in Indian America*. New York: Harper & Row.
Honour, Hugh. 1975. *The New Golden Land: European Images of America from the Discovery to the Present Time*. New York: Pantheon Books.
Hungry Wolf, Adolf. 1973. *The Good Medicine Book*. New York: Warner Paperback Library.
Hungry Wolf, Adolf and Beverly. 1983. *Shadows of the Buffalo*. New York: William Morrow and Co.
Ismaelillo. 1987. "Mayan Visions." *Daybreak* 1(1):20.
Johnson, Tim. 1988. "The Second Coming." *Daybreak* 2(1):14–17.
Kehoe, Alice Beck. 1981. *North American Indians: A Comprehensive Account*. Englewood Cliffs, NJ: Prentice-Hall, Inc.
————. 1985. "The Ideological Paradigm in Traditional American Ethnology." In *Social Contexts of American Ethnology, 1840–1984*. June Helm, ed. Washington, DC: American Ethnological Society. 41–49.

————. 1989. *The Ghost Dance: Ethnohistory and Revitalization*. New York: Holt, Rinehart and Winston.

Kehoe, Alice B. and Thomas F. Kehoe. 1979. *Solstice-Aligned Boulder Configurations in Saskatchewan*. Canadian Ethnology Service, Mercury Series No. 48. Ottawa: National Museum of Man, National Museums of Canada.

Kelly, Lawrence C. 1983. *The Assault on Assimilation*. Albuquerque: University of New Mexico Press.

Krippner, Stanley and Alberto Villoldo. 1986. *The Realms of Healing*. Berkeley: Celestial Arts. (First edition, 1976.)

Lovejoy, Arthur O. and George Boas. 1965. *Primitivism and Related Ideas in Antiquity*. New York: Octagon Books. (First edition, 1935.)

Lovelock, James E. 1979. *Gaia*. Oxford: Oxford University Press.

Lyon, William S. 1986. *Flyer for "Black Elk Speaks Aloud."* Ashland, OR: Southern Oregon State College.

Martin, Calvin. 1987. "An Introduction Aboard the *Fidele*." In *The American Indian and the Problem of History*. Calvin Martin, ed. New York: Oxford University Press. 3–26.

Moldow, Gloria. 1987. *Women Doctors in Gilded-Age Washington*. Urbana: University of Illinois Press.

Neihardt, John G. 1932. *Black Elk Speaks*. New York: William Morrow. (Paperback editions 1961, 1979 issued by University of Nebraska Press, Lincoln.)

Needham, Rodney. 1985. *Exemplars*. Berkeley: University of California Press.

Paulson, Lisa. 1987. High Wind Association flyer, May 22, 1987. Plymouth, WI.

Powell, J. W. 1896. "Report of the Director." In *Thirteenth Annual Report, Bureau of Ethnology, 1891–92*. Washington, DC: Government Printing Office. xxi-lvii.

Reifel, Ben. 1971. "Interview," by Joseph H. Cash, Summer 1967. In *To Be an Indian*. New York: Holt, Rinehart and Winston. 121–30.

Russell, Peter. 1983. *The Global Brain*. Los Angeles: J. P. Tarcher.

Sapir, Edward. 1956. "Culture, Genuine and Spurious." In *Culture, Language and Personality*. David G. Mandelbaum, ed. Berkeley: University of California Press, 78–119. (First published 1916.)

Shorris, Earl. 1971. *The Death of the Great Spirit: An Elegy for the American Indian*. New York: Simon and Schuster.

Smith, Donald B. 1983. *Long Lance: the True Story of an Imposter*. Lincoln: University of Nebraska Press.

————. 1988. "From Sylvester Long to Chief Buffalo Child Long Lance." In *Being and Becoming Indian: Biographic Studies of North American Frontiers*. James A. Clifton, ed. Chicago: Dorsey Press. 183–203.

Storm, Hyemeyohsts. 1972. *Seven Arrows*. New York: Ballantine Books.

Sun Bear. 1970. *Buffalo Hearts*. Spokane: Bear Tribe Publishing Co.

Vecsey, Christopher. 1981. "Introduction," by Åke Hultkrantz. In *Belief and Worship in Native North America*. Christopher Vecsey, ed. Syracuse: Syracuse University Press. ix-xxvii.

Ywahoo, Dhyani. 1987. *Voices of Our Ancestors*. Boston: Shambhala.

Zolla, Elémire. 1981. "The Teachings of Carlos Castaneda." In *North American Indian Studies*. Pieter Hovens, ed. Göttingen: Edition Herodot, 247–53.

11

A Legacy of Misperception and Invention: The Omaha Indians in Anthropology

R. H. Barnes

Emile Durkheim once referred to the revolutionary importance of ethnography to sociological knowledge, despite a tendency in his day, still alive today, to dismiss it disdainfully as dull and irrelevant to everyday human concerns. The United States in the nineteenth century produced a lively and influential body of such descriptive studies of cultures and institutions, carried out by persons with strikingly varied backgrounds and purposes. One of the central and enduring questions of anthropology was born from this work, indeed largely and unconsciously from the pages of a single rather unprepossessing and fairly dry report on the Omaha Indians of Nebraska.

In anthropological habit, the issue is known by the union of two ethnic names. The "Crow-Omaha problem," as it is called, is a topic which has grown up with the academic discipline of anthropology and which shows no signs of going away. Initially the phrase referred to the similarities in social classification and unilineal descent groups within the context of certain culturally recognized marriage preferences in many native ethnic groups of North America.

The Crow and the Omaha both belong to the Siouan family. They differ in that the Crow are matrilineal and the Omaha are patrilineal. These differences carry through in kinship terminology, descent group formation and at least partially in marriage preference. The problem as initially conceived was how to explain the similarities. Does social classification determine group structure and marriage preference, or is the reverse true? Alternatively, is it possible that there is no causal relationship and that the similarities are no more than expressions of the same collective attitude.

Many North American peoples have social forms similar to, and no doubt historically and ethnologically related to, the Crow and Omaha. Anthropologists were content for a time to let the names "Crow" and "Omaha," and the associated social systems, stand for *types* of societies. Why the Crow and Omaha proper were singled out in this way is explained in part by fortuitous historical circumstances and in part by the personal preferences of the anthropologists involved. In an early phrasing of the problem the contrast was drawn between the Choctaw and the Omaha. Robert Lowie, who in the early years of the twentieth century was making important contributions to the debate, happened also to be working on the ethnography of the Crow of Montana. Perhaps for this reason anthropologists picked up the habit of referring to the Crow and Omaha as a shorthand way of alluding to what were really a constellation of related analytic questions.

Unfortunately for particular theories, the similarities identified in Crow, Omaha and other societies of the kind were not constant throughout the range of peoples with the features in question. This circumstance had the effect of opening the possibility of elaborating further theories of an essentially speculative and historical nature attempting to account for how societies supposedly once identical had come to differ so much. It also tempted other anthropologists to claim that the similarities in social classification were entirely illusory and of no consequence whatsoever. Another development was that anthropologists began to identify Crow and Omaha systems not just in the limited area of North America where we can be sure that all cultures have some sort of shared background, but all over the world. This trend brought its own reaction, so that one anthropologist for example declared that, "there really is no such thing as an Omaha terminology, except that of the Omaha themselves, and it leads only to confusion and wrong conclusions to suppose that there is" (Needham 1971:15).

The history of these debates has been competently summarized by several authors, the most recent being in Barnes (1984). For present purposes, the point to be made is that shifting conceptions of the Crow-Omaha problem resulted from the healthy willingness on the part of the profession to reconsider established positions and to adopt new perspectives. Unfortunately, as time went by references to Omaha systems became increasingly casual and speculation increasingly remote from its descriptive base, the original ethnographic record.

For the Omaha, this record includes two ethnographic monographs that deserve to be regarded as anthropological classics. The first is the

Third Annual Report of the Bureau of Ethnology (Washington, D.C.), called *Omaha Sociology*, by the Reverend James Owen Dorsey, published in 1884. The second is the Twenty-Seventh Annual Report of the same bureau, published in 1911 by Alice Fletcher and Francis La Flesche and called *The Omaha Tribe*. These books when taken together helped to make the Omaha one of the best and most fully described of North American peoples in their day. Naturally, they attracted attention of anthropologists working on comparative problems. What most distinguished *Omaha Sociology* was its very full description of the Omaha relationship terminology and a less satisfactory description of the sociology of Omaha clans. It also gave a rather elaborate account of Omaha marriage prohibitions, which frankly is very hard for the unprepared reader to digest and which was largely ignored until Claude Lévi-Strauss stimulated interest in it in 1965 (Lévi-Strauss 1966). *The Omaha Tribe* presented a good deal more information on descent groups as well as a rich general coverage of the culture.

Hinsley (1981:175) has remarked how the Director of the Bureau of American Ethnology, John Wesley Powell, managed to mold Dorsey's ethnographic findings into "appropriate shapes," which means in particular in conformity with the theories of Lewis Henry Morgan, one of the nineteenth century "inventors of kinship" (Trautmann 1987). Dorsey had spent 1871–1873 living as an Episcopal missionary among the Ponca, whose language he learned to speak and who had in prehistoric times formed part of the Omaha community. He was a good practical linguist, having learned as a child to read Hebrew. When the Bureau of Ethnology (later Bureau of American Ethnology) was formed in 1879, Dorsey joined it. Powell had already sent him to collect linguistic and anthropological material among the Omaha for the Smithsonian Institution, and Dorsey lived with the Omaha from July 1878 until April 1880.

Dorsey's writings are indeed characterized by what Hinsley calls his modest and sympathetic temperament. Powell, who was unhappy with Dorsey's lack of a formal background in anthropology, asked him to read Morgan's *Ancient Society*. Dorsey (1884:215) dutifully begins his discussion of Omaha social organization with a quotation from Powell defining the state, followed by a definition of a descent group (gens or clan) which was lifted almost straight from Morgan. Indeed coming as it does at the head of the opening paragraph of the relevant chapter, the reader might suspect that the Director's guiding hand extended well beyond strictly editorial considerations.

Dorsey had it that a gens (patrilineal descent group) or clan (matrilineal descent group) was composed of a number of consanguinei, claiming descent from a common ancestor, and having a common taboo or taboos. Dorsey's comments later brought an implicit refutation from Fletcher and La Flesche (1911:195), who denied that Omaha descent groups were political organizations and observed that, unlike the Latin gens which was Morgan's starting point, its members did not claim to be descended from a common ancestor. Hinsley says that, "while he obediently adopted Morgan-Powell structures and terminology, Dorsey refused to theorize from his data, which as often as not contradicted Powell's expectations."

In fact, he did speculate in ways that were clearly his own, but here too his data undermined the theory. The Omaha tribal circle, as Dorsey encountered it, consisted of two moieties, each containing five named descent groups. These groups (gentes in Dorsey's terminology) were usually further subdivided. When describing descent group segmentation, Dorsey's informants often referred to the number four, an archetypal classifier in Omaha culture, as in many other North American peoples. Dorsey inferred that, "There are strong reasons for believing that each gens had four subgentes at the first; several subgentes having become few in number of persons have been united to the remaining and more powerful of their respective gentes." Though some changes of the kind mentioned did occur in the historical period, Dorsey's conclusion is probably best regarded as the result of his inexperience and the general state of anthropological sophistication of his day. Omaha attitudes and descent group division were far less uniform and systematic than this picture implies, and Dorsey may well have interpreted some Omaha statements incorrectly, believing them to be imbued with the same academic desire for clarity and simplicity as his own thought. Be that as it may, the idea that Omaha descent groups were, at least in the past, uniform, substantial, homogeneous structures (which the evidence now available shows they were not) continued to confuse anthropological arguments well into the twentieth century.

Perhaps the crowning achievement of *Omaha Sociology* is Dorsey's record of the relationship terminology. Though obviously incomplete in some respects, in other ways it might almost be said to be too complete. Like the rest of his work, Dorsey's discussion of the terminology is accompanied by little or no analysis. What he provides is essentially just a set of tables showing the genealogical positions to which terms are applied. It was not until Bowers published books on the Mandan (1950) and Hidatsa (1965) that comparably thorough descriptions became available for any other Siouan peoples.

This aspect of Dorsey's ethnography has generally been admired at a distance. The way he presents it does not make it easily accessible, and for most students the less said about kinship terminologies the better. It is ironic that the better known analytic accounts of Omaha terminology (Radcliffe-Brown 1941 and Lounsbury 1964) have been carried on at a remove, since they actually refer to Tax's material on the Algonquian Fox. Thus when anthropologists say that some people in Africa or Asia have an Omaha terminology, the reader may reasonably doubt that they have bothered to make a point by point comparison with the actual Omaha system. Dorsey's information has recently been reorganized to facilitate consultation (Barnes 1984:132–137).

After *Omaha Sociology* was published, a German jurist, Josef Kohler (1897), gave it extensive attention in a monograph on primitive marriage. Kohler focused on similarities between features of the terminology (what may be called patrilineal equations) and the Omaha preference for taking as a second or later wife, the first wife's sister, father's sister or brother's daughter. All these women belong to the same patrilineal group, and Kohler noticed this fact, as well as the fact that the rather different terminological features and marriage preference of the Choctaw were compatible with their matrilineal groups. Durkheim's review (1897) of Kohler's book set the issues forth more plainly, and the "Crow-Omaha problem" was born, what before Lowie, Kohler would have called the "Choctaw-Omaha problem" had he chosen to express matters that way.

In addition to marriage preferences Dorsey described an alarmingly elaborate list of marriage prohibitions. Until recently readers of his book have left these passages strictly alone. Indeed on the basis of published information it is almost impossible to know what to make of them. During the 1950s and 1960s, stimulated by Lévi-Strauss's classic *The Elementary Structures of Kinship* (1949 and 1969), anthropological interest in systems of positive marriage alliance grew to the point that they became one of the central topics of the profession. The climate was appropriate for asking whether there were comparable structures based on marriage prohibitions, as Lévi-Strauss did in fact in 1965 referring specifically to the Omaha. However, adopting his characteristically distanced, if not disdainful, attitude toward the empirical record, as opposed to the intellectual play with imaginative models, Lévi-Strauss did not attempt to crack the code of this aspect of *Omaha Sociology*.

Being more empirically minded and frustrated with not being able to understand what Dorsey meant, I tried my hand at it. I concluded that the Omaha in fact did not have an alliance system of the kind Lévi-Strauss attributed to them. I also inferred that the Omaha may not have been burdened with quite so severe a set of limitations to choice as at first appeared because, so it would seem, only relationships which are

actually remembered are effectively barred and the Omaha have fairly
brief genealogical memories. To come to these conclusions, however,
which of course are no better than the records on which they are based,
I found to my surprise and actual relief that I had to give a good deal
of attention to the relations between the ethnographers and between
them and the Omaha. I say relief because there were some genuine
mysteries affecting the evidential base, and these mysteries, being personal, were a welcome distraction from abstract analytic concerns.

Dorsey died unexpectedly of typhoid fever in February 1895 at the
age of forty-seven. In 1890, six years after the publication of *Omaha
Sociology*, Dorsey announced that he was preparing a monograph on
Indian personal names that would also contain Ponca and Omaha genealogical tables. These genealogies were to illustrate not only personal
names, but the kinship system and marriage laws as well. Completion
of the project was prevented by his early death, but manuscript dic-
tionaries of Omaha and Ponca personal names, together with complete
Omaha genealogies up to the 1880s and partial Ponca genealogies survive
in the National Anthropological Archives, Washington, D.C.

Dorsey may have begun compiling Omaha genealogies while he was
in the field, but evidently he had not finished the work by the time he
published *Omaha Sociology*. Two Omaha, Samuel Freemont and George
Miller, visited Dorsey in Washington in 1888 and 1889 to help him revise
the genealogies. A consequence of this chronology is that when Dorsey
published his monograph he may well not have had crucial information
now available in the genealogies for testing statements about marriage
prohibitions.

Dorsey's specifications of marriage restrictions are more elaborate
than anything of the kind ever published on related American Indian
groups, and no other authority on the Omaha has given information of
comparable extent. In a few pages Dorsey set out such a list of constraints
that he was led to ask how it was that an Omaha could ever find an
eligible person to marry. Internal evidence suggests that this crucial
section derives almost entirely from two informants, Joseph La Flesche
and Lewis Morris (or Two Crows), who visited him in Washington in
1882 to help him revise the book for publication. In keeping with his
open, but somewhat uncritical, attitude toward information given him,
Dorsey frequently recorded in the book statements by La Flesche and
Two Crows in which they correct or disagree with information from
other Omaha. Both Edward Sapir (1938:7) and Frederica de Laguna
(1957) later commented on the possible implications of this evidence of
disagreement among informants. When taken together with the fairly
ample published and unpublished information about Omaha personal-

ities now available, they provide an opportunity for going behind the surface of published ethnography, giving it a critical extra dimension and potentially greatly increasing our understanding both of the Omaha and of how ethnography and anthropology work—but not without a great deal of effort.

What has not, until recently, been attempted is to examine the statements of these two men about marriage in light of their own lives to gauge just how sound is their information. Joseph La Flesche, or Iron Eye, is one of the most well known Omaha of his era. Having been adopted into the Elk clan and the Omaha tribe by a principal chief named Big Elk, Joseph La Flesche himself became for a time a head chief of the Omaha. His father was French Canadian and his mother was variously reported to be a Ponca with family connections to the Omaha or actually an Omaha. He had several wives simultaneously, and three illustrious children, including a woman medical doctor (Dr. Susan Picotte), as well as Susette "Bright Eyes" La Flesche who became nationally known through campaigning for the welfare of the Ponca tribe (Clark and Webb 1988), and Francis La Flesche, joint author of one of the classic Omaha monographs.

Liberty (1978) has written of Francis La Flesche as "the first professional American Indian anthropologist," but she has also devoted an article to his role as an "informant" (1976). Francis La Flesche grew up speaking Omaha and was born early enough to participate in Omaha rituals and the annual buffalo hunt. During Dorsey's period on the reservation he was a trusted and reliable informant, having been educated in the Presbyterian mission school, about which he later wrote a book. His relationship with Alice Fletcher was considerably more complex.

Alice Fletcher had trained in anthropology as a private student of Frederic Putnam, who was director of the Peabody Museum of Harvard University. Thomas Henry Tibbles and his wife, Susette La Flesche, came east in 1879 seeking support for the Ponca who had been forced to move to Oklahoma. Fletcher persuaded Tibbles to guide her on a tour of the Omaha, Winnebago, Ponca and Santee Sioux reservations. She later spent much time carrying out allotments of land for the Omaha, the Winnebago and Nez Percé. During the Omaha allotment, at which she was assisted by Francis La Flesche, she also began her study of Omaha culture. Mary Copley Thaw endowed a lifetime fellowship at the Peabody Museum for her in 1891 and also helped her to purchase an apartment in Washington, D.C. In the same year Fletcher adopted Francis informally.

Francis had begun working as a copyist in the Office of Indian Affairs in 1881. In 1891 he attended the National University, earning the LL.B. in 1892 and the LL.M. in 1893. In 1910 he transferred to the Bureau of Ethnology, which sent him to work in Oklahoma. From 1920 until retirement in 1929, he was officially employed as an "ethnologist" of the Bureau. He published a distinguished series of anthropological articles and monographs of entirely his own production, including four annual reports of the Bureau of American Ethnology on the Osage. *The Omaha Tribe* seems to have been set to paper by Fletcher, but the substance is plainly mostly due to La Flesche.

Mark (1982) has given an unusual interpretation to their relationship. Instead of simply emphasizing how their mutual support and cooperation led to their individual and joint achievements, she sees as well an element of mutual competition. For Mark, Francis La Flesche struggled as a Native American for recognition as a professional anthropologist, while Alice Fletcher, who was striving toward a similar goal against the professional restrictions then placed on women, for a considerable period held him back. At this distance in time, it is difficult to judge the accuracy and fairness of this view, for Mark is clearly reading more into their circumstances than the evidence strictly warrants.

Francis La Flesche enters into the Omaha case therefore in three principal ways: (1) partly as a participant and therefore subject, (2) as an informant, like his father, both to Dorsey and to Fletcher, and therefore as a native interpreter of culture, and (3) as a professional ethnographer and analyst. In all three respects, he had something to say relevant to understanding his father's account of the marriage rules.

Dorsey (1884:255–256) begins the passage in question by describing the people whom Joseph La Flesche, Two Crows and some of the relatives of Two Crows could not marry. Dorsey says that Joseph's mother belonged to the Black Bear group of the Ponca tribe. He also names the Ponca descent group of his mother's mother and even of his mother's mother's mother. All three Ponca descent groups were prohibited to Joseph, though Dorsey writes that the Omaha Black Bear group was not prohibited, because it belonged to a different tribe from that of his mother. In several places Dorsey referred to the fact that Joseph was Ponca by birth, only having become Omaha by virtue of adoption. His younger brother Frank, namesake of Francis La Flesche the son, remained with the Ponca and became a chief of the tribe. Frank La Flesche's mother was also Ponca, but a different woman than Joseph's mother.

Dorsey intended that this information merely illustrate the rules, and it looks substantial enough. Unfortunately, the question of Joseph's mother's tribal membership was a sensitive family issue with political implications. When Dorsey was preparing his study of personal names

he requested information from Francis concerning the rights in children
following divorce, tactlessly phrasing the question in terms of occur-
rences within the La Flesche family. Francis wrote back a short letter
refusing to cooperate and complaining that Dorsey had already published too many personal details in Bureau of American Ethnology
reports. "Some things you have published about me which I did not
wish published but you took the liberty to do so."

In response to a hostile anonymous review of *The Omaha Tribe* which
brought up the old charge that Joseph La Flesche was not an Omaha
but a Ponca, Fletcher and Francis La Flesche (1912) spelled out the
objection. They referred first to the statement that Joseph La Flesche
was a Ponca and second to an account the young Francis had given
Dorsey describing how Joseph's installation ceremony as a head chief
had been broken off and left incomplete because a ceremonial pipe had
been allowed to drop. Fletcher and La Flesche attempted to refute their
critic by offering a genealogy showing that Joseph's mother was actually
an Omaha. This genealogy, the only evidence that she was Omaha, was
taken from a family friend, Samuel Freemont, in the last year of his life
(1906). Dorsey's earlier, unpublished genealogies, on which Samuel
Freemont had worked in 1888, do not confirm her Omaha membership,
nor the assertion that she belonged to the Black Shoulder descent group.
Joseph's wife Mary Gale said on several occasions that his mother was
a Ponca. Furthermore, Joseph's half-brother Dwight Sherman, who shared
the same mother and who figures in the genealogy under discussion,
gave testimony six months after the Fletcher and La Flesche letter was
written in the Court of Claims in September 1912 affirming that he was
one-half Ponca, his mother being a Ponca and sister to a Ponca chief.

Family sensitivity on this point relates to the circumstances in which
Joseph gained and later lost the head chieftainship, the details of which
cannot be gone into here, though these in no way qualify his reliability
as a knowledgeable participant in Omaha culture. The uncertainty about
the mother's actual family connections derives from the fact that she
tired of her French husband's long absences while away trading and
divorced him. She then married an Omaha man, but both were killed
by Sioux in 1847. Joseph's father married another Ponca woman, who
became the mother of the elder Frank La Flesche. Fletcher and La
Flesche attributed the genealogy of Joseph given by Dorsey to Frank,
but if that were true, it would mean that Frank at least had violated the
rules, for his wife belonged to one of the restricted groups. The Omaha
tended to suppress memory of dead relatives, especially women. If a
woman died when her children were young, "it is probable, that, at
maturity, they will have forgotten even her name" (Fletcher 1883:395).

Though Joseph did not speak English, he did speak French and participated in the French world of commerce along the Missouri River. Ironically, he was a Franco-Indian Métis drawn into Omaha society where he was, through his adopted status, uneasily situated though influential. His son Francis, whose mother was entirely Omaha, moved from full participation in the declining traditional Omaha culture of his childhood eventually into full participation in twentieth-century English speaking American professional life, earning in the end (1926) an honorary LL.D. from the University of Nebraska. We misunderstand the Omaha ethnographies, not to mention Omaha history, if we view Joseph La Flesche only in terms of his assumed Native American identity and neglect the obvious fact that by traveling with his father he learned to participate in his father's world too, eventually enabling him as trader to the tribe to secure his chieftainship, despite competition from a similar Métis, Logan Fontenelle. On the other hand, the temptation to see in Francis only the traditional Omaha can lead to grotesque results. Liberty (1976:106) has noted that a photograph taken of him in the Bureau of American Ethnology dressed in office attire with a buffalo robe draped over his shoulder was retouched for his obituary in the *American Anthropologist* to remove any sign of his bow tie, white collar, trousers and polished shoes. The retouched photograph visually labels him the archetypal Indian. Perhaps Francis's interest in Pan-Indian political organization and the Native American Church (Liberty 1978:46) indicates that his life was more of a piece with his professional career than any attempt to separate his orientations into traditional and modern would suggest.

Since the evidence conclusively confirms that Joseph La Flesche's mother was a Ponca, the assertion by Fletcher and Francis La Flesche that she was an Omaha can be dismissed, with the reservation that she clearly did have family ties to the Omaha and it is through these ties that Joseph La Flesche may have been physically related to the Big Elk who adopted him into the tribe. Therefore the evidence he gave Dorsey about marriage prohibitions can after all be taken at face value. The situation is somewhat different respecting Dorsey's other illustration of the rules, taken from the family of Two Crows.

Dorsey lists the descent groups from which Two Crows, his father and his grandfather had taken women. Though Two Crows was free to take further wives from the same group as his first wife, he was not allowed to marry women belonging to the same descent lines as his mother and his grandmothers. His brothers shared the same prohibitions. The son of Two Crows was prohibited the same lines plus that of his own mother. All these prohibitions were passed on to the grandson of Two Crows in so far, and this is an important reservation, as living persons could remember the connection. In other words, the prohibitions would have been cumulative and increasing in number were it not for the fact that as one generation replaced another, the descent group affiliations and even names of more distant relatives were routinely forgotten.

Following the examples, Dorsey gives a more formal statement of the marriage restrictions. These are very elaborate and if obeyed in a mechanical way might well have made it extremely difficult for an Omaha man or woman to find an eligible partner. There is no evidence, however, that they really had trouble of this kind, although it is known that adults were careful to see to it that young people did not make inappropriate choices (as they still did in 1930, see Mead 1932:80). Elsewhere (Barnes 1984:162–175), I have discussed the formal implications of the various rules and concluded that the Omaha did not really have such extensive restrictions as anthropologists have thought. The appearance of extreme restriction results from the circumstances of Dorsey's discussions with Joseph La Flesche and Two Crows in 1882 and the way he wrote up their information as a set of impersonal rules. What they actually seem to have been trying to tell him is that men of the same local line but of different generations ought not to marry into the same groups as long as close kinsmen in these generations are still living or the memory of the tie is fresh.

In any case the details of this rather intricate examination do not need to be repeated here. What I wish to do now is simply to draw attention to an important weakness in the evidence given by Two Crows. Although Two Crows would have been aware of the problem, Dorsey may well not have been in the position to appreciate it until he completed his work on Omaha genealogies four years after *Omaha Sociology* appeared. From these genealogies and scattered references in various publications, the following picture of the family of Two Crows emerges. The family belonged to the Mottled Object segment of the Leader descent group. Two Crows told Dorsey (1890:399) that his paternal grandfather had been killed during a raid on the Pawnee around 1778. His father, Fear-Inspiring Buffalo Bull, was attacked and apparently killed by an unknown tribe in 1840 (Fletcher and La Flesche 1911:99). Dorsey's genealogies indicate that this man had several daughters, but he does not give their names nor indicate their number, which suggests that they may well all have been dead and, in keeping with Omaha habit, have been generally forgotten by the 1880s.

Two Crows was born in 1824 or 1826 and, according to his gravestone at Macy, Nebraska, died on March 4, 1894. He also had seven brothers.

An elder brother, Stands-at-the-Front, died in a battle with Dakota in 1849 or 1850, while looking through a loop-hole he cut in a tent skin to fire through (Dorsey 1890:431). This man's wife married another of the brothers, Buffalo-Bellowing-in-the-Distance. A marginal note in the genealogies laconically comments "killed by Sioux." Of the remaining brothers, Walking-in-Groups had died by October 21, 1878 (Dorsey 1890:502, 692). I have no record of the deaths of Flying Crow and Artichoke, but infer they were dead by the 1880s. The latter seems not to have married and is noted as having had "no issue." Evidently, therefore, the only two siblings of Two Crows alive in 1882 were the ones Dorsey mentioned as sharing the same prohibitions. These men were Standing Swan, who lived until April, 1914, when he was killed by a young man while both were drunk, and Dakota, commonly referred to as Sioux Solomon, who by 1914 had died of alcoholism.

Two Crows had a very mixed career typical of the position of the tribe during this period. He was respected in his community and thought to speak the purest Omaha. He had been a successful warrior and was a leader in the Buffalo Dance Society; but, although he was not a Christian, he was an active member of Joseph La Flesche's modernizing group. Dorsey wrote that, "He says just what he thinks, going directly to the point," but Fortune thought he had deliberately withheld from Dorsey important information about the Buffalo Society.

Dorsey not only stated that Standing Swan and Sioux Solomon shared the restrictions ascribed to Two Crows, but named the groups from which their wives came as proof of conformity. These facts were accurate, but the genealogies later available show that Two Crows was not telling the whole story. In fact five of his seven brothers actually married women from prohibited groups, although since two had the same wife, only four women were involved. In two other cases, the women in question were second wives. Only one of the men alive in 1882 was currently involved or becoming involved in such a liaison, and in this case the potential for embarrassment between Two Crows and Joseph La Flesche was great enough to insure that they would say nothing about it to Dorsey. Sioux Solomon's second wife was a woman from the Black Bear segment of the On the Left Side descent group. She was named New Moon Returning, but was also known as Alice La Flesche Solomon. She had been the second wife of Joseph's son Francis, who divorced her in 1884 for adultery, naming two prominent Omaha men as correspondents.

Francis married this woman in August, 1879. Some authors (Green 1969:177; Mark 1982:499) have confused her with his first wife Alice Mitchell, daughter of He-who-is-Brave (or Henry Mitchell) of the Pipe segment of the Black Shoulder descent group. She and Francis were married on June 26, 1877 and she died in 1878 (Dorsey 1890:692). Since Green has suggested that the death was only symbolic and that she was the same as Alice La Flesche Solomon, it should be noted that the genealogies of 1888 both show her as married to Francis and note that she was "dead," while the second woman lived until July 3, 1914. Francis petitioned for divorce on November 6, 1883, but the couple were already estranged by the end of 1881. Francis had recently been appointed to the Indian Bureau and late in that year, according to Green, he returned to the mission on government business, where he ignored wife and child, while paying enough attention to a young woman teacher to cause a scandal, leading the woman to leave her job. His father-in-law, Little Prairie Chicken or Horace Cline, was affronted by his behavior and by the fact that Francis ignored Omaha custom and did not present him with gifts. He then went to the mission and took a horse belonging to Francis and several from his sister.

Possibly Sioux Solomon had not entered the picture by 1882, but it is equally possible that he had and that the whole painful affair lent an extra dimension of caution to the discussion of marriage that Dorsey, who had not been on the reservation since April, 1880, was not at all or not fully informed about. Francis later married (in 1908) and divorced a half-Chippewa woman who then settled a few doors down the street from Francis and Alice Fletcher in Washington. Even his close association and frequent traveling with the much older Alice Fletcher led to gossip on the reservation.

It is not unusual of course for people to break the rules of their society and to conceal the fact. But the present question is to establish what were the rules and to what degree they were deemed binding. No one has claimed for any other Siouan tribe that their rules were so elaborate as the Omaha, and the only evidence of that kind derives from Two Crows and Joseph La Flesche, who were possibly misunderstood by Dorsey, but who certainly were not telling everything of relevance from within their own families. The whole passage therefore is suspect. It is certainly a weak basis to sustain speculation such as that by Lévi-Strauss that representations of Crow-Omaha systems require an extra dimension or that their restrictions on marriage have the effect on a small population of resulting in a system of unconscious prescriptions. When readers come across references to "Omaha alliance" in remote places of the world, it would be well for them to remember the mystery of Joseph La Flesche's mother, the discreet silence by Two Crows about some of his sisters-in-law, and the embarrassment about Francis La Flesche's second wife.

Because the two classic Omaha monographs were so unusual in their day, they were widely cited and referred to by anthropologists with speculative ends in view. Thereafter they continued to attract attention as much for their academic fame as for the immediate appropriateness of the ethnographic record. As time went on anthropologists tended to consult this record less frequently, and to treat the Omaha as an established and essentially well understood social type, overlooking the fact that our knowledge of the Omaha has not advanced much beyond what was available in 1911 (the major exceptions being works by Mead and Fortune, both published in 1932) and has certainly not kept pace with developments in twentieth century ethnography. Earlier writers tended to stay closer to the facts and their speculations tend to be more accurate than those of later authors.

A thorough review of the published and unpublished information has permitted a double check, both on the evidential status of the ethnographies and on the current state of anthropological theory where it takes up issues of relevance to these ethnographies. On the whole the ethnographies come off better than current theory. Certainly the record does make it possible in many respects to test and correct theories in ways that had not until recently been attempted. Furthermore, despite disagreements and differing interests and styles among the three main ethnographers, not to mention their vastly different backgrounds and occupations, the basic features of Omaha culture do come through their sometimes conflicting reports.

Ironically, Dorsey's rather deadpan reiteration of disagreements among informants allows us a century later to open up the ethnographies and see mid- to late-nineteenth century Omaha life, as it were, three dimensionally. Of course what we see will have a lot to do with late-twentieth century preoccupations. But the main thing is that ethnography which long ago had a formative impact on anthropological understanding and then to a degree began collecting dust on library shelves has once again come alive and had an impact. There is actually plenty of scope for progress by persons who wish to learn the Omaha language and to carry the reassessment further into those other topics also richly covered by La Flesche and his two partners. It is fair to infer that the lessons for anthropology have not yet all been perceived or learned and that the profession will find occasion in future to look once more at *Omaha Sociology* and *The Omaha Tribe*.

References

Barnes, R. H. 1984. *Two Crows Denies It: A History of Controversy in Omaha Sociology*. Lincoln and London: University of Nebraska Press.

Bowers, Alfred W. 1950. *Mandan Social and Ceremonial Organization*. Chicago: University of Chicago Press.

———. 1965. *Hidatsa Social and Ceremonial Organization*. Bulletin 194, Bureau of American Ethnology. Washington, DC: Government Printing Office.

Clark, Jerry E., and Martha Ellen Webb. 1988. "Susette and Susan La Flesche: Reformer and Missionary." In *Being and Becoming Indian: Biographic Studies of North American Frontiers*. James A. Clifton, ed. Chicago: The Dorsey Press.

Dorsey, James Owen. 1884. *Omaha Sociology*. Third Annual Report of the Bureau of Ethnology (1881–1882). Washington, DC: Government Printing Office.

———. 1890. *The Cegiha Language. Contributions to North American Ethnology*, vol. 6. Washington, DC: Government Printing Office.

Durkheim, Emile. 1897. "Review of Josef Kohler, Zur Urgeschichte der Ehe." *L'Année Sociologique* 1:306–19.

Fletcher, Alice C. 1883. *Observations on the Laws and Privileges of the Gens in Indian Society*. Proceedings of the American Association for the Advancement of Science 32:395–17.

Fletcher, Alice C., and Francis La Flesche. 1911. *The Omaha Tribe*. Annual Report of the Bureau of American Ethnology, vol. 27. Washington, DC: Government Printing Office.

———. 1912. "Communication." *American Historical Review* 17:885–86.

Fortune, Reo. 1932. *Omaha Secret Societies*. New York: Columbia University Press.

Green, Norma Kidd. 1969. *Iron Eye's Family: The Children of Joseph La Flesche*. Lincoln, Nebraska: Johnsen.

Hinsley, Curtis M. 1981. *Savages and Scientists: The Smithsonian Institution and the Development of American Anthropology, 1846–1910*. Washington, DC: Smithsonian Institution Press.

Kohler, Josef. 1897. *Zur Urgeschichte der Ehe: Totemismus, Gruppenehe, Mutterrecht*. Stuttgart: Enke (1975 edition. *On the Prehistory of Marriage: Totemism, Group Marriage, Mother Right*, ed., R. H. Barnes, trans. R. H. Barnes and Ruth Barnes. Classics in Anthropology. Chicago: University of Chicago Press).

Laguna, Frederica de. 1957. "Some Problems of Objectivity in Ethnology." *Man* 57(228):179–82.

Lévi-Strauss, Claude. 1949. *Les Structures élémentaires de la Parenté*. Paris: Presses Universitaires de France.

———. 1966. *The Future of Kinship Studies*. Proceedings of the Royal Anthropological Institute of Great Britain and Ireland for 1965.

———. 1969. *The Elementary Structures of Kinship*. J. H. Bell, J. R. von Sturmer, and Rodney Needham, trans. London: Eyre and Spottiswoode.

Liberty, Margot. 1976. "Native American Informants: The Contribution of Francis La Flesche." In *American Anthropology: The Early Years*. John V. Murra, ed. (1974 Proceedings of the American Ethnological Society) St. Paul: West.

———. 1978. "Francis La Flesche: The Osage Odyssey." In *American Indian Intellectuals*. Margot Liberty, ed. (1976 Proceedings of the American Ethnological Society) St. Paul: West.

Lounsbury, F. G. 1964. "A Formal Account of the Crow- and Omaha-type

Kinship Terminologies." In *Explorations in Cultural Anthropology*. W. H. Goodenough, ed. New York: McGraw-Hill.

Mark, Joan. 1982. "Francis La Flesche: The American Indian as Anthropologist." *Isis* 73: 487–510.

Mead, Margaret. 1932. *The Changing Culture of an Indian Tribe*. New York: Columbia University Press.

Morgan, Lewis Henry. 1877. *Ancient Society or Researches in the Lines of Human Progress from Savagery Through Barbarism to Civilization*. New York: Holt.

Needham, Rodney. 1971. "Remarks on the Analysis of Kinship and Marriage." In *Rethinking Kinship and Marriage*. Rodney Needham, ed. (Association of Social Anthropologists Monograph 11) London: Tavistock.

Radcliffe-Brown, A. R. 1941. "The Study of Kinship Systems." *Journal of the Royal Anthropological Institute* 71(1): 18.

Sapir, Edward. 1938. "Why Cultural Anthropology Needs the Psychiatrist." *Psychiatry* 1:7–12.

Trautmann, Thomas. 1987. *Lewis Henry Morgan and the Invention of Kinship*. Berkeley: University of California Press.

12

Validity Is Not Authenticity: Distinguishing Two Components of Truth

Richard de Mille

Editor's Note

While he was a student at the University of California, Los Angeles, Carlos Castaneda reported ten years of Sonoran field work, not in scholarly journals but in three best-selling popular volumes, the third of which was accepted in 1973 as his formal dissertation for the Ph.D. in anthropology. In 1975, Richard de Mille, psychologist and writer, was reading Castaneda's volume, about "don Juan," the now-legendary Mexican Indian teacher of universal wisdom, when he was struck by a stupendous scientifio-literary realization: Castaneda's sage of the sagebrush was an imaginary person, and those eclectical metaphysical conversations in the desert were academic allegories. For the next six years, de Mille pursued Castaneda up and down library stacks and across the realms of discourse, until he had produced Castaneda's Journey *and* The Don Juan Papers. *These books, well received by scholars and public alike, drill the bones of* Uclanthropus piltdunides castanedae *and everywhere strike baloney—though of course many of Castaneda's fans, with or without Ph.D., still like to believe that Carlos and don Juan roamed Sonoran sands together, catching jack rabbits with their bare hands while discussing Husserl and Wittgenstein. Some credit Castaneda with telling the "truth" because they like his ideas, others because in his fables they recognize some of their own or others' ethnographic findings. The following essay explains why truth in anthromancing is not always what it seems.*

Time's 1973 cover story raised serious questions about Castaneda's truthfulness. Where had he really been born and when? How solid a being was don Juan? Were the books fact or fiction? Rebuking *Time* for setting its "hired leeches" on Castaneda's works and person, a reader declared the don Juan story "no less true or honest" if wholly invented. Should don Juan prove imaginary, wrote Peter Matthiessen in *The Snow Leopard*, "then spurious ethnology becomes a great work of the imagination; whether borrowed or not, the teaching rings true." "The most vividly convincing documents I have read," Carl Rogers told fellow psychologists, "come from one man, Carlos Castaneda." "He may be lying," hedged *New Age*, "but what he says is true." Truth, apparently, is not a simple matter.

When a *Los Angeles Times* book reviewer said *Castaneda's Journey* (de Mille 1976) had offered evidence "strong enough to sow seeds of doubt in the firmest bedrocks of belief," an exasperated reader charged him and me and skeptics in general with missing the point, which was that Castaneda had provided a system of thinking meant precisely to break readers out of the bonds of having to ask whether metaphysical books are based on fact. "If the system is valid," our correspondent said, "its source is rather irrelevant." I answered that philosophy is not the only game in town; some people wish instead to play anthropology, where sources are not only relevant but sometimes crucial (see chapter 11).

"Either Castaneda is recording an encounter with a master . . . or else he is himself that master," wrote Joseph Margolis, a professional player of the philosophy game; "in this sense, it makes no difference whether the books are a record of an actual encounter or whether Castaneda is the author of a clever fiction." I gladly grant Margolis his point if strictly confined to the teaching of metaphysics, but in the game of science it makes a big difference whether or not a field report is based on actual trips to the field.

Psychoanalyst Elsa First distinguished naïve skeptics who reject the don Juan books simply because they report anomalous or apparently supernatural events from more knowledgeable skeptics who find Carlos's desert novitiate simply too good to be true—don Juan too much the oriental guru, his teachings too close to Sufism, Tantric Buddhism, or the Hindu chakra system. "This could well be explained," First countered, "by the fact that the 'natural mind' everywhere perceives similarly" (see chapter 9). The point was well made, and the explanation in terms of worldwide mysticism must be seriously considered, but in the end, after further conceptual analysis and an examination of particular evidence, it will definitely be rejected.[1]

When poet Robert Bly wrote in the *New York Times* that Castaneda "ransacks the work of genuine researchers like Michael Harner" to prepare his "spiritual goulash" and that his "thefts" are convincingly documented in *Castaneda's Journey*, Harner emphatically protested what he said was the mistake "of assuming that similarities between Casta-neda's material and that published by others on shamanism is due to plagiarism by Castaneda"; "apparently," Harner continued, Bly and de Mille "are unaware that remarkable parallels exist in shamanic belief and practice throughout the primitive world."

In keeping with Harner's wish that those who write about Castaneda should be better informed, I have by this time read several books beyond Harner's own outstanding works on the Jivaro—books by such au-thorities as Bean and Saubel, Furst, the Leightons, Myerhoff, Opler, Petrullo, Sharon, Steward, and Underhill—and I think I have now grasped the general outlines of shamanic belief and practice. While I was writing *Castaneda's Journey* I had barely dipped into Eliade, who tells us, for example, that "the shamans lay the novice on the ground and cover him with leaves and branches." Don Juan did the same to Carlos, of course, covering him first with branches, then with leaves, and then with earth. Such a parallel Harner no doubt had in mind to illustrate his conception of Castaneda as a source of valid ethnographic ideas, and there is certainly nothing in the example to raise anyone's suspicions, but other parallels are more richly textured.

In her 1968 dissertation, Barbara Myerhoff described the ritual peyote hunt in the sacred land of the Huichol ancestors. After the baskets had been filled, the shaman told his party of hunters they must all leave as quickly as possible, for it was dangerous to remain there. "We were puzzled," Myerhoff wrote, "but fell into our places at the end of the line and found ourselves barely able to keep up, for the group was nearly running."

In his 1973 dissertation, also know as *Journey to Ixtlan*, Castaneda described a night spent in the hills practicing the "gait of power." Having frightened Carlos sufficiently with ghost stories and bird calls, don Juan announced he was ready to leave. "Let's get out of here," he said and began to run. Carlos wanted to stay in the hills until dawn, but don Juan retorted "in a very dramatic tone" that to stay there would be suicidal. "I followed him," wrote Castaneda, "but . . . I could not keep up with him, and he soon disappeared in the darkness ahead of me."

Harner would surely have no trouble with this example. Fear of holy places, he might say, is universal. When people are afraid, they run. The less fleet have a hard time keeping up with the more fleet. It's really quite simple, if you're not blinded by a passion for turning honest reporters into clever hoaxers.

Very well, then, the example is not evidential. But what about don Juan's "gait of power"? Where did that come from? In *Magic and Mystery in Tibet* (published in 1932, reissued in 1971) Alexandra David-

Neel described the *lung-gom-pa* trance walker: "The man proceeded at an unusual gait and, especially, with an extraordinary swiftness." In *Journey to Ixtlan* (published in 1972) Castaneda averred: "He then proceeded to demonstrate a special way of walking in the darkness, a way which he called the 'gait of power.'"

"Sunset and clear nights," David-Neel wrote, "were favorable conditions for the walker." "The gait of power is for running at night," don Juan whispered in Carlos's ear.

Commenting on David-Neel's account in *his* 1971 book, *The Way of the White Clouds*, Lama Govinda added: "The feet seem to be endowed with an instinct of their own, avoiding invisible obstacles and finding footholds, which only a clairvoyant consciousness could have detected in the speed of such a movement and in the darkness of the night." Castaneda went on to say (in 1972): "My body seemed to be cognizant of things without thinking about them. For example, I could not really see the jagged rocks in my way, but my body always managed to step on the edges and never in the crevices, except for a few mishaps when I lost my balance because I became distracted."

"There is no greater danger," Govinda concluded, "than the sudden awakening to normal consciousness. It is for this reason that the *lung-gom-pa* must avoid speaking or looking about, because the slightest distraction would result in breaking his trance." "The degree of concentration needed to keep scanning the area directly in front had to be total," concluded Castaneda; "as don Juan had warned me, any slight glance to the side or too far ahead altered the flow."

Those of us who judge the don Juan books a hoax will see obvious literary influence working in these passages, but those for whom don Juan remains authentic will see instead the workings of the universal mystic mind. Psychologist Michael Gorman, for one, found it fascinating that "a Polish count, an Indian philosopher, and a Yaqui sorcerer" all took the central human error to be confusing one's own way of looking at the world with the way the world actually is. Don Juan, you may recall, said one's view of the world arises from "a description, which is given to us from the moment of our birth." What I find more fascinating here than don Juan's sharing of an abstract idea with Korzybski and Krishnamurti is his sharing of concrete language with Edward Sapir, who said that one's view of personal conduct arises from "arbitrary modes of interpretation that social tradition is constantly suggesting to us from the very moment of our birth."

Apparently deaf to such verbal resonances, numerous writers have marveled at don Juan's traditional mysticism or psychodelic lore. "Interestingly enough," comments Marlene Dobkin de Rios, "many of the insights Casteñeda gleans from his teacher seem to have widespread application in other societies where plant hallucinogens are used. This is perhaps due to the limiting parameters of the drug itself, insofar as they effect man's central nervous system in a patterned way." A plausible hypothesis, if one has confidence in the authenticity of Castaneda's reports. Lacking such confidence, one suspects the common psychodelic themes arose not from characteristics of drugs administered by don Juan but from the contents of books read by Castañeda. Does this suspicion make any difference to the validity of don Juan's teachings? Does it matter whether they came directly from don Juan to Castaneda or directly from a book to Castaneda? Unfortunately it does make a difference. An observer who cannot be trusted to tell us where and how he got his information cannot be trusted to preserve the integrity of that information either. Don Juan may not only be imaginary, he may also be handing us a line. An expert on plant hallucinogens will no doubt recognize some valid elements in don Juan's psychodelics, but an expert who trusts don Juan's authenticity may go beyond expertise to accept invalid elements invented by Castaneda, such as the famous smoking of the mushroom.

If anthropologists can be misled, what will happen to non-anthropologists? Elmer Green, psychophysiologist of yoga practices at the Menninger Foundation, found it "interesting" that don Juan's teachings paralleled those of Sufist Jacques Ramano, who taught that truth is to be lived, not merely talked about. He thought it "entertaining" that Eastern metaphysics had been succinctly expressed in the independent teachings of a Mexican Indian, don Juan. He was intrigued by don Juan's idea of "the double" and thought his calling the true self "a cluster" was "remarkably similar" to Gordon Allport's idea of "functional autonomy." I agree that if an actual *curandero* came up with a series of ideas also found in books by Robert Ornstein, Otto Rank, D.T. Suzuki, and Gordon Allport, his sources would be worth looking into. The correspondence, noticed by Green, between the solar-plexus chakra and don Genaro's tentacles would surely make scientists sit up, and take notice, if they believed don Genaro existed. When one believes the two dons to be imaginary, however, what one finds interesting and entertaining is Castaneda's remarkable success in pulling the wool over otherwise sharp professional eyes. At one point Green ponders the similarity between don Juan's "path with heart," the Tibetan heart chakra, and Jesus' comment that a man is as he thinketh in his heart. Suddenly one wishes for don Juan's own reflections on such reverence.

"Don Juan," I whispered, "did you know that according to Jesus a man *is* as he thinks in his heart?"

Don Juan forgot about stalking the rabbit and stared at me in amazement.
"You must be kidding!" he said.
"I'm not kidding, don Juan."
Sadly he shook his head. "It's very clear to me," he said, "that Jesus didn't
see. Otherwise he would have known that a luminous being doesn't think in his
heart. He thinks in his *tonal*." He looked at me suspiciously. "Have you been
going to mass again?"
I laughed. "You know better than that, don Juan. It's something I read in
Elmer Green's book."
"God damn it!" Don Juan threw his hat to the ground and stomped on it.
"I knew it! If you'd stop reading those books and listen to *me*, nobody could
say you were stealing ideas. Don't you see that?"
"I see it, don Juan," I said apologetically, "but many things in the books I
read agree with things you say."
"Is that so." He squinted through the bushes looking for the rabbit, which
had dragged itself away while we were talking.
"For example," I persisted, "Green says the Sufis teach that truth is to be
lived, not merely talked about."
Don Juan nodded. "They're right about that. Talk is cheap."
I reached for my notebook. "Is that a sorcerer's saying?" I asked.
"Is what a sorcerer's saying?"
"Talk is cheap."
Don Juan chuckled. "You heard a sorcerer say it, so it must be a sorcerer's
saying."
I wrote it in my notebook.
"You want another one to go with it?" he said.
"Sure," I said.
"Actions speak louder than words," he said.

To me the most surprising support for Castaneda has come from Mary
Douglas, whose "Authenticity of Castaneda" (de Mille 1990:25–31),
exemplifies a widespread failure to distinguish two components of truth:
authenticity and validity.

Validity, in this discussion, refers to the correspondence between the
content of a scientific report and some established background of theory
and recorded observation. A report is judged valid when it agrees with
what we think we know. When people thought the world was flat, reports
that the hull of a departing ship would disappear before its sail had to
be ignored, denied, or explained away. When people thought the world
was round, such reports would be accepted and cited to prove its round-
ness. The actual shape of the world, round or flat or cubical, does not
come into the definition; only the correspondence between the report
and the established theoretical and empirical knowledge about its shape.

Authenticity, in this discussion, refers to the provenance of the report.
Did it arise from the persons, places, and procedures it describes?

Though these definitions are quite conventional in science, some scientists apparently do not keep them clearly in mind. An example may

be useful. If (hypothetically) some anthropologists have reported, and most believe, that Ojibwa shamans use *Amanita muscaria* mushrooms in curing rites, then my report that I have participated in such a rite on MinissKitigan (Garden Island) in the Michi-Tchigamig (Lake Michigan) may easily be accepted as a true report, and any details I add to the current description of the rite may also be accepted and become part of the anthropological literature on shamanism. If, after a few months, it is alleged that the closest I have been to Garden Island was when I picked up my new Hudson Hornet in Detroit in 1953, a shadow of doubt will fall across my report, and my added details may be questioned. If I then write a letter to the *American Anthropologist*, admitting that I have never set foot on MinissKitigan but citing specific pages of the forthcoming *Puhpohwee for the People* for my added details, my original report will be judged *wholly inauthentic*, but my added ethnographic details may be judged *wholly valid*, on the authority of Keewaydinoquay, a well-recommended Ojibwa shaman, who is the author of the book I stole my ideas out of. Needless to say, any further reports I write will be treated with great skepticism.

Validity and authenticity, then, are substantially, though not completely, independent components of truth. Validity cannot be achieved without authentic observing and reporting, by someone, somewhere, some time, but when authentic-and-valid reports are available in a library, a clever pretender can put together a wholly inauthentic report (like *The Teachings of Don Juan*) containing many valid details (such as the idea that sorcerers try to steal each other's souls). Since most people, including anthropologists, care more about validity (which is theoretical and therefore interesting) than about authenticity (which is a rather boring practical condition for obtaining valid information), they tend to take authenticity for granted whenever they read a report whose content seems valid to them. I believe this is exactly the error Mary Douglas fell into.

Not the only error, however, for she reasons that anyone who writes as naïvely as Castaneda can hardly be fooling us. Could such a bumpkin have invented don Juan? Of course not! Her attempt to assess Castaneda's authenticity by analyzing his style, and through his style his character, fails because Castaneda's style does not simply or fully reflect his character. He is not in fact naïve but merely writes that way when describing the thoughts and comments of the fictive character I call Carlos-Naïf.

Ralph Beals made a similar error when he reasoned that don Juan must exist in some form or other because Castaneda had started talking about him way back in 1960. Could anyone keep up the charade year after year if there were no don Juan at all? Of course not! The inference failed because Beals did not guess the very wide difference between Castaneda's character and that of persons he was accustomed to dealing with in the university. As Castaneda has said: "My life is weird—more weird than it looks."

Such failures to read character may be expected. We normally assume other people are like ourselves. What I did not expect scholars to do was to infer don Juan's authentic existence or Castaneda's credibility from the validity of particular ethnographic contents scattered throughout the don Juan books. Douglas argues against judging the books bogus (inauthentic) on the ground that don Juan's attitude toward life and death is (she believes) alien to our own (and therefore like the attitude an anthropologist might expect to find in a pre-literate Indian culture). This is clearly inferring authentic provenance from valid content: if don Juan says things we expect Indians to say, or things we expect non-Indians not to say, then don Juan must exist. It does not follow.

Don Juan's "philosophy of ascetic mysticism," Douglas says, "is enough evidence of truth in the tale." Manifestly she infers don Juan's existence from the quality of his teachings. Having accepted him as an authentic source of Indian lore, she invites her colleagues' attention to his techniques for inducing different kinds of visual experience: techniques of squinting, focusing and unfocusing, and rapid sideways scanning. "From these ideas," she says, "we are likely to get advances in anthropology."

At the very least, Douglas fails to say which aspect of truth she is talking about and leaves the false implication that don Juan's teachings came to Castaneda more or less as Castaneda said they did. It may be, as she says, that from ideas of squinting, scanning, or focusing, whatever their sources, one could get advances in self-development or spiritual training or even anthropology, but that is quite different from saying that these ideas arose in a particular Indian culture, perhaps a league of sorcerers, and that anthropologists should take them seriously as ethnographic findings.

Douglas dismisses "the temporary discomfiture of a few professionals" who get nervous when new approaches to fieldwork are proposed, but she overlooks a source of discomfiture more important to scientists than innovation, which is the well-grounded suspicion that one is reading fake field reports, which at least one respected colleague has called authentic.

Scholars for whom English is a second language are doubly unlikely to hear echoes of Opler and Petrullo, Suzuki and David-Neel in Castaneda's prose. Correspondences between don Juan's teachings and other people's writings "cannot simply be plagiarism," writes a German scholar,

Dennis Timm, "because the worldwide correspondence of magical experiences is an ethnological banality."[2] De Mille, Timm says, should have assessed his own deficient personal power before trying to write about the power of don Juan; de Mille is so preoccupied with proving Castaneda a thief "that he falls directly onto the open knife of his own argument."

I wrote to Timm that his disputatious knife cuts either me or him depending on whether one finds correspondences only of magical phenomena or correspondences also in the words describing the magical phenomena. I offered three examples. Timm replied that by trusting evidence of that kind Western scientists had trapped themselves in their own preconceptions. To support his position, he quoted Mary Douglas on the authenticity of Castaneda—which brings us full circle.

Don Juan's teachings, Timm said, are an esoteric matter, to which scientific generalizations have no access. "Scientific verification of the 'teachings' is impossible," he declared. "A confirmation of what Castaneda experienced can be established only by a 'special consensus,' which can be reached only by sorcerers."

I suspect Timm is quite right about the difficulty of confirming Carlos's experiences, but disconfirming Castaneda's field reports is well within the power and scope of science and is a worthy end in itself. I hope Timm will eventually grant that point, and then go on to a realization of greater import to him, which is that an esoteric document is more likely to reward the spiritual or magical seeker if it has arisen from the experiences it describes rather than from the imagination of a fiction writer, no matter how much magical literature that writer may have read. If there is no background of experience for the teachings of don Juan (Paul Heelas wrote), then we must judge don Juan (or, I would add, Castaneda) to be "a charlatan engaged in indoctrination."

Timm gives low marks not only to me but to Hans Peter Duerr, in whose much milder criticism of Castaneda he finds a betrayal of "alternative science." In the summer of 1963, anthropology student Duerr made a trip to the Southwest to explore rock-caves at Puyé. While waiting for a Greyhound bus in the Albuquerque station, he fell into a conversation with a Tewa *yerbatero*, an Indian who was very learned about plants. After some small talk, Duerr asked whether the Indian could help him find a family in one of the pueblos north of Santa Fe that would take him in for a few months, because he wanted to learn about the ritual dances in the subterranean kivas. The Indian lifted his head, looked Duerr squarely in the eyes—Duerr does not say, "with a stupendous look"—then smiled and told him the most suitable pueblo for his learning would be "el pueblo de Nuestra Señora la Reina de los

Angeles," where the university libraries had plenty of information about kiva dances. Stung to the quick, Duerr hopped a bus going west and pursued his further studies of Indian lore "in the libraries of Los Angeles and other unfortunate places": fit preparation for a critic of Castaneda.

Unlike Mary Douglas, Duerr did not take Castaneda's arch naïveties for a sign of authenticity. "Even an American college student cannot be so foolish," he told himself. The many passages portraying Carlos Naïf, Skeptic, Etic, Western-Rationalist he found "stylized for didactic reasons." The talking animals belonged in fairy tales. Don Juan was too much the noble savage, Eastern guru, or grandfatherly superego. Once he had penetrated Castaneda's style to glimpse the trickster-teacher beneath, Duerr went on to link validity and authenticity in a sounder way than Douglas had done.

Though he gave Castaneda the benefit of many doubts, Duerr found his magic half-baked at best. Having himself flown on the wings of the Datura plant, Duerr did not recognize Carlos's affair with the devil's weed.[3] He challenged Carlos's invincible stupidity in not ever being able to distinguish hallucinations from ordinary reality. He was suspicious of don Juan's mushroom smoking. He criticized Castaneda for distorting and exploiting the ineffable experience one has at the borders of reality. "Coyote always spoils everything"—he quoted a Paviotso shaman.

Finding *in*valid content in the books, Duerr inferred their *in*authenticity from that content. This is not a foolproof kind of inference but (for reasons I shall discuss) it is more likely to succeed than inferring authenticity from validity. The ploy was cutely capsulated in a letter I received from a poet who knew the books were fiction the minute she read don Juan's statement that a sorcerer can go to the moon but can't bring back a bag of rocks. "Don Juan would not have said *that*," she wrote. "He might have said a sorcerer *doesn't* bring back a bag of rocks. The difference is crucial, if we are to believe don Juan is impeccable." Here a poet's intuition of impeccability cannot tolerate certain discrepancies; so she concludes Castaneda is making up the story. Inauthenticity inferred from invalidity.

Since validity and authenticity are not wholly independent components of truth, we can try to predict one from the other but, as Mary Douglas has unintentionally shown, such prediction is hazardous. The figure *Categories of Truthfulness* represents the prediction problem by a four-fold table, in which I have classified eight well-known works as either valid-authentic (+ +), valid-inauthentic (+ −), invalid-authentic (− +), or invalid-inauthentic (− −). These assignments are not, of course, absolutely correct, since a work classified in one category

FIGURE 12.1

Categories of Truthfulness

	AUTHENTIC (+)	*INAUTHENTIC* (−)
	(+ +)	(+ −)
VALID (+)	*An Apache Life Way* —Opler 1941 *Peyote Hunt* —Meyerhoff 1974 *Return to Laughter* —Bowen 1954	*The Teachings of Don Juan* *A Separate Reality* *Journey to Ixtlan* —Castaneda
	(− +)	(− −)
INVALID (−)	*The Mountain People* —Turnbull 1972	*Gold of the Gods* —von Däniken 1973

may exhibit some characteristics of another category, but I think they are defensible.

Anthropological works will be assigned by most judges to the valid-authentic category, which should not surprise us, since the profession of anthropology is dedicated to producing honest reports that are theoretically correct. Assigning the majority of works to any other category would be an admission of general failure in the field, and so would be rather unlikely. This does not mean that most anthropological works are theoretically faultless or perfectly honest but only that they satisfy some explicit or implicit standard of theoretical correctness and reportorial honesty. They pass inspection on both counts. How severe the inspection should be is another question, which I shall not address.

The first two works I have chosen to illustrate the valid-authentic category are ethnographic reports. The third, *Return to Laughter*, is a work of anthropological fiction based on the author's professional experience in the field. All three are classified as valid, because their ethnographic content has been accepted as generally correct; all three, in other words, agree with what anthropologists think they know. All three are classified as authentic, because no one contends they did not arise from the persons, places, and procedures they describe. The first two claim to be ethnographic reports; the third claims to be a work of fiction, in which the persons and places are fictitious (though realistic) and the procedures combine field observation and fiction writing. All three have been used to teach anthropology. Students enjoy *Return to Laughter* because of its narrative appeal; professors do not hesitate to use it as a text, because they think it validly portrays experiences of fieldwork and validly describes features of a particular society.

Pseudo-anthropology is also a thriving field; so a great many books could be assigned to the invalid-inauthentic cell of the table. I have chosen one outstanding example, Erich von Däniken's *Gold of the Gods*, a tale of archaeological discovery in South America. "To me," writes von Däniken, "this is the most incredible, fantastic story of the century. It could easily have come straight from the realms of Science Fiction if I had not seen and photographed the incredible truth in person."

In 1972, von Däniken claims, explorer Juan Moricz personally conducted him on a tour of some tunnels 800 feet below ground, where he saw a hoard of golden artifacts, of which some samples had also been collected at Cuenca, Ecuador, by a priest named Crespi. Challenging the authenticity of von Däniken's story, Moricz himself later said he had never taken von Däniken through the tunnels but had only told him about them. Challenging its validity, archaeologist Pino Turolla said the eccentric Father Crespi's "priceless artifacts" were junk made by local Indian smiths out of materials such as the copper toilet bowl float Turolla spotted in the collection. Moricz's expedition to the caves had found stone carvings but none of the gold promised by a long-standing legend. If von Däniken did not visit the tunnels, his story is inauthentic; if there was no gold in the tunnels, his story is invalid as well (assuming a skeptical theory of El Dorado legends).

The ease with which one can assign many works to the like-signed (+ + and − −) cells of the table may give an impression of strong positive correlation between validity and authenticity, but I think the impression is wrong. Working against such a correlation is the general fallibility of theories and (to a lesser extent) of documented observations, both of which are frequently contradicted by accurate new observations they did not predict. More pertinent to an essay on Castaneda is the fact that any writer of an inauthentic report, whether he is a hoaxer or some less flamboyant cheater, does well to include as much valid material as he can, from whatever source, to make his report more plausible to such informed readers as professional colleagues or dissertation committee members. Conversely, an honest reporter is bound to make some mistakes and can easily make a lot of them. The weakness of theory, the existence of cheaters, and the ubiquity of error must reduce the correlation between authenticity and validity and may reduce it to the point where prediction of individual cases is at best a waste of time.

Honest errors in reports can arise from at least two sources: misperception of events, and unsound interpretation of events correctly perceived. Neither of these bear on authenticity; both bear on validity. I shall discuss them in order.

Misperception of events is no doubt less frequent than misinterpretation of events correctly perceived, but misperception raises questions more obviously relevant to the books of Castaneda, which offer tracts on social-science interpretation under the guise of stories about an apprentice's perceptions and quasi-perceptions of at least two kinds of non-social worlds, an ordinary (though not realistic) desert world and a nonordinary world of sorcery or magical vision. Since Castaneda substitutes visualizing for conceptualizing, thus turning Edward Sapir's social world into don Juan's natural and visionary worlds, we are obliged to consider the hazards of misperception in social science.

A paradigmatic illustration of seeing what is not there and not seeing what is there comes reportedly from a Viennese psychiatrist, Alexander Pilcz, who documented the East Indian rope trick by recording it with a motion picture camera. As the camera turned, Pilcz and several hundred other witnesses saw the following sequence of events. A fakir and a small boy walked into their midst, and the fakir tossed a coil of rope up into the air. The rope stood by itself. The boy climbed up the rope and disappeared at the top, whence his arms, legs, trunk, and head soon fell separately to the ground. The fakir collected these remains in a basket, climbed the rope carrying the basket, and disappeared at the top. After a decent interval, the fakir and the smiling, reassembled boy descended the rope. The rope fell like a pole and shattered. The broken pieces formed themselves into a rope again. The fakir and the boy took a bow.

Like the rest of the audience, the previously skeptical Pilcz was very impressed by this performance, but when the film was later projected, it showed the following sequence of events. The fakir tossed the coil of rope up into the air, whence it promptly fell down again in the normal way. For the rest of the time, the fakir and the boy stood beside the fallen rope doing nothing at all.

In Castaneda's terms, we have here two separate realities: a nonordinary reality experienced by Pilcz and the audience during the performance, and an ordinary reality experienced by Pilcz when the film was projected. We also have an opportunity to rank them or choose between them if we like. Players of the philosophy game may decline to choose, declaring their full satisfaction with the mere existence side by side of two kinds of reality. Occultists will no doubt say the fakir didn't want his trick recorded on film, and so projected an alternative sequence of images into the camera by thoughtography; if they are well-read occultists, they will mention the name of Ted Serios, a documented thoughtographer. Scientists, including anthropologists, will be inclined to take the film version as the correct one and the experience of the audience as an hallucination; if they like vacuous explanations, they may say the hallucination was caused by mass hypnosis. Anomalists, such as parapsychologists, will take the film version as a normal standard, but they may suspect what the audience saw had some substance to it all the same, of a kind not understood by them or anyone.

Well, what actually happened? Did the rope stand stiff or fall down? Did the boy climb up or remain on the ground? To answer such questions one needs a reality framework, and one needs to prefer that framework to any other. Though metaphysicians may declare they cannot answer such questions, practical people have no difficulty answering them. First, however, one must subscribe to the reality framework that is most familiar to everyone, Castaneda's ordinary reality, which philosophers William James and, later, Alfred Schutz called the "paramount reality." I have called it the "boss reality," because if you don't do what it wants to do, it will knock you flat, and eventually it will knock you flat whether you do what it wants you to or not. Don Quixote's giants were Sancho Panza's windmills, but either way they unhorsed Quixote.

However much they may like to contemplate standing ropes, flailing giants, or heads turning into crows, scientists have to keep at least one eye on Pilcz's film, Panza's windmills, or the ordinary world of Carlos-Skeptic. The rules of science require them to ground any investigation in the ordinary, communicable reality, as Castaneda purported to do when he assigned calendar dates to the events in his imaginary fieldwork. Scientists are not forbidden to study or enter alternative realities but only required to tie their research at some points to the ordinary world. Apparent hallucinations like the rope trick and apparent anomalies or paranormal events like ESP and psychokinesis are quite acceptable objects for scientific study. Charles Tart even proposes that drugged or hypnotized experimenters might sometimes succeed where those in normal states of consciousness have failed. But whatever phenomena science approaches and whatever means it uses, its procedures and reports must to some extent be grounded in the ordinary reality. "The closed sub-universe of scientific reality," wrote Alfred Schutz, "although necessarily different from that of common sense, of everyday life is, also necessarily, tied to the process of empirical verification within the common-sense world in which we live and which we take for granted as our paramount reality" (Schutz 1964:152). If a report is to have any authenticity, the narrator must have known in the ordinary way who conducted the experiment or observation, where it was conducted, and what means where used. To take an extreme example, a report of a dream must include the information that it was a dream; a dream reported as fieldwork is not authentic.

The fact that these points need to be discussed at all shows the recent influence of phenomenology, reintroducing the old idea that private thoughts are data for social science. Contemporary phenomenologists may object to this simple characterization of their methods, but I think some such conception has rendered certain social scientists incapable of distinguishing—or has helped them to avoid distinguishing—Castaneda's allegories from legitimate field reports. An erstwhile member of one of his graduate committees and still his stout defender, Theodore Graves said, "Castaneda's purpose was *not* to write factual ethnography but to convey the subjective experience of confronting a radical challenge to his notions of reality" (in Strachan 1979:91). Does this mean, I asked, that the don Juan story is creative writing having no necessary connection with an actual old Indian? No, he replied, though Castaneda organized, interpreted, and presented his facts creatively, he is a factual reporter. A few more factual reporters like that, and social science will be finished. In offering his cultural materialism as the paradigm for social science, Marvin Harris found in Castaneda the perfect club with which to belabor phenomenologists. By doing fieldwork in his head for fourteen years, Castaneda became the phenomenologist to end phenomenology.

Despite a renewed interest in what is real and how to recognize it, a more likely source of error and target of criticism is still the misinterpretation of ordinary events correctly perceived. Colin Turnbull's *The Mountain People* is a famous target, which I have assigned to the invalid-authentic cell of the table. Turnbull lived in Uganda with a starving tribe called the Ik, whose behavior he found utterly repulsive. The experience distressed him deeply, and he wrote a very successful book about it, which told the story of his distress and described the horrible life of the Ik.

The Mountain People is authentic because nobody has said Turnbull invented his observations. Fredrik Barth did accuse him of creating "a systematically false record" of his fieldwork, but Turnbull indignantly and successfully rebutted that charge, while Grant McCall wrote: "I do not wish . . . to imply . . . that I believe it to be a fiction. I am not . . . questioning the observations that he makes, or his competence to record them. Where I differ from Turnbull is in the interpretation of these data."

Turnbull admits he was baffled by the Ik. Their suffering laughter seemed bizarre to him. "I am simply not qualified to assess it," he wrote; "all I have done is to attempt to describe it." Having said, as an interpretation of the way he saw them living together, that the Ik had "no culture," Turnbull then granted that their gregariousness and laughter might have been signs of culture he had failed to grasp. "I . . . have been in other pretty trying circumstances," he said, "but have never quite lost my anthropological cool as I did with the Ik."

Though Turnbull's critics said his book painted an invalid portrait of the Ik, some of them praised him for giving a picture both authentic *and* valid of the trouble a fieldworker can get into and the emotional turmoil he may have to endure. More than that, some said all fieldwork is fraught with difficulties like Turnbull's, if usually less severe, and they admired his courageous exposure of trials and shortcomings common to all fieldworkers. A. K. Mark gave Turnbull and Castaneda similar credit for examining the fieldworker as closely as the informant; Carlos-Skeptic's perennial quandaries were likened to Turnbull's frank confessions. On a less positive note, Vincent Crapanzano dismissed Turnbull and Castaneda as shallow popularizers duped by idioms of the age, Turnbull by "facile politics," Castaneda by "the 'heavy' mysticism of the young drop-out." Beyond such similarities Mark and Crapanzano over-looked an important dissimilarity. Turnbull's fieldwork was conducted in the ordinary world, and a film of it by Professor Pilcz would have shown the Ik. Carlos's fieldwork was conducted in a world of fantasy, and a documentary film of Castaneda's life from 1960–1974 would not have shown don Juan. With the exception of those who will say don Juan could make himself invisible to Pilcz's camera, this brings us to the fourth cell of the table, where Castaneda's first three books are (perhaps too favorably, but necessarily for this discussion) classified as valid-inauthentic. I omit his fourth and fifth books, which are anthropologically less valid.

Castaneda's inauthenticity has been, I think, conclusively established in various ways by me and Hans Sebald. Contradictions within the supposed field reports, and between the reports and the desert environment they claim, convince most readers that the story did not arise from the persons, places, and procedures it describes. Additional evidence comes from many instances of obvious foraging in other people's published works. By now the more interesting question is how much and what kinds of validity the don Juan books have.

One has little difficulty finding valid ethnographic content in Castaneda's initial trilogy, some of which apparently derives from the very books by Opler and Myerhoff that occupy the valid-authentic cell of the table. Looking at the name Opler in the Alleglossary (a list of published sources Castaneda apparently used to ground his fictions in other people's facts)[4] we see ten items listed, of which those titled Campfire and

Place demonstrate literary influence, while those titled Enemies, Gesture, Guardian, Power, and Rule contain ideas found in the trilogy, though they may fall short of proving imitation. Anthropologist Walter Goldschmidt, who wrote the foreword to *The Teachings of Don Juan*, was very impressed by don Juan's parable about the four enemies of a man of knowledge. While I think Goldschmidt should have felt more skepticism about don Juan's authenticity, or should have been more frank about the skepticism he felt, I recognize that the similarity between Opler's and don Juan's treatment of fear, clarity, power, and old age, which readily confirms the suspicions of a skeptic like me, can equally bolster the confidence of a believer (perhaps like Goldschmidt) when taken as signs not of imitation but of cultural diffusion or universal mind.

Turning to the name Myerhoff, we see seventeen items listed, of which ten are common to Castaneda's trilogy and *Peyote Hunt*. None is particularly evidential, which helps to explain why Myerhoff, before reading *Castaneda's Journey*, found confirmations of her own work in the trilogy rather than imitations. When she read *Tales of Power*, however, Myerhoff was offended by what Castaneda had done with tonal and nagual, "two beautiful indigenous concepts" she thought he had utterly perverted. To Indians, tonal and nagual are fateful or metamorphic animals; to don Juan they are quasi-Buddhist notions of potentiality and actuality, or latency and manifestation. The nothing (nagual) that creates the something (tonal) is recognizably an East Indian idea. In Amerindian cultures, the world is explained as a product of transformation, not of creation *ex nihilo*; nature is fashioned out of dust by a superhuman potter,[5] not manifested out of nothing by an indescribable principle. Encountering don Juan's oriental abstractions in *Tales of Power*, some formerly sympathetic anthropologists sadly concluded Castaneda had abandoned legitimate anthropology for phony mysticism, while at the same time mystically inclined readers were rejoicing over don Juan's finally getting down to business and giving them the true teachings. Whether a report is valid or not depends on the theory to which it is referred.

Much earlier, skeptical anthropologists had discovered invalid ethnographic contents in the trilogy as well. Most obvious was the so-called Yaqui way of knowledge spuriously offered by the subtitle of *The Teachings*. Despite authoritative declarations by Yaqui specialists Edward Spicer, Ralph Beals, and Jane Holden Kelley that the don Juan story had nothing to do with Yaqui culture, the Yaqui misnomer refused to die. Non-anthropologists and careless anthropologists went on and on referring to don Juan as "an old Yaqui sorcerer," and as late as 1977 the *American Anthropologist* complaisantly reproduced Simon and Schuster's full-page advertisement calling *The Teachings* and *A Separate Reality* studies of "religious practices of the Yaqui Indians," which they certainly are not. Castaneda's disingenuous disclaimers of any intent to suggest don Juan's way of knowledge was really a Yaqui way made the misnomer all the more inexcusable, both originally and in perpetuity.

Where did the misnomer come from? I should guess don Juan's vague connection with the Yaqui tribe was a device for superficially imitating genuine ethnography while getting round certain requirements such as travel to the field and the burdensome labor of cultural descriptions. The Yaqui were not so far away that an impoverished student might not claim to visit them in his automobile. When his first committee chairman, Ralph Beals, grew leery of thousand-mile weekend round trips, Castaneda simply abandoned him and went looking for a less critical chairman. As for cultural incongruities, the Yaquis had been exiled from their homeland for many years, so don Juan might have picked up all sorts of non-Yaqui knowledge during his travels in other parts of Mexico. Tolerance of the Yaqui misnomer by the University of California Press is harder to explain, but I have tried to make sense of it in chapter 13 of *The Don Juan Papers*.

Next is don Juan's so-called sorcery. If the old wizard wants to call himself a *brujo* (sorcerer) or even a stockholder, that is his idiosyncratic privilege, but when Castaneda calls him a sorcerer, that is a scholarly or perhaps anti-scholarly error. As Beals made clear, don Juan is not a sorcerer in any accepted anthropological sense. Sorcerers are feared and hated by other members of their community because they employ evil spirits or magical projectiles to make people sick; don Juan is a hermit who has no enemies and employs his plant allies to discover other worlds and ontological essences. Far from being a sorcerer, he is a rather benign, mystical magician.

Other errors can be listed. Indians do not "sew" lizards with agave fiber and cholla thorn. Before *The Teachings*, they refrained from smoking mushrooms. Indians do not quote Lama Govinda on trance running and, so far as anyone knows, have not learned to levitate beside waterfalls by means of tractor beams projecting from the solar-plexus chakra. They don't bother to stalk rabbits bare handed, and they don't call peyote "mescal."

In view of such fallacies, the reader may think it unfair to classify Castaneda's trilogy as valid while Turnbull must languish among the invalids. I justify this merely illustrative classification in the following way: considering Turnbull's professional respectability and actual fieldwork, *The Mountain People* is surprisingly invalid; considering Castaneda's hoaxing and don Juan's insubstantiality, the trilogy is surprisingly valid, as a reading of the Alleglossary will show. The same cannot be said of *Tales of Power* or *Second Ring*, whose crude distortions of Indian culture belong with von Däniken's priceless toilet float. Whether *Tales* or *Ring* deserve any credit as valid mystical writing is another question, which is answered in *The Don Juan Papers*, where Philip Staniford croons a mellow *Yes*, while Agehananda Bharati sounds a thundering *No* (de Mille 1990:147–153).

What are the hazards of prediction between authenticity and validity? Having no actuarial tables, I can offer only my common sense opinions. Within the constraints imposed by weakness of theory and ubiquity of error, a report accepted as authentic has a fair chance of being generally valid. Conversely, since hoaxers and other consistent cheaters who can produce convincing reports are greatly outnumbered by reasonably honest reporters, a report accepted as valid is likely to be authentic. This sounds reassuring, but it means that skillful hoaxers and cheaters will be accepted along with the honest reporters. Castaneda profited from this ambiguity.

A report judged inauthentic (from evidence bearing directly on authenticity) may be filled with garbage like *Gold of the Gods* or only larded with it like Castaneda's trilogy. An inauthentic report is not likely to be generally valid; reporters who misrepresent their sources will not hesitate, when it suits them, to distort their sources' information.

These three kinds of prediction, if made at all, have little utility. Maybe Indians smoke mushrooms, maybe they don't. Neither certain knowledge that Castaneda is a hoaxer nor firm belief that he is not can give us the answer. Conversely, Castaneda may be an honest reporter, but his correct assertion that sorcerers try to steal each other's souls does not prove him honest: he may have read about soul stealing in Michael Harner's "Jívaro Souls." The one prediction I put stock in is predicting inauthenticity from invalidity in those cases where many invalid observations (rather than interpretations) are found. In *The Don Juan Papers*, Robert Carneiro carries out this exercise while debunking a popular adventure tale called *Wizard of the Upper Amazon*. Carneiro succeeds because he has a lot of prior information that bears on validity and finds in the book many observations that contradict his prior information.[7] He concludes the adventurer was a liar.

Owing to the general weakness of theory, even this fourth kind of prediction can lead one astray. Elsa First's naïve skeptics rejected the don Juan books because they reported paranormal events. If ESP and psychokinesis are self-evidently absurd, the books can be judged inauthentic (or perhaps merely invalid, where an honest observer may have been fooled) because of this absurd content. But if ESP and psychokinesis are not absurd, don Juan could be debunked for the wrong reason.

To help in such assessments, sociologist Marcello Truzzi systematically distinguishes narrators, narratives, and events. *Narrators* can be *credible* like Opler, Myerhoff, Bowen, and Turnbull or *noncredible* like Castaneda and von Däniken. *Narratives* can be *plausible* like (for the most part) *The Teachings of Don Juan* or *implausible* like *A Separate Reality* (which readers attuned to story-telling quickly recognized as fiction because of the manner in which the story was told). *Events* can be *ordinary* like Professor Pilcz's film of the rope falling down or *extraordinary* like his vision of the rope standing up. The three dimensions are formally independent.

Applying Truzzi's scheme to the don Juan books, one can say that in 1968 a credible Castaneda published a fairly plausible *Teachings* describing the ordinary existence of a rather unusual hermit. In 1977 a notoriously noncredible Castaneda published a somewhat implausible *Second Ring of Power* describing very extraordinary events, such as materializations, levitations, and out-of-body combat. During those ten years Castaneda grew less and less credible as more and more of his autobiographical anecdotes contradicted independent records and each other. His trilogy was widely reclassified as implausible when *Castaneda's Journey* analyzed its internal contradictions. His tales grew more and more extraordinary as he turned away from anthropology and toward occultism. It is instructive to note, however, that *Second Ring*, his most occult book up to 1977, is implausible not because of its very extraordinary events but because of a few minor contradictions in the text. The trilogy, which contains many more contradictions that *Second Ring*, is therefore much less plausible, as an account. Application of Truzzi's scheme should reduce errors of naïve skepticism and naïve subscription alike.

Discussing validity and authenticity for months with various Juanists and Castanedists, I have met some typical objections, which I shall now list, along with my answers.

1. *Inventiveness is limited.* Much of what Castaneda claims must actually have happened to him, because no one could invent such outlandish adventures. *Answer:* The objector is obviously not a reader of fantasy or science fiction. Arthur C. Clarke has not been to the moon, but he did write *2001*; astronauts have been there but did not write it. *A Voyage to Arcturus* is far more outlandish than *Tales of Power* or *Second Ring*, yet no one believes David Lindsay

went to Arcturus or had the visions he describes, except as a writer has visions. After reading the potsherd of Amenartas telling of the pillar of fire that brings eternal youth to the queen who stands in its flames, L. Horace Holley, fictive narrator of *She, A History of Adventure*, says: "My first idea [was] that my poor friend, when demented, had composed the whole tale, though it scarcely seemed likely that such a story could have been invented by anybody. It was too original." "The idea that I concocted a person like don Juan is inconceivable," Castaneda said. "He is hardly the kind of figure my European intellectual tradition would have led me to invent. The truth is much stranger. I didn't create anything. I am only a reporter." In the tradition of fantasy writing, Castaneda voices straight-faced doubts that anyone could invent the marvelous tale he has just invented.

2. *Castaneda is in good company.* Colin Turnbull writes imaginatively, but no one has accused him of making up his data. *Answer*: My point exactly: no one (except Barth, who was rebutted) has accused Turnbull, many have accused Castaneda. While both have been praised as bringers of truth and condemned as purveyors of falsity, Turnbull has been praised for authenticity and condemned for invalidity, whereas Castaneda has been praised for validity and condemned for inauthenticity. One is accused of honest mistakes, the other of slyly hiding his sources.

3. *Fact is fiction.* Since both informants and fieldworkers are rather unreliable, no ethnography is strictly factual. *Answer*: Error, misinterpretation, and fudging are not the same thing as gross fabrication. A tolerable degree of spuriosity can be distinguished from an intolerable degree. The don Juan books are accused not of being unstrictly factual but of being strictly unfactual.

4. *Castaneda's basic claims have not been disproved.* We have no conclusive evidence that Castaneda has not experienced odd events. *Answer*: Neither have we conclusive proof that the mysterious white man who two-thousand years ago walked from tribe to tribe throughout America healing the sick, raising the dead, and teaching Jesus' gospel in a thousand languages was not in fact Jesus. The objection puts the burden of proof not on Castaneda, where it belongs, but on the community of scholars, where it does not belong.

5. *In some form or other, don Juan could exist.* It doesn't matter if don Juan was not exactly as he appears in the books. Castaneda could have had one or more teachers whose essence he portrayed in the figure of don Juan. *Answer*: The vaguer don Juan becomes, the more likely his existence. If he was just an ordinary man Castaneda met, then certainly he exists. The don Juan books, however, are not at all vague. They are exact, and for the purposes of science at least must be judged in their exactness. The only don Juan we

know is the one Castaneda gave us. If he is really a combination of Maria Sabina, Suzuki, and Ramon Medina, one is better off reading *Mushrooms*, *Russia, and History*, *What is Zen*? and *Peyote Hunt*.

6. *No coin has only one side*. Insofar as the don Juan books are valid, they must have arisen from authentic observation and are, in that sense, authentic. Validity cannot be divorced from authenticity. *Answer*: Distinguishing wives from husbands is not divorcing them. Seed cannot be divorced from flower, yet anyone can sort seeds from flowers without error. To say, correctly, that authenticity and validity are not completely independent is not to say we cannot formally distinguish them as components of truthfulness and assess them by different tests. When information is sparse, we may not be able to test them, but that is not an excuse for discarding the categories or the tests. Error terms in mathematical prediction do not cause us to renounce predictions; on the contrary, they make us confident of prediction where error terms are small and cause us to look for more information where they are large. Predictions and judgments do not have to be perfect to be worth making. Counterfeit coins have two sides, too. The don Juan books do not acquire any authenticity of their own by incorporating the valid contents of authentic books by other writers.

7. *All's fair in samadhi and satori*. Mystical experiences cannot be adequately described in factual reports. Castaneda was trying to communicate the ineffable, so he had to resort to novelistic interpretations. *Answer*: This objection confuses the ineffability of the mystical experience (which is a matter of validity, or how the experience is to be correctly described and understood) with the question whether the narrator himself actually had the experience (a matter of authenticity). However ineffable the experience, there is no intrinsic difficulty in saying whether one has had it. Saying one has had it when one has not had it is inauthentic reporting. Since so many of Castaneda's falsifiable claims have in fact been falsified (such as the claim that his chronology was authentic or the claim that his adventures occurred in the Sonoran desert), we are ill advised to gratuitously credit his unfalsifiable claims (such as claims of having mystical experiences).

8. *Fieldnotes are private*. Never in all my years as a graduate student did a member of the faculty ask to see my fieldnotes. Fieldnotes belong to the person who writes them. Castaneda had every right to keep his fieldnotes to himself. *Answer*: Fieldnotes are private in the sense that they are the literary property of the writer and are not to be published without the writer's consent. On the other hand, they are public in the sense that anyone who enters the scientific community to do research undertakes an obligation to preserve his data intact and unaltered, to submit them for examination when

asked to do so by qualified colleagues with a legitimate scientific interest in them, and, if there is opportunity, to deposit them with a suitable common custodian, as in a museum or library, when he can no longer preserve them or no longer wants them. Fieldnotes are the primary data of anthropology. They are part of the scientific record. Refusal to submit them for examination violates the norms of scientific conduct and amounts to prima facie evidence of fraud. The fact the fieldnotes are sometimes (defensibly or indefensibly) taken for granted does not reduce the fieldworker's obligation to serve as their custodian in the interest of science. While your committee obviously trusted you, as most committees trust most candidates, Castaneda's first chairman grew suspicious. "I pressed him to show me some of his fieldnotes," Beals wrote, "but he became evasive and finally dropped from sight." Unlike some of his successors, Beals acted responsibly to forestall scientific fraud. Competent, responsible examination of Castaneda's fieldnotes must have resulted in his disqualification from candidacy, or at least in the disqualification of *Journey to Ixtlan* as a dissertation reporting anthropological fieldwork, whether or not it might have been accepted on some other basis—say, as a literary work of interest to anthropologists. The committee members who did not ask to see the fieldnotes before signing what purported to be an account of fieldwork, or who examined them and found nothing wrong with them, were either negligent or, as Beals put it, naïve.

9. *Personal knowledge*. All this talk about Carlos's missing fieldnotes is asinine. I have seen them. They exist. Or did before they were destroyed when his basement flooded. I saw them in many notebooks and boxes during many wonderful hours in 1965 when Carlos and I were discussing both his apprenticeship to don Juan and my fieldwork among the Scotoma tribe, which Carlos always seemed to understand better than I did, though he said he had never visited the Scotoma. Wherever I had a blind spot, Carlos instantly helped me to see through it. I will always be grateful to him, and I resent these attempts by people who have never even met him to blacken the name of a sincere, studious, gifted man with accusations of fraud that must be motivated more by a desire to make a fast buck out of a bad book than to make any contribution to knowledge. *Answer*: By 1965 Castaneda had been working on his opus for five years. His habit was to write in notebooks, so by 1965 he had a pretty big collection of them. Since he was writing about imaginary fieldwork, his manuscript looked a lot like fieldnotes. As far as I have been able to discover, however, only twelve pages of those "fieldnotes" have ever been examined by a skeptic, the pages he sent to Gordon Wasson, which I examine again in chapter 40 of *The Don Juan Papers*. Here I need only say that those pages correspond with

certain passages of *The Teachings* in just the way an early version
of an invented story corresponds with a later version. No careful,
informed examiner would have taken them for fieldnotes. You were
inexperienced in those days and had no reason to doubt Castaneda's
sincerity, but now you have an opportunity to realize that you have
known one of the great hoaxers of the century.

10. *Subjectivity is science.* Some who are convinced that *Journey to
Ixtlan* describes imaginary events accuse Castaneda of professional
malpractice in offering the book as a dissertation, but they do not
understand the latitude of science. It would be malpractice only if
he did not *intend* to give an honest account of events *as he experienced them.* The entire text could be the product of a psychotic
episode and still be an acceptable phenomenological account. De
Mille's proof that the events are imaginary is, in my opinion, a
purely speculative web of inference, but even if Castaneda's committee had read the argument in 1972 and been convinced by it,
they could not have proved an intent to deceive. Castaneda could
still have believed he was telling the truth, and therefore, *would*
have been telling the truth, about what he experienced. *Answer*:
Phenomenological accounts may be useful in science, but their use
does not abrogate the rule that a scientific report must somewhere
be tied to ordinary reality. Though they may be of interest to scientists and may deserve academic recognition in some special category, subjective accounts that have no explicit objective framework
at all are not scientific reports and should not be confused with, or
endorsed as, scientific reports by doctoral committees. If Castaneda's committee suspected he was a gifted madman, they should
not have treated what they thought were his ravings as though they
were simply another sober report from a sane fieldworker. Nor was
it their duty to prove him either psychotic or dishonest; the burden
of proof was on him. The contradictions between *Teachings* and
Ixtlan were sufficient grounds for disqualifying the dissertation as a
scientific report.

11. *Fiction is truer than fact.* Fictionalized treatments add dimensions
of truth that factual reports inevitably lack. *Answer*: This is a fashionable but tricky proposition. Rodney Needham urged fellow ethnographers to strive for the empathic penetration and literary discipline displayed in novels by George Eliot, Gorki, and Dostoyevsky.
Thus, he said, their interpretations might partake of the humane
significance imaginatively sought in art and metaphysics. Despite
"professional misgivings on ethnographic grounds," Needham at
first found in *The Teachings* "a remarkable example" of such striving, exhibiting "a gift that is peculiarly apt" to the interpretation
of alien forms of experience, but he later had second thoughts
(1985:188–218). As the novelist needs to observe like an ethnog-

rapher, so the ethnographer needs to write like a novelist, if he is to capture the elusive, fragile, mythic cultural products of the archetypical unconscious mind. By seeming to fulfill such aspirations, Castaneda elicited praise from at least two outstanding anthropologists, first a rather reckless endorsement from Mary Douglas, later the circumspect and short-lived appreciation of Rodney Needham. Though I will readily agree that Dostoyevsky is a more sensitive interpreter of human behavior than the typical scientific anthropologist, many fiction writers distort behavior as much as they portray it. Bowen and Castaneda both wrote fiction, but we have no reason to assume their fictions are equally true to life. Castaneda's cultural cargo is a collection of oddities whimsically adapted from several disparate traditions. His dramatic personages are broad caricatures synthesized "for didactic reasons." Don Juan embodies not only the animistic, concrete thinker I call "don Indian" but also the academic abstractionist I call "the Indian don." An allegorical struggle between direct knowledge and rational discourse is frozen solid for ten years, as Carlos-Apprentice and Carlos-Skeptic fail to merge into one person. While Castaneda offered this miracle play as a factual memoir, Laura Bohannan (writing as Elenore Bowen) turned her ethnography into fiction. If she had then published her novel as a factual report, she would have gained nothing in validity but lost everything in authenticity. Eventually her book would have wound up in a bin with many other novels masquerading as history. False true-stories are, of course, inauthentic by definition. Beyond that, as Clifford Irving, David Rorvik, and Jay Anson have amply shown, they are often also massively invalid: bad company for a good book like *Return to Laughter*.

While novels as well as ethnography can be both valid and authentic, novelistic ethnography raises questions about trustworthiness and utility. The reader is not sure what kind of information he is getting. If, for example, I toss off a few cocktail comments about babies playing with scorpions, your ears will prick up and you will immediately wish to be told whether I am novelistically evoking the fact that babies often engage in dangerous play, or trying to warn you without alarming the other guests that I can see your very own baby sitting this minute on the flagstones in the garden playing with something that looks to me very much as though it might be a scorpion. In the one case, you will sit back in your chair and hear the rest of my ruminations; in the other, you will leap to your feet and rush to save the baby. Such distinctions matter. If don Juan ever existed, some anthropologist besides Castaneda should look into his existence, or into the existence of similar novel sources of ancient wisdom. If don Juan is only a plastic medicine man, a literary device for our allegorical instruction, field trips to find him can be left to hippies and other new-age enthusiasts (see chapter 10).

Scientists need to know whether they are dealing with credible or non- credible reporters. "Is this writer a liar?" is neither a trivial question nor one that should be evaded by appeals to the ineffability of mystical experience, the universality of phenomena, cultural diffusion, the truthfulness of novels, or the problem of subjectivity in the philosophy of science. It is a question scientists must sometimes ask if they don't wish to be led astray.

Castaneda is a fit object of such questioning, for though he collects valid ethnic elements, he likes to play around with them. For instance, his *spirit-catcher*, a loop of cord don Juan plucks to call out the spirit of the water hole, combines two devices described respectively by Furst and Meyerhoff (de Mille 1990:432): the *soul-catcher*, a loop of rope a shaman carries to collar wandering souls, and the *bow drum*, a musical bow and arrow with which a Huichol shaman warns the invisible ancient ones that a party of *peyoteros* was approaching. Such literary invention may be art, but it is neither science nor valid ethnography. The fact that a handful of specialists can see through don Juan's spirit-catcher to the original elements beneath will not help a myriad of trusting undergraduates who learn from Castaneda's books about a supposed community of mystical magicians quaintly miscalling themselves sorcerers and wandering around an air-conditioned desert positing koans and twanging their loops.

As validity comes originally from authenticity, so invalidity springs often, if unpredictably, from inauthenticity. Coyote is a tricky teacher. "In parts, at least, of California," wrote Hartley Burr Alexander, "his deeds are represented as almost invariably beneficent in their outcomes; he is a true, if often unintentional culture hero" (1964:227). To keep the California faith, then, let me add that, intentionally or not, by forcing us to look anew into the subtle relationships between validity and authenticity, Castaneda has made a substantial contribution to social science. From these ideas, one might even say, we are likely to get advances in anthropology.

This essay was reprinted with the author's permission from the new edition of his book, *The Don Juan Papers: Further Castaneda Controversies* (Belmont, CA: Wadsworth, 1990). Complete sources and citations for this chapter are given in the references and notes for chapter 6 of the *The Don Juan Papers* (de Mille 1990). Here, as elsewhere, I distinguish *Carlos* from *Castaneda*. Castaneda is the author of best-selling books about Carlos and don Juan; Carlos is a young anthropology student, whose amazing story is told in books by Castaneda. They are not the same person. Carlos was born in Brazil in 1935, whereas Castaneda was born in Peru in 1925. Carlos's father was a professor of literature named C. N. Castaneda, but Castaneda's father was a goldsmith named C. B. Arana. Carlos's native language was Portuguese; Castaneda's was Spanish. And so on.

Notes

1. See Alice Kehoe's thoughts about "the natural mind" and Euro-American fantasies about *Natürvolker* in chapter 10.
2. Modern anthropologists have more than a little reason to be wary of "world-wide ethnological correspondences." See R. H. Barnes's essay, Chapter 11, which stresses that knowing the special circumstances of key informants—like don Juan—is of critical importance in assessing the merits of raw ethnographic data.
3. Confirming Duerr's impression, Siegel (1981) finds that Castaneda's purported experiences with psychodelic mushrooms and Jimson weed (*Datura*, or Devil's Weed) are psychopharmacologically invalid, and therefore not to be accepted as authentic.
4. See the Alleglossary in *The Don Juan Papers*.
5. An example of transformatory creation is offered by Sam Gill in chapter 8, where God, having no place to put his foot down in a watery world, scratches up sand from the bottom and makes the land and rocks.
6. See note 3 for Siegel's similar inference.

References

Alexander, Hartley Burr. 1964. *The Mythology of All Races*. Volume X. North American. (First published 1916; reprinted in 1944 and 1964). New York: Cooper Square.

de Mille, Richard. 1976. *Castaneda's Journey: The Power and the Allegory*. Santa Barbara: Capra Press.

———. 1990. *The Don Juan Papers: Further Castaneda Controversies*. Belmont, CA: Wadsworth.

Needham, Rodney. 1985. *Exemplars*. Berkeley: University of California Press.

Schutz, Alfred. 1964. "Don Quixote and the Problem of Reality." In *Collected Papers II*. Nijhoff. 135–158.

Siegel, Ronald K. 1981. "Inside Castaneda's Pharmacy." *Journal of Psychoactive Drugs* 13:325–31.

Strachan, Don. 1977. Reviews of *Castaneda's Journey*. *Los Angeles Times* Book Review, February 6.

———. 1979. "In Search of Don Juan." *New West* 4(3):90–1.

13

Ethical Advocacy Versus Propaganda: Canada's Indian Support Groups

John A. Price

Technically, propaganda is any widespread promotion of particular ideas; but the common connotation is that advocacy of ideas carried to an extreme can become unethical and lead to distortions in the promotion of special views and images. Propaganda typically uses stereotyping for political or commercial ends (Price 1973). The presentations are too biased, too selective to tell the whole truth. Emotional appeals may be substituted for a fully reasoned, balanced analysis of issues. One result is that even honest, ethical, and reasoned political advocacy can become tainted and discredited by association with the propaganda of fanatic proponents of any cause.

Such problems occur when advocates abandon fundamental principles of serious research and responsible social action. Sometimes they fail to do complete research on the relevant issues, or they do not maintain a critical stance in judgments about the truth of rumors and hearsay until they have been substantiated. Sometimes overly dedicated champions do not assemble a full array of verified facts in an entirely honest and well rounded way. On the contrary, they present only that evidence and information which supports the position they are endorsing. Similarly, the more zealous advocates concentrate on a narrow range of confrontational styles of social action strategies for achieving their goals, excluding the possibility, for example, of quiet negotiations that might be more effective in the long run than attempting to force policy changes by embarrassing public officials.

Increasingly, we have witnessed these and other tactics used by Canada's historically most important native support group, called The Indian-Eskimo Association of Canada (IEA) at its founding in 1960. This advocacy group later changed its name to The Canadian Association in Support of the Native Peoples (CASNP) in 1972, and then The Canadian Alliance in Solidarity with Native People (still CASNP) in the 1980s. This essay provides an overview of modern native politics in Canada, some general features of modern native political values and rhetoric, and a brief case history of the CASNP support group. The following table gives an overview of information about natives from the 1981 Census (Statistics Canada 1984). About 2.2 percent of Canada's population were then enumerated as native people, a figure five and a half times greater than the 0.4 percent Indians that were counted in the 1980 U. S. Census.

Canada's policies for the management of Indian communities were based mainly on stereotyped thinking about small band type organizations, the most frequent form of native social organization in this nation. Given this narrow conviction and emphasis, with the homogenized universalization of rules and regulations characteristic of state level bureaucracies, the administrative practices of Canada's Indian Department were particularly destructive of the traditional political systems and operations of tribal and chiefdom level societies. In contrast, in the United States larger, multi-community tribal level societies as a general rule were the model for American policy. Therefore, in the United States

TABLE 13.1

Native People in the 1981 Canadian Census

Population (1,000s)

Status	Non-Status	Métis	Inuit	Total	Non-Native
293	75	98	25	491	23,592

Claim A Native Language As Mother Tongue (Per Cent)

On/Off

Reserve

| 46.6%/18.0% | 9.5% | 13.9% | 74.1% | 28.7% (Average) | — |

1980 Per-Capita Income ($1,000s)

| $7.1/$8.8 | $9.9 | $9.5 | $8.3 | $8.6 | $13.1 |

High School or Higher Education

| —/— | — | — | — | 28.7% | 52.8% |

native peoples historically have had much more experience with self-determination—in the sense of internal management of their political affairs—than Canadian natives, having since the early nineteenth century been encouraged to develop their own written constitutions, law codes, tribal courts, police forces, and the like. The "tribal" orientation in the U.S. Indian policy and management also meant that American Indians by-and-large were awarded much larger reservations than was the case in Canada. Hence, the Indians of the United States have some eight times more trust land per capita reserved for their use, under the protection of the federal government, than Canadian Indians.

This historical acceptance of greater political self-determination for Indians in the U.S., combined with the slower rate of acculturation and urbanization of natives in Canada, has led Canada's native policies to lag about twenty years behind those of the United States. For example, the following are the initial dates for several salient government events in the two countries.

	U.S.A.	Canada
Indian in Senate	1907	1958
Indian in Lower House	1944	1968
Citizenship to All Indians	1924	1960
Per Capita Grants to Students	1934	1954
Land Claims Commission	1946	1969
Alcoholic Beverages Allowed	1951	1967
Termination Policy Attempted	1953	1969
Indian Bill of Rights	1968	None
Indian Religious Freedom Act	1978	None
Indian Child Welfare Act	1978	None

The acculturation of Canada's native peoples has been a selective process, as is also true in the United States (Price 1979, 1984, 1988). One dimension is that, generally, the more an Indian cultural trait conflicted with the practices of the dominant society, the more quickly and completely it disappeared, both in practice and from memory. Some examples of extreme conflict are traits such as cannibalism, infanticide, geronticide, scalping and the collection of other body-part trophies, inter-tribal warfare, plural marriage, sacrificial torture and killing of prisoners, and slavery. These traditional practices dropped out early in the history of relations between Indians and the Canadian and American nation-states; and modern native political and poetic rhetoric, when not avoiding any mention of them, vehemently denies their existence or attributes their origins to "the White man." Thus when burned and broken human bones are found in the trash of archaeological sites of the Huron, Neutral, and Iroquois the policy is to treat them legally in the same category as animal bones. In contrast, several permits and reburial rites are required for regular burials, and Indian activists regularly protest the "desecration" of such sites by archaeologists.

When native cultural practices were in only moderate conflict with those of the dominant society, and were institutions of central importance, they often did survive in some modified form. Here one thinks of such revitalized institutions as the Northwest Coast potlatch, the Salish Guardian Spirit Ceremonial, the Plains Sun Dance, and the Iroquois Longhouse Society. However, the most successful institutions of modern native life society are neither ancient nor traditional: they are practices recently invented that in a general way draw on some combination of native tradition and broader Canadian and American influence, interest, and demand.

The modern Powwow is a striking example of such a recently invented pan-Indian "tradition," as are contemporary native political organizations (local, regional, national, and international). Some of these syncretisms are specific to particular cultures, such as the Inuits' soapstone sculpture and print making and the Ojibwa-Cree school of painting. Moreover, the central themes and pronouncements of native political and poetic rhetoric emphasize mainly issues and forms that elites of the majority society most respect. Among these much stressed, broadly acceptable politicized cultural themes, certainly the most popular is that Indians are truly the first-comers, the Original People, the really native Americans. Other themes almost as frequently expressed are the ideas that the native peoples of North America practiced representative democracy long before immigrants from Europe enjoyed such liberties (see chapter 6), that they lived in peaceful cooperation in communities based on equitable sharing rather than competition and inequality (see chapter 8), that they practiced "geopiety" and lived in ecological harmony with "Mother Earth" (see chapter 7), and that they have fine traditions of oral literature and the visual arts and crafts.

The rhetoric of Indian support groups and of allied Indian leaders involve concerted efforts to present acceptable special interest group images. But even when politically sophisticated Canadians—recognizing the political motivations in such pronouncements—discount some of the hyperbole in such pronouncements, there have been serious difficulties in public acceptance of native political views. This is so because the demands made by activists on behalf of Indians often conflict with general Canadian values and cultural features. The fundamentals of democratic life, the separation of religion and politics, industrialization, urbanization, and policies universally applicable to the whole citizenry are among the particular points of friction.

The Canadian political left and related social activist political groups greatly value material, political, and social equality; they tend not to mix religion and politics; they are anti-sexist; they align themselves with international movements; they are anti-racist; they tend to be oriented to urban life, industrialism, and labor unions; they oppose the killing of seals, whales, and other wild animals; and they tend to be anti-militaristic. Thus while the political left might want to support Indian causes, they must deal with mixed signals. This is especially so in the peace and ecology movements because so many natives peoples are quietly proud of the their heritage in warfare and because hundreds of thousands of native Canadians still depend upon harvesting fish and game. Moreover, native people often include religious issues as legitimate aspects of their political activities. Native conferences, for instance, typically begin and end with prayers and religious references are commonly found in the speeches. Moreover, they are the most rural of Canada's ethnic groups, the least industrial, the least unionized, and the most vocal in defense of special rights not available to other Canadians.

Native people have been particularly "undemocratic" in several substantial ways, adding further sources of friction with potential supporters. They have insisted on a constitutionally entrenched special status as *the* aboriginal people of Canada, a people entitled to numerous rights beyond those granted to the citizenry at large. Similarly, they make extensive special claims on Canada's economic and political systems through modern interpretations of old treaties, demanding such privileges as special hunting and fishing rights, exemption from taxation, free medical services, freedom to cross and recross the international border with the United States (because of an article in the 1794 Jay Treaty between the United States and Great Britain), and a wide latitude as regards political self-determination.

Indians have been successful in acquiring freedom from most Canadian taxes (Bartlett 1985). Indian bands have a taxation status like municipalities, being generally immune from external taxation, while entitled to raise their own real estate and business license taxes—charged against both Indians and non-Indians living or operating on Indian lands. Indian corporations based on Indian reserves do pay taxes on goods purchased off their reserves, although Indian bands per se are generally exempt from taxes. Such exemptions do not apply to all those counted as natives, for Inuit, Métis, and non-status (not federally registered) Indians do pay taxes in the same way as all other citizens. But status

Indians are exempt from federal and provincial taxation on reserve land, personal property on reserve land, and income received while working on reserve land. Similarly, scholarships paid by the Department of Indian Affairs to Indians for attending universities are deemed to be paid on a reserve and are thus not taxable. All these special categorical aids and exemptions represent points of controversy between Indian and non-Indian Canadians.

Indian exemptions from provincial sales taxes are somewhat variable from province to province. Historically, British Columbia has had the most repressive policies of any province in Canada and taxes everything it can, except sales to an Indian purchaser at a store located on a reserve. On the other hand, Saskatchewan has an official tradition of positive policies toward Indians, although it also has by far the highest arrest rates of Indians and the lowest favorable public sympathy in national opinion surveys. Saskatchewan exempts almost all purchases by Indians from sales taxes, on or off reserves and irrespective of place of delivery. Between these two extremes of British Columbia and Saskatchewan, most provinces exempt Indian purchases from sales taxes for consumption or use on a reserve, particularly when they are delivered right to the reserve. But liquor, tobacco, gasoline, electricity, and telephone services tend to be taxed.

The federal government now spends $2.9 billion a year on its programs for Canada's status Indians and Inuit. In addition, there are hundreds of millions available in provincial programs benefiting Indians, and more benefits resulting from provincial, excise, sales, and income tax exclusions for natives. Moreover, there are now over 750 successful Indian businesses in Canada, many started with loans from the Indian Economic Development Fund or the newer (1983) native managed Native Economic Development Program. Given these facts, their unique land and treaty rights, their special place in the new Canadian Constitution, and national programs to promote Indian businesses and to employ native people, we can say that they have certainly achieved the "citizen plus" status that native advocates have fought for over the past generation.

After Canadian native peoples were granted citizenship in 1960, with a new Bill of Rights, the rhetoric of advocates was quite modest, calling for economic and political equality, simple legal justice, adequate medical and educational programs, and so forth. Nonetheless, as native political organizations acquired genuine political power and these calls for equality began to be realized in the 1970s, the rhetoric of advocates increasingly shifted to newer goals and in some instances took on a new stridency.

More and more these aims included specialized issues: the plight of

Indians in prisons; and issues that involved a combination of social protests—such as the women's movement and the native movement's effort to eliminate discrimination in the Indian Act of Canada. In significant ways, the aims and interests of Indian activists coincide with those of other special interest groups, as when the ecology, peace, and native movements joined forces to eliminate the use of Labrador as a training ground for NATO pilots. Other specialized aims of Indian activism include defending cases of alleged injustice against individuals. One such has been the the case of the American Sioux political leader Leonard Peltier's sentence in an American prison; another the sentencing of Sergeant Clayton Lonetree to thirty years incarceration for espionage, larceny, and conspiracy while guarding United States embassies in Moscow and Vienna; and a third the case of Donald Marshall, a Micmac who served eleven years in prison for a murder, of which he turned out to be innocent when the actual murderer at last confessed. Native support groups, similarly, are always willing to beat the publicity drums for any such particular claim of injustice against native groups and individuals, whether land claims, hunting and fishing rights, hydroelectric development projects, or what have you.

In these increasingly specialized, multiplying ways, native advocacy over the past decade has moved from the general to the specific. In the same period, organizations staffed and conducted exclusively by native peoples have taken control of most of their own advocacy. Those which are managed by non-Indians, or which include non-Indians in their membership and in leadership roles, commensurately, have been supplanted and forced to become minor voices in the whole native advocacy industry. It is among those displaced from their earlier positions of prominence where we can see the more flagrant abuses of advocacy rhetoric: frank, unmitigated propaganda which bypasses the intellect and strikes directly at the the public's emotions. The new non-Indian Indian activists, in open competition for an influential voice in the direction of native affairs, are involved in direct competition for positions of power. In this developing political contest it is difficult for serious scholars, such as applied anthropologists, who hew to professional standards of evidence, research, and pragmatic advice, to find a place for themselves with others interested in the future of native Canadians, and to have an influence on social policies.

Selections from John A. Price's Additional Work Notes for "Ethical Advocacy Versus Propaganda"
Michael Price, Complier

A mixed Native and non-Native organization political organization I have been associated with over the years has evolved from a research and political lobbying [group] to unresearched advocacy and uncritical propaganda on behalf of what is seen as any pro-Native cause. In the early 1960s, the Indian-Eskimo Association of Canada (IEA) did research on many problems of native peoples and acted as a national political lobby for Native interests. In the later 1960s it helped stimulate the development of Indian centers and the formation of Native political organizations. By 1970, the Eskimos had formed *Inuit Tapirisat* [Eskimo Brotherhood] of Canada (ITC) and there was a working alliance of Native organizations, particularly through the National Indian Brotherhood (NIB), for [a legitimate voice] on behalf of federally registered Indians, and through the Native Council of Canada for non-status Indians and Métis. The Native associations required that the IEA change its name, because it appeared to denote an official Native organization. In 1972 the name was changed to the Canadian Association in Support of the Native Peoples (CASNP), and the head office was moved from Toronto to Ottawa, to more effectively pursue a political lobbying function.

With greatly expanded federal support, the all-Native associations had an explosive growth in personnel and programs. And they recommended that the government stop funding CASNP. The government agreed and CASNP was forced to close down most of its research operations . . .

The IEA, later called CASNP, has had a long history as a Native support group. Always based primarily in Toronto, it had branch offices and chapters in Ottawa, Winnipeg, and Edmonton. Though it always had some Native members, who were encouraged to run for positions on the Board of Directors, most members and officers were non-Natives. These came mainly from Native Studies specialties in academia, church groups, and social service agencies, together with some individuals just interested in Native affairs.

The IEA was created in 1959 by a committee of the Canadian Association for Adult Education, and was supposed to educate the public about Native issues, to encourage Natives to form national political associations, and to advocate and lobby for Native associations. The IEA held conferences and workshops where Native people could speak to largely non-Native audiences on the issues of the day (Ponting and Gibbins 1980:chapter 10).

The IEA's early lobbying efforts were concerned with such issues as: (1) establishment of the Indian Claims Commission, (2) removal of Indian Affairs from the Department of Citizenship and Immigration, (3) improvement of Native housing, (4) Native hunting rights, (5) a nation-wide survey of contemporary Indian life (that resulted in the influential Hawthorne-Tremblay report), and (6) federal funding of a network of urban Indian social services and recreational centers.

Early issues of the IEA's *Bulletin* describe such things as: (1) activities of Native associations, (2) scholarships and job openings for Natives, (3) educational kits, (4) the activities of the IEA's northern field agents, such as Wally Firth, a Native who piloted an IEA airplane on various research, political, and economic development missions in the Northern Territories in the 1970s, and who later became a politician in his own right, (5) government projects that would affect Native areas, and (6) the association's library services and publications.

Articles in these early issues of the *Bulletin* were well researched and conveyed the complexity of the issues discussed. For example, Jeannette Fauell's (sp?) court battles starting in 1979 to recover the Indian status she automatically lost when she married a non-status Indian, were shown in terms of their historical, legal, and political complexity, not just as an issue of right and wrong. It took fifteen years of conferences and court cases to resolve the issue raised by her case, and now with Bill C-31 of 1985 some 76,000 women and their children who lost their Indian status through marriage [to non-Indian status men] can be reinstated.

The [IEA's] research base in Toronto was aided by its rapidly expanding library on Native peoples, particularly its holdings of 140 Native periodicals, [collections of] government reports, [files of] newspaper clippings, and a variety of peripheral documents that were unavailable in any other library. A clipping service was started in which microfilm copies of [newspaper] clippings were organized by topic and annually distributed to other libraries throughout the country.

By 1971 this IEA resource was being described as "the best library of its kind anywhere." It had 130 publications for sale, including the influential *Native Rights in Canada* (IEA 1970), and kits for schools and public libraries. The IEA was holding workshops for teachers and social workers, operating a Native speakers bank, presented a joint brief with the National Indian Brotherhood to the Canadian Senate's Committee on Poverty, and was helping the Canadian Eskimos to form and incorporate *Inuit Tapirisat* [Eskimo Brotherhood] of Canada.

In this period federal funding for, and the political influence of, Native organizations was rapidly expanding. But then the IEA went into a decline, with something of a push from George Manual, the head of the National Indian Brotherhood. The IEA had encouraged several Native organizations to appoint one of their members to the IEA's Board of Directors. It has often been assumed that the IEA's financial crisis was caused by Manual's recommendations to federal agencies to stop funding the IEA; that may have helped, but in 1971 only 14 percent of IEA funding came from government grants. It was primarily the decline in donations from business, and from IEA's 200 private and 227 organizational members, and the expense of employing Native field workers and maintaining an office in Ottawa that led to years of financial decline.

[Years later] in 1978–1979, when IEA had reorganized as CASNP, the successor organization got 57 percent of its annual budget of $450,000 from government grants. Then, when the government reduced its grants to CASNP, its programs had to be cut back again.

[Meanwhile], in 1968 the Board of Directors of IEA met with the boards of the National Indian Brotherhood and the Canadian Métis Society in order to coordinate IEA's activities with these two national associations. [Then] some Métis complained that the IEA was competing for members with these organizations. There was [also] a general objection to the IEA name, because of the implication it was a fully Native organization. There were [additional] complaints. One was that the IEA was not always obtaining the approval of local Native associations when it went into their areas and did research. The IEA was accused of using Native people in token ways, to serve on its Board of Directors as "Indian dressing" [so as] to get grants and to provide legitimacy to a basically non-Native association. The Native organizations were concerned that they had no power and that individuals who presented themselves as Natives [should] in fact be authentic representatives of the Native people.

The IEA agreed to reserve a certain number of positions on their Board for the Native organizations. The IEA [then also] changed its name to the Canadian Association in Support of Native Peoples, to answer the criticism of presenting itself as a group of primarily native people. Soon after this change in name was made, however, the National Indian Brotherhood boycotted making any appointments to CASNP's board and continued this boycott for several years. The IEA/CASNP, under criticism from the NIB for competing with it for funds, adopted a policy of never applying for funds from Canada's Indian Affairs department or from the Native Secretariat of the Secretary of State, withdrawing forever from competition with native organizations for funds. [For a time, IEA/CASNP maintained] very good relations with the *Inuit Tapirisat* of Canada, fairly good relations with the National Association of Friendship Centers, and fairly poor relations with the largest and most powerful Native group, the National Indian Brotherhood.

Ponting and Gibbins (1980) discuss the politics of the early history of IEA and CASNP. They give a fourfold analysis, following the style of Talcott Parsons' "Four Needs": support to Native organizations in cultural matters, helping in White-Native relations, political lobbying, and providing resources. CASNP's support of Native organizations was aimed toward: (1) preservation of culture, as by teacher training workshops for curriculum development and workshops for the operation of urban Indian centers; (2) enhancing the integration of local communities through publications and speakers sent to Native groups; (3) political support of Native defined goals, often with submissions to government policy commissions in which there was a Native interest. Until the 1980s, CASNP remained oriented toward research and education and left politics to Native organizations. So it also, (4), provided resources such as Native scholarships and publications and workshops for Native organizations in such matters as fund raising, media relations, and operating a speaker's bank. Ponting and Gibbins end by describing the demise of CASNP, due to its displacement by fully Native organizations and by church groups, philanthropical foundations, and educational institutions.

In the 1974–1975 Annual report, CASNP's Education Director wrote "more people are looking for a factual and easily accessible source of information to counterbalance the mere reporting of events in the media. This role is one which we and Native leaders across the country see, with CASNP making major contributions and consolidating its efforts . . . In the upcoming year we will place an increased emphasis on the development and provision of accurate, unbiased information to the media and the general public in the hope of alleviating misunderstanding and fears based in ignorance."

Ponting and Gibbins conclude that CASNP achieved its original paternalistic goal of contributing to the development of Native organizations and [that] it finally was no longer needed by Native people and died of success. But CASNP did not really die; [instead] it went into a long term decline and then emerged again as a smaller, more radical and more political organization.

Changing its name to Canadian Alliance in Solidarity with Native People, and taking a more militant stance, the reborn organization kept its old acronym, CASNP. It continued to address legitimate Native complaints, but its pronouncements were not based on much research, they lacked a balanced consideration of issues, and did not suggest a well developed strategy of social action to correct injustices. The result was that CASNP took on a kind of frustrated, propagandistic cast, expressing a feeling of alienation from the majority society.

As a case study of this change in CASNP's style, I will use one issue of the organization's quarterly *Bulletin*, for Summer/Fall 1987. This will give readers a sense of the variety of issues addressed by this non-Native, Native lobby.

In this issue of the *Bulletin* one story involved the Oneida Council of Chiefs. Based in Canada, but claiming to represent Oneidas in Wisconsin, Ontario, and New York, they had a claim before the U.S. Federal courts in New York to regain six million acres of land in twelve counties in the state of New York. They said they would consider occupying state parks and unused state land if New York did not help to resolve the clam in their favor (see chapter 15).

Another report involved the Lac la Croix Indian Band at Forêt Francis, Ontario, which wanted to operate motor boats in Quetico Provincial Park, and in the American waters of Lac la Croix in Superior National Forest, in order to fish and earn a living. Their current, temporary right was set to expire in 1988, when motors were to be banned so as to preserve the "wilderness experience" of visitors to these parks.

One report concerned the United Church of Canada, which issued a formal apology to the Native peoples of Canada for failing to "recognize, learn from, and share in native spirituality, and for the resulting destruction of dignity, cultures, and spirituality."

Another involved an Indian warning:

> Canadians [that they] are always searching for roots, since the culture they brought with them when they immigrated here did not grow well in our soil. So they did their best to eradicate what was already flourishing here when they arrived . . . and the killing of our culture continues . . . you Canadians are now crying about the threat to your cultural sovereignty. What has already been done to us is about to be done to you [by the Americans]. Canada is like South Africa in some ways. Before the Europeans came Indians had no unemployment, welfare, alcoholism, children's aid societies, prisons, or mental hospitals . . . Indians were herded into 'Reservations' and had to have a pass to leave the reserve. South African officials actually studied the Canadian reservation and "status" systems when they set up apartheid. Indian children were snatched and incarcerated in church boarding schools in attempts to "Christianize" them. Potlatches and powwows were outlawed . . . in South Africa the Europeans are outnumbered by non-Europeans by more than 5–1. Who knows whether . . . the Canadian people would have extended the vote to all Indians in the 1960s if they had been outnumbered [as in South Africa].

One story told how the Ontario government was examining a fishing agreement with the Treaty Indians in the Northwest part of the province, around Kenora and Dryden. These fishing rights were opposed by the local tourist resort owners. "The tourist operators, a majority of whom are Americans, organized public meetings and stirred up a lot of white-sheeted, cross burning images among the gentle townfolk of Dryden. During a January 22 meeting, speakers demanded abolishment of Aboriginal treaty rights and armed resistance to the enforcement of these rights." A native woman from Grassy Narrows [reserve] responded by a letter to the editor of the local newspaper, *The Daily Times and News*, [writing]:

> only the bad side of Indians is portrayed in the local paper . . . . We are always labeled as drunks, thieves, or irresponsible people . . . . Wages from our people are almost all spent with local merchants in Kenora . . . . Kenora receives close to $20,000,000 each year from the lands . . . . We own nothing. We don't even own our houses on the reserves or the land, or any business that exists on the reserve . . . nor do we have access to mortgages to attain improved housing! I have seen American operators in the past here . . . our resources are continually [taken] across the border, leaving nothing here except our lakes, which are being fished out . . . .

Another told of uranium mining in Saskatchewan. In the Cree language, uranium is called *dada thay*, meaning "death rock." In June 1985, the Cree, Chipewayan, and Métis who live near Wollaston blockaded a road as an anti-Death Rock demonstration, after it was found out that areas in Wollaston were contaminated with a radioactive isotope up to 237 times the legal limit. Most of the energy development projects in Canada are in northern areas where Indian and Métis communities are concentrated . . . . The U.S. now accounts for 24 percent of the province's $600 million [per year] uranium industry. Saskatchewan ships 400,000 pounds of uranium [per year] by truck to the Kerr McGee Sequoyah uranium processing plant at Gore, Oklahoma, home of the Cherokee nation.

Also noted was a petition to the Prime Minister and the Minister of Indian Affairs and Northern development:

> There are 53 Native languages spoken in Canada. At the present rate of acculturation, it is estimated that within ten years only three languages will survive: Ojibwa, Cree, Inuktitut . . . . We will insist that Ottawa immediately improve the quality and number of first language programs available to Native people on and off the reserves . . . . The newcomer society has forced the denial of First Peoples' language.

This issue of CASNP's *Bulletin* reported that the Windy Boy [reserve] on Lyell Island in the Queen Charlotte Islands, home of the Haida Indians, [was a place with] a rich and beautiful ecology that is threatened by clear-cutting logging operations. The Haida had been blocking the logging roads and there were seventy-eight arrests:

> The logging of Lyell Island continues without reduction or modification. Reflecting its biased pro-industry make-up, the appointed Wilderness Advisory Committee recommended sacrificing Lyell Island, including up to 80–

90 percent of the Windy Boy watershed, and to preserve the rest as a National Park.

In 1983, a mine on Gauning Island on the west side of Monesby Island was closed down. In August 1987 the federal and provincial governments and the Falconbridge Mining Company signed an agreement with the Haida giving them the thirty-nine hectare island, including housing for about 350 people, a hospital, a hotel, and a recreational complex.

Another report concerned an airfield at Green Bay, Fairbanks, that was being used as a NATO training base, particularly for the high-speed, low-level flying that is necessary to fly under the level of radar detection systems. This creates massive sonic booms as the planes sweep above the ground faster than the speed of sound. The government claims that "The only humans present are occasional Inuit families who hunt and fish out of small camps on a seasonal basis. When occupied, these camps are carefully avoided by the low-flying aircraft. However, the Inuit have asked for solidarity from, among others, the Canadian and European peace movements, other native peoples, and native support groups, ecologists, and the churches."

The Inuit were also the focus of another report. In March 1987 eight Inuit were arrested for illegal hunting and possession of caribou. This is part of the statement they gave on the day of the arrest. "To judge our hunting of caribou as illegal is to judge our whole way of life as illegal. As a people we have been made to feel as foreigners in our own land. We believe deeply that the foreign law is not our law and the right claimed by others to govern us and to dispose of our lands and our resources is not legitimate. We recognize no authority on our land but God and the wishes and direction of the *Ishemit* [elders]."

Leonard Peltier, an [American Lakota] political leader, was in his house on the Pine Ridge reservation in South Dakota in 1975, when rifle fire from outside the house killed two FBI agents, who were coming to issue an arrest warrant on a person they believed to be in the house. Peltier fled to western Alberta, but was arrested in 1976 and returned to the U.S. where he was convicted of aiding and abetting in the deaths of the FBI agents. Today there is a large international movement that defines Peltier as a political prisoner and is moving to have him freed . . . claiming (1) he should have been given political asylum in Canada, (2) the charges were FBI "frame ups," (3) the extradition hearing was based on circumstantial evidence, (4) the U.S. government falsified documents and withheld crucial evidence, (5) he spent three years in solitary confinement in an institution notorious for using shock therapy and behavior modification on inmates, (6) a human rights commission in Spain honored him for "defending the historical and cultural rights of his people against the genocide of his race," and (7) he is not getting adequate treatment for an eye problem in prison.

CASNP, allied with the International Conference on Penal Abolition, [argued that] Native people make up an inordinately high proportion of Canada's prison population. In one highly publicized case, Donald Marshall, a Micmac wrongly served eleven years in prison for murder before the White man, Roy Ehsanz, who committed the crime, confessed, and Marshall was released. "In contrast to Marshall's life sentence for second degree murder, Ehsanz got one year for manslaughter."

These reports in CASNP's *Bulletin* reveal an implicit political strategy, which is propagandistic in design and execution. [Some of] the specifics of this strategy are as follows:

1. Present issues in terms of the nature and concerns of the majority society (Canadian identity concerns, competition with the United States).
2. Stress Native ecological or environmental wholesomeness and relatedness (appealing to environmental activists).
3. Maintain a high moral and religious position (appeals to church groups).
4. Do not discuss negative features of Native societies, such as political factionalism (do not offend Natives).
5. Claim a large mandate and a large constituency (one example of propagandistic exaggeration).
6. Use extreme cases, drawn in stark blacks and whites, and personalize as a way of dramatizing.
7. Omit any facts that might complicate the simplified image intended.
8. Accept Native statements as unfettered truths.
9. Play the victimization theme often.

Note

1. In late November, 1987, John A. Price agreed to write an essay for this book. A few weeks later, in December, he sat down and finished a thick abstract of the essay he planned to submit, a draft containing the core of his ideas and interpretations. In addition, he wrote many pages of working notes, intended as the basis for fleshing out his first draft. At that moment, neither he nor anyone else suspected he was fatally ill. Within a few agonizing weeks he was gone, a shocking loss to his family, friends, and profession. Later, while sorting through John's papers, his son Michael Price found the abstract and sent it to this book's editor. With some minor copy-editing and correcting, published with the permission of his family, this essay is the draft John was trying to finish in the last days of his life. Always the consummate professional scholar, it is not the revised and triple-checked final draft he would have submitted. In particular, it does not include the closer look at the *Canadian*

Alliance in Solidarity with Native Peoples he planned. But it does contain the core of information, ideas, and conclusions John A. Price wanted published in this book. A selection of his work notes is appended.

References

Bartlett, Richard H. 1985. "Taxation." In *Aboriginal Peoples and the Law*. B. W. Morse, ed. Ottawa: Carleton University Press.

Canadian Alliance in Solidarity with the Native Peoples. 1985–1987. *The Phoenix*. Toronto.

Canadian Association in Support of the Native Peoples. 1972–1977. *Bulletin*. Toronto.

Indian-Eskimo Association of Canada. 1971–1972. *Bulletin*. Toronto.

Ponting, J. Rick, and Rodger Gibbins. 1980. *Out of Irrelevance: A Socio-Political Introduction to Indian Affairs in Canada*. Toronto: Butterworth.

Price, John A. 1973. "The Stereotyping of Indians in Motion Pictures." *Ethnohistory* 20:153–171.

———. 1979. *Native Studies: American and Canadian Indians*. Toronto: McGraw-Hill Tyerson.

———. 1984. "Government Policies and Programs Relating to Urban Indians." In *The Dynamics of Government Programs for Urban Indians in the Prairie Provinces*. R. Breton and G. Grant, eds. Montreal: Institute for Research on Public Policy.

———. 1988. *Indians of Canada: Cultural Dynamics*. Salem, WI: Sheffield Publishing Co.

Statistics Canada. 1984. *Canada's Native People: 1981 Census*. Ottawa: Supply and Services Canada.

14

Inside BIA: Or, "We're Getting Rid of All These Honkies"

Stephen E. Feraca

"—and that means you, too!" He who fired this barb was a young mixed-blood with a law degree, an American of partial Indian ancestry, then newly employed with the Bureau of Indian Affairs (BIA) at its headquarters in Washington. His target was a full-blood, an American totally of Japanese ancestry, a Nisei born in California. This "Honkey," unlike the bearer of the law degree, had many years of professional experience in the administration of Indian Affairs. She had also, along with her entire family, experienced the supreme injustice and ignominy of internment during the Second World War.

Again in contrast with the belligerent Indian American who cannot speak the language of his tribal ancestors and is divorced from their traditions, the Japanese American is fluent in her ancestral tongue and fully literate in its complex writing system. Many tribal visitors, because of her physical features and the obvious non-European character of both her given name and surname, regarded her as Indian, and probably do still. They were confirmed in their belief to a large degree by the genuinely personal attention she gave to all the many tribal delegations with whom she came in contact.

This confrontation between the two employees, if it can be so-called, occurred at the beginning stages of the new emphasis on Indian preference in the BIA and the Indian Health Service (IHS). Many people, Indian and non-Indian alike, found that particular threat to be highly amusing. I did not, but an Afroamerican coworker became almost hysterical at the prospect of attaining honkeyhood. Half-jokingly, she resolved to find Indian ancestry in her genealogy but was warned that this would not suffice. Indian preference had been limited to one-quarter blood for initial appointments in the BIA, and later in the IHS when health services became separated from the Bureau. We all thought that with preference extended to promotions and training the same quarter-blood criterion would apply. The situation, however, became even more unpalatable and unworkable than it would have been if limited to the mythology of blood quantum.

These developments came during the mid-1960s, with the opening of the abuses of affirmative action (that is, officially sanctioned discrimination) in academia, in government, and in much less formal institutions of American society (see Glazer 1987). The BIA, close to the seat of federal power and particularly vulnerable to the wants of its own special-interest lobby, reflected the attitudes and policies of the dominant society sooner and quicker than other institutions. Affirmative action, meaning Indian preference, was bound to rear its ugly head but, as always in the field of Indian affairs, with a peculiar visage. In an official sense it began with a memorandum of May 3, 1966, from the Commissioner of Indian Affairs to all BIA chiefs. Most employees shrugged; a surprising number have forgotten it; I and others saw the handwriting on the wall.

A confused, blatantly racist, extraordinarily offensive atmosphere had surrounded the seating of the first Indian in this century, and the second Indian in history, in the Commissioner of Indian Affair's chair. Commissioner Robert L. Bennett's first bureau-wide memo, mentioned above, was titled "Indian Employment." One cannot ignore the impression that this individual, of Wisconsin Oneida extraction and a long-term member of the society of professional Indians, a person reared in the Bureau's Haskell Indian Institute, had been waiting a long time.[1] The document stated in its most pertinent part:

> We have always considered that Indian preference has applied only in the initial appointment process. We have taken the position that, as in the case of veteran's preference, it has no force in connection with promotion and training opportunity . . . I am sending this memorandum to you because I believe we have not been concerned enough with the Indian after he is employed. We have let his employment drift along after having given him his preference in appointment. I do not believe we can continue this. Too often I have seen an Indian and a non-Indian compete for promotion and the opportunity goes to the non-Indian because he is better qualified. While we must always endeavor to select the best qualified person for the job, we also must help the Indian to be among the best qualified.

During the next two years quarter-blood preference was applied in the filling of vacancies and in general recruitment in a growing climate of inconsistency and fear. Among other unsavory features was the spectacle of people who had never seen a tribal roll, and who did not know whether they were enrolled, feverishly trying to establish their blood quantum. To achieve a quarter-blood status they were enlisting the services of Whites who were familiar with useful records, including some with a flair for genealogy. Some of the exercises performed in that discipline, and in pedigree mathematics, were ludicrous. Tales of the individuals who added a $\frac{3}{32}$nds father to a $\frac{3}{64}$ths mother to achieve a better than one-fourth "blood" status are legion.

Then a blockbuster hit—a Memorandum of Agreement dated April 26, 1968, between the BIA and IHS. Titled "Maximum Utilization of Indians," it was cosigned by Commissioner Bennett and the Director of the Division of Indian Health. Reaching all the way back to an Act of June 30, 1834, a century earlier than the Indian Reorganization Act of 1934 (which statute would have in itself sufficed), this poorly drafted paper confirmed our suspicions about the future of professionalism in the specified agencies, and in other positions in Interior and Health, Education and Welfare (HEW) within Indian program fields. Using a quarter-blood cut-off earlier in the text, the second "policy" point read:

Maximum use will be made of trainee type positions and restructuring positions when feasible to permit Indians to qualify for appointments. For non-professional positions, in particular, when positive efforts have failed to produce a fully qualified candidate and there is an Indian preference eligible [i.e., applicant] available who is believed to possess the ability to perform the duties of the position satisfactorily but who does not fully meet the established qualification standards both agencies will utilize every means available to *restructure* such positions in an attempt to permit the Indian preference eligible to meet the requirements of it [emphasis mine].

I submit that no other federal agency would have countenanced such a monstrous declaration. Forgetting for the moment the non-Indians directly affected, exceedingly few individuals regarded this policy statement as offensive to Indians.

Although indisputably many of his fellow Haskell alumni and other Indian staff actively supported the commissioner, others were derisive. They were professionals with varying backgrounds in tribal tradition, or none at all. They appreciated the first preference that had been extended to them, but although most began their careers as clerks they had risen to responsible positions. In my view, some remained clerks regardless of grade, and far too many remained "country boys (or girls)," but this has nothing to do with Indianness. It is, indeed, a major problem encountered throughout the federal bureaucracy, where successive promotions often come with longevity, not growth in technical and administrative skills.

Those from Haskell Institute were loyal to the old school tie but some thought it had outlived its usefulness. Some were thoroughly critical of the speech and work habits of the younger graduates. This institution, located in Lawrence, Kansas, began as an off-reservation boarding school with a curriculum aimed at preparing reservation Indians for participation in the national work-force. In practice, it trained young Indians for careers in the BIA. My own mother-in-law, her brother, and two of her sisters graduated from Haskell; and all but one sister entered the Indian Service in low-level jobs, as typists and the like. Lacking the legally required one-quarter blood-quantum minimum, they were, however, permitted to attend, as were many other marginal "Indians." They were all at the time strangers to any Indian community other than that formed by the Indian Service bureaucracy itself. Indeed, there is such an animal.

Haskell has for some time been a glorified high school with nominal community college status. One reason that young Indians—from reservation communities or elsewhere—are drawn to it is simply that tuition, board, and room come free. There are still many students enrolled who do not derive from reservation communities. The "old guard" Haskell graduates, many of whom were essentially Euroamerican in both ancestry and culture, have practically disappeared from the Indian scene, and some of them from this world. Among them were, as contrasted with too many of today's professional Indians, competent, conscientious, and hard-working administrators. One, for example, was an Oklahoma Choctaw who was noted for being "unalterably opposed to spending a dime for off-reservation Indians" (his words in my presence). He was high-ranking and influential, and personally went out of his way to help in establishing a much-needed child welfare program for Florida Seminoles (it was a failure, however, through no fault of the Bureau). Not atypically in this respect (but we can't all be perfect), he also said of a BIA—multi-tribal conference, "It was a real nice affair—no Indian dancing or stuff like that." Oklahoma Cherokees and Choctaws were the most visible and powerful of this old guard. One such "Choctaw," whom I first met at a Sun Dance in South Dakota, admitted that he had no Indian ancestry whatsoever but he did exhibit a healthy appreciation for tribal traditions among those who did. Unfortunately many were they who had no such sentiments and cared less. A few were, as privately labeled by the noted anthropologist Gordon Macgregor, "culture destroyers," and MacGregor certainly was including non-Indians in this condemnation.

I am suggesting that Indians, genuine or spurious, are no better qualified than others to understand the dynamics of Indian societies and to gauge and cope with their needs. For instance, a Nisei with an anthropological background, Hiroto "Zak" Zakoji, achieved much success and well-deserved respect for his grass-roots person-to-person involvement with and sensitive analysis of some truly staggering sociopsychological conditions among Plateau and Northwest Coast tribes. (No, the Bureau is not and never has been loaded with Japanese Americans.)

I am not suggesting that Indians are intrinsically less qualified, but if non-Indians need highly special training, experience, and sensitivity in confronting these often exceptionally difficult problems so do they. Such knowledge and skills are not acquired through biological inheritance. The older Indian element, graduates of Indian Service schools or not, would generally agree. It need hardly be said, however, that it is a great rarity for younger Indian people of any level of sophistication to admit today that any qualification beyond that of an Indian identity is needed. Much of all this is lost on the poorer, less educated but mature reservation residents. Typical of their attitudes are the comments of several Florida Seminole women who approached me in a group before the beginning of what was to be a greatly enhanced summer recreation and learning program. These ladies, all mothers of teenagers, were working or visiting at the tribal commercial village. One woman pointedly asked who was under consideration for jobs as counselors for both the grade- and high-school programs. When I mentioned a few names, including a college graduate and some graduating high school seniors, she said unqualifiedly, "Don't get any Indians." All the other women present echoed this sentiment but I was constrained by my own and BIA policy to ignore them. I did add (as volunteer workers) a young White couple pursuing graduate degrees, and another young White woman borrowed from a county program. That the Seminole mothers knew what they were talking about was shown by later events, itself a sad commentary. The Seminole counselors would not try and could not control the kids enrolled in this program. On the other hand, the non-Indian volunteers tried and were unsuccessful, with painful results: both of the dedicated young women were assaulted.

Louis R. Bruce, a Mohawk-Sioux, succeeded Bennett as commissioner. Immediately upon Bruce's confirmation, during Richard M. Nixon's first term, the Indian preference policy reached new levels of stridency. About a year after he took office, Bruce said in Binghamton, New York, that of the twenty-three top positions he found in the Bureau, none was occupied by an Indian, but under his aegis soon there were twenty such positions, seventeen of them filled by Indians (Morello

1970). His claims were preposterous. Although their ranks had been thinning, the old guard Indians were veritably much in evidence when Bruce took office, and the deputy commissioner on deck, John O. Crow, epitomized the Haskell influence. But Crow was no friend of Bruce and his ilk, who loudly proclaimed that at last Indians had taken over the BIA. During the same Binghamton address Bruce said also that Indians are "fighting only to be heard. We don't want to hurt anybody—just to be recognized. That's what our red militants are doing." Bruce's stewardship was an utter disaster. His appointees were not only by-and-large militants and total strangers to administration, novices intent on reinventing the wheel, they actually sanctioned the use of federal office space, support facilities, and travel expenses for representatives of the American Indian Movement. To show their gratitude, in 1972 these young militants occupied and wrecked the BIA building, provoking the demise of Bruce and company, and ending as well Deputy Commissioner Crow's distinguished career of service to Indian people. The situation was so bad under Bruce that we lesser, long-service fools in the Bureau thought that the discriminatory Indian preference policy would go out the door with him. No such luck; the pressure that Bennett, Bruce, and Interior Secretary Rogers B. Morton responded to with this racial preference policy continued, as did the policy itself.

On June 26, 1972, Secretary Morton, together with Bruce, issued an edict containing the boldest statement yet: "Where two or more candidates who meet the established requirements are available for filling a vacancy, if one of them is an Indian, he shall be given preference in filling the vacancy." As noted by a then newly organized group of BIA employees, Dedicated Americans Revealing the Truth (DART), the statement "who meet the established requirements" did not mean *equally* qualified. Just before the application of this new garnish to the preference policy, the National Federation of Federal Employees had protested vigorously to the secretary in opposition to any discrimination based on race. Later, however, this employees union proved unwilling to do real battle for the BIA's non-Indian segment of its membership. Non-Indians then began to pay increased attention to the activities of DART.

During this turbulent period federal government agencies, state institutions, and larger private employers everywhere were experiencing the thrust of affirmative discrimination in the form of quotas, or the threat of them, or of arbitrary employment decisions that produced the same results. Even before the Morton-Bruce declaration some highly irrational things were being said and done, absent any official sanction, to promote the interests of selected Indians. When a notably professional

White branch chief expressed his frustration about filling some positions, his supervisor—a White Haskell Cherokee—advised that she "always thought there was a lot of talent in the mail room." The mail room and some other operations in the BIA headquarters were almost entirely filled with individuals, usually rather young and uneducated, recruited directly from reservations. These and many secretarial positions were and are truly low-paying jobs.

Yet even with Black unemployment the problem it is in the Washington metropolitan area, the Bureau has no compunctions about filling these slots with people who have to be transported from places as distant as the Navajo Reservation. The protesting branch chief was engaged in extremely complex work pertaining to tribal government. Needing skilled and experienced help, he openly scoffed at any suggestions that he canvass the mail room. Further concerning Blacks in this context, I have discussed the nature of Indian preference with only a few Blacks, including a federal personnel officer. All except one woman, a BIA employee, fully accepted Indian preference in the capital city and everywhere else. For a long period my own small branch contained no Indians, but did include two Blacks and two Nisei, one of the latter a clerk-typist whose output was nothing less than prodigious. When acting as branch chief for an extended period, I was chided for maintaining an "integrated shop." One of our people was a young, dark-complexioned historian with somewhat craggy features. Our regular chief of many years once said half-seriously, "I sure wish Mike looked more like an Indian." This sort of thing is really not funny. This young man, a Ph.D. candidate and a specialist in Indian political history, got out when it became only too evident that professional advancement in the Bureau was impossible for anyone who could not or would not claim an Indian identity.

Those were the times that saw the beginnings of the placing of "natives" in Indian cultural studies programs. It was also the era of such witless concepts as the development of courses in Swahili for Black students. American Blacks largely derive from West Africa. Swahili began as an East African Bantu language laced with Arabic. The Swahili classes emptied as quickly as college classes in Indian languages. On a much lower academic level, a woman from a British Columbia reserve expressed her shock at discovering that the Teton Sioux language was being taught to children in a grade school in the western part of the state of Washington. The proponents of this form of fake nativism were unable to find an instructor in the local tribal language, but the kids were learning "Indian." This is not funny, either. On a South Dakota campus a dear friend and colleague, a White native of that state who had spent his life in the study of Northern Plains ethnohistory, was summarily replaced by two thoroughly Americanized mixed-bloods who proceeded to achieve fame in the development not of meaningful Indian studies classes, but some astronomical travel and telephone bills.

The Honkey world, having witnessed such excesses only briefly mentioned above, riveted its attention on the *De Funis* and *Mancari* cases. Marco De Funis is a Sephardic Jew who challenged the emerging policy of affirmative discrimination, or reverse racism, and Carla Mancari is an Italian-American, who in fact hails from the region of my paternal ancestors. She battled furiously as gladiator in this legal arena, where the better class Christians, instead of joining the victims of discrimination, played the part of hungry lions. Although an organizer and later a shop steward of the union representing the BIA, I resigned because when things became truly intolerable that organization did not perform as expected. I was also one of the most vociferous opponents of Indian preference, but I did not formally join Mancari in her suit; and that I will always regret.

Mr. De Funis was the student who, graduating *magna cum laude* in 1971 from the University of Washington, applied for entrance to law school there. After being rejected he learned that thirty-six applicants with lower test scores than his were admitted. They were Blacks, Hispanics, Filipinos, and Indians. De Funis sued, a lower court finding in his favor. The Washington law school then appealed and was upheld by the State Supreme Court. Meanwhile, court orders enabled De Funis to attend law school. The case reached the U.S. Supreme Court in 1974 but was declared moot because of De Funis' admission to law school. He was by that time in the final quarter of his last year, the school assuring the court that he would graduate. We who were selfish enough to wish that he had not been admitted found ultimately, as described later, that insofar as Indian questions were concerned it would not have mattered anyway. William O. Douglas was one justice who dissented, saying, "If discrimination based on race is constitutionally permissible when those who hold the reins can come up with 'compelling' reasons to justify it, then constitutional guarantees acquire an accordion-like quality." [2] The *Mancari* suit had already reached the Supreme Court. Our hero was Justice Douglas, who was going to save the Indian people from further patronization, and the rest of society while he was at it.

Carla Mancari was, at the time, one of many non-Indian education specialists at the BIA's Albuquerque, New Mexico, South-western Indian Polytechnic Institute. She was a founder of DART and a principal behind the effort to place a hold on all personnel actions until the courts were able to settle the Indian preference issue. Her courage is unquestioned, but she knew little of the workings of Indian society, especially of tribal governments and the history and nature of the definitions of tribal membership. I like to think that I and others knowledgeable in the fields of tribal organization and enrollment would have been able to contribute data and analyses beyond the racial issue. But the suit brought by Mancari against Secretary Morton was, I must admit, essentially of a racial nature in the minds and hearts of all concerned. Indian views did not much differ from ours. Whatever proclamations disguise or legitimize this form of government sanctioned discrimination it remains fundamentally a question of racism. The U.S. Supreme Court thought otherwise.

A decision in *Mancari* was reached soon after the disappointing and frustrating *De Funis* case. Mancari had won in the District Court on the grounds of Indian preference being implicitly repealed by the 1972 Equal Employment Opportunity Act. The case was, as anticipated by all, appealed to the Supreme Court. That body held on June 17, 1974, among other startling things, that the Equal Employment Act, as an extension of the Civil Rights Act of 1972, was "largely just a codification of prior anti-discrimination Executive Orders, regarding which Indian preferences had long been treated as exceptions . . . "[3] Indians are bound to be, in just about everyone's view, different. Indians are not, as many Americans (especially Mormons) persist in believing, descended from the ancient Israelites. I am, however, in examining the extraordinary image of Indian people in this country and Canada, frequently reminded of the old story of the Jewish boy who asks his scholarly grandfather if Jews are like other people. The old gentleman lifts his eyes from his talmudic studies to reply, "Yes, but more so."

The *Mancari* decision was unanimous. Justice Douglas, therefore, let us down, but along with the other eight magistrates did so in a manner that beautifully skirted those constitutional issues about which so many watchers expected a thorough and conclusive review. Stripping the decision of historical elements and jargon, what emerges from the bare bones of *Mancari* is that Indian tribes do not constitute ethnic, sociological, or racial entities but self-governing sovereignties; and the United States is responsible for the positioning of members of such sovereignties in those federal agencies charged with the enhancement of such sovereignty. What a far cry from the honest paternalism expressed to me on a June afternoon in 1954 upon arriving for the first time on Pine Ridge Reservation. Although hired as a summer laborer, I was admonished by the second-in-command at the agency that particularly because of my interest in Indian tradition I was expected to "make life better for our Sioux people." I was not in much of a position to do that but, urged on by my new friends, I did take advantage of my non-Indian status, in nearby Nebraska, to illegally buy an awful lot of beer for their consumption. In fact, I did so the first night there, in the company of my great friend the late Clarence Janis, bearer of one of the oldest French names known to the Sioux and one of the finest traditional Sioux singers.

In the *Syllabus* of *Mancari* two basic findings are cited: firstly, that Congress did not intend to repeal Indian preference by the Civil Rights Act (as if it had been given any thought); and secondly, that Indian preference "does not constitute invidious racial discrimination in violation of the Due Process Clause of the Fifth Amendment but is reasonable and rationally designed to further Indian self-government."

If it is reasonable to apply Indian preference wholesale on a purely political basis, then it is eminently unconscionable to have Navajos involved in the affairs of the Utes, Sioux similarly empowered to manage the affairs of Blackfeet or Crows, and so forth. It would be reasonable, however, for the entirety of Crow Agency to be staffed by Crows; the Minneapolis Area Office to be populated by all the Chippewas necessary to handle strictly Chippewa business; and precisely the same divided arrangements prevailing in the Washington headquarters. The Pine Ridge IHS Hospital would, we should expect, be staffed with Oglala Sioux (except that medical officers are exempt from the preference policy, fortunately for the patients). God forbid that a Crow orderly be employed at that hospital. Such would not only tend to violate principles of Oglala self-government, the Crows have a healthy penchant for recalling intertribal warfare. Ridiculous? Of course it is; but since the court said nothing to Congress or the secretaries of Interior and HEW about the implementation of the policy many ridiculous actions were taken. Some of these really approached the nonsense sketched above. I do not know of any that strengthened the capacity for self-government of the several tribes but they certainly—hardly in keeping with the impossible idealism and romantic abstraction of the court—strengthened Indian racism.

Mancari in truth elated most Indians but neither they nor non-Indians immediately realized how loose and newly extended a definition of Indianness was made possible, indeed, virtually mandated by the decision. When legal and other minds were agonizing over the drafting of implementing regulations it remained clear that the affected agencies were still thinking in racial terms. "Certificates of Indian Blood" were for years after the 1974 decision still being required of Indian applicants with little attention being given to the factor of tribal membership *per se*. Only slowly did managers, applicants, and others begin to grasp that the political nature of the matter allowed for Indian preference to be extended to all members of tribes—White members, Black members, four-fourths blood members, thirteen sixty-fourths blood members, and the many thousands who would have to dig deeply for a distant ancestor with an Indian name. Not until the end of 1977 did the BIA at last publish rules for the definition of the term "Indian" for employment purposes. Long before then the racist climate had become completely unbearable.

Characteristic of the blatancy of some of the abuses was the notice of a combined Bureau of Indian Affairs and Indian Health Service party, to which only Indian employees were invited. I must remark that the only "Indian" item on the reception's limited menu was "fry bread." I have never seen the proper adverbial form "fried" employed in any of the innumerable meeting and Pow Wow notices that mention this item. Most Indian people and members of the larger society seem oblivious to the pre-Columbian absence of the makings of this distinctively modern Indian delicacy. There was no wheat cultivated in the Americas, this form of bread being adopted by Indian people from the French and Spanish.

It was not necessary to travel any distance beyond our own modest division in the BIA's Washington offices to find examples typical of the repressive racist atmosphere. Abuses in personnel actions were not unknown before the coming of Bennett and his policies, nor was it unknown for the Indian Service to harbor both Whites and Indians who had little more than contempt for reservation people. There were, however, Indian and non-Indian bureaucrats who in those days said "no" to Indian leaders when any other response would have been patronizing. There were Indian and White Agency superintendents and other officers who took their jobs damned seriously. They seemed to have had some silly notion that they were employed not by the tribes but by the federal government, in service to all Americans.

Truthfully, well before Bennett's arrival on the scene and absent any fanfare there was a move on to recruit qualified Indian graduates, not always with complete success. Representatives of a large Midwestern university, while arranging contractual services for our division, advised us that a recent law graduate there employed, a Chippewa characterized as a real whiz, might be attracted to the field of tribal government operations. Both Indian and non-Indians involved were anxious to recruit this man who arrived without delay, lugging his omnipresent, massive, bulging briefcase. He was given a specific and complex assignment, made an appearance late on a few afternoons, and then disappeared— to the great relief of those personally responsible for him. It was learned soon afterwards that he had a severe problem with alcohol and had produced nothing for the university. The Bureau had, in a word, been conned. The university people had served themselves doubly, getting rid of an incompetent by bumping him upstairs, while avoiding any accusation of discrimination.

Not long after the formal announcement of the expanded racial preference policy there arrived, again in the same office, a young man who supposedly was a member of one of the many tiny southern California "tribes." To me and others his claimed identity was extremely suspicious, not only because he appeared and behaved as non-Indian as was conceivable. I checked. The group from which he derives is totally unorganized and has no membership criteria. The official enrollment ended with a 1940 reservation census. He was born in 1941; his name was added to the census by a White field staff member only when he showed up seeking Indian preference. This individual who is not, and under the circumstances cannot be, a member of any tribe, and who has little Indian ancestry, has had—in addition to his initial appointment—at least two promotions based on Indian preference. He was, moreover, incompetent and his ignorance of Indian society reached a level just above that of bedrock. Two or three doors away from his shop was another new employee who was in his own speech "a Indian" working on his "doctorial dessertation [sic]," his academic program being federally funded. Although assigned to tribal enrollment activities, he flatly refused to continue an important enrollment research project, admittedly tedious in certain respects. This work was to have been performed under my supervision; I completed the portion that was expected of him and most of the rest of this lengthy project. No one would touch him, least of all his White branch chief, a professional of many years experience who had acquired a real fear of those Indians on her staff. She and I and others who declined to make an issue of the matter were all wrong. The employee eventually went on to better things in Indian programming, always by virtue of Indian preference, and in time was indeed invested with a doctorate (or is it "doctoriate"?).

By no means exhausting the horror stories within our own corridor (as this is about aspects of the Indian world I have not mentioned cases like that of the psychotic White secretary), I vividly recall the "summer student," a longhaired boy from Oklahoma with distinctly Indian features. He positively refused to return so much as an ordinary greeting delivered by any White staff member and sulked throughout the employment period. After his return to school were found in his desk copies of letters and memoranda he had written. They had been directed to the Equal Employment Opportunity Office and bitterly complained about the absence of Indians among the women who ordinarily supervised him. This unfortunate young person was tragically depriving himself, all the more so because he wrote excellent prose.

Anyone who thinks that such painful experiences as those few described above further Indian programming, tribal self-government, or the aspirations of young Indian people eager to work and to learn has several more guesses coming. On one occasion, when lunching in the Interior cafeteria, I was treated to an unsolicited condemnation of Indian preference voiced by a tribal leader seated at the adjoining table. Indian both culturally and phenotypically, he was justly proud of his success in steering programs toward his previously neglected tribe. He fully admitted that he had strongly supported Indian preference, anticipating that the policy would attract specialists with a genuine knowledge of social and economic needs. Observing that "We expected the best and got the worst," the strongest such charge I have ever heard, he ticked off the names of several undesirables also known to me. The rest of his remarks echoed the points made in a paper a few of us Honkies signed and delivered to Interior Secretary Andrus. We wrote that it was nearly impossible in our branch to fill vacancies left by two non-Indians. We said that this was becoming endemic to the Bureau, and "as a result of the ambiguous manner in which the Indian preference policy is administered the situation can only rapidly worsen due to attrition." There was no response.

I am among the ranks of those who have often begged for the opportunity to select and train Indian students and newly graduated individuals in all the fields in which I have been employed, beginning in adult education and community development on Pine Ridge Reservation. The closest I ever came to any such opportunity was to help in "sensitizing" sanitation engineers in the Health Service (but they were my age and White), and training a young, totally acculturated Indian woman, for too brief a period, in the processing of Indian claims awards. She was not selected by me and although she proved to be an excellent worker, I would have sought someone with a background more characteristic of reservation Indian society. On Pine Ridge there was at that time no chance to train an Indian assistant or even to establish such a slot. My successor was the whitest of Whites, a run-of-the-mill shop teacher looking for the promotion he received with no affinity whatsoever for adult education or community work. I understand that he functioned largely as a truant officer, something I had avoided like the plague. Added to the irony was that he got to use the brand-new agency car that was delivered one week before I was transferred. My position had not been assigned a vehicle. For more than three years I had to borrow the superintendent's car, catch rides from other BIA staff or from IHS people with similar destinations, or use my own.

At the Seminole Agency in Florida the tribal member on my staff I considered to be most promising became the president of the tribal board less than a year after I arrived. He spoke both native languages used by the Seminoles, and was much more aware than I could ever have become about the overwhelming sociopsychological problems of many individuals and whole families. On a Florida reservation one of the more public drunks, an alligator wrestler when he worked, produced children by both of his wife's daughters from a former marriage, and twins by one of his daughters from that wife, all living in the same household. Immediately after my arrival in Florida, I undertook arrangements for transportation and other business involving Seminole children scheduled to attend BIA boarding schools in Oklahoma. When I registered astonishment at the disproportionately high numbers being shipped away from their homes, my assistant explained that many of those being processed were the victims of severe family situations. She took pains to point out that the agency regularly sent the youngest teen-age girl from the incestuous family away to school to save her from the fate of her sister and half-sisters. (What is done for other Floridians to combat this kind of horror, not having a Bureau of Indian Affairs?)

The lady lamented, however, that neither she nor anyone else had ever been able to persuade the girl to remain in Oklahoma through the summer months, although a job for her could be arranged through the boarding school. The following year I mentioned to this girl's half-brother, well educated in the formal sense, that I intended to do everything possible to place her in an Oklahoma job, appropriately supervised by Bureau field staff (I failed; she came home as usual). He conveyed to me that he could not understand why I was so intent on keeping her away from home. This man succeeded to my position. The tribes and the local communities have little hope, except accidentally, of being competently served and educated, in the broad sense of this word, absent the careful recruitment of individuals who are qualified well beyond any position-description sheets. Today all such advertisements emphasize detailed Indian preference statements. The local, often isolated Indian communities starving for information, attention, and encouragement ordinarily do not care where any employees come from or about their racial characteristics. Of course, most tribal politicians—their attention fixed on the power center in Washington—can be counted on to say that they do.

Kelsey T. Kennedy, personnel officer at a Bureau field installation, wrote a letter of August 11, 1975, to all members of Congress enclosing a copy of a "petition," really a paper titled "Indian Preference—An American Apartheid." The covering letter states that the enclosure "seeks an end to the discriminatory, inequitable, and un-American policy of total Indian preference as practiced in the BIA today." Kennedy says also, "Although I do not presume to speak for Indians, I believe this petition is in the interest of Indians and of all Americans." Noting that at the time it was being circulated the federal government was fighting for the desegregation of Boston's public schools, the paper reads in an opening paragraph:

> Although the government's apartheid policy for Indians is being pushed with equal vigor, most Americans are not aware of this policy because it has little impact on their lives. When this policy does attract public attention, efforts are made to conceal its malignant and pernicious nature and to make it appear benign and beneficial. Such slogans as "Indian self-determination," "Indian involvement," and "tribal assumption of programs affecting Indians" have become the catchwords to disguise Indian apartheid. Out of a vague sense of guilt and without any first hand knowledge of the situation, most non-Indian Americans react positively to such expressions as clear evidence of their government's determination to improve the lot of Indians.

Kennedy brought the house down with the following observation, the noisiest applause coming from those of us who were sickened by the political games being played with the lives of Indians:

> Although Indians have been the victims of many past injustices, the solutions to today's Indian problems will not be found by turning back the clock or trying to undo the past. Solutions must be found within the context of the total American society of today. The popular stereotype of the Indian brave riding his trusty steed and shooting buffalo with his bow and arrow has no resemblance to the current realities of American Indian life. The future belongs to the Indian who can understand, adjust to, live with, socialize with, cooperate with, and compete with his fellow Americans of all races. The assumption that the Indian can be made whole by apartheid, by insulating him from his non-Indian neighbors and creating special Indian-made and Indian-operated social and political mechanisms to serve him is an unproved and unsound assumption. *It smacks of social experimentation* [emphasis mine].

Referring to the Morton-Bruce announcement of June 1972, Kennedy, who was surely knowledgeable of the BIA employment situation, held that with Indian preference limited to first appointments the 18,000 BIA force of the time was, nonetheless, two-thirds Indian. He emphasized that Indians, therefore, had achieved the 66 or so percent employment in the Bureau's work-force through merit. When Kennedy was writing, the quarter-blood criterion was generally still being employed. With the dissemination of the 1977 regulations, Indianness in this context was expanded to all enrolled tribal members, consistent with *Mancari*, irrespective of the degree of their European or African ancestry.

In principle, membership in most tribes is based on some degree of Indian ancestry, however remote. However, there are many exceptions, and I refer to both Whites and Blacks. The Oklahoma Cherokee and Seminole tribes still contain enrolled Freedmen—Afroamericans descended from their former slaves. I do not know of any such enrolled "Indians" who have applied for Indian preference—but I am waiting. The regulations, however, inconsistent with *Mancari* and fundamentally racist, are based on the language of the 1934 Indian Reorganization Act (IRA), which includes persons who are descendants of members of tribes who were residents of *any* reservation on June 1, 1934. My wife has never lived on any Chippewa reservation, having been raised among her tribe's ancestral enemies, the Sioux. If she had been born just a little earlier our children, who are not enrolled with any tribe, would be afforded Indian preference—and that would be ludicrous. The preferential list, again following the IRA, includes people of Alaskan Eskimo and Indian descent, making clear that any quantum of blood suffices, without regard to tribal membership. It further embraces anyone of one-half blood derived from tribes indigenous to the United States. This means that, for example, persons with New York Seneca fathers but White mothers, who are not admitted to this matrilineal tribe's membership, are still given preference if the father is classed as a full-blood.

What have been the employment results of the bitterness, the confusion, and the damage to Indian programming of all these years beginning with Bennett's first, deathless memorandum? During the fiscal year 1985 the total Indian complement of the BIA was just over 75 percent. This includes a great many fully acculturated, phenotypically White individuals, nominal Indians or Indians "by definition," who are, more significantly, not the products of any Indian community. Naturally, no statistics are readily available for such variables. As the employment grades descend, the Indian percentage rises (so, too, does the level of cultural traditionalism). The higher reaches of BIA positions are reserved for those least Indian culturally, while the percentage of Indians at less than Civil Service Grade 6 is almost 97. In the BIA's education office we find the lowest Indian figure, roughly 43 percent, this despite the incessant din created by those who insist that only Indians can possibly understand Indian children. These days practically all Agency superintendents, all the BIA Area directors, and many of the IHS field office heads are Indians. The IHS director is a White Kiowa and the BIA head is a White Cherokee.

More than twenty-five years ago the associate commissioner of Indian affairs, a White anthropologist, told a gathering of his colleagues that the superintendents had become "handmaidens to the tribal chairmen." He should have included the area directors, and if he thought that the picture was bad at that time he would have been truly repelled if he had stayed around for a few more years. There was a time when serving one's own tribe as agency superintendent was anathema, a notable exception in the 1940s being Crow agency.

A specially debilitating feature of Indian preference, a practice preceding Bennett's tenure, is that of tribal councils reviewing and passing on all candidates for the higher-level field positions, and many of the lower ones. With all too great frequency the tribes demand and get their own members for superintendents and other positions, with the question of conflict of interest being raised—and ignored—every time. But this practice is, after all, entirely consistent with *Mancari*. The tribes are usually getting, including area directors, individuals who are more Americanized than the old Haskell elite. Together with all other exacerbated problems, nepotism, an old story in the BIA, has reached an alarming rate with whole families being employed, often at the same installation. But they are all "Indians," more-or-less. Yes, but the involvement and influence of individual Indians is thereby lessened. Leave it to the Teton Sioux (who have been responsible for so much Indian policy) to set a standard that, fortunately, has not so far been followed by others. A few years ago on Pine Ridge the posts of tribal chief and agency chief were shared by full brothers, but their mother was a Creek.

Congress by the late 1970s at last began to examine the Indian preference mess insofar as some problems were concerned, one of which was the plight of non-Indian BIA and IHS personnel. Members of Congress noted that morale was shattered; many highly qualified staffers had left; others had nowhere to go and, denied promotions themselves, had to endure the spectacle of the advancement of the new and the less competent. It became acutely embarrassing for managers, Indian and non-Indian, to turn away well-qualified non-Indian applicants (or to quietly advise them, as I did, not to bother responding to a position advertisement). The powers that be, still entrenched, had developed a technique disbelieved by non-Indian applicants. For a given position opening, assuming several non-Indian candidates and one Indian candidate, only the Indian, despite minimal qualifications, would appear on the certification list presented to the selecting office. However, in a few offices non-Indian professionals were actively, if surreptitiously recruited. In one of these shops, almost wholly and compromisingly White, an applicant was quickly assisted in establishing his remote Cherokee ancestry and, in this instance, his tribal membership. He is a highly professional person, but an Indian in no more than the legal sense. Federal Court decisions and administrative practice are causing otherwise proud, well-qualified people to graft new roots on their family trees, solely to achieve positions they deserve on the basis of their own merits.

Congresswoman Gladys Spellman from Maryland and Senators Stevens from Alaska and Percy from Illinois, among others, became aware of the injustices and the gross failures of the whole system and began to allude to the dissatisfaction also expressed by Indian leaders. Simultaneously they were of a mind, reluctantly so because of the potential of setting a bad precedent, to ease the burden of the affected non-Indians. I do not know of any politician who seriously considered amending the Indian Reorganization Act and other statutes containing Indian-preference provisions. The political hazards of such a bold step would be too heavy to bear.

The so-called remedy, for which we all are expected to remain grateful, was to legislate the "Honkey Out Act" of December 5, 1979. The legislation made retirement for non-Indians within certain categories somewhat attractive. In my own case it permitted an early retirement— without full benefits—after twenty-five years of service regardless of my age. It also provided for those employees who reached fifty-five years of age within five years of the date of the act to make a decision about taking advantage of the provisions, unless a waiver was secured for one year. The act was recently (and very, very quietly) amended to permit those who had reached the mandatory class to continue for another five years. Today there is only a handful of these die-hards left, since the legislation encouraged an exodus of the "Old Honkies" in December 1984.

I followed the crowd two months later. With their passing, and mine, the BIA soon fell apart, a fact only now entering the consciousness of journalists and the Congress. I have much respect and sympathy for those few professionals, Indian and non-Indian, still with that agency. There remains an unjust and as usual unforeseen ramification. I refer to the Indian employees who never received Indian-preference in any form, including initial employment when the quarter-blood criterion was in vogue. They are being told they cannot retire under the act. Included are the employees who became officially enrolled tribal members long after they entered the Indian Service. Often enough their tribes only lately established formal enrollment criteria. These people are among the innocent victims of these discriminatory policies. So, too, are most of the others who have been granted preference in hiring and promotion on the basis of race, although they and patronizing Americans may not yet be aware of it.

Nowhere else within the minority-preference syndrome, legal or otherwise, has the principle of affirmative discrimination been so applied. In its first BIA applications it was unique; and it is now found in every federal agency containing an "Indian desk" or even an "Indian interest" of any kind, such as Housing and Urban Development and the Smithsonian Institution. It is also found in state agencies handling special Indian programming of all types, and includes our universities, private and public. And it is found in the Vatican. When Kateri or Catherine Tekakwitha, a Mohawk, was approaching beatification, the step before canonization, the Church admitted that there were no *bona fide* miracles to be ascribed to her intercession. In all other cases miracles have been necessary to achieve beatification—but not for an Indian, and there were no other Indian candidates. She was beatified in 1980 amidst much pomp and ceremony including a Catholic Indian pilgrimage to Rome to see the Pope, who had waived the standard qualifications, expressing the Church's own version of affirmative discrimination. I was unaware of any ethnic or racial preferences to be found among the company of saints. Non-Indians who have made their way up through the ranks, like San Francesco of Calabria, of whom it is still said that a day he did not work a miracle was a miracle, are fortunately not concerned about promotions on the basis of their ancestry. They did not ascend heavenward through the branches of their family trees.

This essay is an excerpt from the author's forthcoming, *"Why Don't They Give Them Guns? The Great American Indian Myth."* 1990. Lanham, MD: The University Press of America, used by permission of the author.

Notes

1. For an official biography of this "effective bureaucrat who worked within the system rather than as a leader," see Ellis 1979.
2. *De Funis et al.* v. *Odegaard et al.*, 416 U.S. 312 (1974).
3. *Morton et al.* v. *Mancari, et al.*, 417 U.S. 535 (1974).

References

Ellis, Richard N. 1979. "Robert L. Bennett: 1966–69." In *The Commissioners of Indian Affairs, 1824–1977*. R.M. Kvasnicka and H.J. Viola, eds. Lincoln: The University of Nebraska Press. 325–31.

Glazer, Nathan. 1987. *Affirmative Discrimination: Ethnic Inequality and Public Policy*. Cambridge, MA: Harvard University Press.

Morello, Steve. 1970. *"Getting 'More Than Words'."* Binghamton, New York Press, October 27.

15

When Fictions Take Hostages

Alan van Gestel

On February 5, 1970, in the United States District Court at Utica, New York, there was born a phenomenon remarkable in American jurisprudence. On that day the first of an aggregation of lawsuits commonly called the Eastern Indian land claims was filed. An organization calling itself the Oneida Indian Nation of New York claimed ownership to roughly 100,000 acres of land, approximately 872 of which were then occupied by the counties of Madison and Oneida, New York, and asked the court to declare the counties trespassers. The great bulk of the county land constituted a giant spiderweb made up of portions of the local highway systems. The complaint charged that in 1795, 175 years before its filing in court, and before the counties of Madison and Oneida even existed, the State of New York purchased land from the Oneida Indian Nation in a transaction that was illegal because it did not have the technical approval of the federal government.

A little over two years later, on June 2, 1972, another Indian community, the Passamaquoddy Tribe, filed a complaint in the United States District Court in Bangor, Maine. In this second case the Indians sought to compel the help of the federal government in bringing suit against the State of Maine and private landowners for over 12 million acres of land, more than half of the entire state. The transaction that formed the basis for the Passamaquoddy complaint occurred in 1794, 178 years before its filing and when the State of Maine did not exist. In 1794 what is now Maine was a district of Massachusetts and the land involved was under its jurisdiction.

With the filing of the Oneida and Passamaquoddy lawsuits, the Eastern Indian land claims began in earnest. In the next eighteen years, through 1988, states east of the Mississippi witnessed a cascade of over thirty lawsuits by groups of Indians, all seeking, in one way or another, to "recover" from states, counties, cities, towns, and private landowners over 35 million acres of land. The predicates of the claims are acts, or failures to act, by one or more of the sovereign states in their dealings with various Indian tribes or groups, the latter being the objects of benign neglect by their guardian, the United States of America.

Understanding the issues and who the adversaries are in these litigative wars is of the utmost importance. They are fought over rights and liabilities shared among three different kinds of political entities— the government of the United States, the government of the individual state containing the land in question, and the government of the Indian community bringing the lawsuit. Significantly, those who are threatened with the greatest loss are not any of the governments involved. They are, instead, the innocent and law-abiding citizens who live under the clouds of these legal battles. None of the people whose land is the target of these claims were even born until many decades after the purchases in question were completed. Why must they receive this procrustean treatment?

A catalog of some of the major claims that have been litigated or are still pending will give a picture of what is involved. If some claims are left out of this catalog is not meant to suggest they lack importance but merely to indicate that a description of all claims is not necessary to make the point. As already noted, the first Oneida claim involved approximately 100,000 acres in New York's Madison and Oneida counties, and the Passamaquoddy case clouded the title to 12 million acres in the State of Maine. A later Oneida claim, based on preconstitutional transactions with the State of New York, lays claim to almost 6 million acres spread through twelve counties in the central and northern part of that state, running from the Pennsylvania border in the south to the St. Lawrence River boundary with Canada. The Oneida are not the only claimants in New York State, as is evidenced by a 64,000–acre claim brought by the Cayuga in Seneca and Cayuga counties, an 11,600–acre claim brought by the St. Regis Mohawk, principally in St. Lawrence County, and a claim to a six-square-mile area in southeastern Madison County and southwestern Oneida County by the Stockbridge-Munsee.

The Mashpee claim in Massachusetts involved all the land in the entire Town of Mashpee, approximately 15,000 acres. In Florida the Miccosukee claimed 5 million acres, as did a similarly threatening challenge by the Seminole Tribe. Then the Chitimacha Tribe in Louisiana entered the fray, seeking recovery of 3 million acres, while, in South Carolina, the Catawba Tribe campaigned in the courts to recover 144,000 acres in the northwestern corner of that state. Other claims involving smaller land areas have been threatened, filed, resolved or settled in Connecticut, Massachusetts, New Jersey, New York, Rhode Island, Virginia, and Vermont.

While the total area subjected to these claims is difficult to determine, in part because references in the various complaints are often made to purchases vaguely described in documents literally centuries old, 35 million acres is a conservative estimate. Thus, the land areas that are the subject of these claims are vast, encompassing geography as great as entire states larger than the size of Maine or South Carolina or entire countries larger than Austria, Hungary, Ireland, or Scotland.

No mere abstract right to remote, unoccupied tracts is at issue in these courtroom offensives. At risk are titles to innumerable homes, businesses, municipal facilities, schools, colleges, universities, hospitals, and other public services. In addition, if the Indians' lawsuits are successful, throughout the eastern part of the country the stability of state and local taxation programs could be cast into immediate disarray, with consequent disruptions extending far beyond the areas claimed. The financial and sociological consequences would be disastrous and widespread. The personal fiscal security of a great many individuals and families, as well as that of business and governmental obligations, could be fatally impaired or wiped out. The hopes and investment-backed expectations of hundreds of thousands, perhaps millions, of blameless citizens, would be dashed. What was vacant and unimproved land when the Indians "owned" it is now enormously valuable property benefiting, and benefiting from, the industry, investments, and development of many generations of people, businesses, and governmental bodies that did not even exist when the asserted wrongs were supposedly committed.

Attorneys for the Indians proceed with superficial simplicity evoking generally sympathetic public reactions. They demand that their clients be "restored" to "immediate possession," a demand which ignores that by no means all Indians affected are aware of, much less support the cases, and which obscures the fact that no single or simple order could be fashioned to grant such relief. The cases represent legal activism on behalf of causes thought to be noble, with tactics generally invented and defended by the attorneys, not their clients. Yet, given the dislocations and disruptions that would inevitably result, and assuming the order of the court which made it would be obeyed, the federal judge would have to provide for and oversee innumerable contingencies and ramifications. In effect, the court would have to establish itself by judicial fiat as a kind of "transitional government" and appoint its officers as unelected vice-regents to manage a transfer which could take many years.

It is not "merely" a restoration of possession to real estate that would flow from such a final judgment. Because of peculiarities and fictions which abound in Indian law, the courts, in actuality, are asked to create entirely new sovereignties out of major portions of the states involved, with political and social ramifications of inconceivable complexity.

Perhaps more darkly for our judicial system, which relies on public obedience to its mandates, the ultimate result of Indian victories could instigate civil disobedience on a massive scale. Courts would be well advised to proceed with caution before issuing orders which may not be obeyed and cannot be enforced. It was, coincidentally, an earlier Indian case[1] which is said to have produced the disobedient response from President Andrew Jackson: "John Marshall has made his decision, let him enforce it."

Once before, the Supreme Court faced the issue of deciding the question of the rightful government of one of the states. In declining to do so it pointed out some of the pitfalls involved:

> [I]f this Court is authorized to enter upon this inquiry as proposed by the plaintiff, and it should be decided that the charter government [of Rhode Island] had no legal existence during the period of time above mentioned,— if it had been annulled by the adoption of the opposing government,—then the laws passed by its legislature during that time were nullities; its taxes wrongfully collected; its salaries and compensation to its officers illegally paid; its public accounts improperly settled; and the judgments and sentences of its courts in civil and criminal cases null and void, and the officers who carried their decisions into operation answerable as trespassers, if not in some cases as criminals.
>
> When the decision of this Court might lead to such results, it becomes its duty to examine very carefully its own powers before it undertakes to exercise jurisdiction.[2]

In many of the Eastern Indian land claims the plaintiffs also seek from the present-day landowners the "fair rental value" of the land claimed "for the entire period of [their] dispossession." These amounts, if they could be determined at all, would be staggering. The result of an execution on such judgments could only be countless personal, business, and municipal defaults. These are not cases where the treasury to be tapped is that of the United States[3] or the sums to be paid, although large, are manageable. Enforcement of the judgments would dwarf the largest and most complicated, expensive, and time-consuming bankruptcy proceedings and business reorganizations on record. Those judgments would constitute, by judicial order, some of the greatest transfers of wealth ever seen; transfers from the present day landowners to the "successors in interest" of Indian communities, themselves of doubtful existence when the transactions in issue occurred.

The problem facing the courts in Indian cases was thoughtfully and sensitively addressed by Chief Judge Warren K. Urbom of the District of Nebraska:

> [White Americans] may also ask themselves questions: How much of the sins of our forefathers must we rightly bear? What precisely do we do now? Shall we pretend that history never was? Can we restore the disemboweled or push the waters upstream to where they used to be?
>
> Who is to decide? White Americans? The Native Americans? All, together? A federal judge?
>
> Who speaks for [the Indians]? Those traditional people who testified here? Those [Indians] of a different mind who did not testify? The officials elected by [the Indians]?
>
> Feeling what *was* wrong does not describe what *is* right. Anguish about yesterday does not alone make wise answers for tomorrow. Somehow, all the achings of the soul must coalesce and with the wisdom of the mind develop a single national policy for governmental action.[4]

The plantiffs in these cases characterize themselves as Indian "nations" or "tribes" who are "the direct descendants" of aboriginal Indian communities who inhabited the claim areas centuries ago. These Indians claim to be the owners of, and to have the exclusive right to possession of, all their ancestors' aboriginal territory. The parties being sued are actually hundreds of thousands, perhaps millions, of individuals, business entities, municipalities, governmental agencies, schools, colleges and others who now assert various interests in and occupy the land.

The Treaty of Paris of 1783, concluding the American Revolutionary War, made no provision for the Indian allies of either Britain or the United States. Thus, the claimants in one of the largest of the cases[5] have alleged, the Continental Congress took separate steps to adjust relations with the Indian tribes pursuant to authority delegated under Article IX of the Articles of Confederation.

A significant portion of Article IX provides:

> The United States in congress assembled shall have the sole and exclusive right and power of determining on peace and war, except in the cases mentioned in the Sixth Article [having to do with the invasion of a state] . . . entering into treaties and alliances . . . of regulating the trade and managing all affairs with Indians, not members of the States, provided that the legislative right of any State within its own limits be not infringed or violated.

On September 22, 1783, Congress passed a "proclamation" prohibiting and forbidding all persons from making settlements on lands inhabited or claimed by Indians "without the limits or jurisdiction of any particular state" and from purchasing or receiving any gift or cession of "such lands" unless expressly authorized and directed by the United States in Congress assembled. The 1783 Proclamation also provided that every "such purchase or settlement" not having the authority of the United States would be null and void and that no right or title would accrue in consequence of any "such purchase, cession or settlement."

The United States Constitution became effective on the first Wednesday of March 1789.[6] Unlike Article IX of the Articles of Confederation, the Constitution contained language which made clear the absolute power of the federal government to regulate affairs with Indians. The debates at the Constitutional Convention reflect the intentions of the Framers— to commit the sole and exclusive power to manage Indian affairs to the federal government, thereby freeing the Constitutional Charter from the conflicting claims of state power which had plagued the Confederation. The Constitution vested in the Congress the power to regulate "commerce . . . with the Indian tribes."

The First Congress passed the first of a series of Indian trade and intercourse acts, codifying federal jurisdiction over Indian land transactions under the new Constitution. There has been a form of Indian trade and intercourse act continuously in force from July 22, 1790, to the present. The current version of the Act provides in part that:

> [n]o purchase, grant, lease, or other conveyance of lands, or of any title or claim thereto, from any Indian nation or tribe of Indians, shall be of any validity in law or equity, unless the same be made by treaty or convention entered into pursuant to the Constitution.[7]

Most of the Eastern Indian land claims assert that the United States did not authorize or participate in the negotiation of the land purchase transactions between the States and the Indian tribes, nor did it ever later ratify the purchases.

These cases, if successful, will overturn almost 200 years of real property law and transactions and affect "immediate possession" or the "fair market value" of millions of acres of land. They seek to do so despite the enormous changes to the parties and the land that have occurred in the intervening centuries. Indeed, two of the cases[8] seek to do so despite the fact that the claims involve transactions which took place before the founding of the government that established the courts in which the cases are pending. These transactions occurred, generally, at times when there was no national government worthy of the name, and the only laws to apply and courts to apply them were the laws and the courts of the thirteen original states. In these pre-constitutional years the sovereignty of the thirteen states was unimpaired by membership in anything like the present federal system, established by a constitution deriving its powers and legitimacy directly from the American people.

The Indians who are suing are twentieth-century groups composed of twentieth-century people who do not themselves claim they were cheated or defrauded by the present landowners. They claim instead to be "successors in interest" (succeeding to the rights of their ancestors by being born into the tribe) to eighteenth-century Indian communities which in the eighteenth century, they claim, were cheated and defrauded by an eighteenth-century political sovereignty. The Indian "governments" then ceded vacant, wild, and for the most part uninhabited land on the frontier of a new and struggling country; their successors now want to "recover" vastly improved and fully inhabited property in the hearts of stable and prosperous states.

Most of the present landowners can trace their ancestry only so far back as Ellis Island or other ports of debarkation for America's great immigrant population. Even those with roots that reach to the Mayflower or the Half Moon can hardly be charged with active malice toward the Indians of the eighteenth century. All current landowners acquired their property in utter innocence of these ancient Indian claims. Not a single man or woman who has been sued had any hand in the motives or methods of the land purchases by the various states occurring one or two centuries before their birth. Today's landowner defendants are nothing less than hostages in a power struggle between three governments— federal, state, and Indian.

Judge Nichols, of the United States Court of Claims, made an apt point in a 1978 Indian claim. He said:

> Though the role is relatively new for courts, historians have long been assessing the morality of statesmen, warriors, and prelates of the past. They have learned how to do it in a more sophisticated way than is often found in court opinions. For example, let me quote from Macaulay's essay on Machiavelli—

> Every age and every nation has certain characteristic vices, which prevail almost universally, which scarcely any person scruples to avow, and which even rigid moralists but faintly censure. Succeeding generations change the fashion of their morals, with the fashion of their hats and their coaches; take some other kind of wickedness under their patronage, and wonder at the depravity of their ancestors.

> It pleases us to consider the Indian a protected ward as to his present needs, and a wronged victim as to the past. We wonder at the depravity of our

ancestors because they had a different view. Our ancestors might have wondered at our depravity could they have enjoyed the gift of prophesy.

The whole essay is a superb example of Macaulay's technique in passing moral judgment on the past, and I cannot recommend it too highly. But it has not been universally accepted. Lord Acton, of the generation that followed Macaulay, may be taken as representing a contrary approach. He is best known to Americans today by the famous quote, become a cliché, about absolute power corrupting absolutely. This he tossed off as an aside in a personal letter to the Reverend Mandell Creighton, who had displeased Acton by being too easy on long dead Popes in his "History of the Papacy." Acton took the occasion to expound his favorite thesis, which was that it is the duty of the historian to avenge the evil and wrong of the past, by harsh denunciation of its principal actors. In doing this, his standards are those of the present, because right and wrong do not change, like fashions in coaches and hats. Thus he would judge everyone from Attila the Hun to Zoroaster strictly by the standards of a Victorian English gentleman. See *Essays on Freedom and Power, Lord Acton*, selected by Gertrude Himmelfarb, Gloucester, Mass. 1972.

We have a good deal of Actonism with us today. Thus, we do not own slaves, or countenance others owning them, but Thomas Jefferson did, and therefore his memory is deemed by many not worthy of respect or veneration. Ironically, Acton himself defended slavery in an essay written in 1861, and therefore by his own technique of moral admeasurement, he was wicked too. Much of our contemporary Actonism is based on sheer ignorance, or the view that history is "not relevant," but Acton himself was enormously learned. Our national sport of discovering and denouncing the depravity of our ancestors has both knowledgeable and ignorant practitioners.[9]

That the landowner defendants have been figuratively seized as hostages in the political battle between the Indian, state, and federal governments was proudly proclaimed by Professor Robert N. Clinton of the University of Iowa Law School. In August of 1981, Professor Clinton replied to an earlier version of this essay (van Gestel 1981) which criticized there, as here, the use of innocent landowners as pawns in this intergovernment struggle. Commenting on the Oneida and Cayuga lawsuits in New York, Clinton said:

The litigation is necessary to afford the tribes the necessary bargaining leverage to achieve their not unreasonable demands in a political arena which has historically ignored them and even now is structured in a fashion antithetical to their interests . . . [T]he threat of the eastern Indian tribes to actually litigate and enforce their seemingly valid claims to large land areas in the east is necessary to create the required bargaining strength needed to have long ignored demands redressed. No country and no good attorney should be expected or required to negotiate from a position of weakness by unilaterally giving up or being forced to abandon a major bargaining strength [Clinton 1981].

The Eastern Indian land claims present an unusual and complex set of problems for the courts. Difficult issues of first impression have been raised and addressed; complicated, sometimes confused and often foreboding areas of the law have been surveyed and traversed. Legal fictions created earlier have been built upon. And all the while, a strange and unusual guilt complex derived from notions of past treatment of native Americans by the "invading" Europeans clouds the ability of modern courts clearly to see and apply legal and equitable concepts to protect the unoffending landowners. There is with these Indian claims no better example of the oft-quoted maxim that hard cases make bad law.

Until the advent of the Eastern Indian land claims, most Indian litigation took place in midwestern and western states and generally involved claims between Indian groups and the United States government. The basis for most claims had to do with rights under treaties, relations with Americans on and around reservations, and claims to water and mineral rights. Some of these cases involve Indian groups resettled in what was to have been a permanent "Indian Territory" (eastern Kansas and Oklahoma) under the Indian Removal policy of the 1830s. Other western cases involve groups awarded rights, guaranteed by federal treaties, to reserved remnants of their former lands. In most such treaty dealings, the semblance of formal negotiations between the United States and "governments of domestic dependent nations" were observed, although the United States soon adopted a policy of assimilation and direct management of these populations that bypassed whatever political institutions had prevailed in earlier years. It is litigation over those treaties, and the rights claimed to flow therefrom, that generally comes to mind when people think about Indian land claims.

By contrast, the Eastern Indian land claims are generally not based upon treaties or any other formal relationship with the federal government; and they do not involve rights on or about Indian reservations. They principally involve claims to land that has been inhabited and developed by non-Indians for 150 or more years. Usually the land was first acquired by purchase by one of the states when the country was first being developed and settlement began moving west. West at that time, of course, meant west of the Hudson River in New York or west of the Appalachian Mountain chain, but was still considerably east of the Mississippi River. Thus, what is being litigated are the rights to fully developed and inhabited land which has not housed an Indian tribe's corn fields or witnessed a hunting or fishing expedition for two centuries or more.

That the Eastern Indian land claims must be taken seriously is apparent from the consequences of the Passamaquoddy claim in Maine.

There, the Indians, by settlement, were granted 350,000 acres and a monetary package of $81 million.[10] A much more recent resolution of an Indian land claim (albeit in Tacoma, Washington) involves the Puyallups. On August 27, 1988, a group of Puyallup Indians, numbering some 1400, voted to accept an out-of-court settlement valued at over $140 million.[11]

Another indication of the seriousness of Indian land claims appears in the December 17, 1980, opinion of Judge Lumbard in *Mohegan Tribe* v. *Connecticut*.[12] There, speaking for the Second Circuit Court of Appeals, he said:

> In the past few years numerous suits have been brought by Indian Tribes still residing in eastern parts of the United States.[13] These tribes have asserted claims to large tracts of land in the East, thereby throwing into uncertainty the validity of land titles throughout the area . . . To date, the Indians have been largely successful in their legal battles regarding their claims to eastern lands. Defenses based upon state adverse possession laws and state statutes of limitations have been consistently rejected. The only grounds upon which the states have thus far succeeded in defeating Indian claims is to show that plaintiffs in these suits do not properly represent an existing tribe which can be proved to be the legitimate descendant of the original landholding tribe.[14]

In order to appreciate why such claims are often successful, some basic ideas of Indian land law must be understood. Very early in American judicial history a legal fiction was created which caused Indian tribes to become defined as "distinct, independent, political communities" qualified to exercise powers of self-government and having other prerogatives by reason of their tribal sovereignty.[15] A legal fiction is a situation, circumstance or status contrived by the law to permit a court to dispose of a matter. It is an assumption of fact made by a court as a basis for deciding a legal question. Roscoe Pound, in his great work on jurisprudence, points out, aptly for the present discussion, that while fictions have played an important part in legal history,

> We must not forget that they are a clumsy device appropriate only to periods of growth in a partially developed political organization or society in which legislation on any large scale is not possible. They are not suited to later times and developed systems. In a period of growth, when ideas are few and crude, they enable a body of law to be molded gradually, without legislative action, to meet immediate wants as they arise and to conform to the requirements of cases as they arise.

> After a certain state of legal development, on the other hand, fictions retard growth and clog development. In a rational age, an age of substance rather than form, when legal doctrines are logically worked out and a body of

learned jurists is at hand to apply and develop them, fictions may confuse and conceal the substance of legal precepts. In a sense they were devised to conceal the substance when the substance was not regarded as of legal consequence. They may operate still to conceal the substance after later ideas have made the substance almost the only thing of legal consequence [Pound 1949].

In *Worcester* v. *Georgia*,[16] decided in 1832, one year after the Cherokee Nation case, the Supreme Court declared that a weaker power does not surrender its independence by associating with a stronger power and accepting its protection. Conquest of the Indians did, however, render tribes subject to United States law, which by the Constitution vests in Congress the ultimate power of dealing with Indian tribes.

There were more legal fictions invented in the Supreme Court's Indian decisions of the 1830s. The relationship between the federal government and the Indians was then characterized as that between guardian and ward. This, of course, was a wholly fictitious construct of Chief Justice Marshall. As a direct result of the concepts espoused by Marshall, a tribe has been given at the same time some aspects of a sovereignty and certain rights—those of a childlike ward—protected by the "parental" United States. It is this concept of separate sovereignty which has brought to Indian country tax-free gasoline and cigarettes, high-stakes bingo and freedom from many state criminal laws. Conversely, the United States has assumed broad authority to deal with a tribe and its interests, as well as obligations to provide protection against any invasion of those interests by third parties, including the individual states. This special, but fictional, relationship has led courts to find state-created limitations on the enforcement of claims to property to be inapplicable to the property rights of Indian tribes.[17]

The notion of an Indian "tribe" or "nation" is itself a legal fiction much the same as the idea that a corporation is a person. The term "tribe" or "nation" as used in connection with Indian groups in the United States has a vast number of definitions and connotations. Some are ethnological, some are legal, some are historical, and some are a mixture of all of the foregoing.

In the early years "nation" did not have the political-legal meaning given it in later years. Instead, "nation" was synonymous with "a people" or "race." In modern social science usage, the earlier usage of the word "nation" had the meaning of phrases such as "identity group" or "ethnic group" today, without the connotation of political autarchy. For an anthropologist to call the Pequot of Connecticut a "nation" is an intellectual atrocity. The sixty-five people living on the modern reservation called Pequot are all descendants of one woman, their collective great-great grandmother. Technically, they constitute a bilateral descent group.

In 1979, the United States Court of Appeals for the First Circuit discussed the legal definition of a tribe in the context of a claim for the recovery of real estate based on alleged violations of the Indian Trade and Intercourse Act. The court ruled that because of wide variations among tribal groups living in different parts of the country under different conditions, the definition of "tribe" should remain broad and flexible. The court went on basically to approve a definition included in a charge to the jury which applied the principles laid down in an earlier Supreme Court opinion.[18] That definition is as follows:

> By a "tribe" we understand a body of Indians of the same or similar race, united in a community under one leadership or government, and inhabiting a particular though sometimes ill-defined territory . . . [19]

The definition's four elements: (1) "same or similar race"; (2) "united in a community"; (3) "under one leadership or government"; and (4) "inhabiting a particular though sometimes ill-defined territory"—leave much to be explained. Nevertheless, this is the most recent definition applied by a court in the context of a real estate claim by an Indian tribe. Similar concepts have been applied in earlier cases.[20]

The State of Connecticut once argued with considerable vigor that the Trade and Intercourse acts had geographical applications limited to "Indian country" and so did not apply to lands within the states. This contention was rejected by the Connecticut District Court;[21] and the Second Circuit Court of Appeals, on December 17, 1980, affirmed that holding.[22] The Supreme Court itself has stated that the Trade and Intercourse Acts "apply in all States, including the original 13." [23]

Another twist in Indian law that poses serious problems in presenting a defense relates to the allocation of the burden of proof. Although ambivalent in meaning, "burden of proof" generally refers to the responsibility for persuading the trier of fact—the judge and jury—that an alleged fact is true. When the time for decision comes, the jury, if there is one, or the judge without a jury, must be guided how to decide an issue if their minds are in doubt. The party having the burden of proof will fail if the jury or judge is unpersuaded or left in doubt about the existence of a fact.

A little known federal statute,[24] first enacted in 1822, allocates the burden of proof in all trials about the rights of property in which an Indian may be a party. The 1822 statute mandates that when an "Indian" is on one side and a "white person" is on the other—and those are the precise words of the statute—the burden of proof shall fall upon the "white person" whenever the Indian shall make out a presumption of title in himself from the fact of previous possession or ownership. In 1979, 157 years after its passage, the Supreme Court added still more fictions when it construed the word "Indian," as used in the statute, to include Indian tribes, not just individual Indians, and the word "white person" to include all non-Indians regardless of color and status or as either human or nonhuman (such as a corporation).[25] Peculiarly, the court excluded from the reach of "white person" the sovereign states of the United States. Thus, the burden of proof, which in cases involving facts that occurred 150 to 200 years ago can often be determinative, has been thrust upon the only truly innocent party in these Indian land claims—the present-day landowner. At the same time the individual states, which were the perpetrators, if any wrongdoing ever occurred, do not suffer the same impediment.

The interpretation of the burden of proof statute was facilitated by an extraordinary application of legal fiction. The fiction that enables a community of Indians living as a tribe to constitute a sovereignty, a domestic dependent nation, permitted the court to avoid the blatant racism otherwise implicit in using "Indian" and "white person" as criteria for applying the law (see chapter 14).

The shifting of the burden of proof to the defendant is highly unusual in American jurisprudence—and in the situation presented by the modern Indian land claims, wholly unnecessary, even on moral grounds. The Indian plaintiffs can hardly be considered as disadvantaged in the modern federal court. The rules and principles of law are on their side, as is much of the case law. Public sentiment as reflected in the press and the academic world favors Indians in such cases. Indian cases, also, are richly subsidized by the federal government, large private foundations, church groups, and other institutions, so that most of the long-committed, specialized legal expertise works for Indian groups. There are exceedingly few lawyers with expertise among the defense bar, and no publically financed firms such as the Native American Rights Fund with its considerable resources, standing ready to defend landowners and others affected by these cases. Further, when such defenses are mounted, they are almost automatically attacked by well-organized Indian support groups—including the media, church groups, academics, and public officials—on moral, legal, political, racial, and other grounds (see chapter 13). The most common accusation hurled at those who defend landowners and local units of government in the courts is that they are "racist," certainly a questionable tactic in a political system that prides itself in supporting the rights of defendants.

Additionally, Indians have nearly monopolized the available anthropological and historical research expertise. This is so because of the
sentiments of most academics, because of the heavy level of funding
available to hire them, and because when they "help" Indians they are
praised by their institutions and colleagues. By contrast, those scholars
who are called to serve the defense often come under intense pressure
both within and outside their institutions to refrain from participation.
In a judicial system that relies upon an adversarial process which assumes
that the truth will emerge from two well-presented opposite positions,
the situation can become entirely unbalanced.

A fundamental and pervasive difficulty with the Eastern Indians' claims
is that they ask courts to decide issues not well suited to judicial resolution, to grant relief not appropriate for an appointed tribunal, and
incapable of judicial administration. Thus, a question initially faced was
whether these cases are justiciable. The courts were asked to decide
whether the claims presented and the relief sought were of the type
which admit of judicial resolution. These difficult issues were squarely
addressed by the United States Supreme Court in its second decision in
one of the Oneida cases. An explanation of that important decision is
vital to an understanding of Indian land claim law.

In 1977, Federal Judge Edmund Port of the Northern District of New
York ruled that New York State had violated the Trade and Intercourse
Act in a 1795 purchase of 100,000 acres from the Oneida Indians. Later,
in 1982, Judge Port assessed damages against the counties of Madison
and Oneida for trespassing on the Oneida Indian lands in the years 1968
and 1969. Finally, in 1983, Judge Port ruled that the counties were
entitled to indemnification and reimbursement from the State of New
York for any amounts that they may ultimately have to pay to the
Indians. The basis for Judge Port's 1983 ruling was that the State of
New York, and not the counties which did not even exist at the time,
was the ultimate wrongdoer and, therefore, in equity, the state should
bear the cost of the loss. The Second Circuit Court of Appeals affirmed
all of the rulings by Judge Port.[26]

The Oneida case was argued next before the United States Supreme
Court on October 1, 1984.[27] On March 5, 1985, the Court handed down
its decision. In an opinion supported by five justices and dissented from
by the remaining four, the High Court ruled that Indian tribes and
nations have a common law right to sue in the federal courts for the
recovery of land illegally appropriated from them, that the claims are
justiciable in the federal courts (even though they may create new sovereignties), and that there is no state or federal statute of limitations

which bars these claims even though they are brought centuries after the acts on which they are based.[28]

Justice Stevens dissented and was joined by Chief Justice Burger, Justice White, and Justice Rehnquist. The theory of the dissent was that the equitable doctrine of laches should bar a claim brought so many years after the facts on which it is based. Laches is a theory which requires a court to look at the relative equitable positions of the parties and attempt to determine whether it is fair to permit a claimant to sue long after the date of the incident in question. A laches defense includes consideration of whether there were open and innocent changes of circumstances on the part of the person being sued on the assumption of the validity of his position. Courts have traditionally found it inequitable to permit one person to stand by silently and watch another who believes he has rights in himself to make significant changes to the land and then come forward with a claim. Justice Stevens closed his dissent with the following words:

> The Framers recognize that no one ought be condemned for his forefather's misdeeds—even when the crime is a most grave offense against the Republic. The Court today ignores that principle in fashioning a common law remedy for the Oneida Nation that allows the Tribe to avoid its 1795 conveyance 175 years after it was made. This decision upsets long-settled expectations in the ownership of real property in the Counties of Oneida and Madison, New York, and the disruption it is sure to cause will confirm the common law wisdom that ancient claims are best left in repose. The Court, no doubt, believes that it is undoing a grave historical injustice, but in so doing it has caused another, which only Congress may now rectify.[29]

Remarkably, seven justices joined in a portion of the Oneida decision which reversed Judge Port's findings for indemnification in favor of the counties against the state. They held that the Eleventh Amendment to the United States Constitution barred a suit in federal court against the State of New York. Since there is only a limited right or law permitting such a suit in a state court in New York, it appears that this part of the Supreme Court's ruling effectively prevents the counties from recovery for the wrongdoing of the State of New York.

The results of the 1985 Oneida decision, together with earlier rulings on other points of Indian law, are that an Indian community which can prove itself to be a "tribe" has a common law claim to recover land which it sold hundreds of years ago, without any limitations or similar time bar, against blameless present-day landowners. Those landowners have no effective right to sue the real wrongdoer, their state government, for reimbursement even though that state government is the entity which broke the law when dealing with the Indian tribe's predecessors. The same state government, it should be noted, has forced its citizens—private landowners—to pay taxes and abide by laws and regulations which it would have had no right to impose if the land really belonged to an Indian sovereignty. One could hardly be critical of those landowners who, when attempting to make sense of the rulings by the courts, agree with Dickens' Mr. Bramble when he said that "the law is a ass, a idiot" (Dickens 1838).

The legal absurdity of some of the recent decisions is highlighted when one realizes that these kinds of claims can only be brought by a legally created fiction, an Indian tribe. Neither an individual Indian nor a group of Indians without the status of a tribe has standing to sue for tribal land.[30] And if the individual Indian brought suit for land he claimed to be his own, he would face the same legal impediments that apply to non-Indians, including the bar of the statute of limitations or laches if he waited too long before starting suit.[31] Indeed, in many of the Eastern Indian land claims wending their way through the courts, individual Indians and their families who are themselves private landowners, like their non-Indian neighbors, are hostages to the process. Thus, a fictional entity, an Indian government, can sue an individual and take his land away if a century or more ago the state government bought the land from an Indian "tribe" without the permission of the United States government. And, the only nonfictional entity, the landowner who loses his land because of the state's ancient transgression, has no right to sue the state for indemnification.

Why must the Supreme Court play judicial brinkmanship with the lives and fortunes of the hostage landowners? Even it, after making its extraordinary and far-reaching ruling in the Oneida case, seems to realize where the true responsibility lies. After stating the law, the five justices in the majority added an intriguing final footnote to their opinion:

> The question whether equitable considerations should limit the relief available to the present day Oneida Indians was not addressed by the Court of Appeals or presented to this Court by petitioners. Accordingly, we express no opinion as to whether other considerations may be relevant to the final disposition of this case should Congress not exercise its authority to resolve these far-reaching Indian claims.[32]

The meaning of that footnote is far from obvious. What guidance, if any, does it give to a trial court faced with one of these kinds of claims? Does it mean that in some way a judge ruling in favor of Indian claimants can nevertheless apply "equitable considerations" to limit the relief available? Does it mean to suggest that the relief may be limited? Can the judge say to the Indian tribe that it wins but it cannot have the land back? If so, what does it get from the victory—and from whom?

This footnote is a stunning example of the dilemma faced by modern courts in struggling with ancient Indian land claims and the legal fictions on which they are based. Courts want very much to compensate native Americans for ill-treatment of their ancestors in the past. At the same time, the Supreme Court at least seems, albeit in a somewhat abstruse way, to recognize that it is not fair to place the burden on the innocent landowner. The court agrees that these claims call for resolution by an elected Congress, not an appointed judge. Again, it was Chief Judge Urbom who made the point eloquently in the *Wounded Knee* cases. He said:

> I feel not shirking of duty in saying that formulation of such a national policy should not be made by a federal judge or the handful who may review his decision on appeal. Four reasons press me to that conclusion.

> First, a strength of the elective process is that the citizenry may choose those who mirror their thoughts, and an amalgam of many thus elected is more likely to reflect the conscience and wisdom of the people than a few who are appointed.

> Second, legislative bodies have investigative tools for listening to a wider community than do courts for ferreting out the deeper consciousness of the body politic.

> Third, relations with American Indians are rooted in international relations . . . including the laws of conquest and of treaties developed over centuries, not by courts, but by executive heads of nations through negotiations. The United States in its early history accepted in its dealings with other nations the European concepts. Perhaps it should not have done so in its relations with the American Indians. But it did. Changing now, after nearly two centuries, is a matter of massive public policy for broader exploration than courts are able to provide. Essentially, the issues here have to do with the methods of shifting power from one group to another—by war, threat of war, economic pressure or inducement, verbal persuasion, election, agreement, or gradual legislative encroachment. The acceptability of each method should be decided by the citizenry at large, which speaks directly or through its elected representatives.

> Fourth, the people of the United States have not given me or any other judge the power to set national policy for them. By the Constitution the people have assigned governmental powers and have set their limits. Relations with Indian tribes are given exclusively to the executive and legislative branches. Perhaps it should be otherwise, but it is not. When and if the people amend the Constitution to put limits on the executive and legislative branches in their affairs with Indian tribes the federal courts will uphold those

limits, but in the meantime the courts cannot create limits. In short, a judge must hold government to the standards of the nation's conscience once declared, but he cannot create the conscience or declare the standards.[33]

On October 31, 1988, a three-judge panel in the United States Court of Appeals for the Second Circuit in New York rendered a decision in one of the largest and most complicated of all Eastern Indian land cases, which may prove to be a beacon of reality in assessing the viability of these ancient claims. The case involved the claim to almost 6 million acres of land by the successors in interest to the Oneida Indian Nation. The case was predicated upon the assertion that the State of New York illegally purchased the land in 1785 and 1788 without getting the express permission of the central government under the Articles of Confederation. It thus involved a preconstitutional transaction. The decision, perhaps for the first time, required a federal court to interpret the meaning of the Articles of Confederation, that failed charter which later required "We the People . . . to form a more perfect Union" under the constitution that became effective in March of 1789. After an extraordinarily detailed analysis of the events leading up to and reasons for the Articles of Confederation, as well as their failure, the court concluded that the historical evidence indicates that the Articles of Confederation, along with the 1784 Treaty of Fort Stanwix and the Proclamation of 1783, which were also interpreted in the decision, are properly construed not to prohibit or require the assent of Congress for New York's 1785 and 1788 purchases of Indian land from the Oneida.[34] Throughout the lengthy opinion, the court set down many lessons, all historically sound, and in a truly pragmatic way genuinely wise, which could provide the solid basis for at last disassembling the fictions that seem to confuse and conceal the substance of the legal precepts which should apply in determining these complex cases.

In appraising these Indian complaints, based as they are on eighteenth- and nineteenth-century actions and fictions, it is important that clear meanings not be distorted by the gloss of twentieth-century perceptions. These are not instances of current wrongs measured by statutes or a constitution whose meaning has evolved over the passage of time. Nor do they present instances of the federal government acting in collusion with some giant corporation cutting back on a reservation's boundaries or overlooking the plain language of a solemn treaty. The rights of the landowners must not be ignored because a court may regard the actions of our predecessors in a manner dictated by today's accepted views and practices. The courts must be ever careful to view the law and the actions alleged with a sensitivity to how they would have been viewed at the times of their occurrence and to the "justifiable expectations" [35] of the current landowners, whose total innocence must be acknowledged.

Courts are not free to give untrammeled effect to their personal or policy preferences. As Justice Cardozo succinctly said: "The judge, even when he is free, is still not wholly free. He is not to innovate at pleasure. He is not a knight errant, roaming at will in pursuit of his own ideal of beauty or of goodness. He is to draw his inspiration from consecrated principles" (Cardozo 1921).

What is the position of the federal government in these cases? After all, it was the federal government as guardian which, if anyone, failed the Indians generations ago; and it is the federal government today which is the embodiment of the national conscience. The federal record is dismal, confused, inept and almost wholly unresponsive. By stark contrast to the Canadian government,[36] the United States, to date, has done little to assume the responsibility for and burdens of the Indian land claims. When the Indians sought relief, the federal government ignored them. When the beleaguered landowners seek to join it as a defendant it hides behind the doctrine of governmental immunity, that is, the government cannot be sued without its permission. Even in those few cases that have been settled, such as in Maine, Rhode Island, Florida, or Connecticut, it has played a reluctant role, joining in only after the parties themselves have, because of the enormous burdens of the litigation, negotiated a settlement with concessions by guiltless landowners. In addition, the United States has, as in the instance of the Oneida cases, provided funding to the Indians' attorneys for purposes of bringing the suits.[37]

There is something fundamentally wrong in the stance taken by the United States government. "By standing on the sidelines as Indians and non-Indians fight these bitter court battles, the federal government has encouraged the impression that Indian advances can be made only at the expense of non-Indians who did not commit the acts alleged as the basis of the suit" (Hutchins 1980). It is neither equitable nor fair to force landowners to defend themselves against ancient claims that are in no sense based upon any wrongdoing on their part while the United States sits on the sidelines or, worse yet, assists in the prosecution.

This essay is an expanded and updated rendering of a chapter included in *Iroquois Land Claims* (Syracuse, NY: Syracuse University Press, 1988). By permission of Syracuse University Press.

Notes

1. *Worcester* v. *Georgia*, 31 U.S. (6 Pet.) 515 (1832). This story that Jackson made such a statement is likely apocryphal. He was accused of doing so

before the Cherokee case was decided by his Whig political opponents, including the attorney for the Cherokee, who alluded to this in his argument before the Supreme Court. However, once the Court had rendered its judgment, President Jackson had no legal power to enforce the Court's decision and did not do so. See Prucha 1984 Vol. 1: 212–13.

2. See *Luther* v. *Borden*, 48 U.S. (7 How.) 1, 38–39 (1849).
3. See *Yankton Sioux Tribe* v. *United States*, 272 U.S. 351 (1926).
4. *United States* v. *Consolidated Wounded Knee Cases*, 389 F.Supp. 235, 238–239 (D.Neb. and D.S.D. 1975).
5. *Oneida Indian Nation of New York* v. *State of New York*, 860 F.2d 1145 (2d Cir. 1988).
6. See *Owings* v. *Speed*, 18 U.S. (5 Wheat.) 420, 5 L.Ed. 124 (1820).
7. 25 U.S.C. §177.
8. See *Oneida Indian Nation of New York* v. *State of New York*, 860 F.2d 1145 (2d Cir. 1988) and *Stockbridge-Munsee* v. *State of New York, et al.*, 86–CV-1140 (N.D.N.Y. Oct. 15, 1986).
9. *United States* v. *Oneida Nation of New York*, 576 F.2d 870, 883–884 (Ct. Cl. 1978).
10. See Maine Indian Claims Settlement Act of 1980, Pub. L. No. 96–420, 25 U.S.C. §§1721–1735.
11. *New York Times*, August 29, 1988, p. 1.
12. 638 F.2d 612 (2d Cir. 1980).
13. See e.g., *Oneida Indian Nation* v. *County of Oneida*, 414 U.S. 661 (1974); *Mashpee Tribe* v. *New Seabury Corp.*, 592 F.2d 575 (1st Cir. 1979); *Epps* v. *Andrus*, 611 F.2d 915 (1st Cir. 1979); *Oneida Indian Nation* v. *County of Oneida*, 434 F. Supp. 527 (N.D.N.Y. 1977); *Schaghticoke Tribe* v. *Kent School Corp.*, 423 F. Supp. 780 (D. Conn. 1976); *Narragansett Tribe* v. *Southern Rhode Island Land Development Corp.*, 418 F. Supp. 798 (D.R.I. 1976); *Joint Council of the Passamaquoddy Tribe* v. *Morton*, 528 F.2d 370 (1st Cir. 1975); *Chitimacha Tribe* v. *Laws*, Civ. No. 77–0772–L (W.D.La.); *Catawba Indian Tribe* v. *South Carolina*, No. 80–2050–C (D.S.C.).
14. 638 F.2d at 614–615.
15. *Cherokee Nation* v. *Georgia*, 30 U.S. (5 Pet.) 1 (1831).
16. 31 U.S. (6 Pet.) 515 (1832).
17. See *County of Oneida* v. *Oneida Indian Nation of New York*, 470 U.S. 226, 240–244 (1985). *Western Pequot Tribe* v. *Holdridge Enterprises, Inc.*, CA H-76–193 (D. Conn. 1977); *Oneida Indian Nation* v. *County of Oneida*, 434 F. Supp. 527, 541–43 (N.D.N.Y. 1977); *Schaghticoke Tribe* v. *Kent School Corp.*, 423 F. Supp. 780 (D. Conn. 1976); *Narragansett Tribe of Indians* v. *Southern Rhode Island Land Dev. Corp.*, 418 F. Supp. 798 (D.R.I. 1976).
18. See *Mashpee Tribe* v. *New Seabury Corp.*, 592 F.2d 575, 582 (1st Cir. 1979).
19. *Montoya* v. *United States*, 180 U.S. 261, 266 (1901).
20. See *United States* v. *Candelaria*, 271 U.S. 432, 442–443 (1926); *The Kansas Indians*, 72 U.S. (5 Wall.) 737, 756 (1867); *United States* v. *Wright*, 53 F.2d 300 (4th Cir. 1931). See also *James* v. *U.S. Dept. of Health and Human Services*, No. 85–417 (D.D.C. Aug. 4, 1985) which urged consideration of the specially prescribed procedures for recognition of tribes developed by the Department of the Interior.
21. *Mohegan Tribe* v. *Connecticut*, 483 F. Supp. 597 (D. Conn. 1980).

22. *Mohegan Tribe* v. *Connecticut*, 638 F.2d 612 (2d Cir. 1980).
23. *Oneida Indian Nation of New York* v. *County of Oneida*, 414 U.S. 661, 670 (1974).
24. 25 U.S.C. §194.
25. *Wilson* v. *Omaha Indian Tribe*, 442 U.S. 653 (1979).
26. *Oneida Indian Nation of New York* v. *County of Oneida*, 719 F.2d 525 (2d Cir. 1983).
27. The case was argued on behalf of the counties by the author of this essay, Allan van Gestel, and on behalf of the Indian claimants by Attorney Arlinda Locklear of the Native American Rights Fund in Washington, D.C.
28. *County of Oneida* v. *Oneida Indian Nation of New York*, 470 U.S. 226 (1985).
29. *Id*. at 273.
30. *Epps* v. *Andrus*, 611 F.2d 915 (1st Cir. 1979); *Mashpee Tribe* v. *New Seabury Corp.*, 592 F.2d 575 (1st Cir.), *cert. denied*, 444 U.S. 866 (1979).
31. *Schrimpscher* v. *Stockton*, 183 U.S. 290 (1902); *Felix* v. *Patrick*, 145 U.S. 317 (1892).
32. *County of Oneida* v. *Oneida Indian Nation of New York*, 470 U.S. 226, 253 n.27 (1985).
33. *United States* v. *Consolidated Wounded Knee Cases*, 389 F.Supp. 235, 239 (D.Neb. and D. S.D. 1975).
34. *Oneida Indian Nation of New York* v. *State of New York*, 860 F.2d 1145 (2d Cir. 1988).
35. *Rosebud Sioux Tribe* v. *Kneip*, 430 U.S. 584, 605 (1977).
36. In August, 1973, the Canadian government, through the Minister of Indian Affairs and Northern Development, announced that it was prepared to negotiate comprehensive land claims with aboriginal groups where their traditional and continuing interest in the lands concerned could be established. The Government of Canada thus committed itself to the resolution of comprehensive land claims through the negotiation of settlement agreements. No hostages were necessary to inspire action in Ottawa. Through its Comprehensive Land Claims policy Canada seeks to ensure consistency between that policy and other federal policies for aboriginal people and has dedicated itself to an equitable application of the policy to guarantee the overall fairness of settlements. A full description of the Canadian plan is contained in a booklet entitled "Comprehensive Land Claims Policy" published under the authority of the Hon. Bill McKnight, P.C., M.P., Minister of Indian Affairs and Northern Development, Ottawa, 1986.
37. Annually, the United States government, through the Department of the Interior, provides funding to a private Indian legal office called the Native American Rights Fund. NARF is counsel for the Indian groups who have brought most of the Eastern Indian land claims. Some of the funding is specifically earmarked for land-claims litigation.

References

Cardozo, Benjamin N. 1921. *Nature of the Judicial Process*. New Haven, CT: Yale University Press.
Clinton, Robert N. 1981. "The Eastern Indian Land Claims: A Reply." *New York State Bar Journal* 53 (5) 374–375.

Dickens, Charles J.H. 1838. *Oliver Twist*. Chapter 5.
Hutchins, Francis G. 1980. "Righting Old Wrongs." *The New Republic* (August 30, 1980) 14.
Prucha, Francis Paul. 1984. *The Great Father: The United States Government and the American Indians*. 2 vols. Lincoln, NE: University of Nebraska Press.
van Gestel, Allan. 1981. "The New York Land Claims: An Overview and a Warning." *New York State Bar Journal* 53 (3): 182–185, 212–216.

16

Europe's Indians

Christian F. Feest

Americans tend to be surprised when they learn of the large amount of popular interest in everything relating to North American Indians prevailing all over Europe. Europeans, when asked about the reasons for this strange fact, tend to be somewhat puzzled themselves, and will often point to a special relationship between their own nation and the "Indians." On closer look, however, these "Indians" turn out to be a population inhabiting the European mind, not the American landscape, a fictional assemblage fabricated over the past five centuries to serve specific cultural and emotional needs of its inventors (Lemaire 1986).

In the process of accounting for the "New People" of the "New World" brought to their attention since the days of Columbus, Europeans have made liberal use of classical and medieval notions of peoples marginal to the known centers of the world, submitting the new information to a process of intellectual domestication (see chapter 17). Distances in time and space (themselves considered interchangeable) were equated with differences in kind, making the peoples of the far corners of a Eurocentric world into creatures only marginally human, or the living survivors of a lost golden age—or both. This was probably the easiest way to understand these newly discovered cultural differences; and some evidence suggests the possibility that the indigenous peoples of the Americas defined their first European guests in similarly generalized, antithetical terms.

The power of expectation was such that early European visitors reported sightings of what existed only in their imagination. Unipeds— humanoid monsters with only one leg, described 1500 years earlier by Herodotus for what were then the outward regions of the world—were supposedly seen by the Viking explorers of Vinland. More than five centuries later the existence of such monstrosities was confirmed by Jacques Cartier, based on his misunderstanding of information furnished by the St. Lawrence River Iroquois. Giants were said to populate the area to the north of the Jamestown colony in Virginia as well as the remote spaces of Patagonia. Dog-headed natives were shown on six-teenth-century maps of North America and in illustrated volumes dis-cussing the southern part of the New World. And, irrespective of the ethnographic facts, almost every native population ran the risk of being identified as cannibals, representing a state of moral depravity analogous to the physical aberrations described above. In the sixteenth century, cannibalism was described for the Brazilian Tupinamba, who certainly consumed human flesh, as well as for the Eskimo, who certainly did not. Later, and well into the twentieth-century, when more positive images of Indians came to predominate in Europe, cannibalism still added a bit of spice to the dull if beguiling diet of "noble savagism."

The ambiguous duality of these imaginative constructions is reflected in the use of the medieval image of the "Wild Man" in early illustrations of American Indians, represented as hairy creatures living apart from civilized society but also far from its corruption (Colin 1987). The per-ennial juxtaposition of Indians noble and depraved later provided enough literary tension to keep whole nations happy for a century or more (Borsányi 1987; Rusinowa 1987), and it supplied all the necessary in-gredients from which generations of writers created novels with Indian subject matter.

Apart from allowing an easy reduction of the tremendous diversity of native cultures in the Americas into a few comprehensible categories, the primary function of the opposing images was (and still is) to serve their creators as alternative models. Fanciful representations of the In-dian, therefore, were commonly used to contrast and highlight value judgments about European society and civilization. Whereas negative stereotypes reinforced belief in the values of European cultures, positive images delivered simple idealized models against which the complex, often unsatisfying realities of the authors' own culture could be scruti-nized.[1]

In the eighteenth-century, Indians began to be featured in European fiction on a large scale but the transition was gradual (Chinard 1934; Bissel 1925). This was so because both the earlier travelers' "eyewitness" reports also contained a significant amount of fictional information, and because some fiction writers (such as Le Beau and other French authors of the period) did indeed have some first-hand experience with indig-enous peoples in North America. Instead of ultimately exposing the images as undisguised fiction, the lively literary treatment helped to contribute to the credibility of the characterizations. In this way, thanks to French writers, the Huron became the eighteenth-century American Indian type specimen. The huge success of fanciful portrayals published as nonfiction, such as the Baron Lahontan's *New Voyages to North American* (1703), Jonathan Carver's *Travels* (1775), or John Dunn Hunter's *Memoirs* (1823), can equally be attributed to the fictitious elements of their descriptions (see chapter 12). By the time journalism began to devote attention to American Indian matters, the temptation to use established and recognizable images instead of fresh descriptions based on an authentically differentiated realism was too strong to be overcome.[2]

When images of "the Indian" were first shaped in sixteenth-century Europe, most of the raw "data" came straight from far south of the Rio Grande. Later, after Europeans first had extensive contacts with North American Indians, the same expectations that helped shape ideas about South American peoples influenced the development of images of native North Americans. This process represents an independent generation of European perceptions of the North American Indian. But a second process was also at work, which Sturtevant recently has called the "Tupinambization" of North American Indians (1988; see chapter 3). This process involved the direct transfer of representations of particular South American tribes, which were used to generate corresponding visual images of North American peoples.

With increasing European exploration of the Pacific Islands in the eighteenth-century, the standard "Indian" image also proved to be independent of the narrow confines of geography and was freely transferred from the continent to the islands of Polynesia. There the Enlightenment harvested fresh evidence for a new improved version of the "Noble Savage." In verses inspired by reports of Captain Cook's voyages, a minor German village poet described the dreamy-eyed admiration felt by a European reader for the inhabitants of the Friendly (Hawaiian) Isles. He had the European visualizing them as sleeping peacefully in eternal bliss in their "wigwams," devouring a hearty meal of bear's meat, ostrich eggs, and coconuts, while using their "patoo-patoos" to chase away the cheating traders. This romantic image the poet contrasted with the "self-confessed" wretchedness of native life on the islands, defined by a continual state of war, by scalping and cannibalism, by a predominant diet of fish, and by substandard housing (Schmidt 1981:179–82). In this way traditional stereotypes of the American-inspired Noble and Ignoble Savage, merely embellished by some local Pacific touches, were used to define the Polynesians' "Indianness."

Two centuries after South American images had been transplanted to the northern hemisphere, a conventionalized North American image became dominant. Visiting Botocudos from eastern Brazil, on display in London in 1822, were dressed sometimes in Plains Indian and sometimes Hawaiian costumes to protect them against the inclement English weather (King 1987). Even George Catlin's South American Indian portraits bear an obvious resemblance to the likenesses of their distant North American cousins—partly, no doubt, because Catlin's South American trip itself was mostly imaginary.

At the same time, the rapidly advancing North American frontier helped shift the focus of European interest from the East to the trans-Mississippi West. New but compatible visual imagery was supplied by artists Karl Bodmer and George Catlin, and found its widest distribution unto third- and fourth-generation derivatives as illustrations for novels. Waves of European immigrants to the United States helped keep alive the concern of those remaining behind for the new circumstances of their friends, relatives, and former compatriots. Much of this information was supplied in literary form. In Germany more than a thousand titles of fiction relating to American Indians were published in the last quarter of the nineteenth-century alone. In France, Napoleon III's attempts to gain a foothold in Mexico caused French writers to forget about the Huron and the Iroquois and to make the Comanche and Apache their new stock heroes and villains, respectively.

Karl May, the most influential nineteenth-century German parent of Indian images, learned his lesson when he wrote one of several German adaptations of Gabriel Ferry's *Coureur de Bois*. Though the whole setting must have attracted May as it did many other German readers, he seemingly drew his own conclusions from the fact of Ferry's being French. If the arch-enemy of the German people was siding with the Comanche against the Apache, the latter necessarily had to be the Germans' potential allies. Winnetou, the "red gentleman" and slightly effeminate Indian chief and companion of the German first-person hero of May's novels, therefore had to be an Apache. This form of cross-identification of allies and enemies continues into the present. Recently, a reform-minded member of Austria's Socialist Party published an appeal for "more Comanches" in his party—if the Apache were friends of Karl May, the ultimate petit bourgeois, the Comanches had to be socialists.

The question of the infusion of national characteristics into the Indian stereotypes of various European counties is related to another perennial issue in the study of Indian-European relations: whether there were any differences in the attitudes of the various colonial powers towards the native populations of North America (see Peckham and Gibson 1969).

In both respects some variations may have existed, despite differences that were probably minor when compared with pan-European similarities in such representations.

Some of the nationalistic views of American Indians appear to relate to stereotypes about the European nations themselves, such as when Hungarians show greater interest in the Indians' horsemanship, Germans in their military skills, and the French in making love to Indian maidens. More importantly, however, the differences have to do with the different roles of European nations in the colonization of North America. If nations which had themselves become colonial powers were a little more prejudiced than those who did without the benefits of overseas possessions, this is hardly surprising. So there has been a theme in German literature relating to America that depicts Germany as the potentially better colonial power, a presumption that made Germany the natural ally of the Indians in their struggle against British or French domination. After the loss of their North American colonies, the French claimed an especially close relationship to the Indians. And predictably, Polish and Swedish novels have Polish and Swedish heroes fighting at the side of their Indian friends.

That the image of the "Indian" in Europe has not remained static over time is, truly, the best evidence for its function in serving changing European needs. Especially in the recent past, the traditional icon of the Indian chief—wisely stoic, commendably militarist, authoritarian in style of leadership—has partly given way to an idealized view of American Indian society as egalitarian, feminist, and committed to peace, spirituality, and unity with nature (see chapter 8). For such reasons, the Hopi appear to have replaced the Sioux as the epitome of Indianness. In some respects, the cultural diversity of indigenous American societies, influential in the rise of such stereotypes in the first place by providing an inventory of alternatives, has also made it easier for a standardized image to flow with the divergent currents of change in European wants.

The "struggle-for-national-unity" theme that pervaded European Indian fiction in the late nineteenth and early twentieth centuries, reflecting the great importance of such issues in many European countries at that time, has almost completely lost its attraction today. The 1887 version of Chief Seattle's speech, a product of American manifest-destiny thinking, never really caught on in Europe (see chapter 7). Seattle's recent adoption as a cult figure by several Christian churches and the World Wildlife Fund, on the other hand, is based on a completely new speech written in 1969–70 by (but never attributed to) Ted Perry, a professor of English at the University of Texas. Perry's revision was immediately further embellished and then disseminated by the Press

Committee of the Southern Baptist Conference, making Chief Seattle into an Adario for the ecologically minded 1970s (Kaiser 1987).

Given the spurious nature of such imagery, there was an understandable desire by critically minded Europeans to at last find and face some facts. Short of taking the risks involved in traveling to the New World, observing live specimens of American natives in Europe was the most obvious way to see for oneself.[3] Columbus may neither have invented the art of kidnaping nor the idea of displaying live human beings to an European audience. But when, on returning from his first voyage, he presented to the King of Spain six survivors out of ten *Indios* taken on board in the Caribbean, he established a precedent that caused many thousands of native people to be brought to the Old World in the ensuing five centuries.

For early European explorers a prime reason for bringing "Indians" to Europe was to supply living evidence that they truly had discovered some hitherto unknown, inhabited part of the world. Evidence was also desired to test various assumptions about the nature of those dwelling in these far-flung places. Those visitors who could make themselves understood were interviewed in the hope of gaining new information about what was then still their country, or at least information that might confirm old prejudices. Portraits and drawings of them were added to books of costumes and to allegorical representations of what were now, luckily, four continents. The newly recognized four continents allowed a variety of correlations with the four directions, four seasons, four elements, four temperaments, four rivers of Paradise, four evangelists, and what not.

Since the intrepid explorers delivered this living evidence along with marketable commodities such as fish, timber, and—all too rarely— precious metals, one of the first good purposes for the use of natives conceived of by Europeans was the exploitation of this "new prey" as slave labor. Especially so the early sixteenth century saw a series of slave raids along the Atlantic coast. However, the same susceptibility to European diseases that caused large-scale depopulation in the New World also contributed to the quick decline of the Indian slave trade. Moreover, although continued on a smaller scale into the seventeenth century, slave raiding was later considered highly detrimental to the cause of peaceful colonization.

A more important reason for displaying indigenous Americans to a European public was to generate sufficient added enthusiasm to attract the capital necessary for colonial ventures. For most viewers, however, such public exhibitions were at least equally important as a source of entertainment. The strangeness of the travelers' habits and their physical peculiarities—including tattooing and artificial head deformation—provided a thrill otherwise offered only by midgets, giants, or calves with two heads. Two "American princes" bearing Creek chiefs' titles, employed as eighteenth-century flashers, were paraded in the 1720s by an Indian trader from Charleston, primarily because of their extensive tattoos. These "princes" tantalized their audiences by wearing long scarlet coats concealing their mysteries. Only after payment of an admission fee would they yank open these garments to bare bodies covered with permanent epidermal images of suns, snakes, dragons, and various other pictographs. Other performers were made to execute scenes from their savage lives—to act out mock marriage ceremonies, use fire-drills to ignite flames, throw their spears, or launch arrows from their bows. The useful talents of the natives could be further demonstrated by letting them paddle their canoes or kayaks on some local river or pond.

As late as the nineteenth century the Micmacs were still telling a story about one of their own who had been taken to France and made to display his hunting skills in front of the king and his retinue. After killing a deer penned in an enclosure surrounded by spectators, not only did he butcher and cook the meat but—at least according to the much later Micmac story—he also ate it, and then defecated in front of the noble audience, therewith completing the nutritional cycle and registering his disgust about having been made a mere object of curiosity (Rand 1894:279).

Sometimes these shows took a competitive turn, with natives aligned against local boatsmen or runners; but more commonly the pedagogical aspects of such displays was emphasized. In the educational exhibition known in Germany as *Völkerschau*, popular in the late nineteenth and early twentieth centuries, serious efforts were made to recreate the actual lifeways of peoples by importing whole native families who would dwell in replicas of their traditional habitations and behave as authentically as possible. Classes of school-children attended special performances as part of their geography courses. In contrast, professional American troupes, such as Buffalo Bill's, were often seen as less educational and more amusement oriented than those promoted by Europeans.[4] However, whatever the aims of the impresarios, for the native performers in these productions their participation increasingly meant an opportunity for gainful employment, while for some promoters the commercialized shows often provided an opportunity to rip off both their employees and the public (Hamell 1987; Wright 1987).

Instead of serving to educate the European public, some native Americans were shipped to Europe to receive a European schooling themselves. An early example is that of Don Luis, a native from the Chesapeake Bay area, who was brought to Spain in 1566 and educated in the hope that he would later lead a group of missionaries to his homeland (Lewis and Loomie 1953). Beginning in the early seventeenth century, French missionaries would send children to France to be reared in the "one true civilization" so they might later become exemplars for their savage brothers and sisters. Some of them became so thoroughly acculturated they ultimately refused to return to America, frustrating the original purposes of their patrons (Dickason 1984:217–21). Even the English in Virginia, who did not spend so much energy as the French on their proclaimed goal of converting the native Virginians, took some juvenile visitors to England and placed them with local families who were to educate them.

The impulse to convert and educate visiting natives remained strong throughout the nineteenth century and continues even today. Bible societies and the local clergy tried their luck, for instance, with some of those who had come to Europe as entertainers. Several natives attended Roman Catholic seminaries in Rome to become priests (McClurken 1988). In recent years, efforts have been made to offer native American students an education in Austrian forestry training schools. Two Oglalas, who came over for a summer course in 1986, discovered that fiction had long before forecast fact: almost a hundred years earlier Karl May had described in his novel *Winnetou* how the son of the Navajo chief by his German wife had been sent to the forestry school in Dresden.

Although most of the earliest visitors to Europe had been abducted, native peoples themselves became increasingly curious about and desirous of learning more of the land whence the kidnapers had hailed. Based on the experiences of two Montagnais brought to France in 1602, who returned to report "of the good entertainment which the King had given them," the chief decided to send his son to France in the following year, where he was installed as the Dauphin's companion. In 1608 Powhatan, the Virginia Algonquian ruler, exchanged his subject Namontack for an English boy, fittingly named Thomas Savage. Namontack was sent to England to give his master a first-hand impression of the place and the people. The Virginia Company of London touted him as Powhatan's son, an Indian prince. Rumors spread that Namontack was to negotiate an agreement about navigation, and that he had been coached not to take off his hat when being introduced to King James. Eight years later Powhatan sent to England another of his advisors, the temple priest Uttamatomakin, who was to take a census of all the trees and people by making notches on a stick. Similar accounts of tally-keeping by native visitors to Europe later became part of the stereotype of the "Indian abroad."

Ever since Namontack's time, many native American political delegations have come to Europe, often goaded by colonial authorities eager to convince their wavering allies of the wealth and power of one or another Great White Father. Most prominent among them were the Four Kings of Canada, one Mahican and three Mohawks, who became a smash hit in London society during 1710—could they have even dreamed that more than two-and-a-half centuries later the "Mohawk roach" would become the trademark of European punks? Sometimes it proved difficult to safeguard such visiting dignitaries from the curious gaze of their European hosts. When London theater owners advertised the appearance of the Four Kings as spectators, the audience turned out to be more interested in the Indians than in the plays (Bond 1952). The landlord of a Cherokee delegation in 1762, for a consideration, would admit visitors to the Indians' dressing room, "which gave them the highest disgust, these people having a particular aversion to being stared at when dressing or eating."

After the American Revolution, only Canadian Indians continued coming to England on political errands, and they have continued to do so until today. One recent delegation, for example, arrived protesting the first draft of the new Canadian Constitution. The establishment of international organizations in Geneva, such as the League of Nations and later various suborganizations of the United Nations, has more recently lured native American representatives across the Atlantic (Rostkowski 1984; 1987). Following the enormous publicity generated in Europe for contemporary Indian causes by the 1973 occupation of Wounded Knee, the American Indian Movement (AIM) was for some years able to establish itself as the sole, true embassy for all native Americans. AIM's representatives were so successful they were able to create a network of European support groups that provided traveling Indian politicians with an organizational infrastructure (Peyer 1987). But during the 1980s, neotraditionalists and even some elected tribal officials have succeeded in breaking into AIM's former monopoly.

Other varieties of Native American visitors have only sporadically made their appearance in Europe. Before World War I, few Indians came to Europe as soldiers on military duty; and although there was always some market for the products of native American artisans in the Old World, such items were rarely sold directly by their producers. But along with the human displays of the nineteenth century developed the practice of selling drawings or carvings produced on the spot, which contributed to the visitors' income. Some European museums have items in their collections obtained from native participants in such shows. Fortunately, not all such specimens have a history quite so grisly as the pair of moccasins, formerly in the City Museum of Brunswick. This footwear had belonged to an Indian in Buffalo Bill's troupe, who was run over by a train between Hanover and Brunswick—the unfortunate showman's moccasins were donated to the museum by the physician who performed the autopsy.

Because of the late acceptance of native American arts into the Eurocentric domain of "art," few Indian artists have sought contact with the European art world until recently. Oscar Howe, the Dakota painter who came to Europe as a soldier, is sometimes described as having been one of the first to actively study art works in Europe, particularly those of Picasso and other cubists. Howe himself has vehemently denied this contention, pointing out that service in the army left him no time to visit museums, and that he was not interested in modern European art, anyway. Obviously, we can see here how the normative power of images helped shape perceptions of reality: Howe simply had to be influenced by the cubists whose work he never saw in Europe.

Since the European public's preconceived notions made the difference between success and failure, close approximation to established stereotypes often determined who would be regarded as an Indian and who not. As quickly as the reality deviated measurably from the imagery, the reality was rejected as misleading by suspicious audiences that had been fooled before, but did not otherwise know how to tell the difference. Distrust and disbelief were mutual in this respect. Often, native people returning from Europe were thought to be liars when giving an account of their strange experiences. It happened to Uttamatomakin when he returned to Virginia in 1617. And it happens to tribal politicians today, who are sometimes suspected by their constituents of having misappropriated tribal moneys and of making up the better part of their reports.

The corollary of this mutual mistrust is that those whose appearance closely matched the imagery stood and stand a better chance of being taken for real, even though they may be impostors. William Augustus Bowles, an American Tory dressed up as an Indian, managed to pass in the upper crust of London's society in 1791 as "commander-in-chief of the Creek and Cherokee" nations. A woman hired as the second-choice substitute by an American entrepreneur displaying Eskimos in Europe in the 1820s, after the leading Inuit woman died and the first substitute, a gypsy, was found less than a perfect choice even if dressed in sealskin clothes, was totally convincing wherever she was displayed and had her portrait taken by an artist at the Prussian court (Wright 1987). A person calling himself Big Chief White Horse Eagle, whose somewhat fictional autobiography was written by a German admirer (Schmidt-Pauli 1931), found it profitable to travel Europe in the 1920s and 1930s, adopting unsuspecting museum directors and chairmen of anthropology departments into his tribe. Photographs show him sporting a feather bonnet, Navajo silver jewelry, and a button reading *Lions Club Pasadena*. A Viennese museum director found him particularly convincing, because the Big Chief had made it a matter of principle not to shake hands with Jews.

Some of the Indian "representatives" who have recently appeared in Europe also have serious problems with establishing their legitimacy. None of them, however, could match the most flamboyant fake Indian politician to visit Europe since the days of Bowles. This party, named *Capo Cervo Bianco* (Chief White Elk), arrived in Italy during the the 1920s, claiming to be on his way to the League of Nations to represent the Iroquois of upstate New York. He was received by Mussolini and for a time managed to live richly out of his believers' purses. Chief White Elk's downfall came only after a serious error in judgment and a unforgivable breach of Italian etiquette: he was taken to court, de-feathered, and exposed as an Italo-American by the name of Edgardo Laplante after he had dishonored an Austrian countess who had earlier presented him with a Bugatti racing car.

These days, most of the dubious characters in the Indian show business belong to the Faculty of Medicine. Whereas Indian medicine men were usually featured in nineteenth-century fiction as cunning charlatans con-spiring to keep the otherwise noble savages from adopting Christianity, today many Indians—authentic or spurious—work the Greater Europa Indian Medicine Men Circuit selling sweat lodges, sun dances, and heal-ing ceremonies to European customers disenchanted with both Christian churches and bureaucratized health-service (see chapter 10). Their suc-cess is completely independent of traditional knowledge, just so long as they can impress a public bamboozled by the books of Carlos Castaneda and other descendants of the Baron Lahontan (see chapter 12). Attempts have been made by various native American organizations, sometimes themselves of clouded competence in this matter, to publish blacklists and warnings against "unauthorized" medicine men visiting Europe.

Some of these fake visitors look like they came straight out of the ever-popular Indian novels, those fictions that had predisposed their audiences into accepting them in the first place. The Huron character in Voltaire's *L'Ingénu* turned out to be a Frenchman, after all, yet his unadulterated "Huron" straightforwardness continued to win him the hearts of the ladies and the fierce enmity of the government.

Even more revealing is the account of Winnetou's visit to Dresden in Karl May's *Satan and Ischariot*, written during 1894–1895, not long after Buffalo Bill's Wild West Show had been in town. According to the novel, the first-person narrator is attending a weekly meeting of the local singing club, when two unannounced guests call at the door. One of them, "a strangely dark complexioned man . . . with looks one could be afraid of," dressed in a dark suit, lifts his high-topped hat to expose his long, full hair "falling over his back like a cloak." Now even the skeptical singers need no further proof to accept the visitor as the famous Winnetou. Karl May next has his favorite Apache gentleman request a performance of German music, and the choir is pleased to oblige. In the meantime Winnetou orders a beer, which "he likes to drink, but with moderation." Winnetou does not comment on the music, "but as I knew his personality, I knew quite well how deep an impression the German song had left on his soul," the author has his narrator tell us. After coming home, May takes two peace pipes from the wall, which they smoke together, before Winnetou's departure from Dresden on the morning train. Although nothing else is reported about the chief's reactions, the message to the reader is clear enough—an Apache chief who likes German songs and drinks beer in moderation must be a kindred soul.

A related incident dealing with an encounter between competing image-makers and image is supplied by May's widow. This document pertains to her recollections of the meeting between her husband and the Indians of Buffalo Bill's show. The Mays had gone to see the Wild West performance in Dresden in 1906, and on Colonel Cody's invitation had visited behind the scenes before the show got under way. The author, it must be noted, had yet to visit America, yet regularly claimed in writing to have performed all the incredible feats described in his "tales of travel" and to be able to speak and write "the Indian languages of the Sioux, Apache, Comanche, Snakes, Utahs, Kiowas." In Klara May's account, Karl was introduced to the Indians and immediately started to speak earnestly to their chief in a foreign, presumably native American language. After a time, the American image-maker, Cody, interrupted the conversation: "You are an idealist, my dear," said he, patting his German rival's back, "the only valid law is that of the strong and clever!" To Klara it seemed as if the facial expression of the Indian suddenly changed—"and hate seemed to flash in his beautiful dark eye."

There can be no doubt that Indians visiting Europe did have some effect on European attitudes toward the indigenous populations of North America. It may be suspected, however, that it was mostly the illusions of reality conveyed by the visitors' performances which helped convince the public of the accuracy of its preconceived notions. The Indians' views of Europe as reported since the visit of the Four Kings of Canada and into the nineteenth century belong to the European literary tradition of fashioning exotic foils who criticize European society (Bond 1952; Mulvey 1987; Napier 1987). In addition to such literary projections, a certain amount of self-fulfilling prophecy may have been involved. Being treated either as noble or as a savage could, indeed, have produced the predicted behavior from the visitors.

Almost every European nation lays claim to having a special relationship with "the Indians." During the seventeenth century, English colonial propaganda tried to draw parallels between the ancient Britons and the natives of Virginia in their present wild and heathen state. Other models stressed the analogy of historical or existential experience as the basis for a distinctive bond of mutual understanding. This sometimes involved the belief in a genetic or linguistic relationship, one older example of which was the story of the "Welsh Indians" supposedly descended from the legendary Prince Madoc's crew. A recent example of a supposed ancient linguistic linkage is the published claim of shared ancestry between Hungarian and a California Indian language. Among the existential roots of such analogical "relationships" between a European nation and "the Indian" are the sense of a shared pantheistic view of nature as among Russians (Vaschenko 1987), the shared fate of a country divided, occupied, and deprived of self-determination as has been the experience of the Poles (Nowicka 1987), or the shared struggle for national unity as for the Germans. Whatever the key terms of the analogy, European nations have had no difficulty in finding a special bond with Indians in their own distinctive heritages.

So far as Germans are concerned, we may also stress that the Indian image has been significantly shaped through the products of German printing presses since the sixteenth century. However, "the Indian" represented as *Naturvölker* has several older prototypes (see chapter 10). Just as the Germanic tribes described by Tacitus were once the "Indians" of the Romans, so too were the Scythians the "Indians" of Greek civilization even before them. For German audiences, however, the special relationship defined was not so much based on superior information or on parallel histories as it was on similar "racial" ethos. In an analysis of Karl May's treatment of Indians (in which the difference between imagery and reality is totally neglected), an author, who during the Nazi period would write novels in which the heroism of Indian leaders was explained by their assumed Viking ancestry, concluded as follows:

> In Winnetou Karl May delineates the Indian drama. It is also the German drama. Winnetou is the noble man of his race—he knows about the purity of the blood, the longing, and the hope of his brothers, but they have to flounder because they are worn down by discord . . . This is Indian, this is

also German. Who has grasped the meaning of the Indian drama has also grasped the meaning of the German drama.

Reports about Lakotas who wanted to be buried in Germany notwithstanding, references to Germans in Lakota war songs suggest that the sentiments may not have been mutual (Conrad 1987:467–68; Theisz 1987). During World War II, it is said, many Germans felt betrayed by their "allies" on learning that native Americans were serving in the U.S. army to fight Germany.

The desire to become one with the "Indians" is not only expressed in literary form, as in a brilliant short text by Franz Kafka, it is also manifestly present in the wish of European women to marry Indian men. This impulse is contrary to the commonly observed aversion to such marriages in the actual colonial confrontation, but today it has become a way to raise a superior brood of mixed-blood heroes. In addition to some prominent cases of such unions, a colleague at a museum in the Canadian Plains reports that every summer significant numbers of German females arrive on his doorstep asking for directions to the nearest eligible Indians whom they might take as spouses.

A few years ago, a couple in Germany was unable to convince the authorities that it would be appropriate to name their baby girl "Winnetou" (they ultimately settled for Louise). This is not an isolated case: German playwright Carl Zuckmayer in earlier years succeeded in having "Winnetou" officially listed on his daughter's birth record. Outsiders not familiar with the popularity of Karl May's hero may still be surprised that people would want to bestow that fictional Apache chief's name on their female offspring at all.

The deeply felt identification of Europeans with "Indians" was obviously independent of the amount of actual contact. Johann George Seume, an eighteenth-century German poet and impressed British mercenary in the American Revolution, a transplanted soldier sometimes stationed in Nova Scotia, would later refer to his "half-Huron personality" without ever having encountered any Hurons other than the Baron Lahontan's philosophic Adario and his perennial literary progeny.

This sort of identification in turn created a basis for all European attempts to simulate an "Indian" lifestyle. Given the nature of the underlying ideology, these endeavors among all such "Indian hobbyists" involve, at least in part, the acting-out of living fiction. But we cannot ignore that, so far as the French and British are concerned, some roots of the movement may be traced to their colonial experience. French traders and *coureurs de bois* often became "White Indians" themselves, although this assumption of new ethnic identities was hardly appreciated by the authorities at the time (Jacquin 1987). Eighteenth-century British army officers stationed in North America, such as Sir John Caldwell, and officers of the British Indian Services, such as Guy Johnson, would occasionally dress as Indians for various reasons, commonly political. If such masquerades served some additional philosophical purpose or particular ego-need, it was certainly different in intent from that of the American patriots of Boston Tea Party fame.

European dressing up as Indians (other than for the purposes of Renaissance festivals or later ballets and theatrical performances) dates from the seventeenth century, at least. In 1686, William Byrd, a Virginia trader, supplied one of his English correspondents with "an Indian habit for your boy, the best I could procure amongst our neighbor Indians." That playing "Indians" was possibly considered kid stuff is also illustrated by the example of an Indian who had been presented with European clothing by the king of France: he reciprocated by sending an Indian outfit for the young Dauphin. Whether this was done at the suggestion of the missionaries, and whether it is related in spirit to John Locke's dictum that "in the beginning all the world was America," can only be guessed.

By the late nineteenth century, people dressed as Indians had become a regular feature of the annual Fall Fair parades in Leipzig. Contemporaneous accounts clearly point to what were then called "ethnological displays" or *Völkerschauen* as the source for this new craze. Around 1910, Dresden had its first Indian hobbyist group, the "Club Manitou," and this passion for pretending to be wild Indians soon spread like wildfire. Today, membership figures in Indian clubs in West Germany run into the lower tens of thousands, enough to stock a mid-size reservation (Conrad 1987; Bolz 1987). Clubs are also active all over eastern Europe, from the German Democratic Republic to the Soviet Union, where All-Union powwows have been held since the early 1980s. Many such clubs are also found in northern and western Europe.

For its devotees, Indian hobbyism is far more than the faithful reproduction of exotic material culture. Exhibition of hobbyist products have been held in several ethnographic museums, for instance, giving the artisans a legitimacy they would not otherwise have. Although life in the simulated Indian encampments is limited to weekends and summer vacations, the hobbyists' "Indianness" extends into their daily lives, thoughts, and religious beliefs. Curiously, in their own way, European hobbyists are transvestites in the cultural domain, if not in gender roles, and it is fitting that some of the best German bead and quill work today is done by males, just as it was done by berdaches in traditional Plains Indian societies.

Not all such cultural transvestites are as successful as Archie Belaney, the Englishman who became Grey Owl, a figure even today widely regarded as the epitome of "the Indian." A German review of his works published in 1936 stressed that no non-Indian writer could ever hope to become so one with nature as Grey Owl, and that his call for a return to a simpler, peaceful life in the face of the ravages of World War I had found an unbelievably strong reception in Germany. Traumatic war experience as a motivation to look for a counter-image, a more satisfying exotic version of the "real world," has not been confined to survivors of World War I's horrors. It has also led some veterans of the Vietnam War to "discover" their Indian identity, notably including some of the "Indian medicine men" now touring Europe.

One root of the European Indian support group scene was the early and more broadly based human rights movement, such as the Anti-Slavery Society. In its specific development, narrowly relating to American Indians, however, it seems to be based on the broader common identification of Europeans with Indians. At least some of the political activists played the part of natives in "Cowboys and Indian" when they were children, and there is a partial overlap of support group and hobbyist activities and publications. There is a tendency by some support group people, who stress political issues, to look down upon the mere imitators of native lifeways, whom they see as hopeless and socially irrelevant romantics. But while trying to make their interest in faraway people relevant to the modern political-economic problems of their own culture and society, Indian support group activists necessarily run the danger of bending the facts to suit their needs, and so of being hardly more realistic themselves (see chapter 13).

To some extent, European scholarly interests in the native population of the Americas are based on this popular culture foundation. Some academic "Indian specialists" came out of the hobbyist movement and others serve as advocates in Indian support groups. All are potential sources of information for either group, performers or activists, despite a certain amount of the ritualized anthro-bashing by Europeans sympathizing with native Americans which has become fashionable in the wake of Vine Deloria's polemics. But it is obvious that all academic approaches, no matter how politically detached and theoretically innovative, are ultimately part of a European and not an indigenous American tradition of looking at the world. Anthropology as propagated by Franz Boas, whose attention was itself directed to the Northwest Coast by a group of Bella Coolas visiting Germany in 1885–86 (Haberland 1987), made explicit use of the otherness of cultures that are studied by participant observation. It is not at all unusual for anthropologists absorbed in the otherness of Indians to identify themselves with the interests of the people they study.

In politics, a widespread Fascist fascination with the Indians was related to the widely accepted image of the Indian chief as a symbol of leadership. Similarly, the American Indian Movement's insistence (or at least that of certain of AIM's special pleaders) on the importance of "being of one blood" and "worshiping Mother Earth" has plucked sympathetic chords in the hearts of various dubious nationalist groups all over Europe.

By and large, however, the traditional European pairing of pro-Indian and anti-American sentiments may be found today on the left of the political spectrum. After the American Revolution and well into the twentieth century, conservative governments and their supporters wasted no opportunity for pointing to the treatment of American Indians by the United States government as indicative of what others might expect from the young Republic. In the 1820s and 1830s, the Austrian consul in New York regularly reported to Metternich, the reactionary chancellor of the Habsburg monarchy, on Indian affairs (Kasprycki 1988). In the same years, European Catholic missionaries always stressed it was the same American government that dealt unfairly with both the Indians and the Catholic Church. Those European immigrants, on the other hand, who had come to the United States to enjoy the liberties they could not find at home, spoke strongly in favor of United States Indian policies (Rusinowa 1987).

After World War II, when the United States had become the major conservative force in Western Europe, using its influence to project American views of history into textbooks and the media, anti-Americanism became a largely leftist pursuit, and pro-Indian sentiments traveled in its company. The fulminations of the American Indian Movement were seen by the radical left as a national liberation movement, so posters of Sitting Bull were placed next to those of Ché Guevara. One of the most visible groups active in the Italian student revolt of 1978 called themselves *Indiani metropolitani*, dressed in store-bought Indian outfits made for children, delivered their political messages in the jargon of the film *Little Big Man*, and published a manifesto entitled "Was there anybody more of an Indian than Karl Marx?" (Mariani 1987).

Not everyone may share the notion that Marx was an Indian. There are even East German jokes dealing with the occasional confusion of Karl Marx with Karl May:

"I've been reading *Das Kapital* by Karl May," says Franz.

"No. No!" replies Gregor, correcting him, "Karl Marx wrote *Das Kapital*, not Karl May!"

"Yes. I see. You may be right," replies Franz. "I'm already well into Book III and not a single Indian has shown up yet."

But Indians are regularly cited as models by and for Europeans, whatever their position on the political spectrum, and whichever their cause. One characteristic of the old and continuing relationship of Europeans with the "Indian" is, indeed, the perpetual willingness to accept their own centuries old expectation that the Indian has a worthwhile "message" for everyone. Frenchman or German, nationalist separatist or conservative industrialist, all are ready to listen to the most absurd statements if validated by an association with Indianness. In the final analysis, what to Europeans (and to Euroamericans, as well) might seem to be a countercultural battering ram derived from a brush with the exotic, turns out to be a homegrown fantasy embellished with the trappings of exotic stereotype.

This essay is based in large part on the editor's postscript, "Indians and Europe?" in Christian F. Feest, ed., *Indians and Europe: An Interdisciplinary Collection of Essays* (Aachen 1987: Rader Verlag), which contains a fuller documentation of some of the evidence. Throughout this paper, frequent reference will be made to individual contributions in *Indians and Europe* volume.

Notes

1. Similar observations apply, of course, to the largely derivative notions of "the Indians" by Americans. See Berkhofer 1978.
2. See, Bond 1952, Fiorentino 1987, Schroeder 1987, Riegler 1988.
3. The history of Indian visits to Europe and European reactions to them remain to be written. Foreman (1943) provides and undocumented overview, to which Dickason (1984:205–29) adds material relating to early Indian visits to France.
4. See Mulvey 1987, Létay 1987, Napier 1987, Clerici 1987, Conrad 1987, Haberland 1987.

References

Berkhofer, Robert F., Jr. 1978. *The White Man's Indian*. New York: Knopf.
Bissel, Benjamin. 1925. *The American Indian in English Literature of the Eighteenth. Century*. New York.
Bolz, Peter. 1987. "Life Among the Hunkpapas: A Case Study of German Indian Lore." *In* Feest 1987:475–90.
Bond, Richmond P. 1952. *Queene Anne's American Kings*. Oxford.
Borsányi, László. 1987. "An Emerging Dual Image of Native North Americans During the 19th Century in Hungary." In Feest 1987:287–96.
Chinard, Gilbert. 1934. *L'Amérique et le rêve exotique*. Paris. N. p.
Clerici, Naila. 1987. "Native Americans in Columbus' Home Land." In Feest 1987:415–26.

Colin, Susi. 1987. "The Wild Man and the Indian in Early 16th Century Book Illustration." In Feest 1987:5–36.

Conrad, Rudolf. 1987. "Mutual Fascination: Indians in Dresden and Leipzig." In Feest 1987:455–73.

Dickason, Olive Patricia. 1984. *The Myth of the Savage and the Beginnings of French Colonialism in the Americas*. Edmonton: University of Alberta Press.

Feest, Christian F., ed. 1987. *Indians and Europe: An Interdisciplinary Collection of Essays*. Aachen: Rader Verlag.

Fiorentino, Daniele. 1987. "Those Red-Brick Faces: European Press Reactions to the Indians of Buffalo Bill's Wild West Show." In Feest 1987:403–14.

Foreman, Carolyn T. 1943. *Indians Abroad: 1493–1938*. Norman: University of Oklahoma Press.

Haberland, Wolfgang. 1987. "Nine Bella Coolas in Germany." In Feest 1987: 337–74.

Hamell, George R. 1987. "Mohawks Abroad: The 1764 Amsterdam Etching of Sychnecta." In Feest 1987:175–93.

Jacquin, Philippe. 1987. *Les Indiens Blancs: Français et Indiens en Amérique du Nord (XVIᵉ–XVIIIᵉ siécle)*. Paris: Payot.

Kaiser, Rudolf. 1987. "A Fifth Gospel, Almost: Chief Seattles' Speech(es). American Origins and European Reception." In Feest 1987:505–26.

Kasprycki, Sylvia S. 1988. *Diese unglücklichen Geschöpfe: Briefe des Freiherrn von Lederer an Metternich*". (in press). Wiener Ethnohistorische Blätter

King, J.C.H. 1987. "Family of Botocudos Exhibited on Bond Street in 1822." In Feest 1987:243–51.

Lemaire, Ton. 1986. *De Indiaan In Ons Bewustzijn: De Ontmoeting van de Oude met de Nieuwe Wereld*. Baarn: Ambo S. V.

Létay, Miklós. 1987. "Redskins at the Zoo: Sioux Indians in Budapest, 1886." In Feest 1987:375–81.

Lewis, Clifford M. and Albert J. Loomie. 1953. *The Spanish Jesuit Mission in Virginia, 1570–1572*. Chapel Hill: University of North Carolina Press.

McClurken, James M. 1988. "Augustin Hamlin, Jr.: Ottawa Identity and the Politics of Persistence." In *Being and Becoming Indian: Biographic Studies of North American Frontiers*. James A. Clifton, ed. Chicago: The Dorsey Press.

Mariani, Giorgio. 1987. "Was Anybody More of an Indian than Karl Marx?: The 'Indiani Metropolitani' and the 1977 Movement." In Feest 1987: 585–98.

Mulvey, Christopher. 1987. "Among the Sag-a-noshes: Ojibwa and Iowa Indians with George Catlin in Europe, 1843–1848." In Feest 1987:253–75.

Napier, Rita G. 1987. "Across the Big Water: American Indians' Perceptions of Europe and Europeans." In Feest 1987:383–401.

Nowicka, Ewa. 1987. "The Polish Movement: Friends of the American Indians." In Feest 1987:599–608.

Peckham, Howard and Charles Gibson, eds. 1969. *Attitudes of Colonial Powers Toward the American Indian*. Salt Lake City: University of Utah Press.

Peyer, Bernd. 1987. "Who Is Afraid of AIM?" In Feest 1987:551–64.

Rand, Silas T. 1894. *Legends of the Micmacs*. New York.

Riegler, Johanna. 1988. "Tame Europe and the Mysteries of Wild America: Viennese Press Coverage of American Indian Shows, 1886–1898." *European Review of Native American Studies* 2(1):17–20. Budapest.

Rostkowski, Joëlle. 1984. The Struggle for Political Autonomy: U.S. Indians and the United Nations. In *North American Indian Studies*. 2 Pieter Hovens, ed. Göttingen, 86–98.

———. 1987. "The Redman's Appeal for Justice: Deskaheh and the League of Nations." In Feest 1987:435–53.

Rusinowa, Izabella. 1987. "Indians in the Reports of Polish Travelers of the Second Half of the 19th Century." In Feest 1987:297–306.

Schmidt, Friedrich Wilhelm August. 1981. *Einfalt and Natur*. Berlin. N. p.

Schmidt-Pauli, Edgar von. 1931. *We Indians. The Passion of a Great Race. Big Chief White Horse Eagle*. London.

Schroeder, Aribert. 1987. "They Lived Together with Their Dogs and Horses: 'Indian Copy' in West German Newspapers, 1968–1982." In Feest 1987: 527–50.

Sturtevant, William C. 1988. "Le Tupinambization des Indiens d'Amérique du Nord." In *Les figures de l'Indien*. Gilles Thérien, ed. Montréal: UQAM.

Theisz, R.D. 1987. "The Bad Speakers and the Long Braids: References to Foreign Enemies in Lakota Song Texts." In Feest 1987:427–34.

Vaschenko, Alexander. 1987. "Some Russian Responses to North American Indian Cultures." In Feest 1987:307–20.

Wright, Robin K. 1987. "The Traveling Exhibition of Captain Samuel Hadlcok, Jr.: Eskimos in Europe, 1822–1826." In Feest 1987:215–33.

17

White Ghosts, Red Shadows: The Reduction of North American Natives

Jean-Jacques Simard

Indians and *Whites* do not exist. These words do not mean real people—flesh and blood, sentient humans like those we meet on the street or in the countryside. Indian and White represent fabled creatures, born as one in the minds of seventeenth- and eighteenth-century European thinkers trying to make sense of the modern experience, particularly the European "discovery" of new continents and their populations. Ever since, Indian and White have been entangled with one another in the collective thought of both European and New World peoples, like some artist's image of a mad duo coupled in a dark embrace. To borrow a thought from the Iroquois, Indians and Whites are *false faces* peering into a mirror, each reflecting the other.

For this reason, to understand what it means to be an Indian in the contemporary world requires, also, knowing what it means to be a Whiteman. In this quest I will follow two different but converging lines of argument. On the one hand, I will assert that belonging to a native community (Indian or Inuit) implies having a peculiar place, a class status, in the wider North American society where such communities are found, whether Canadian or American. I will add that such a status means *having no place*. On the other hand, what is popularly described as native "culture," I will argue, bears little relation to the actual way of life of Indians and Inuit, now or centuries ago. Instead, what is depicted as the culture of native peoples represents the absolute opposite of what is thought of as "Western" culture—it is the *Whiteman's shadow*. These two elements—social condition and cultural image—mesh together into a comprehensive picture of North American "nativeness," which I will call "reduction."

I cannot fathom to what extent these thoughts will sound iconoclastic to an American's ear. Even here in Northern Canada—the land of Beaver Dundee and Montreal Jones, where the primordial Mountie, Nelson Eddy, still serenades his paramour, Rose-Marie, as their bark canoe quietly glides across a Hollywood movie set full of quaint half-breed trappers baptized Pierre but always called "Frenchie"—such ideas still seem wholly unnatural. Conventional wisdom, the long-accepted images of Indian and Whiteman, is that strong. An account of a personal experience will illustrate where I am coming from.

I never knew I was a "Whiteman" until two decades ago when I set foot in the small Cree community of Wemindji, on the east coast of James Bay. Then a shade over twenty years old, I always had thought I was a French Canadian from the boondocks of the Lake St. Jean area, 120 miles north of Quebec City. Nevertheless, the local Crees soon made me to understand I was a Whiteman. So I tried to act like one, groping my way around, not knowing exactly what was expected of me. After a couple of years, still feeling strange in dealing with "Them" by way of the so-called Whiteman supposedly lying inside me, I took refuge from such weirdness in bureaucracy and academia. Moving south into a comfortable office, I associated with other "Whitemen," in Quebec's office of Northern and Native Affairs. To learn how to take care of "Natives" properly, I went back to college.

Anthropology was then *the* major for those who wanted to learn more about non-White others. During my introductory course, a Belgian professor mentioned in passing that a chief, familiar to the public as *the* Indian's spokesman, was not "authentic" because he had adopted the "Whiteman's ways." That such people were "not true to their culture" was news to me. The only examples I had known and lived with for two years were just plain Indians, irrespective of age, sex, education, linguistic talents, travel experience, occupation, or status in the community. They still looked, thought, and behaved in ways that seemed "Indian" enough to make this French Canadian, at least, feel truly alien and uneasy in their midst.

Commenting to this effect in response, I added that, besides, this naive student saw the very Indian chief the professor mentioned as an entirely "authentic" representative of most of today's Indians. From my observation, none of them lived or thought like the nature-bound, mystical, primitive communist, hunter-gatherers the professor identified as "true" Indians. Were they any more "false Indians" than the professor was a "false Belgian" because he was not born to the college trade? A short, snappy exchange ensued between professor and student. So that is how I became a sociologist, not an anthropologist.

For two score years since I have dedicated my scholarly pursuits (and a steady involvement with some Inuit political leaders) to answer and settling two questions: How can one be an effective Whiteman? How can one be a false Indian? These boil down, I think, to a single issue: How can one be what one is not? "There be Dragons," the old medieval maps used to say about the margins of the known world. In my profession, as in the other social sciences, we fight the dragons of the unknown with a weapon called theory.

Among the first truly "modern" North American Indians were some refugees from the survivors of the once mighty Huron (Wendat) confederacy. Devastated by epidemic disease carried from Europe, then invasion by New York Iroquois armies, some surviving Huron refugees fled their traditional domain on Lake Huron's Georgian Bay to take refuge in Sillery. Sillery was a small settlement controlled by the Jesuit Fathers on the fringe of the main fort of Quebec, then capital of a fledgling North American French empire. That empire had been first successfully established with the help—among others—of the Huron.

What made these Huron expatriates, and others like them in the same era, "modern Indians?" By 1650 they lacked the demographic and geographic foundations for maintaining their older way of life. The original kinship based social and economic networks that had held their communities together were shot full of holes. As of 1650 their very survival depended on the those they called the "People-of-the-Wooden-Boats" or the "Bearded Ones"—Europeans. They had lost their earlier strength and value as allies and partners in the developing colonial society built on the fur trade and military expansion. They had become a people without a significant place; a community in internal exile. They also represented the future of other native peoples all over the continent.

Before the end of the seventeenth century, the Jesuits founded two other refugee Indian settlements of the same feudal type. Between 1665 and 1667 one was established on lands facing Montreal. Called "By-the-River" (*Kanawakhe* in the Mohawk idiom), it consisted of a few Mohawks converted to Roman Catholicism and many captives taken by these and other Iroquois from surrounding tribes. Rejected by their own people, these converts were allies and trading partners of Dutch and British Protestants along the Atlantic seaboard. After 1680, roving bands of Abenaki refugees from New England, cruelly beaten by the Puritans in what is known as King Philip's War, drifted toward the mouth of the Chaudiere and Richelieu rivers, where they collected and formed the third Jesuit-managed settlement.

The Jesuit Fathers saw an enormous opportunity in these small refugee communities. We must beware of judging their actions three centuries ago by today's values and standards. It is too easy—and wrong—to censure the missionaries of yore as cultural conquerors, bent on pushing their faith and values down the throat of unwilling natives. That without a doubt they were; but compared with others of their time the Fathers were still the Good Guys.

Jesuits went out of their way to live among the Indians, learning their customs and language, the better to adapt their preaching to the collective sensibilities of their new flocks. In contrast, traders, military, and colonial administrators looked at them askance. They saw the Black Robes as "Indian lovers," as having "gone native." The Jesuits in turn thundered at secular officials for their exploitation of the Indians, for peddling alcohol, and for their indiscriminate sexual use of native women. First of all foot soldiers of the Company of Jesus, they answered directly to the Vicar of Christ, over and above the crowned heads of the rising imperialistic nation-states of Europe, and so their loyalties were suspect. In modern terms, they may better be seen as universalistic, Christian humanists. For them, all humans were equal under God. Even the heathen *Sauvage* had a soul to save, just like Christians. Of more significance, these Jesuits were convinced that deep down, once shed of their superstitions and their untamed, wandering ways, Indians had a purer, natural, childlike soul, uncorrupted by the vices of "civilization"—greed, self-interest, power.

This was precisely the grand chance these missionaries saw in the refugee communities. There it would be possible to *settle* the wandering bands, the better to teach them new trades and true knowledge of godly revelation, to mend their unrefined habits and protect them against the dissolute influence of the "Francoys," and to allow their underlying "natural" goodness to emerge. These Jesuits believed that, by carefully managing the lives of refugee Indians, they could produce ideal communities inhabited by freely sharing, god-fearing, selfless, peaceful agriculturalists, living in harmony with themselves and nature. The chance the Jesuits grappled with was to recreate humanity as it was before the Fall of Man. They thought they were building a new Garden of Eden.

"Indian Reductions," the Jesuits called such new native communities. These they expected would become a perfect model, not only for the inspiration of other "wild" Indians, but for all humankind. We can now see this was never to be. However, the Fathers *did* invent one of the prototypes for what would become known as the Indian reservation. In a wider, more important sense, they also created a forerunner of the major pattern for dealing with indigenous peoples of the continent, later elaborated and refined by both the Canadian and American states.

I have suggested that Indians in "reductions" were people without a place: internal exiles. This was not the case for their contemporaries, other Indians living elsewhere, outside these few tiny church managed communes. For many years other Indians enjoyed significant prestige and influence on the fringes of colonial society. In truth, without Indian allies in war and as trading-partners, the French could never have planted and defended as long as they did the greatly overstretched network of Forts and Trading Posts that reached all the way from the Gulf of the St. Lawrence River across the Great Lakes and down the Mississippi River to its mouth.

The still unreduced Indians occupied an essential strategic position in the political economy of New France. They were a military balance-of-power; they produced significant economic resources; and they knew this full well. For many years they played their political cards smartly, wisely exercising their economic leverage; but when the fur trade gave way to real estate and resource development (farming, lumbering, mining, town building) the bonds between Indian communities and *their* environments became dysfunctional—as regards the interests of the emerging Canadian and American nations. Increasingly so, nomadic hunting-gathering Indian bands were a nuisance. More so, the sedentary communities of farming Indians were a serious obstacle. And multi-tribal confederacies like those of the Iroquois were out and out competitors of the empire and nation-building Europeans of the eighteenth and nineteenth centuries.

Thus the special relationship between native societies and their habitats had to be broken, so that their land could become real estate, its resources commodities, both property used or exchanged for money-making. It was not as *people* that the Indians had to go, understand, but as *natives*. What had to give way was culturally distinctive communities located on and identified with their own territories. In the geographical sense of the term, it was as the "first *nations*" that Indians had to be transformed, so that new nations—Canada and the United States—could be raised up anew on the expropriated ground.[1]

Three solutions to the "Native Question" (in the United States, the "Indian Problem") were possible. Although new diseases imported from Europe resulted in major epidemics and much depopulation, *extermination* of Indians generally was never a deliberate policy sought by French or English colonists. However, from time to time authorities did attempt to wipe out particular native societies, as did the French at the height of warfare with their main enemies, the Fox, and English colonists with the Pequot. In both Canada and America the ideal of benevolent treatment of native peoples blocked adoption of any such ruthless policy.

A second possible policy was *assimilation*. Assimilation, in the main, involves abolition of the special legal status attached to the social category of native, with the goal of absorbing Indians into mainstream society politically and socially. Through the 1930s, this was the major policy aim in the United States, and it resurfaced again in the 1950s under the so-called "termination" program. In Canada until 1867, that colony's boundaries were not secure enough and the country too sparsely settled by British immigrants for the Crown to afford abandoning the special loyalty of its Indian subjects. In this long era, British authorities feared and had to cope with both an external threat—an expansionist United States, and an internal one—the separatist tendencies of its own population. The loyalties of Indians were then seen as a counterweight against both hazards. Nonetheless, throughout the continent many thousands, who in the late twentieth century might well be proclaimed legitimate Indians, individually and as family groups did abandon native modes of existence and identities to become indistinguishable from other Canadians and Americans. However, the most important obstacle to widespread assimilation was the remaining native communities themselves. Most just did not move toward the mainstream. Instead, they kept to their own, uninterested in the idea of "emigrating" into the new nations newly building on the very ground their ancestors had inhabited.

This left one practicable "solution": corralling Indians in small, specially defined territories, legally designated "Indian Country." Historically, Indian Country was beyond the settlement frontier and consisted of huge, yet unappropriated territories. Eventually, it became a multiplicity of tiny disconnected parcels out in the boondocks, the badlands, or the wilderness, segregated from the surrounding society. There the central governments of Canada and the United States assumed the responsibility of sustaining Indians in these rustic ghettos.

There was little use attempting to *exploit* Indians as forced labor, as the Spanish did in Mexico and South America; they were not plentiful enough to bother with this option, even had Canadians or Americans been so disposed. These small populations were not organized as aggressive, prosperous states, so *dominating* them in the classical, imperialistic sense as in South and East Asia was more of a burden than anything else.[2] So as the lands of one native society after another were acquired and opened to settlement by newcomers, the fate of all became that of the original wards of the Jesuit Reductions. Indians in Canada and the United States have become internal exiles, refugees in the country formerly exclusively theirs, a "useless" people with an ambiguous part in the developing nation states. Unwillingly, their fate was to be without *any* significant place.

The verb "reduce" (and the noun "reduction") comes from Latin roots meaning "leading back" or "driving back." Its synonyms are "lesser, decrease, abate, diminish, shorten, impoverish, curtail." Reduce also signifies "subdue" or "conquer," "abridge" or "classify." Here is a case where plain language is good enough for theoretical purposes. *Reduction* of the North American natives means that the colonial process has not only limited their geographic range but reduced their sociological horizon as well. They have been incorporated into the system of social stratification of North American nation-states as a social race, one whose allegedly inbred, eternal character makes it a somehow different *kind* of species, predestined to at least partial irrelevancy in the surrounding, historically changing real world.

Reduction began with the land itself. Somehow indigenous peoples had to be excluded from the physical space into which the new North American societies were spreading. This is the *geographical* aspect of reduction, developed in the idea and practice of reservations. Indian reserves are restricted estates wherein formerly wide-ranging populations were confined, sometimes more-or-less voluntarily, sometimes following uprooting and transportation from their original territory. In practice, the environmental quality and size of reservations commonly have been insufficient to provide enough land and resources for native societies to sustain anything approximating a traditional subsistence economy, or the development of an agricultural-ranching economy, or to reconstitute themselves economically in some alternative manner.

Thus many reservation communities have so far failed to develop the hinterland-urban pattern of land occupation found elsewhere. Those reservations such as the great territory of the Navajo that seem huge, compared with the tiny band reserves of Southwestern Ontario, and those which are "sitting on treasures" of minerals or oil, are quirks of economic and demographic history. When first established they were isolated, and technological, industrial or demographic development was not advanced far enough to mandate the exploitation of such resources. These tracts were then seen as worthless—irrelevant—pieces of land. Today, the same is true for the Barrens of Canada's Northwest Territories and most of the Arctic.

I have implied that the "reservation" is more than a geographic-political fact; it is also an idea. Ever since the Jesuit reductions, they have been defined as havens against a surrounding alien, heartless "White" world. On reservations, according to this widely accepted view, Indians could live among their own, remain true to their traditional selves, find their authentic soul. The reservation, as a uniquely preserved native estate, has in part become an imaginary substitute for the ancestral lands of their forbearers. Today, some scholars and other advocates of the Indian cause have started calling reservations "sacred holy lands," apparently seeing them as New Canaans or Zions. In important ways this is not a reference to the real conditions on the parcels where modern Indians live: it is a country of the mind. Even for those contemporary Indians who share this fantasy, there is an unreal quality to it. In truth, accurate memories of lands from which Indians were displaced has dimmed over the generations. The "sacred holy land" representation expresses an increasingly powerful emotional attachment to what remains: Indian-owned land has become a key symbol of old wrongs suffered, and of a special modern identity.[3]

We must also remember that many Indian or Inuit groups were never intimately bonded to a particular part of the landscape, at least not for long. The records of pre-Columbian Indians, whether in native legend and myth or in the archaeological record, are replete with evidence of regular migrations, territorial expansion, displacements, and conquest. Saying this does not belittle whatever genuine attachment or property titles native groups may today rightly claim to parts of this continent. On the contrary, the point is to underscore a fact: the image of an Indian community *tied to one piece of land* is a historical emergent, mainly a reflection of the reservation experience.

Many present day native peoples have incorporated this *geographical reduction* into their own collective and private self-images as an article of faith. They are convinced that the segregated ethnic estate concept is essential to their survival in Canadian or American society. Of course it is and, just as truly, of course the reservation is not such an essential to survival as distinctive identity groups. Reservations are essential to maintaining the status quo, the persistence of an existing set of relationships and prerogatives. But many Indian groups have maintained their identities and organizations over the generations with no land base whatever. Nonetheless, young people born and reared in urban areas, seemingly assimilated into the "Whiteman's world," often say they must return to the reservation to "get back to their roots" or "find their true selves."

The geographic reduction of native North Americans was tied to their *demographic* reduction. There are two sides to this aspect of reduction. First, the natural rate of population expansion was stunted by biological and man-made conditions. Second, the demographic growth of native communities has been, and still is, legally and ideologically restricted.

The people today enumerated as Indian and Inuit in the United States and Canada now total about the same as the estimated population of the continent when Columbus arrived. During the intervening five centuries the world's population multiplied fourfold, that of the developed countries by a factor of ten. Even my own group, the French Canadians, though not among the richest of North Americans, became *sixty-four* times more numerous than they were when Canada was a French colony. The stability of the total native population alone illustrates the appalling effects of epidemics, famine, war, and poor living conditions. Some local native groups disappeared entirely; others were greatly thinned; and a few recovered and expanded far beyond their earlier size—the Navajo, for example, now number more than twenty times their early historic size. Nonetheless, the continent's native populations, as a whole, had to wait improvements in diet, housing, and health care of the 1950s to start growing substantially again.

The second type of factor affecting the demographic expansion of native communities consists of ideological and legal restrictions. Because of the limits on living space and other resources allocated to them, there has been an increased emphasis within existing, officially recognized "tribes" or "bands" on exclusiveness, the rejection of statutory "outsiders," endogamy, hiring preferences, and other means of limiting membership. Descendant of mixed "outsider-insider" conjugal unions, not to mention any kind of immigrant to the reservations, may be seen as deviously encroaching on older community members' rights to land, government aid and services, treaty rights, and other proprietary assets. These concerns have been much enhanced during the last decade—in Canada, by pressures of Métis and non-status Indians, and in the United States, by the policy of adding whole new "tribes" to those formerly recognized.

One additional demographical note is this: the fertility rates of most Indian and Inuit populations, which contributed much to their recent growth, are now tapering down toward demographic equilibrium (a trend universally related to the growth of consumption and to the widening range of individual opportunities).

The end result is that, today, the Indian or Inuit brand is applied to people who not only belong to a geographically reduced group but, by the same token, to one whose numbers are too few to provide the troops necessary for economic self-sufficiency, the political self-responsibility, and the self-expressive cultural vitality that nowadays spell practical, self-contained community life, let alone "nationhood."

Canadian listeners to the last televised constitutional conference on aboriginal rights learned, for example, that there were 185 such Indian "nations" in British Columbia alone, averaging a few hundred people each, all of them supposedly reaching for some modicum of "sovereignty." All due political rhetoric aside, it is hard to see how such tiny pool of able-bodied people could furnish on their own the *inbred* specialized human resources to staff the schools, health facilities, public utilities, courts, police forces, staple industries, commercial establishments, political parties, media, voluntary associations, and other institutions that even an imaginary North American small town needs to sustain itself as a continuing social-political entity in the modern world.

Deliberately turning one's back to historical change is not inconceivable—the flourishing Amish communities of Pennsylvania and other states have done it with surprising success, for instance. But the Amish go back to the Anabaptist movements of the fifteenth-century European religious reformation. Their obstinacy has also been an historical constant, which has not been the case of any of the nativistic, mystical, "back-to-the-roots" episodes of American Indian history. That is why pick-up trucks and T.V. dish-antennas are far more typical of present-day reservations than horse-and-travois or shaking tent performances.

It was far easier for the Jesuits of the seventeenth-century to dream of small, utopian, self-sufficient communes than it is, in the late twentieth, to establish viable "sovereign nations" of a few hundred souls. Though it would be presumptuous to put a precise figure on the minimal population size a contemporary polity must have before it can even pretend to provide for its own the most basic institutional framework for meeting the average, everyday social needs of its members, over 20,000 is certainly a conservative estimate. Few "tribes" or "bands" come close to that size.

Parasitic petty-states may be viable as gilded tax-havens for the rich-and-famous, but one may doubt—notwithstanding what some Indian officials seem to believe—that gambling casinos and bingo parlors will suffice to transform the hundreds of bantam "nations" of the North American "Third World" into so many Monacos. Once "monocoazation" is excluded, that leaves but two standard alternatives for increasing the demographic base of native polities: taking in out-group immigrants or fusing several smaller local communities into wider social-economic-political units. Both solutions were practiced by precolonial native groups but have become almost inconceivable under the reduction system.

Even when historical conditions accommodated small, self-contained communities, it was common for Indian communities to increase (or seek to maintain) their ranks through out-marriage and the adoption of captives—including many Whitemen until lately. The biological ancestry as well as the cultural heritage of modern Indian and Inuit has been rather sharply diluted by intensive interbreeding and interaction with newcomers. And up to this day, all Indians or Inuit settlements—even those most remote from metropolitan life—have included a constant and often growing proportion of Whitemen who form an integral part of these communities' social organization and everyday life. Most of these outsiders never fully integrate into these communities, however, because of the systematic barriers erected by the reduction system along the already hard to cross colonial-ethnic boundary line.

Traditionalism, here, corporatist tribal militancy, there, and political-economic inequalities (whether Outsider over Native or the reverse) everywhere feed intergroup tension and formal, if not actual, repulsion. This makes for an inverted, scaled-down reproduction of the Black-White problem the late Swedish economist, Gunnar Myrdal, called, in a famous book of the 1940s, *The American Dilemma*. For while the native social world, even at the local level, includes and often depends on the services of a permanent and inescapably "White" minority, the real "Whitemen" living within Indian and Inuit communities are doomed to remain an ever alien minority made up of transient, colonial-like "birds-of-passage."

In the past, local groups of native peoples did come together and form wider, multiethnic political and economic entities—the Six Nations Confederacy is but one example that comes to mind. But the present reduction system is not conducive to such development, since it bonds ethnic belongingness to discrete territories, officially defined "tribal" identities, and shares of redistributed state and public resources. Land, natural resources, and access to the public purse are, in practice, distributed in a highly uneven manner, related to the vagaries of historical-geographical circumstances and the degree of political shrewdness in lobbying for funds, instead of being shared out on the basis of population size and need. So it is not at all uncommon to find Indian "tribes" of radically different size, and great disparities of wealth, bitterly competing with one another for rights to territory, including the valuable natural resources located therein, and for the plethora of grant programs made available by national and state or provincial governments. The long-standing, acrimonious dispute between the Navajos and Hopis over their respective land rights is but the most conspicuous example of such disputes. What is less well known is that the same area is also occupied by tiny remnants of a different people indigenous to the same territory, Paiutes who are not officially recognized as a "tribe" and who have no territorial rights whatever. As we will see, other features of the reduction system also undermine the possibility of transethnic solidarity for purposes of viable economic-political development.

One may view the geographical and demographic curtailment of natives, together, as the biophysical or *ecological* level of retrenchment, on which all further aspects of the reduction system stands. Next in order is *economic reduction*. Most reservations have never been a practical economic proposition. Denied access to their former range and resources, their ranks depleted by illness and death, the productive social fabric of native societies was shredded. The history of the decline of the fur trade reflects such developments. In the western Great Lakes this occurred early in the nineteenth century; in sub-arctic and arctic Canada, dependency on the fur trade collapsed only recently, in the middle of our own century. Early or late, Indians who had come to rely on production of furs to fulfill rising expectations for new standards of living experienced economic collapse. No longer could they provide for themselves by producing raw materials for European and American markets, less so did they have the resources, manpower, and skills to begin new productive ventures to keep up with the increasing living standards of their neighbors.

For most Indian communities, treaty negotiations blessed and legitimized their dispossession and made them into dependents of the American or Canadian states. The provisions of these treaties, starting in the late eighteenth-century, created in rudimentary form the shape of a liberal welfare state in Canada and the United States. Indians, thereby, were to become the first welfare dependents in North America. Their destiny would be barely to eke out a scant subsistence, if that, on the sidelines of the most unprecedented period of industrial development in history. So, until recently, most Indians living on reservations drew a scant subsistence from public relief, cottage-industries, government-supported programs, marginal trapping, hunting and fishing, and whatever arts and craft products the local and national markets took a fancy to.

Some kinds of economic activities have long been thought of as inherently "natural" for native peoples. The oldest and most persistent of these is renewable resource harvesting of fish, game, and wild plant foods and materials. To this were added community-based small business with a wildlife or handicraft bent, service sector employment as guides for sportsmen or tourists, and entertainments in the forms of Wild West shows, powwows, seances, and other "cultural" performances. Lately, research into oral traditions about land occupation long ago has also become a kind of cottage-industry. In 1983, after a formal meeting with all Indian chiefs of his province, Quebec's Premier gave each one a present: a fine, $39.95 Buck knife (U.S. made). This was intended as symbol of the Indians primordial "cynegetic" (hunting) vocation. The chiefs did not reciprocate with the gift of a Japanese-made electric cattle-prod, as their own symbolic testimony to other Quebecers' instinctive calling for farming and hydroelectric engineering.

Some Canadian tribes, and most in the United States, have also started selling tax-free cigarettes; but the real money-makers for Indians in both countries are high-stakes bingo emporiums and gambling casinos. People have to make do with the economic opportunities at hand, surely. In this instance the tribes are profiting from their peculiar legal status by economic operations in the service sector, exploiting the minor vices of other Canadians and Americans. However, it is important to note that such enterprises, besides their unproductive, parasitic nature, confirm the peculiar "extraterritorial" status of the reservations. Such "economic development" strategies, therefore, directly contribute to the perpetuation of the reduction system.

The few increasingly well-to-do "Bingo tribes," in this regard, are like those of an earlier era who found tremendous underground windfalls in oil and natural gas reserves. Like these earlier beneficiaries they make up a small minority, and their good fortune makes the squalor and dependency of the majority of other reservations the more striking. Why do these apparent economic success stories maintain the reduction system? Because, once again, the development of native peoples is tied directly to their special land-holding status and the "natural" accidents of history and geography. Such economic "improvement" is not based on collective or individual entrepreneurship, technical and managerial know-how, judicious planning, production and investment, economies of scale, the quality of manpower, or on other substantive enhancements and achievements.

Often the "bound to nature" version of economic reduction has been incorporated into the self-images of many individual Indians. They, like other Canadian and Americans, commonly see natives employed as professionals, managers, office or store personnel and other white collar types as somehow less genuine than those who live "close to nature, off the land." Sometimes young Indians who are members of tribes where such employment is the overwhelming rule will seek out "their roots" in the company of other, less developed, "more traditional" native communities. Another aspect of this internalized "rhythms of nature" reduction is the standard rationalization for the unreliability and instability of some Indian students and those employed in desk- and clock-bound jobs. Such behavior is excused on the grounds of an irresistible, "culturally normal" urge to abandon work or studies to answer nature's call in tune with "Indian time." Because of the imperatives of sustaining the day-to-day operations of modern tribal institutions, there is, as a result, a heavy reliance on the services of outsiders, whose tardiness or absenteeism is not so easily explained away or tolerated. Modern Canadian and American legislation dealing with native land rights, like the *Alaska Settlement Act* or the *James Bay and Northern Quebec Agreement*, also reflect this stereotype. These contain many pages detailing renewable and wildlife resources,[4] long lists of "traditional activities," and many stipulations about royalties to be received by natives for future natural resources development projects, but they skim over other imperatives of modern economic organization and planning (statistical research, savings-and-loan or investment banking, just to mention a few).

Even the newer, well meaning versions of native economic reduction (like resource royalties or gambling services) rest on very shaky grounds, theoretical or practical. They unthinkingly subscribe to the obsolete nineteenth-century "law of comparative advantage," which prescribed that nations should specialize in the exploitation of whatever valuable assets they were uniquely provided with by their natural and historical circumstances, and that other countries did not have in such abundance. The comparative advantages of Indian and Inuit "countries" in that sense, would be land rights, special legal privileges, and distinctive traditional abilities and knowledge. One must notice how eerily this economic calling overlaps with other symbolic dimensions of the reduction of native peoples: geographical (the Native is tied to the land) and, as will be pointed out shortly, juridical (the Native should be constitutionally apart) and ideological (the Native is culture heritage bound).

By themselves, however, "natural" comparative advantages are not sufficient to sustain long-term, collective, political economic sufficiency. It depends on how such advantages are *exploited*. And that, in turn, rests on the qualities and use of *human* resources—advantages such as specialized skills and technical-scientific knowledge, general level of information and education, organization and management, ability to read and respond to market signals or the will to defer gratification.

Historically, following the boom-and-bust cycles which have marked the fortunes of native communities, government has always stepped in, expressing the centuries old paternalistic theme for managing Indian affairs. When oil royalties, or bingo income, or grant supported enterprises fail, Indians again become needy wards, and again government provides. What is provided goes far beyond additional grants to prop up tribal businesses, relief for unemployed families, or social and health services. From the top down, government has wrapped a bureaucratic swaddling-cloth around these communities, constricting most aspects of their everyday life. This is no temporary cocoon from which a healthy moth will eventually emerge to fly off independently. It is a perpetual impediment, preempting the blossoming of responsible, self-managed polities. These comments introduce another layer of curtailment: *political* reduction.

In eastern Canada, the basic political organization of most aboriginal societies before Jacques Cartier's 1534 exploration was of the seasonally nomadic "band" type, gathered under the leadership of headmen and occasional war-chiefs. For most purposes, these small communities were self-regulated by myth, customs, kinship obligations, and consensual palavers. The mere creation of sedentism—fixed settlements—and the establishment of rudimentary government services undermined the relevance of previous political structures. This new situation called for formal, community-wide institutions for which there was no traditional precedent. Quickly, the state and its bureaucratic institutions slipped in to fill the void. For the practical purposes of administrative communication and management, elective local bodies called "Band Councils" were set up. These served as go-betweens, standing betwixt the people and government functionaries. Actually, these Councils were, and remain, the basic cell of the federal Indian Affairs administration. In those parts of Canada where larger, more politically complex tribes and chiefdoms were the rule (Haida, Tshimshian, or Tutchone of the Northwest, Iroquois Six Nations Confederacy in the East) these long established, autonomous political systems were suppressed or outlawed, and resistance was crushed by the threat or application of state power.[5]

Such transformations of native political systems were pursued with the cant of paternalistic superiority. Nonetheless, ever since the mid-nineteenth-century, the motto of government "Indian Agents" has been to "work themselves out of a job." This has proven a remarkably difficult goal to achieve. Managing Indian affairs, on the contrary, has turned out to be an increasingly labor-intensive bureaucratic enterprise. Today, many thousands of federal and provincial civil servants are still at work, promising soon to work themselves out of the job of overseeing native communities. At the same time, they are busy training their own replacements, seeking additional funding and new staff positions. The call of bureaucracy remains—More Money! More Jobs! More Projects! This litany substitutes for the development of forthright local political responsibility all across reservation country.

In both Canada and the United States, recent years have witnessed a blurring of the distinction between native leadership and government appointed administrative personnel. This came about through the recruitment of increasing numbers of Indians and Inuit into government service. Also contributing to this trend has been the devolution of government services: the assignment of responsibility and authority for managing programs to local or regional units of Native government. So it has come to pass that Indian bureaucrat now regularly serves Indian client, often enough a kinsman or fellow band member (see chapter 14). So it is that the line dividing state administrative apparatus from locally controlled political institutions has almost disappeared. Nowadays it is not only difficult to differentiate between community *leadership* and *native staff* of agencies responsible for native affairs, it is also near impossible to separate *politics* from *fund-raising*, *policy* from *programs*, *local government* from *central bureaucracy*. These trends represent a form of *administrative* reduction, with the parties supposedly served by program or government stuck somewhere along one side of a seamless administrative spider's web. Such a system promotes intense conflicts of interest. Indians tied to central government through dependency on government jobs can hardly exercise their responsibilities as *citizens* of self-governing political communities. They have to be content with being, more or less, ineffectual *clients* of a patronizing superstructure, one that confounds democratic process with bureaucracy.

In this sense, a century before other categories of citizens, Indians were anointed with a political Head Start program. They got first crack at what, during the 1960s, would be indiscreetly called "participatory democracy." During the heyday of the technocratic welfare state in that period, underprivileged minorities, dependent on government patronage for survival, were obligated to take a direct part in "managing their own affairs" through active "involvement" (consultation, representation, or straight hiring) with the very bureaucratic agencies whose beneficiaries they were. The official slogan of this 1960s craze was "maximum feasible participation," although critically minded observers later modified this to "maximum feasible misunderstanding."

In that decade (and since) scientific advisors, social engineering "experts," "managers," and "consultants" wheeled and dealed between granting agencies and "the poor." In their new relationships with such real folks these middle-class professionals found a niche where they could carry out their own power-struggle against the existing system for allocating government resources to interest groups. What such experts needed to encourage native peoples toward maximum feasible participation was a useful stereotype about "the Indian." This was provided with the conviction that normal "White" politics was alien to the true nature of Indians. Participatory democracy, on the other hand, was a different matter, a style that would be inherently appealing to the continent's "original self-governing peoples." This thinking found its ultimate expression in the United States in 1975, when Congress passed the *Indian Self Determination and Education Act*.

In both Canada and the United States, long before the central governments gave formal sanction to such developments, numerous Indians saw opportunities for imitating the styles of social science experts. Taking their training in boot camps inculcating the skills of grantsmanship and the social change arts, they enlisted in the War Against Poverty as foot-soldiers and started working their way up the ranks. The result was intense, sometimes bitter, as yet unresolved competition for the limited resources (grants, jobs) available, open combat between Indians claiming birthright and outside experts asserting their educational achievements. Among North American anthropologists and their professional allies, a compromise was offered at the 1989 annual meetings of the *Society for Applied Anthropology*, the theme of this conference being "collaboration." Under this new motto, academics promised to help Indians (and other dependent groups) do their thing, if natives (that is, their clients) will allow social scientists to do theirs.

Such mixed administrative-client relationships have created a technocratic system in purest form. Therein native leaders/managers and Native Affairs academics/bureaucrats each proclaims esoteric authority for identifying and a free hand in addressing the "true needs" of Indian and Inuit people. A profoundly ambivalent love-hate relationship dominates interactions between these "inside" and "outside" components of the Native affairs technostructure. But together they stand, so it is asserted, against the heartless and culturally chauvinist majority. Among themselves they regularly struggle over control of budgets and programs within their own jealously guarded administrative ghetto. Their influence reaches so far into local Indian communities as to block important political debate and action. Programs and policies promising "power to the people," thereby, have left ordinary Indians and Inuit still powerless, their affairs closely managed by the new technocratic oligarchy, including a significant number of native managers.

In a system of government by law, not men, political reduction cannot rely exclusively on administrative containment or bureaucratic fiat; it must have a *juridical* basis. This rests on what is called "Indian status," defined by special laws marking off a social category called "Native" (in Canada) or "Indian" (in the United States), a category set apart from all other citizens of the two countries. Though people legally defined as Native or Indian formally hold full citizenship, with all attending rights and privileges, they are also—constitutionally—placed under the exclusive if mixed jurisdictions of both tribal (Insider) and central (Outsider) governments. Just as Indian reserves have an extraterritorial status in the provinces and states which are responsible for land and resources under the Constitution, so to do individual natives have a special status as a "protected category."

In this fashion, Canada's *Indian Act* and American law officially discriminate on the basis of race, for in both systems it is biological ancestry or pedigree—the "blood in a person's veins"—that determines eligibility for that special status.[6] Thus Indian status consecrates a North American version of *apartheid*, a legally defined racial apartness that is popularly defended as marvelously benevolent. That "Indian status" does not mark legal recognition of any person or group's *ethnic identity* must be stressed. Instead, it defines particular genetic communities, each bonded to its geographic homeland. Those social-political entities— called Bands, Tribes, or Indian Nations—consist of a population of statutory Indians and a reservation—the homeland proper. Irrespective of laws making Indians full citizens, these legally defined wombs really produce second-class citizens, whose main sanctuaries elsewhere are urban Indian islands, the archipelago of service jobs and programs maintained by the federal governments for the exclusive benefit of Natives, and the peninsulas of native studies programs in colleges and universities.

Philosophically, Canada's *Indian Act* is too close for comfort to South African apartheid legislation and to the late nineteenth-century "Jim Crow" laws of America's southern states. However, because it applies to a small, supposedly primordial, "naturally different," easy-to-love, "archaic" minority instead of a large one like the Blacks, such official racial segregation is seen as enlightened. Understandably, natives themselves tend to cling to the fundamental tenets and the special privileges of such legislation. In Canada, until recently, the offshoots of *Red* ova fertilized by *White* sperm were deemed unfit for Indian status, a matchless illustration of how far paternalistic political decisions can be molded by biological madness. Against the will of most band councils (who feared overcrowding of their reserves and depletion of their resources) this Canadian law was changed.

Today, the first generation "mixed-blood" progeny of Indian Status/ Non-Status couplings can acquire official Indian Status—providing they apply for it. People who lost their Indian status generations ago through so-called "emancipation" policies of decades past also now insist on having it back. Additional thousands descended from the emergent ethnic group called *Métis* in the fur-trade era, never recognized as status Indians, have joined in. Again, this is understandable, for their ancestors suffered ecological, economic and administrative reduction like their Indian contemporaries among whom they lived. The Métis, having shared the fate, now want to enjoy the apparent advantages of their Indian affines. And following centuries of being a native people ironically defined apart from other native peoples, the Inuit were also placed into the statutory category of Indian by a 1939 Canadian Supreme Court decision.

The 1983-1987 round of constitutional conferences on aboriginal rights in Canada clarified the right to native "self-government," a right to be entrenched in the first law of the land. It would still have an ethnic-genetic foundation and would still imply exclusive federal jurisdiction over natives and their territories. The idea was not to eliminate or modify the basic tenets of the *apartheid* system, but grant more autonomy, inside the system, to the Indian and Inuit "homelands." Largely in consequence of such historical administrative segregation and juridical demarcation, all natives have come to share a common past and future place that sets them off from the non-native majority. Their collective relationship with the state is not like that of others, the mere citizens. They see themselves, in effect, as *underground nations* amidst a *foreign*, Canadian nation and want this to be converted into a and recognized as a special, *international-like* relationship. Since foreign affairs are the domain of the federal government, entrenching the exclusive federal native status in a revised Canadian Constitution, and attaching to it the right to self-government, would be a symbolic grant of native sub-nationhood.

Given its historical premises and ignoring practical problems, the logic of this position is impeccable. However, it is hard is to see how, under contemporary circumstances, each group of a few thousand people, much less the tiny local bands of several dozens, can effectively reach for the status of an "independent nation," especially so when, at the same time, advocates of Native independence also strive jealously to retain constitutionally guaranteed privileges of "aboriginal rights," prerogatives seen as a type of natural law entitlement. On such pragmatically limited, philosophically contradictory, shaky foundations, the goal of genuine sovereign self-government for such pocket-sized polities cannot be much more than sham.

One seemingly promising alternative would be for native communities to fuse into much larger, supralocal ethnolinguistic units, and to federate themselves under common political institutions coinciding with provincial, state, or even national boundaries. This would expand the territorial and demographic foundations of their collective sovereignty. In Canada, this would require a new, third level of self-government linked to existing provincial and federal divisions. Creating such "autonomous regions" would require a major revamping of the Canadian Confederation. However, such new political units would also have to be of an open, public nature, with all *residents* accepted and treated as equal citizens, without regard to "Indian" or other racial-ethnic status. Accordingly, majority rule—may that majority be ethnically Native or not so—would have to prevail. Working against the prospects for any such territorial federation, however, is the enduring strength of local group identity, loyalty, solidarity, and political interests, and the deep-seated opposition of Indian versus Whiteman. In both Canada and the United States, such divided, parochial interests remain far stronger than regional or national identifications. In both countries, as well, the sacralization by Indians and their supporters of chauvinistic ethno-genetic (or aboriginal) identity, rights and entitlements persists as a preeminent objective.

Twenty years experience studying and occasionally working with Canada's native peoples have left me with a strong impression. Notwithstanding official rhetoric, *at least for the time being* few contemporary Natives are truly willing to bear the full responsibilities, and the consequences, of genuine political autonomy. One exception may well be the Eastern Arctic Inuit, who seem dedicated to building a regional, representative government, one incorporating all residents of the area. But their project is not advanced enough to show if they really wish to avoid continuing and additional entanglement in the institutional reduction inherited from the colonial era.

So far, I have tried to explain how the whole historical edifice of native reduction rests on the material cornerstone of territorial dispossession and resource expropriation. Once exiled from the spaces into which Canadian and American societies would expand, a multilayered economic, administrative, and juridical "hot house" had to be built over their geographical reductions to maintain and contain them in an artificially controlled atmosphere, protected from the world—where everyone else in North America lives. Like orchids in Canada's northlands, the price of such protective reduction has been and is dependency. As a prime condition of their perpetuation, dependency has seeped into all aspects of Indian and Inuit social life: economic, political, psychological, etc.

However, instead of looking at the reduction system solely as rising from material forces upwards to the incorporeal sphere of supreme law and natural rights, I now propose viewing it the other way around. Seen from the top down, the whole reduction apparatus is held together by an ideological linchpin. In this sense, the dominating summit of native reduction consists of a body of powerful symbols, images, and fictions. Together these depict the True Native as a primeval being, one uniquely and perpetually bound to pristine nature and a remarkably durable, inarguably ancient cultural heritage. So powerful are such mental images that *any* type of social transformation can be interpreted as a catastrophic threat to the Native's natural destiny and authentic soul. Harsh necessity thus becomes virtue as the *Invented Indian* merges with real Indians. Bound to the reservation and exiled from the dimension of space, they are accordingly castaways from the exigencies of time. Just as they are physically out-of-place in modern North American society, so are the also ideologically denied the experience of history. Because of the phantom image of *The Indian*, Indians are made into a timeless people.

Three things must be kept in mind regarding this "True Native" image. First, I am presenting a simplified sketch of shifting historical ideas about the first settlers of the Americas. This depiction can be no more than a bare skeleton of centuries of changeable imagery: it is an abridgement. But then, one simple, vernacular interpretation of "nativeness" has persisted for centuries, despite the tendency of intellectuals to amend its superficial features. So my own caricature is reasonably true to the core of the lasting image of "The Indian." Second, the *Invented Indian* cannot be understood by itself, in its own terms: this is but one side of a coin whose other side bears the unearthly features of the *Invented White Man*. Third, this enduring image—a set of stereotypes—is still widely accepted as authentic and valid. Indeed, the image is accepted on both sides of the ethnicity playing field by *Them* and *Us*. That is, those who behave as accomplices in perpetuating this "natural" opposition, insist on, define and deal with one another through images of "Indian" and "Whiteman." The White Ghost has a distorted Red Shadow and, inseparably, vice versa.

Whatever historical variability or transformation has occurred in icons representing the True Native, there have been several constants. These are evident in an unbroken expressive chain starting half a millennia ago, when modernizing Europeans "discovered" the misnamed "Indians" of the Americas and first began holding them up to a mirror, discovering a marvelously reversed clone of themselves as "Whitemen" [7] Of these constants three are particularly relevant to my discussion:

1. *The Images are Monolithic*. Whatever peculiarity is attributed to one native tribe is generalized and extended to all, and to every individual member thereof. On the other side of the token, all Whitemen are fused into one.
2. *The Twin Images are Logically Obverse*. Whatever features are defined as typical of *The Native*, they display a simulation that is the absolute reverse of *The Whiteman*'s moral ideal for self and community (at any one time!). This rule applies whether the *The Native* is seen as morally better or worse than the *Whiteman*, whether the icon represents a *Noble* or a *Wild Savage*.
3. *The Images Represent Archetypes*. "Spontaneous, Natural, Timeless, Original" have been the most common ways of characterizing the

True Indian as human beings, identifying what is specific to them, with the additional provisos that True Indians live close to and in harmony with nature, and are just as agreeably fused with one another socially in conflict-free, consensual communities.

Illustrations of the application of these constants are not hard to come by. Readers need only to jot down what they think they know about The Indian, what they have been told authoritatively to think about The Indian, or what they think they know about The Whiteman in relation to The Indian. If this at first proves difficult, consider the example of the college professor in an ethnic education course who informs her students: "Indians have personal names but they are kept secret and Indian children don't want us to use their names. So in class, how should can you call on an Indian child?" The reversed imagery should be obvious: The White Child prefers and expects to be addressed by name; the Indian Child does not; Indian names are sacred; White names are secular. Or consider how the Whiteman's historic social relationships with the Indian are almost invariably characterized in print. The list of adjectives used for such purposes reads like a roster of Christian sins or virtues: Greed, Charity, Cruelty, Benevolence.

Such stereotypes are not unique in thinking about Indians. Similar styles and attitudes are found in characterizations of other diametrically opposed social categories, whether religious, political, hierarchical, racial, or some other kind. Christian/Jew, Liberal/Conservative, Upper Class/Lower Class, Asian/White, and Male/Female are examples. Such thinking is fundamental to mere discriminative cognition, but is also behind prejudice, intolerance, bigotry, intergroup conflict, racism, nationalism, and chauvinism of all kinds. In such categorical contrasts, the attributes of those on either side can be understood only by reference to the characteristics of the other: they are part of one whole identity, "Us" *and* "Them." Thus, the much-favored modern definition of the Whiteman as a materialist, morally delinquent, environmentally estranged, socially alienated creature is a historical emergent, one that cannot make sense without reference to the opposite traits of the True Indian.

This all began at the moment of first contact between Europeans and the already long-established residents of the Americas. During their Renaissance era, the native peoples on the eastern shores of the Atlantic had only recently been reborn as Europeans. When their first transatlantic voyages approached they were, as well, on the verge of a Great Enlightenment. As this brilliant illumination appeared, massive upheavals already racked their lands: technological shocks, disturbing innovations, huge population expansion, unbelievable economic growth, transformational nation-building, sometimes violent religious renewal. Transoceanic (and transcontinental) voyages of discovery were part of these sweeping transformations. The infant Europeans were pondering what was becoming of *them*: What was God up to? With the benefit of five centuries of hindsight we can give a secular answer to this question. As of 1492, Europeans were starting to experience the birth pangs of one of the most tremendous mutations of human society and culture in history: the dawning of the Modern Epoch.

Among the first cogent explanations of this alchemy was one called the "Social Contract," authored by England's Thomas Hobbes and France's Jean Jacques Rousseau. Man, they revealed, once lived only in a "State of Nature": like wolves preying on each other, said Hobbes; like lambs, spontaneously flocking together, countered Rousseau. Then "once upon a time" the human condition mysteriously changed: well behaved, well policed society was invented. Good sense prevailed, according to the very English Hobbes: to curtail their brutal passions, people gave someone (the State, Absolute Monarchs) the authority to rule them, making them behave with an eye on the common good, not bestial self-interest. Ever the Frenchman, Rousseau took a contrary stance: Man's egoist impulses were otherwise freed from the inherently altruistic bonds of natural community. How to maintain order in the new, potentially agonistic order? By signing a covenant with everyone else, Rousseau explained, a contract that was truly social because it subjected self-interest to an embryonic "General Will." Where, then, lay the power to carry out that wondrous contract? Authority was delegated to the State, responded Rousseau.[8]

To drive their point home persuasively, Hobbes and Rousseau had to invent two central characters, the very same two lead players who still dominate the contemporary world stage: The Whiteman and The Native. Being modern "scientific" thinkers, they had to ground their argument empirically, on hard facts. Their data consisted in part of descriptions by others of the condition of the new-found American Savage, whom they described as living close to their imagined "state of nature." Thus, in the armchairs of an English and a French philosopher was born The Indian, portrayed by them as exactly the reverse of the newly modernized European, The Whiteman. One side of this two-way mirror was the undomesticated Savage: spontaneously whatever he was because, like animals, he was still part of nature. On the other side stood Civilized Man: artificially what he was, the product of deliberate, reflective will-power.

How this transformation was evaluated depended on fundamental moral judgments about humankind. If in the beginning man was naturally bad, then (according to Hobbes) civilization or the "social contract" was a best buy for an imperfect world. On the other hand, if man was originally good, then the "social contract" was the lesser of two primordial evils, man's loss of innocence being the worst (thought Rousseau). Similarly contingent on such moral assessment of the human condition, the "natural native" would be seen in one of two archetypical ways. If naturally bad, the native was brutal, promiscuous, cruel, uncouth—a wild savage to be mercifully domesticated (or otherwise subjugated). However, if original man was judged inherently good, the philosophic yield was the Noble Savage, that eternal witness to the intrinsic wholesomeness of Man before the rise of the social contract and civilization. Thus the Noble Savage was a major archaeological find uncovered by two philosophers' spades. He was a museum specimen that had to be protected, preserved, and displayed as living testimonial to what "artificial" civilization destroys. Forever he would exhibit what civilized Man had ravaged; he was expected to serve as an enduring model for natural social conditions before the Fall, an exemplar for those seeking their restitution.

Subjected to such philosophical assaults, real North American natives during the United States and Canada's colonial and early national eras were trapped in a genuinely Hobbesian predicament. They represented an obstacle to the conquering spirit of modern culture and society. For many years homesteaders or miners, Bluecoats or Mounties, directed by the state and serving the state's interests, had a field day with Indians. Today the unenlightened Whitemen, as condemned by Rousseau's liberal urban posterity, are mainly those undeserving rural poor, the red-necked working class and small-town entrepreneurs who endure on the margins of genuine economic achievement and real political power, competing with Natives for a slice of the government pie. Those now vying with the modern Noble Savage also include sportsmen, wilderness buffs, and natural resource developers resenting the privileged access natives have to the environmental commons and its natural fruits, privileges granted to Indians and protected by the state, grants that continue to serve the state's interests. These opponents of special rights awarded to the social category called "Indian" stand on an old European-American value, the Enlightenments' ideal of "equal rights for all," and use this principle to pick the lock protecting Natives in the remaining "virgin" areas of North America. These competitors often express a Hobbesian view of the Native, as an uncouth, promiscuous, lazy, drunken welfare parasite. At the moment, though there is much divisiveness on such issues among Canadians and Americans, most opinion leaders in the mass media, joined by some key political movers and shakers, embrace a Noble Savage image and the inherent rightfulness of special rights for the Native; but this position is strongly opposed by many of those whose welfare is directly affected by such categorical aids. For Rousseau's progeny, the only Good Indian is one who looks and talks like a Noble Savage; for others the only Good Indian is one who, like themselves, buys a fishing license and observes catch limits.

In no small part this development owes to the replacement of Bluecoats and Mounties (brandishing sabers) by bureaucratic caretakers and academic guardians (whose weapons are ball-points and word-processors). These latter specialists in Indian affairs are today's Jesuits. While the Rousseauan view of the Noble Savage has been translated by them into the idiom of modern social science, real Indians almost everywhere remain riveted to contemporary reductions, now called reservations, and thus insulated from the real world. In the marginal areas of North American society, among those whose business it is to watch over the fate of Indians, Jean-Jacques' Native, however glamorized by social science cosmetology, has become the key symbol in a dominant social service ideology.

Because the descendants of this continent's original peoples are no longer a political-economic obstacle *to* national progress, they have been assigned a distinctively new cultural part to play. Now their unique calling is to mirror disenchantment *with* progress. The Noble Savage today portrays civilization's discontents and the guilty conscience of the dominant. Just twenty years ago Robert F. Berkhofer, Jr., wrote:

> Since Whites primarily understood the Indian as an antithesis to themselves, then civilization and Indianness as they defined them would forever be opposites. Only civilization had history and dynamics in this view, so therefore Indianness must be conceived of as ahistorical and static. If the Indian changed through the adoption of civilization as defined by Whites, then he was no longer truly Indian according to the image, because the Indian was judged by what Whites were not. (1979:29)

Indian reservations (and similarly protected refuge zones such as native studies programs) stand, therefore, to the human kingdom as botanical or zoological gardens do for exotic, archaic, and endangered species of flora and fauna. Today's reductions are cultural zoos: manmade social hothouses where a wild, natural strain of human cultural-genetic material is artificially nurtured so that coming generations will remember Adam and Eve's fall from grace. They are also supposed to serve as a source for civilization's cultural renewal. This same logic explains why native exhibits stand beside dinosaur skeletons and coel-

acanth fossils in museums of natural history: their place in history is out
of it. Indians are thus lodged in an anachronous Utopia, which is in no
place, apart from real time.

There is a standardized set of instructions for arranging such con-
servatory exhibits. *We* make our own history; *They* must stay true to
their eternal ethnic essence. *We* teach our children reasoned self-criti-
cism, to keep their young minds open to a changing, multicultural world,
to *make* something of themselves; *They* must forever cling to their precious, inherited, collective uniqueness. For *Us*, mastership of our own
destiny; for *Them*, any change is a menace. *We* cause things to happen
and bear responsibility for consequences; *They* are hapless victims,
voiceless spear-bearers on the historical stage. *Our* guilt, presumed without due-process, is compelling evidence of *Their* innocence. *Our* culture
is oppressive, individualistic, competitive, self-delusional, contrived, artificial, spurious, neurotic; *Theirs*, from the Andean heights of the Inca
Empire to that of tiny Algonquian bands still found in the allegedly
primeval forest, are all perennial models of authenticity, serenity, and
equality, where community is perpetually in harmony with cosmic forces.

By a weird quirk of historical imagination, contemporary Indians have
been forced to bear the "Whiteman's burden," but upside down. *They*
are forever destined to recreate their identity vicariously, as *Our* eternal
opposites. *They* will always be *Our* victims, *Our* guilt ridden, most
Significant Other. *They*, the conjured *True Indian*, is Our Ghost, a
phantasm of innocence past. So powerfully pervasive has this reduction
imperative been that, paradoxically, real natives have long since internalized its symbols and principles as important elements of their own
identities (see chapters 3, 4, and 7). Thus there is a meaningful dialectic
between *Us* and *Them*, although it has a self-perpetuating, stultifying,
vicious-circle cast to it.

In that sense my opening sentence is part false: the Indian *does* exist.
Indians exist as the descendants of original residents of this continent,
over the years much molded by their peculiar status in Canadian and
American societies. Generation after generation they have integrated
into their own practical and intellectual life the dominant culture's Owner's Manual for being Indian. However, I must reiterate, the True Native
stereotype bears little resemblance to the past and continuing diversity
of real Indians. Consider just one prominent element in that stereotype,
"living close to nature." This is a simplistic way of saying that the True
Indian lived in tiny groups of nomadic foragers. It happens that Columbus landed off-shore of continents where millions of natives were town
and city dwellers: think of the Aztecs, the Natchez, the Abenakis, the
Hohokam, the Maya, the Huron. These and a great many more were

perhaps it was just the case that society had just not been so developed. New discoveries had not been made. They did not know about all the technology that now exist. What they did find took a while to be discovered in usage. It was then sold?

sedentary societies whose members spent their lives in human-invented environments—urban habitats, as far *apart* from raw nature as humans can conceivably get. Similarly, today, tens of thousands of Indians are urbanites. Many live in reductions long since embedded in the heart of some vast metropolis, such as the Kanawakhe Mohawk settlement in Montreal. Tens of thousands more live in Indian neighborhoods in New York, Toronto, and Los Angeles. These real Indians today do not scour the countryside for small game and roots. Like other North Americans, they hunt money, jobs, social services, grants, and media attention.

What is false about the "living close to nature" fable is equally false about other ingredients of the True Indian stereotype. Consider the image of The Indian as the world's original environmentalist, "living in perfect harmony with nature." In the far reaches of prehistory, where we would surely expect to find the purest of True Indians, real ancestors of Indians by over-hunting contributed greatly to the extinction of many species of Pleistocene megafauna. More recently, not too long before the first European transatlantic voyages, the sedentary, town dwelling, farming, pyramid building Mound Builders of Ohio and Illinois created their own versions of civilization that peaked and disappeared—brought on by their own destruction of the ecological base on which they were raised. Naive platitudes above inbred environmentalism reduce all the many varieties of real Indians to one cliché, the False Indian. And such stereotypes make many modern Indians seem like traitors to their kind, for preferring bungalows to wigwams as habitations, television viewing to ritual dancing, Kentucky fried-chicken to Indian fried bread, employment as attorney rather than deer hunting. Those few remaining hand-carved cigar-store Indians, now found slowly peeling away mainly in antique shops, are siblings of the equally wooden, ideologically sculpted True Indian still alive and flourishing in the fantasies of many.

Can the same conclusion be turned around for that illusive figure on the other side of this mirror? Is The Whiteman an invention, too? I think so, although this may come as a surprise to some. Let me show how to make this argument, by applying the "close to nature" litmus-test. Though the Sun King of France did not live all that close to nature, nor, for that matter, do Chicagoans today, my own grandparents did. They, halfblooded lumberjacks and halfhearted subsistence farmers, devoured by lice in their temporal domain and by supernatural fears of an otherworldly one, survived much closer to the forces of nature than the Crees of Wemindji I knew up on James Bay in the 1960s. I inherited my ignorance from my grandparents. They also were unaware they were Whitemen. The Crees, devils in store-bought clothing that they are, made a Whiteman out of me.

Now approaches the moment for the punchline to all these unbearably personal reminiscences. For years I meandered through Jargon's Maze (otherwise called the social sciences) before discovering the exit, right in my own childhood backyard. Because Americans are famed for an unquenchable thirst for knowledge about other peoples, especially their picturesque Canadian neighbors, I will not burden readers with facts they already know. But do remember that Canada was originally New France, a fertile if feeble colony conquered by the dastardly British in 1760. Please recall how 60,000 illiterate, fun-loving, French-speaking *habitants* became today's 6,000,000. And surely keep in mind how, in the meantime, this conquered people was reduced to the status of hewers of wood and drawers of water. The way out of my intellectual quandary concerning *Me, Whiteman* versus *Them, Indians* lay through remembering how, when I was a stripling in the small company town where I grew up, *Nous, Canadiens* spoke of *Eux, les Anglais*.

So far as we were concerned, all "Englishmen," were the same, including Anglo-Canadians, Londoners, Sussexmen, Northumbrians, Scots, Irish, Australians, and English-speaking Polish immigrants, whether millionaire industrialists or our brothers' and fathers' coworkers in the paper mill. *They* acted like bosses, the masters of the universe, asking questions and providing answers. *They* were domineering individualists, driven by the love of power, money, and self. *They* were also hypocrites—they spoke in mellifluous tones but with forked tongues, always with a hidden agenda. *They* lived selfishly all by themselves in neat houses, set far from the curb on paved streets, with no more than two children, and one small dog. *They* also had large feet and were nearly all sissies. *They* were materialistic, calculating, prideful, pushy. *They* never treated *Us* on equal terms, as whole persons. *They* could not so much as pronounce properly *boubou* or *chien* or *derrière*. Their world was commerce, industry, technology, business, urban life, cosmopolitan—rootless! *Their* culture was secular humanism, science, mass-media, fashion, free-thinking, competition. *They* could not even agree on one true religion. The only people to be trusted less than *Them* were Jews, because, except for the fact that they were not bosses of anything of consequence, they were the same as *les Anglais*—worse—Jews were even more devious.

What about us, we French Canadians, the *True Canadian*? For one thing, *We* were not only entirely different from "the English" but *had to be so*: *We* were really God's own beachhead on this materialistic, capitalistic, secularistic English-dominated continent. *Our* manifest destiny was bound to family, faith, tradition, community, a life of the spirit, working the land, sticking together to protect our age-old customs, language, and beliefs. Instead of listening to the siren's song of the

English's cities and modern life, *We* had to keep our ears tuned to the voices raising from the graves of our forefathers or thundering down from the Heavens by way of the pulpit. So, when one of *Ours* turned pragmatic businessman or free-thinking intellectual or scientist or power-crazed politician willing to wheel-and-deal with the English in Ottawa, the word was telegraphed to all: here was one who turned away from his own kind, an uprooted traitor, an inauthentic, English-souled, corrupted *Canadien*.

Like my contemporaries, I lived through a complete reversal of this ideology among French-Canadians. From the mid-1950s up to now, peaking during the 1960s and 1970s, Quebec society has been swept by what *les Anglais* tagged a "Quiet Revolution." Led by a technocratic elite of no-nonsense intellectuals and managers, the former French Canadian natives have broken out of their shells, dedicating themselves to the conquest of Big Government, Big Business, Big City, Big Science, Mass Culture. In process, they transformed themselves into a new, dynamic and sometimes overbearing national entity calling itself the *Quebecois*. Were *We* successful? You must have heard: Senator Edward Kennedy came to study *Our* public health insurance system! Robert Campeau just bought Bloomingdale's! Montreal's *Le Cirque du Soleil* swept Los Angeles and New York standing-room only audiences off their feet! Radio-Canada's Frederic Bach got the 1988 Oscar for animated film.

"Culture," for *Us*, as one of Quebec's well-known playwrights then put it, meant "to take on the whole world and translate it for oneself into one's own idiom; and also translating oneself unto the world, and thus putting one's own original imprint (or signature) upon it." The centuries-old strategy of self-protective "*survivance de la race!*" (survival of the "race," or "culture," as we would say today) was turned into an affirmative, "Shoot for the Stars" nationalist strategy.

At what cost? The crumbling of traditional French Canadian beliefs and ways-of-life was one large item on the bill for the Quiet Revolution. With this was also lost the collective feeling of belonging and a secure identity. Quebec now has one of the lowest fertility rates in the western world: at 1.4 children per family, the *Quebécois* cannot foresee demographic replacement. Besides, now our houses are being built farther from the curb, and have puppies running about on neatly trimmed lawns. *We* have become like the *English*!

Here, then, is my punchline. What French Canadians used to call "the English" forty years ago corresponds to what is called "the Whiteman" in the native thought world. There is no denying that both words denoted, with self-protective contempt, a powerful, exploitative, often domineering majority. But on a deeper, more significant and portentous level, both also symbolize, indirectly but expressively, the massive, anonymous, historical forces that have been transforming the world and disturbing peoples' lives since their fortuitous emergence in Europe some six hundred years ago.

In writing about the *Whiteman* and the *Native*, or any variety of *Us* and *Them*, I am describing one part of this historical maelstrom with its multiple revolutions—in the ways people define and relate to their environment, to their own kind and others, and even themselves as social persons. Over the centuries, one group after another has been faulted as responsible for these dramatically painful transformations. Blame has fallen on the burghers of the free, commercial city-states of Italy or the Netherlands, who sowed the seeds of capitalistic industry, trade, commerce, and voluntary associations, and who created the model of the democratic town-meeting. So, too, have been accused the Jews, for propagating their universalistic, reflective intellectual tradition among the neighbors surrounding their ghettos, and for establishing modern credit facilities and banking networks. Calvinist Protestants were also fingered as the perpetrators, for having short-circuited the clergy's broker role between God and the "Chosen," thereby introducing the idea of independent individuals and the selfless, pragmatic accumulation of worldly riches, the very "Spirit of Capitalism." Also favored as culprits were the free-thinking, science-minded, critical intellectuals of the Enlightenment. Other transgressors include Entrepreneurs, variously called Captains of Industry, Lumber Lords, Robber Barons, and—generically—Capitalists or the Bourgeois. What accusation has been lodged against these successive scapegoats? Of being the carriers of a cultural AIDS virus, one that destroyed the immune system of local community and that traditional authority that depended on shared beliefs, continuity of custom, fidelity to heritage, ascribed status, and meaningful links to the supernatural world.

Sociologically speaking, one springboard of this revolution was the constitution of the "free" market as a self-governed mechanism for regulating economic interaction. Such a mechanism of economic exchanges responded not to the prescriptions of tradition, custom, or local polities but to the impersonal, universal, and practical "laws" of supply and demand and the maximization of efficiency and material benefits. This could not have happened without a parallel transformation of ethos. Critical, independent inquiry had to be torn free from the constraints of religious and other forms of social control that supported and sustained conformity. Thus was introduced into social interaction yet another sort of self-regulating, universalistic free market, that marketplace of ideas where the only monarch was pure reason. Working together, these powerful currents created a historical torrent, the unprecedented, now global institutionalization of economic growth, technological innovation, scientific discovery, and critical reasoning.

For want of better words, I will call these central features of this revolution the "modern matrix." The modern matrix—that unregulated market in things and ideas—has fashioned an entirely new relationship between humans and their worlds. Whether the natural, biophysical environment or the historically created world of culture, both have become *objects* subject to the critical scrutiny and the will of humankind. Both physical and social environments are now things to study, analyze, understand, to pass judgment on, to manipulate and transform—objects to *master*. Traditional ideals of the good life and inherited systems of belief and comportment, once transmitted from generation to generation, where people found their place and the meaning of existence through identification with a particular, durable, discrete cultural community, have vanished. Sometimes gradually, sometimes brutally and almost overnight, old social regimes have fallen beneath the weight of the new. Self regenerating communities everywhere have been cut down by the axes of environmental exploitation, which felled the essential material and technological bases for cultural stability, and by the sharp knives of critical questioning and empiricism, which whittled away consensual meanings and norms. Together, these have deforested whole continents of traditional social life. Heritage has become merely one more commodity, the real stuff now made obsolete by the unrelenting "shock of the new."

The modern matrix has delivered, like none before, the promise in *Genesis* of Man's dominion over the Earth. Along the way, the same initiatives that brought forth "enlightenment," material "progress," and "freedom," spread themselves around the world in the wake of colonial expansion. These were first dispensed under the sign of the cross, then education, finally science. The spirit of change was advanced with the clash of swords and words, beneath the banner of "empire," later "building socialism," now "national liberation." Always, the tinkling of gold coins has made sweet music—to the ears of yesterday's "exploiters" and today's "developers." Whereupon the first colonials came home with the assurance that all "Whitemen" were one, that all bore the same splendid burden, this was a surprise to the millions of expropriated peasants and exploited workers of Europe, to that continent's beheaded nobles and defrocked priests. Knowing they shared the costs but not the rewards of that awesome responsibility may have given some small comfort to Europe's ethnic minorities, themselves overwhelmed by the emerging states and elites, all no less "White" than they. Otherwise, witnessing the collapse of their own autonomy and their traditional universes, the Lapps and Basques and Bretons might more swiftly have elected to become True Natives. That they did not suddenly do so is likely due to their difficulty in seeing the causes of cultural uprooting as being the "Westerners" or "Whitemen."

So, among Europe's anguished peoples, other stereotypes were fashioned to explain what was not understood. Like syphilis, newly introduced to Europe by the recently infected homeward-bound crews of the *Santa María* and the *Niña*, this cultural virus was often identified by the brand marks of neighboring nations. For Germans, the new cultural pox was French imperialist rationalism, while for the French it was British business pragmatism. For nearly all Europeans, repeatedly so, in our century appallingly so, the Jew became the perennially hated "alien amongst us" responsible for social ills. The Truly Godly, seeking someone to blame for the incomprehensible money-grabbing, scheming, free-thinking, cosmopolitan, rootless, suspiciously disloyal symptoms spreading in their midst, invented the Jew, who became the Christian's own evil Whiteman.

The modern matrix insists we look to secular not supernatural causes for worldly phenomena and historical events. But few are willing to comply. Not many are content with cool-headed explanations pointing to blind, purposeless, faceless, anonymous, super-individual, underlying social winds and currents as responsible for our being blown about like shipwrecks drifting on the sea of history. The experience of being politically demasted and socially rudderless frightens and disheartens people. So what can *We* do? *We* have one always congenial recourse: *Someone* must be responsible! So *We*, whoever we are, invent the *Christian* and *Jew*, or the *Capitalist* and the *Undeserving Poor*, or the *Savage* and the *Whitemen*, or the *Secular Humanist* or *Queer* or *Communist*, as suits our ethnic, social class, political, philosophical, or sexual preferences. *They* are handy for many such purposes, and can be accused as carriers of the fearsome virus, whatever its alleged symptoms.

Curiously, after acclaiming its wonderful gains the modern matrix generates its own criticism, by and of itself. This ambivalent narcissism feeds on a profound nostalgia for the imagined social life of the past, the cultures its own propagation has destroyed. It stands self-denounced for *alienating* people from one another, from their communities, from their past, and from nature. Its own stellar production—Western or White or bourgeois or materialistic culture—is variously condemned as contrived, counterfeit, disarticulated, disintegrated, inauthentic—an ogre devouring its own children. Wanton pride, the ever-present inclination to play God, is it greatest self-confessed sin.

Almost as soon as the values of universality, rationality, humanity, individuality—the French Enlightenment's heart—spread across Europe, their opposites arose. These were a glorification of the unique, of the deep lying inner character of nations, of the value of prerational sentiments, of the individual as little more than a surface expression of a preternatural collective identity, of the "Souls" of nations—together the core of German Romanticism. This streak of philosophic nostalgia has run through the ideals of Communism on the Left, Fascist nationalism on the Right, and astride both—Populism. Even scientific discourse, allegedly the enemy of sentimentality, has sometimes been threaded with this seemingly antithetical streak. One expression of this was in early twentieth-century anthropology, with its notion of "unique cultural integrity" and its fascination with "authentic archaic societies." Now that anthropology has gone on to other ways of thinking, such fancies have become incorporated into mass culture, launching another round of courtship with the *Noble Savage* among us. Romanticism also still thrives as a counter-cultural ethos, inspiring what may be the most portentous of today's cultural-political undercurrents, environmentalism as preached by the "Greens" or the "Friends of the Earth" movements.

Such cultural, political and intellectual countercurrents do not truly run free of the still dominant matrix, the whirlpool of modernity. They form an integral part of it. They are its very conscience. They would make no sense in another historical context. Only when rampant technological exploitation of resources reached the point of menacing *Man's* place on the planet would this contrary streak of prophetic environmental criticism make itself plausible and find an audience.[9] Notwithstanding the often strident emotionalism of this new ecological romanticism, such criticism is by no means unrealistic or entirely utopian. Real—extraordinarily threatening—problems are addressed and eminently practical questions are raised. In fact, nothing could be truer to the modern matrix than such an antithetical stance, for the hallmark of modern rationality is an invariable dictum: the future is not given once and for all. The remembrance of institutions and environments past can inspire dreams of a better future, for all of *Us* and *Our* global environment. Progress without memory of history is a cul de sac. Deliberate long-term choices and policies are possible. *We* do not have to rest content with piecemeal reactions to present short-term trends and fashions. In this sense, the romantic spirit is modernity's way of reminding *Us* of a fundamental postulate: Man's fate and that of the World is in *Our* hands. No one can be any more modern than that.

Just when the central features of the modern matrix flowed into the consciousness of intellectuals and the public, criticism of some unsavory consequences of modernity appeared. This critique focused on groups most easily seen as unwilling, defenseless victims of free markets and free thinking. These were depicted as both the casualties of development and an absolute cultural alternative. Rousseau's "Noble Savage" was among the earliest of these improvised alters, the philosopher's social touchstone, a vision of Man's infancy.

I have argued that today's "True and Salutary Native," is a lineal descendant—with a detour through the Jesuits' reductions—of Rousseau's imago. But most of those who lived, or are still living, through the torrents of modernization had no flesh and blood Indians nearby to provide living illustrations of what *We*—modern folk—had lost. Listen, for instance, to this call of the wild, coming from a traveler in unchartered cultural terrain, where he found:

A homogeneous world: man and animal and fruit, air and wood and earth, were a single substance whose parts slowly vibrated round its core—the sun.

I stood in the village mud and sensed the organic rhythm of this telluric world—the pulse of the earth and beast and man together. The native, the unsophisticated toiler, has a self-knowledge, humble but authentic. This our Western culture has merely covered and destroyed with a patina of lies. And that is why there is more hope in the uncultured workers of all races.

Cruising down a river with his native guides, the traveler deepened his impressions: "That night a great peace fell upon the boat. We were lifted out of time . . . I tasted the substance of a people" (quoted in Hollander 1981:131).

Who is writing about whom here? A seventeenth-century Jesuit canoeing past Michillimakinac then down the Illinois River on his way to the Gulf of Mexico with a Huron escort? A modern anthropologist paddling north for field research among the Saulteurs in Manitoba? Neither. The writer's name is Waldo Frank. His "tribe" was the Mujik— Russian peasants. The date was the early 1930s. The place? Joseph Stalin's Soviet Union. Excuse my white lie, for having substituted "native" for "peasant" in the quotation, done in the interest of catching your attention.

After so many punch lines must come a brief conclusion. Let me make clear what I did not say and what I have said. I did not suggest or imply that native peoples have no identities of their own, nor that they should turn back on their remaining traditions or forfeit whatever limited rights they may have. Neither did I recommend excusing those Europeans who brought misery to the first inhabitants of America. I did stress that no one today need accept being intellectually accused, financially saddled, or emotionally imprisoned by the historically invented images of *Them* versus *Us*, of the *Indian* being ground under by the *Whiteman*. No individual or group identity can forever satisfactorily be fashioned out of collective stereotypes, however appealing or repugnant they may be. All of *Us* are far more complex and malleable creatures than ideological cliches would make any of us out to be. Allegations of "cultural" or "national" or "racial" or "tribal" essences are shibboleths.

As Jean-Paul Sartre once observed: "one can always make something out of what others have made of one." And I surmise this modern predicament today applies to those who identify themselves as North America's original peoples as well as to everybody else. Indians and Inuit are no more bound to their traditional, supposedly purer "essence" than are people of European, or African, or Asian origins to any variety of "manifest fate." Besides ethnicity—which may or may not continue to reign supreme in the political attention of humankind—there are many other types of social identities which answer as well to that marvelously human impulse for bonding with a group. Identification of self with neighborhood, gender, kin-group, second generation, occupation, "alternate lifestyles," and many other personal options are readily available. These, too, cut across lines of social class or nationhood, easing dangerous frictions between people and casting out loneliness.

I have also stressed that the Whiteman is very much like the Indian. Massive, constant social change damages all human communities. All of Us are injured by the loss of a sense of continuity and belonging, by the disappearance of ways familiar to our grandparents, by the erosion of "habits of the heart." In the maelstrom of the modern world, the experience of cultural disintegration is no stranger to anyone. In the same manner, if the *Native* truly has any "essence" at all, it is like that of the *Whiteman*. *We* are all still innocents vulnerable to many serpents and poisoned apples in the world's much fouled garden. All of *Us* lived exposed to challenges and must struggle to cope so that we can exist. *Ours* is a collective fate, striving to grasp the future and to make it livable for our children, whom we cannot raise the way we were ourselves raised.

There is, at last, a moral to my story: no one need shoulder the historical burdens of guilt for having vanquished or the shame of defeat. Nor must anyone be tolerated who waves the battle flags of self-pride or the bandages of self-pity. But everybody must accept responsibility for changing the hurtful social conditions and misperceptions they share. Everyone should be held answerable, now to one another, tomorrow to our posterity. How otherwise can *We*, *Whiteman* or *Indian*, ever breakout from the bondage of our mutual reductions?

Notes

1. The peasants of England and Scotland suffered a similar fate during what is known as the "enclosures" movement, from the eighteenth century on. They had to be thrown out to make room for the wool-producing, grass-grazing foot soldiers of the budding textile industry—the sheep. The word "peasant" comes from the French *paysan*, whose root is *pays*—country. A peasant, then, is a man-of-the-country, which is pretty close to the meaning of "aborigine" and "native." The uprooted peasants became "labor" for the factories, just as their farms became another mere factor of large-scale production. The key to both transformations, of course, is that money had become "capital."

2. Up to this day Canadian government services provided annually to native communities cost incomparably more—billions for a few hundred thousand people—than whatever they bring into the Canadian economy in the form of wages, profits, interests or taxes. Of course, there remains the incalculable cumulative value of their original contribution—land. But this can be rationalized away by recalling that increased land values are the result of the labors, investments, and know-how the European-Americans applied to it.

3. A parallel could be made with the symbolic meaning of "Next year in Jerusalem" during the Jewish Diaspora, or with the intense longing Palestinian children born and raised in refugee communities express for returning to Haifa or Jaffa, places they have never seen but which, to their mind's eye, appear as earthly paradise.

4. According to by-laws of the James Bay Agreement, Inuit are even forbidden to offer a piece of "nature food" (fish, fowl, or four-legged) as a present to a visiting non-native friend.

5. Among the Iroquois, the tribal political traditions had to go underground, where they took on a quasi-sacred, syncretic character. There they simmered until the Red Power movement of the 1960s brought them back to the surface. The so-called "traditional" or "Long-House People" presently hold the "radical" banner in the political life of the Iroquois reservations, on both sides of (and astride) the border.

6. By contrast, ethnicity proceeds largely from self-identification, not bloodlines. The Finnish law on the education of the Lapps is the only one I have ever seen which takes ethnicity into elegant account; it says approximately: "for the purposes of the present law, a Lapp is whoever says: I am a Lapp." For the 1980 United States census, a similar "self-identification" rule for Indians was applied, resulting in an apparent 75 percent increase in Indian population that decade.

7. It took centuries for the "Whiteman" moniker to catch on. Europeans of the sixteenth-century—who had not yet learned even to identify with a nation-state—mostly saw themselves as Christians, in contrast to heathens and infidels, such as the Moors.

8. This is why it makes no sense to say that any ancient culture was "naturally" respectful of their environment. Extensive environmental degradation came

with greatly increased population and heavy resource exploitation. Deliberate worry about the fate of the globe is a modern phenomenon; it goes with self-propelling technological development.

References

Berkhofer, Robert F., Jr. 1979. *The White Man's Indian: Images of the American Indian from Columbus to the Present*. New York: Vintage Books.
Hollander, Paul. [Robert Silverberg]. 1981. *Political Pilgrims: Travels of Western Intellectuals in the Soviet Union, China, and Cuba, 1928–1978*. New York: Oxford University Press.

Appendix
Criticisms of Nonconformers

Modern Indians, and those closely affiliated with their interests, are not the only people with vested interests in maintaining a protected, orthodox view of themselves. As John Messenger points out for contemporary Irish and African nationalists (1989:115–124), great offensive is often taken at what anthropologists, historians, and other scholars write and say about the groups they study. Following Messenger's useful lead—he collected and assembled a list of Irish criticisms of his writings and treated it as a body of folklore—here is a sample of the verbal sanctions issued against anthropologists and others whose research reporting is deemed injurious or nonconforming. Sometimes sticks, stones, or other weapons are used in defense of the dominant story line, as well, but scholars are especially susceptible to negative words. As Messenger points out, any group's regularly expressed grievances form a valuable, relevant body of data that can be used for understanding them. Not all of these complaints were originally constructed by Indians, but Indians soon enough acquire and use the phrasings; and because they come from multiple sources they are by no means consistent.

1. You are anti-Indian.
2. You are anti-traditional Indian.
3. You are anti-modern Indian.
4. You hate Indians.
5. You don't like Indians.
6. You hate yourself and your White heritage and are taking it out on the Indian.
7. You are a "Wannabe Indian." Your problem is that you really want to be an Indian but you can't be.

8. You are blaming the victim.
9. You don't feel guilty enough about what White men have done to the Indian (i.e., you are not blaming the Victimizer enough.)
10. You are being false to the true ideals of America.
11. You really are a racist.
12. You may not be a racist at heart, but you are mouthing racial stereotypes.
13. You are a liberal, a utopian do-gooder, a romantic.
14. You are acting in an un-Christian manner.
15. Your thinking is utterly corrupted by Judeo-Christian, historicist, lineal, secular, materialistic, and other White biases.
16. You resent the many wonderful features of Indian life not found in White culture.
17. You are angry, crazy, hostile, spiteful, jealous, etc.
18. You are a culture thief or a culture vulture.
19. What you say about Indians can't be trusted because someone with a vested interest harmful to Indians is paying you to say it.
20. You use Indians to get rich or to help your career.
21. You are not truly interested in Indians—you study them only to understand your own alienated self better.
22. You are a reactionary, an apologist for capitalist oppressors, racists, and exploiters, a supporter of colonialism, of neocolonialism, of internal colonialism, of the Hegemony, of the Patriarchy, etc.
23. You are interfering in Indian self-determination or sovereignty.
24. You are unethical—you should only write and say things that are acceptable to Indians.
25. You are an assimilationist who believes in equality.
26. You are ignorant of the true nature of Indianness, tribalism, etc.
27. Indians are individualists; your lofty generalizations have nothing to do with real Indians.
28. You are projecting your own selfish individualism and do not understand that Indians inherently and inevitably are dedicated to group life and goals, abandoning self-interest to collective interests.
29. No White man can ever really understand or think like the Indian and you might as well stop trying.
30. The people you describe are not really Indian.
31. Indians have always lied to and deceived anthropologists.
32. Whatever any Indian says about Indian heritage, history, culture is indisputably true, not to be questioned.
33. Although Indians may have cautiously revealed some trivial features of their ways, they have always carefully concealed the sacred features of their heritage.
34. What you say is only true of a very few Indians.
35. What you say is only true of Indians who have abandoned their real heritage.

36. You do not understand modern Indians; what you say is true of lifeways that disappeared generations ago.
37. You never met a genuine Indian.
38. There are no genuine Indians—Indians are who and what they say they are.
39. What you say may be reasonably true so far as it goes, but you have willfully ignored many vital things about Indians (gender issues, homosexuality, poverty, powerlessness, non-status Indians, unrecognized Indians, twentieth-century Indians, educated Indians, militant Indians, etc.).
40. You are not taking the emic point of view.
41. You do not understand the Indian point of view.
42. By writing and speaking about Indians, you degrade them.
43. There's nothing new in what you say about us Indians—we've always known that.
44. You do not believe in cultural relativity.
45. You are being analytic and objective.
46. By claiming their are standards of truth and objectivity in studying Indians, you are epistomologically primitive.
47. You do not understand that there is no such thing as truth about Indians, there is only discourse or narratives.
48. There is no such thing as unbiased, apolitical, non-partisan observation, interpretation, or thinking about Indians.
49. Humanists, and those who espouse subjectivism, understand Indians better than social scientists obsessed with objectivity.
50. Only friends of the Indian really try to understand them.
51. If you don't help Indians by giving generously, you are their enemy.
52. It takes an Indian to study, understand, explain, serve, teach about, administer, speak for, raise money for, or help the Indian and only Indians should do so.
53. You are denying or concealing the dirty, immoral underside of White history and culture.
54. The White man was (and is) worse than the Indian.
55. Whatever bad habits the Indian may have were learned from Whites.
56. The White man is fully responsible for everything bad that has happened to Indians.
57. You deny that before Columbus Indians lived in sovereign nations, and that Indians today after centuries of struggle are rightfully regaining their sovereign nationhood.
58. You deny that Indians played a crucial role in American history, politics, and culture—as the role model for liberty, freedom, justice, participatory democracy, and the Constitution, as the Saviour of America at critical moments in its history such as at Plymouth Rock and Valley Forge, etc.
59. You don't understand that Indians who became Christians, who

dressed or acted like Whites, who bought land and paid taxes on it, who sought citizenship, jobs, education, and homes in White communities were only doing this as a ploy in order to survive and to protect their innermost Indianness.

60. You do not understand that Indians only took from Whites what they thought was important to them, and that they have always been fully in control of their heritage and destiny.

61. No matter what the Whiteman has done or will do to the Indian, Indians will forever be Indians.

62. No matter how much Indians change socially, culturally, linguistically, and biologically, they will always remain Indian.

63. You do not understand that Indian heritage and identity is carried in the blood that courses through their veins, and you deny that it takes only one drop of Indian blood to make an Indian.

64. You do not understand the common law, or the canons of Indian law, or Supreme Court decisions concerning Indians, etc.

Reference

Messenger, John. 1989. *Inis Beag Revisited: The Anthropologist as Observant Participator*. Salem, WI: Sheffield.

About the Authors

R. H. Barnes is currently university lecturer in social anthropology at the University of Oxford and fellow of St. Anthony's College. He has published on Indonesian and North American topics and his books include *Kédang: A Study of the Collective Thought of an Eastern Indonesian People* and *Two Crows Denies It: a History of Controversy in Omaha Sociology*. He is working on a study of development and tradition in an Indonesian whaling community (about which he has recently made a film with Granada Television of Britain) and on Southeast Asian conceptions of space, time, and number.

Lynn Ceci, Ph.D. (1930–1989) was an avid teacher and writer of anthropology. She carved out a specialty, the settlement patterns of Eastern Coastal Indian societies during the Colonial era, and subsequently became a leading authority on the origin and significance of wampum, shell beads, and Indian corn cultivation. An associate professor of anthropology at Queens College, New York, her *alma mater*, and a member of the faculty of the Ph.D. program in anthropology for the Graduate School of the City University of New York, she was respected as an unusually gifted and inspiring teacher. She was also a prolific writer and published many significant essays and reviews in Anthropology and Archaeology journals. She authored and coedited two books and is represented as a contributor to several others. While being wife, mother, and grandmother, Mrs. Ceci was also honored for her scholarly accomplishments by numerous professional awards, including Sigma Xi, a faculty-in-residence award, a National Science Foundation grant, the Robert F. Heizer Prize in Ethnohistory, and others.

James A. Clifton first became interested in anthropology during World War II, while visiting Pacific Islands under less than pacific auspices. He then studied at the University of Chicago and, after the Korean War and more military field work in Korea and Japan, completed his doctoral studies in anthropology

375

at the University of Oregon. Though originally trained as a Pacific specialist, for some thirty years his research has been concentrated on American Indians. An ethnohistorian and psychological anthropologist, he is emeritus Frankenthal Professor of Anthropology and History at the University of Wisconsin—Green Bay, and is currently Scholar in Residence at Western Michigan University. His books include, *Being and Becoming Indian*, *The Prairie People*, *Star Woman and Other Shawnee Tales*, *The Potawatomi*, and *A Place of Refuge For All Time*.

Leland Donald, when not refreshing his soul by bird-watching or observing the fauna of tidepools, teaches anthropology at the University of Victoria in British Columbia. He is a graduate of Emory University, completed his graduate training in anthropology at the University of Oregon, and has done ethnographic research among the Navajo of Northern Arizona and the Yalunka of Sierra Leone, to which he has added ethnohistorical studies of the peoples of the Northwest Coast of North America. He specializes in studies of social inequality, slavery, and warfare.

Christian F. Feest is curator of the North and Middle American collections at the Museum für Völkerkunde, Vienna, and teaches anthropology at the University of Vienna. He is editor of the *European Review of Native American Studies*; and his most recent books include *Indians and Europe*, *Das rote Amerika*, and *Native Arts of North America*.

Stephen E. Feraca is a Columbia University trained anthropologist who spent his whole professional career as an applied anthropologist and administrator with the Bureau of Indian Affairs. He served as education and community development specialist among the Pine Ridge Sioux and the Florida Seminole; but most of his service was in the Bureau's Washington office in the Tribal Organization Branch. There he was responsible for processing Indian Claims Commission awards and for preparation of enabling legislation for these payments. His latest production is his book, *"Why Don't They Give Them Guns?" The Great American Indian Myth*.

Allan van Gestel is an attorney and legal scholar, specialized in Indian, environmental, and civil litigation. Educated at Colby College and at Boston University School of Law, where he served as editor of the *Law Review*, he is a partner in the Boston firm of Goodwin, Procter & Hoar. He has served as special counsel in investigations of several judicial problems, and regularly works in continuing legal education for attorneys. His Indian law expertise has been expressed in service as chief trial counsel in the defense of most of the Eastern Indian land claims cases in New York, Massachusetts, Rhode Island, and Vermont. A prolific writer and lecturer, he has published essays concerning Indian land claims issues in a variety of legal journals and books, and regularly lectures for university audiences.

Sam Gill teaches at the field of religious studies at the University of Colorado in Boulder. His recent publications include *Mother Earth: An American Story* and *Native American Religious Tradition*.

David Henige is the African Studies Bibliographer at the University of Wisconsin—Madison and has an interest in historical methodology, oral tradition, and textual criticism. He has published on Native American historical demography in *Hispanic American Historical Review*, *Journal of Interdisciplinary History*, and *Ethnohistory*. He is presently completing a study of the sources for Columbus' first voyage.

Alice B. Kehoe is Professor of Anthropology, Marquette University, where she has taught since 1968. She obtained her B.A. from Barnard College and Ph.D. from Harvard University. Her dissertation compared the Saskatchewan Dakota New Tidings (Ghost Dance) religion with Plains Cree and Saulteaux (Ojibwa) religion in Saskatchewan, and she has done ethnographic fieldwork also with Blackfeet in Montana and Alberta, as well as with Fundamentalist Protestants, the "radical Christian right." Among her publications are, *North American Indians: A Comprehensive Account*, and *The Ghost Dance: Ethnohistory and Revitalization*.

Carol Mason earned her graduate degrees in anthropology at the University of Michigan. A leading archaeologist and ethnohistorian, specialized in the study of culture change among Indians during the prehistory and early history of the Great Lakes region, she is Professor of Anthropology in the University of Wisconsin Center System. Among her many writings is her recent book, *Wisconsin Indians: Prehistory to Statehood*.

Richard de Mille, after military service in World War II, was a television director, a copy editor, a science-fiction writer, and a graduate student at the University of Southern California, where he received a Ph. D. in clinical and measurement psychology. He taught in universities, worked in think tanks, and eventually returned to writing. He is the author of numerous scientific, technical, and popular publications, including *Put Your Mother on the Ceiling: Children's Imagination Games*. *Choice* selected *The Don Juan Papers* as an outstanding academic anthropology book of 1980.

John A. Price (1933–1988) was a distinguished scholar and an applied anthropologist. Educated at the universities of Utah, Hawaii, Michigan, and Osaka, Japan, he earned a high reputation for his studies of minorities and social and cultural borderlands in Japan, Mexico, the United States, and Canada. Author of more than a dozen books and monographs, and many essays, he specialized in culture contact and change, urbanization, and economic development. He taught at UCLA, San Diego State University, McMaster University, the University of Toronto, and, from 1980 until his death, at

York University. In the last fifteen years of his career he became an authority on the native peoples of Canada, and on advocacy groups and development programs involving them. Among his books are: *Tiajuana: Urbanization in a Border Culture*; *Native Studies:American and Canadian Indians*; *Indians of Canada*; and *The Washo Indians*. While being husband, father, and good citizen, Dr. Price also acted as consultant to native groups, served on various editorial boards, and was the editor of the *Applied Anthropology Newsletter*.

Jean-Jacques Simard is *professeur titulaire* of sociology at Laval University. Between 1967 and 1972 he worked as community development agent among the Cree and as special assistant to the deputy minister of Quebec on the development of sub-arctic part of that province. He later served as advisor for the Arctic Inuit cooperative movement and for those dissident Inuit who are seeking an autonomous regional status. He is presently research director of Laval University's Center for Inuit and Circumpolar Studies. He is editor of the journal *Recherches sociographiques* and author of *La longue marches des technocrates* and many essays on Quebec society and native affairs.

Elisabeth Tooker is professor of anthropology at Temple University. She is one of the leading authorities on the culture and history of the Northern Iroquoians and her research and writing has particularly concerned these societies. Among her many books and essays about the Iroquoians are *An Ethnohistory of the Hurons, 1615–1649* and *The Iroquois Ceremonial of Midwinter*.

Index

Indian Reorganization Act (IRA), 198, 273, 286. *See also* Retribalization; Segregation; Self-determination
Indian Ring: allies in, 9–10, 258–59, 271–79; anthropologists' involvement in, 6–7, 18; coopting of national festivals by, 25–26; expert witnesses and, 6–7; modern goals of, 262–65; participants in, 14–15, 193–207, 255–69; public opinion manipulated by, 18–19, 258; publishers role in, 20–21; response to papal visits, 27, 196; sanctions used by, 22–23, 161; structure of New Indian Ring, 16–20, 255–69; structure of Old Indian Ring, 16–18. *See also* Literature; Advocacy organizations; Scholars' roles; American Indian Movement (AIM)
Indians, avocational, 193–207
Indian Self Determination and Education Act, 348–49
Indian, semantics of label, 39–40, 44n
Indian status. *See* Tribal Indian
Indian story: biographies used in, 20, 50–51; certifying authenticity of, 30–32; compiled versions of, 29–44, 266, 353–54; contributors to, 18–19, 30–32, 163–64, 193–207, 255–69; defense of, 20–21, 371–74; Euroamerican origins of, 38, 333–68; formulaic nature of, 38–39; functions of in law, 7; 40–41, 300–304; genres used for, 29–30, 193–207; media promotion of, 41–42, 315; moralizing use of, 186–87; polar contrasts in, 38–39; as propaganda, 38–39; publishers role in, 20–21; theoretical nature of, 39–44; *See also* Themes; Indian Story
Indian time, 345–46
Inequality. *See* Stratification, social; Themes
Inipi. See Sweat lodge rite
Innovations, transmission of, 72–73, 95–96, 102, 140–42
Integration policy, 10–11, 52–53, 299, 338–39. *See also* Indian policy
Intercultural roles, 83, 193–207, 217, 255–69, 271–89
Intercultural self-images, 136–41, 313–30, 333–69. *See also* Euroamerican identity; Indian identity
Interest group, modern Indians as, 15–20; 255–69. *See also* Indian Ring

Intermarriage, 49–54, 52–53, 326, 342–43
Inuit (Eskimo). *See* Native Peoples of Canada
Inuit Tapirisat (Eskimo Brotherhood), 262–63
Iroquoian speaking societies, 77, 82, 258. *See also* Cherokee; Huron; Iroquois Indians
Iroquoianization, 148. *See also* Stereotypes; Tupinambization
Iroquois Indians (of New York), 77, 107–25, 147–49, 335

James Bay and Northern Quebec Agreement, 346
Jamestown colony, 49
Jamestown Tricentennial, Pamunkey exploitation of, 59
Jesuits. *See* Missionization: Catholic
John Paul II, 196
Joseph, Chief, 136
Juan, don, 227–52. *See also* Carlos Castaneda
Jurisdictional claims, 294–95

Kafka, Franz, 326
Kanawakhe (Caughnawaga, Mohawk community), 119, 335, 359
Kinship systems. *See* Social structure
Klamath Indians, 1–2, 132
Kwakiutl Indians, 154–55

La Flesche, Francis, 213–14, 217–23
La Flesche, Joseph (Iron Eye), 216–22
Lahontan, Baron de, 145–46, 162–63, 315
Lakota Indian societies, 197, 219, 326
Lancaster (PA) Conference, 111
Land claims, 291–309
Las Casas, Bartolomé de, 182–83
Law of comparative advantage, 346
Law-office history, 7. *See also* Evidence; Indian Story; Truth value
Leadership roles, Indian, 150–51, 163, 201, 255–69
League of Nations, 321; supposedly founded on Iroquois model, 121
League of the Iroquois (the confederacy), 107–25, 343. *See also* Iroquois Indians
Legal fictions, defined: 300–301; 44, 291–309
Legends. *See* Myth, Cultural Fictions
Lévi-Strauss, Claude, 213, 215, 223